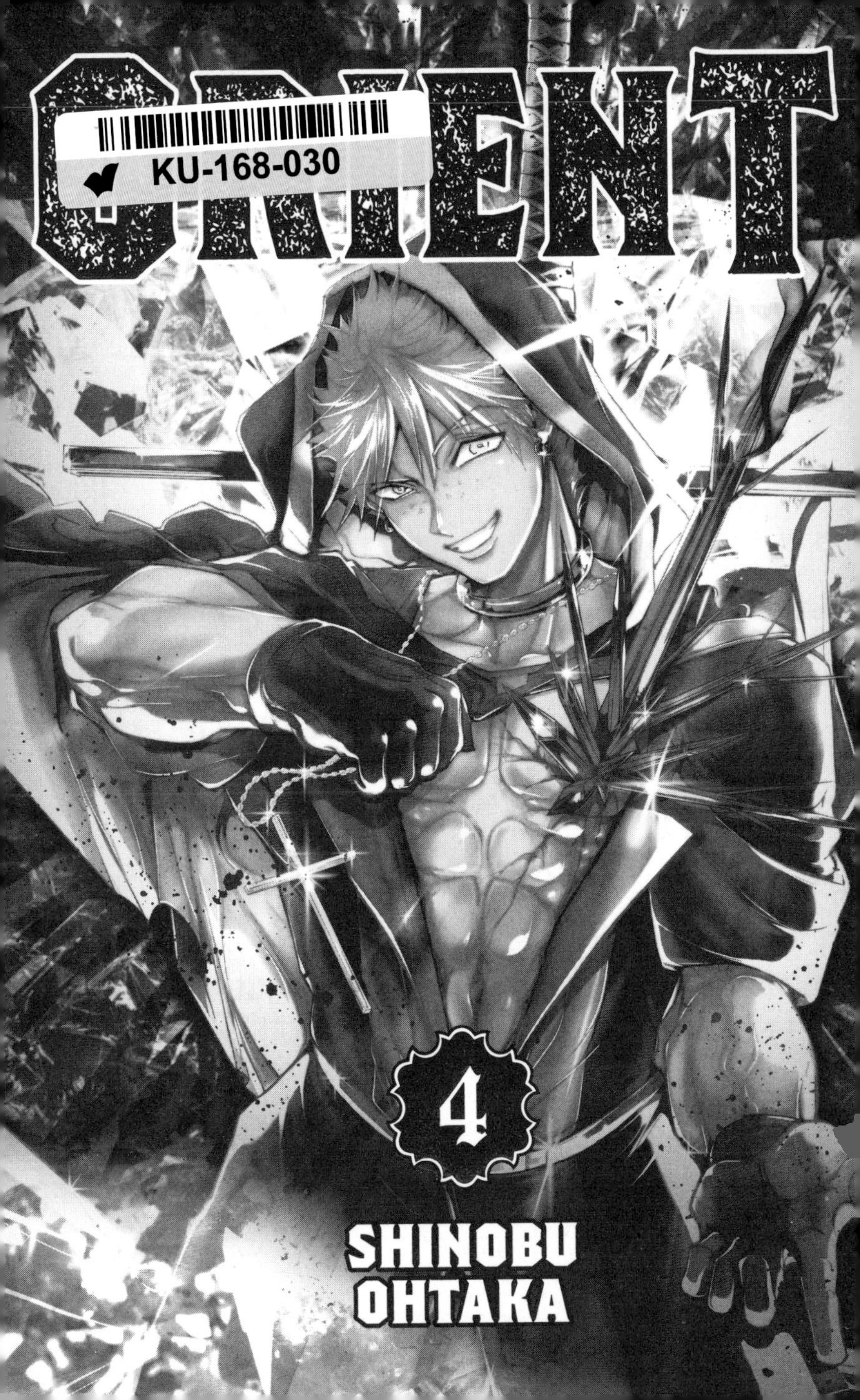
ORIENT
4
SHINOBU
OHTAKA

ORIENT

4

SHINOBU OHTAKA

CONTENTS

CHAPTER 27:
WE FINALLY MEET
77

CHAPTER 28:
THE OBSIDIAN GODDESS
95

CHAPTER 29:
CONVERSING WITH THE GODDESS
113

CHAPTER 30:
LIVING LIKE A CORPSE
131

CHAPTER 23:
THE COLOR OF A SOUL
5

CHAPTER 24:
YOU CAN'T BREATHE UNDERWATER
23

CHAPTER 25:
REKKU YAE-ZAKURA
41

CHAPTER 26:
MUSASHI'S UPBRINGING
59

CHAPTER 31:
THE KATANA
HUNTER
149

CHAPTER 32:
THE WAY
SAMURAI LIVE
167

ORIENT

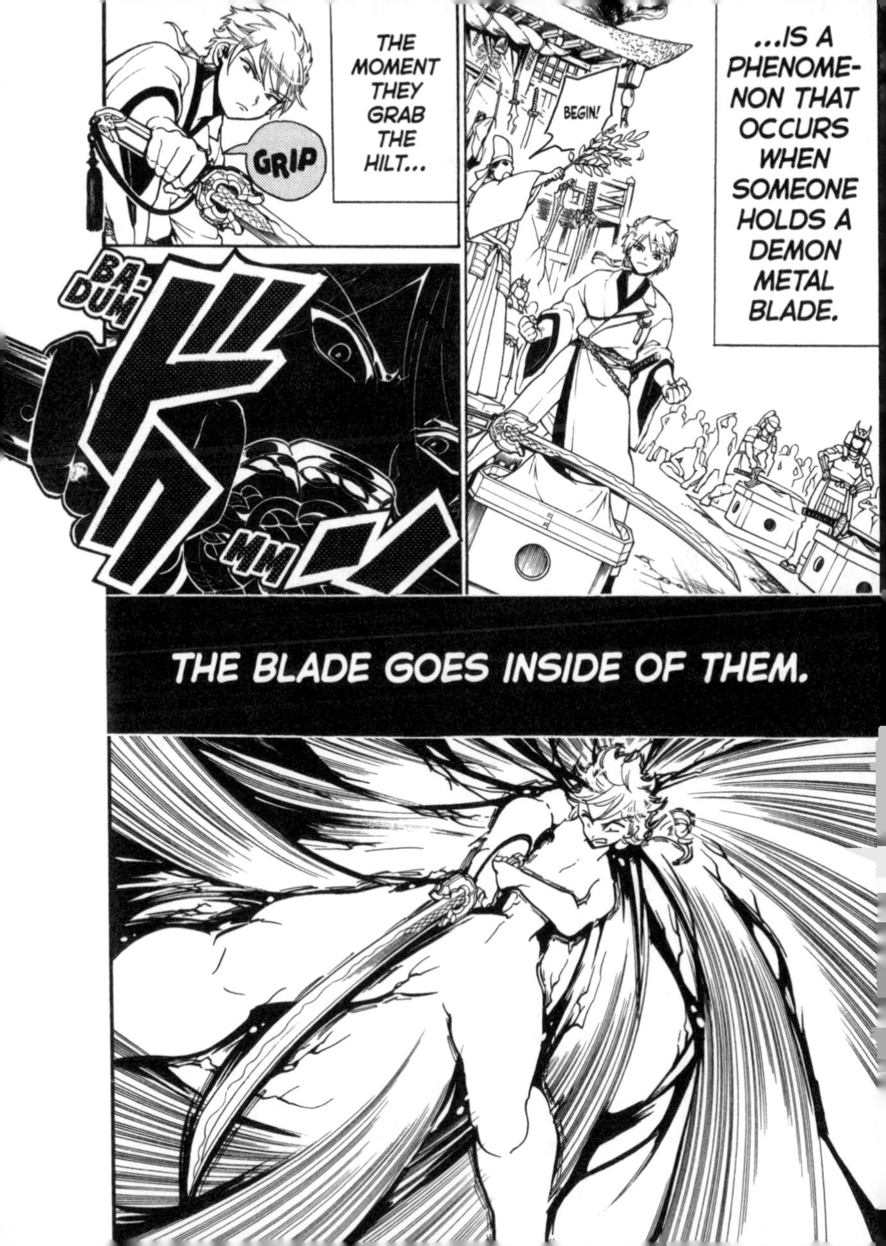
...IS A PHENOMENON THAT OCCURS WHEN SOMEONE HOLDS A DEMON METAL BLADE.
BEGIN!
THE MOMENT THEY GRAB THE HILT...
GRIP
BA-DUM
MM
THE BLADE GOES INSIDE OF THEM.

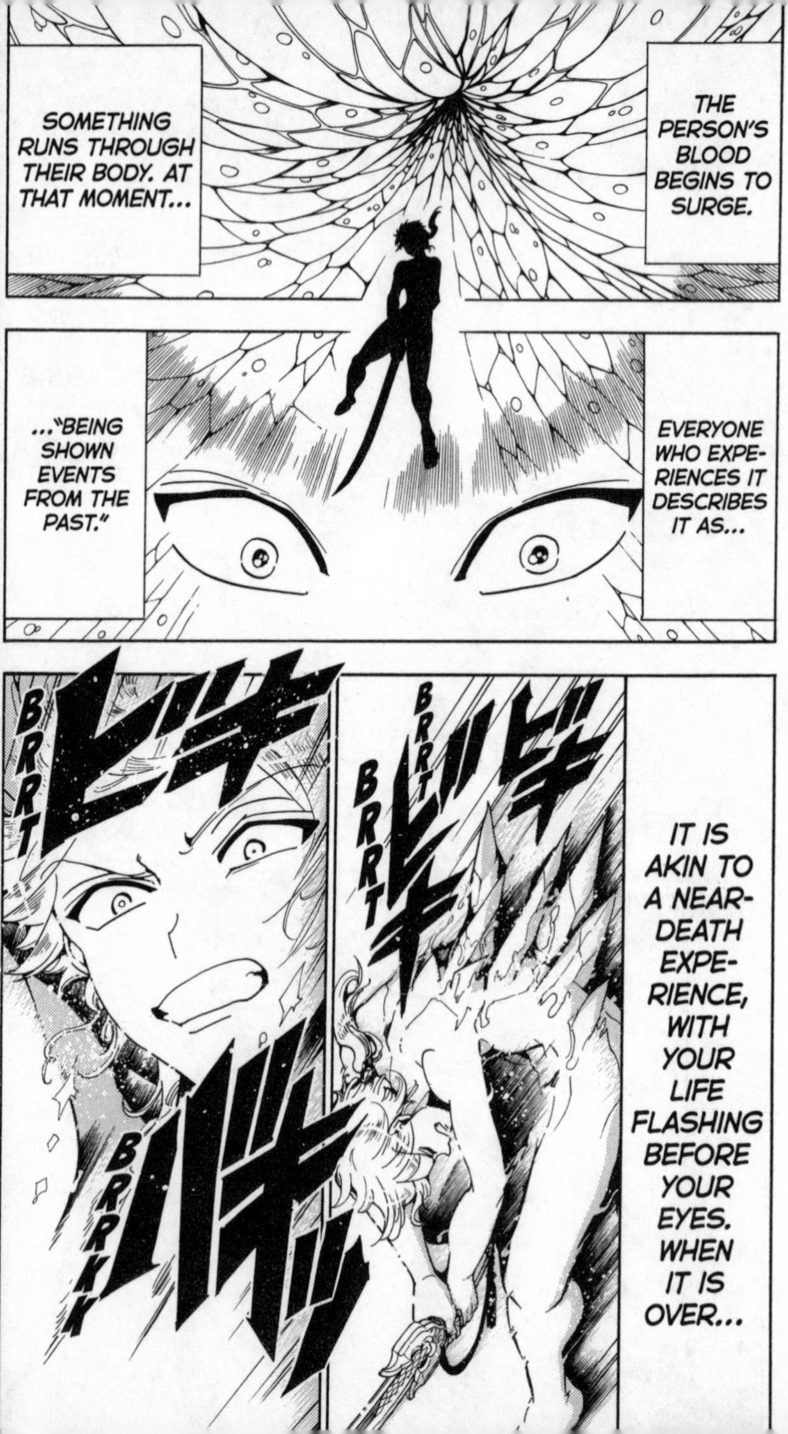
THE PERSON'S BLOOD BEGINS TO SURGE.
SOMETHING RUNS THROUGH THEIR BODY. AT THAT MOMENT...
EVERYONE WHO EXPERIENCES IT DESCRIBES IT AS...
..."BEING SHOWN EVENTS FROM THE PAST."
IT IS AKIN TO A NEAR-DEATH EXPERIENCE, WITH YOUR LIFE FLASHING BEFORE YOUR EYES. WHEN IT IS OVER...
BRRT
BRRT
BRRT
BRRKK

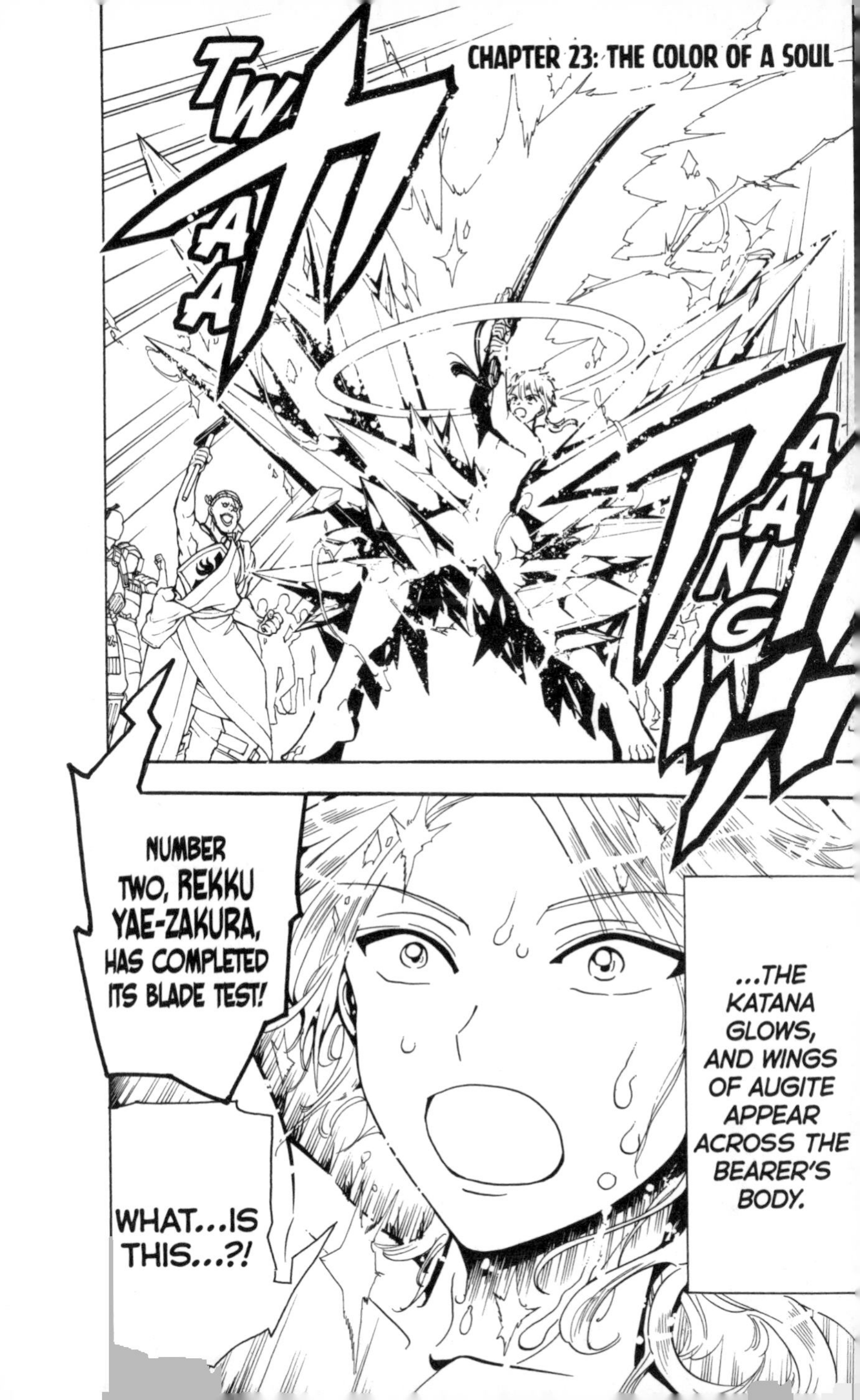
CHAPTER 23: THE COLOR OF A SOUL
AANG
TWAAA
...THE KATANA GLOWS, AND WINGS OF AUGITE APPEAR ACROSS THE BEARER'S BODY.
NUMBER TWO, REKKU YAE-ZAKURA, HAS COMPLETED ITS BLADE TEST!
WHAT...IS THIS...?!

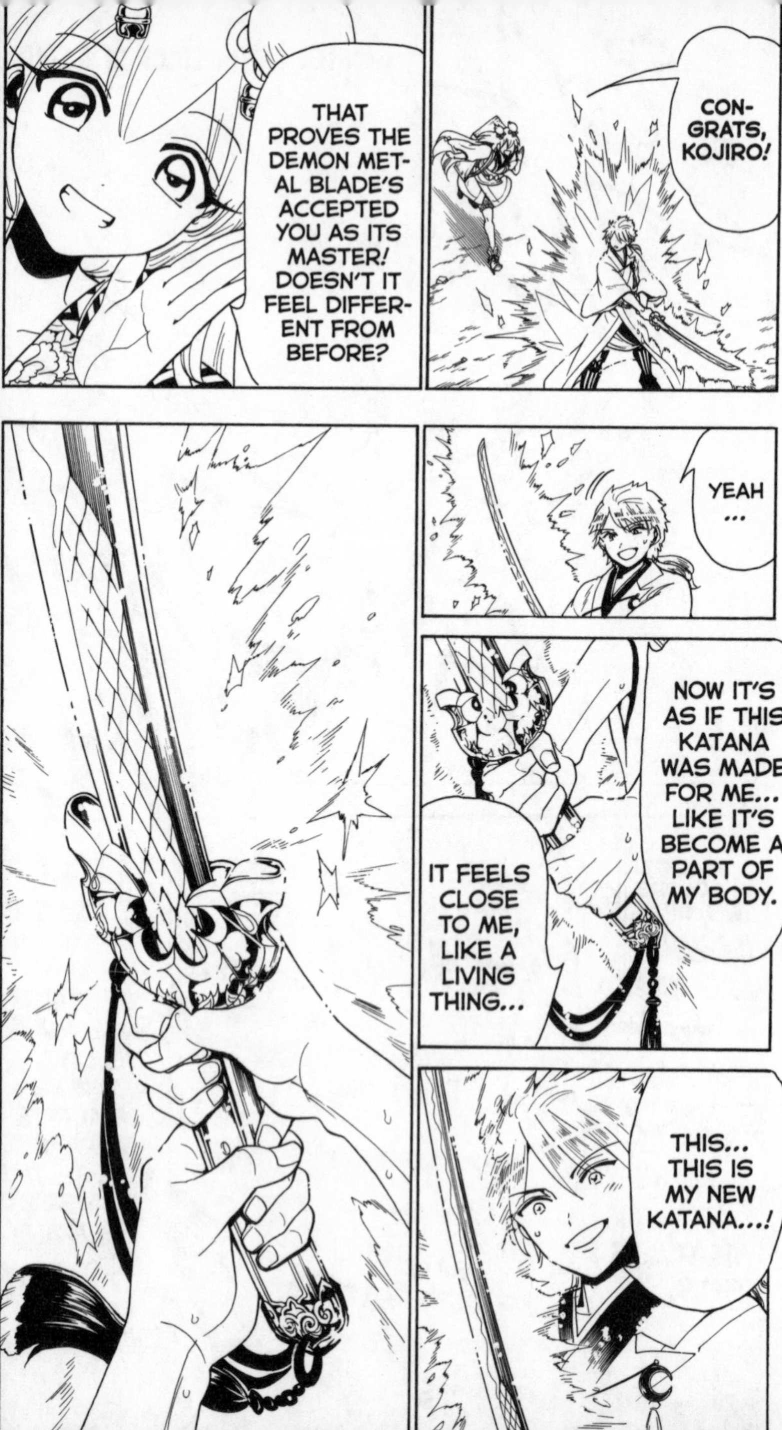
CON-GRATS, KOJIRO!
THAT PROVES THE DEMON MET-AL BLADE'S ACCEPTED YOU AS ITS MASTER! DOESN'T IT FEEL DIFFER-ENT FROM BEFORE?
YEAH...
NOW IT'S AS IF THIS KATANA WAS MADE FOR ME... LIKE IT'S BECOME A PART OF MY BODY.
IT FEELS CLOSE TO ME, LIKE A LIVING THING...
THIS... THIS IS MY NEW KATANA...!

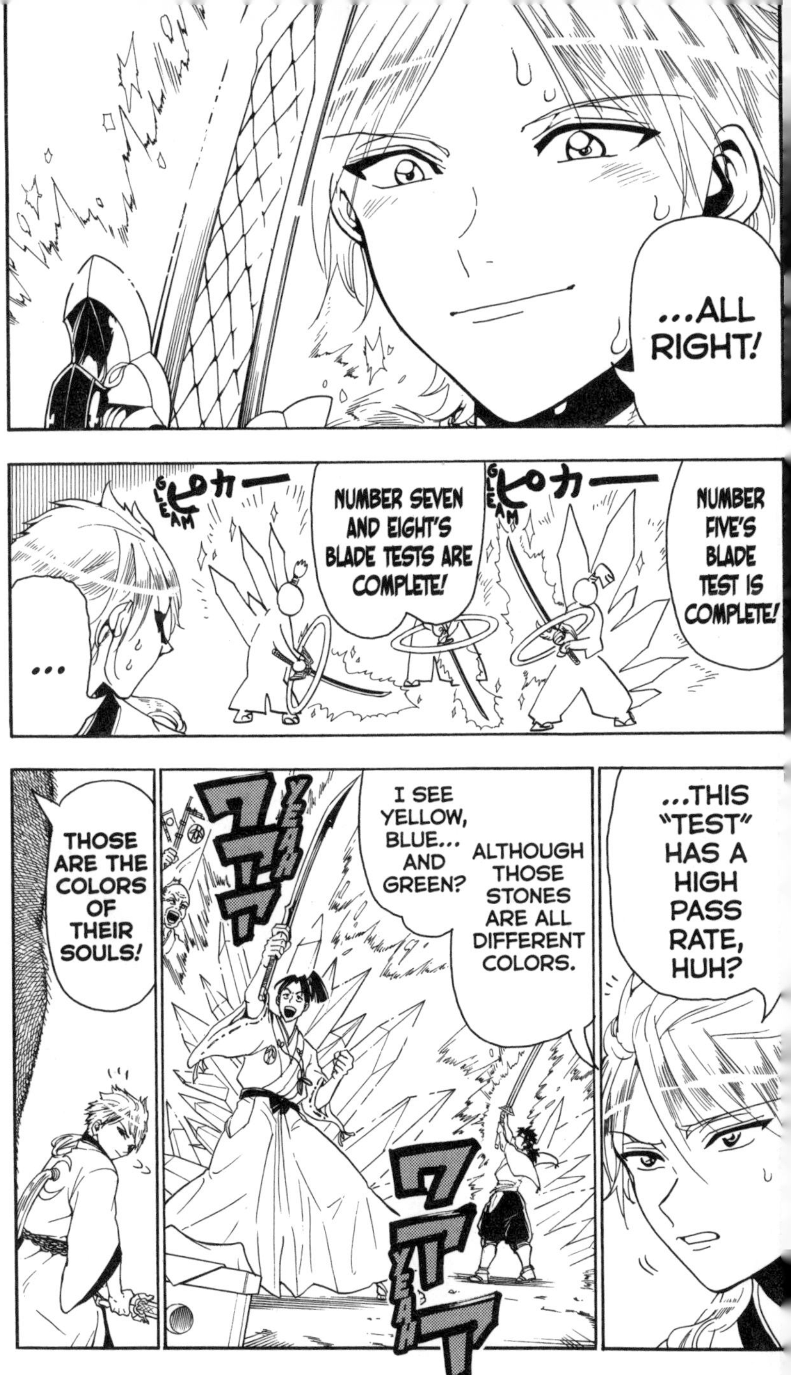
...ALL RIGHT!
NUMBER FIVE'S BLADE TEST IS COMPLETE!
ピカー
GLEAM
NUMBER SEVEN AND EIGHT'S BLADE TESTS ARE COMPLETE!
ピカー
GLEAM
...
...THIS "TEST" HAS A HIGH PASS RATE, HUH?
ALTHOUGH THOSE STONES ARE ALL DIFFERENT COLORS.
I SEE YELLOW, BLUE... AND GREEN?
ワァァ
YEAH
ワァァ
YEAH
THOSE ARE THE COLORS OF THEIR SOULS!

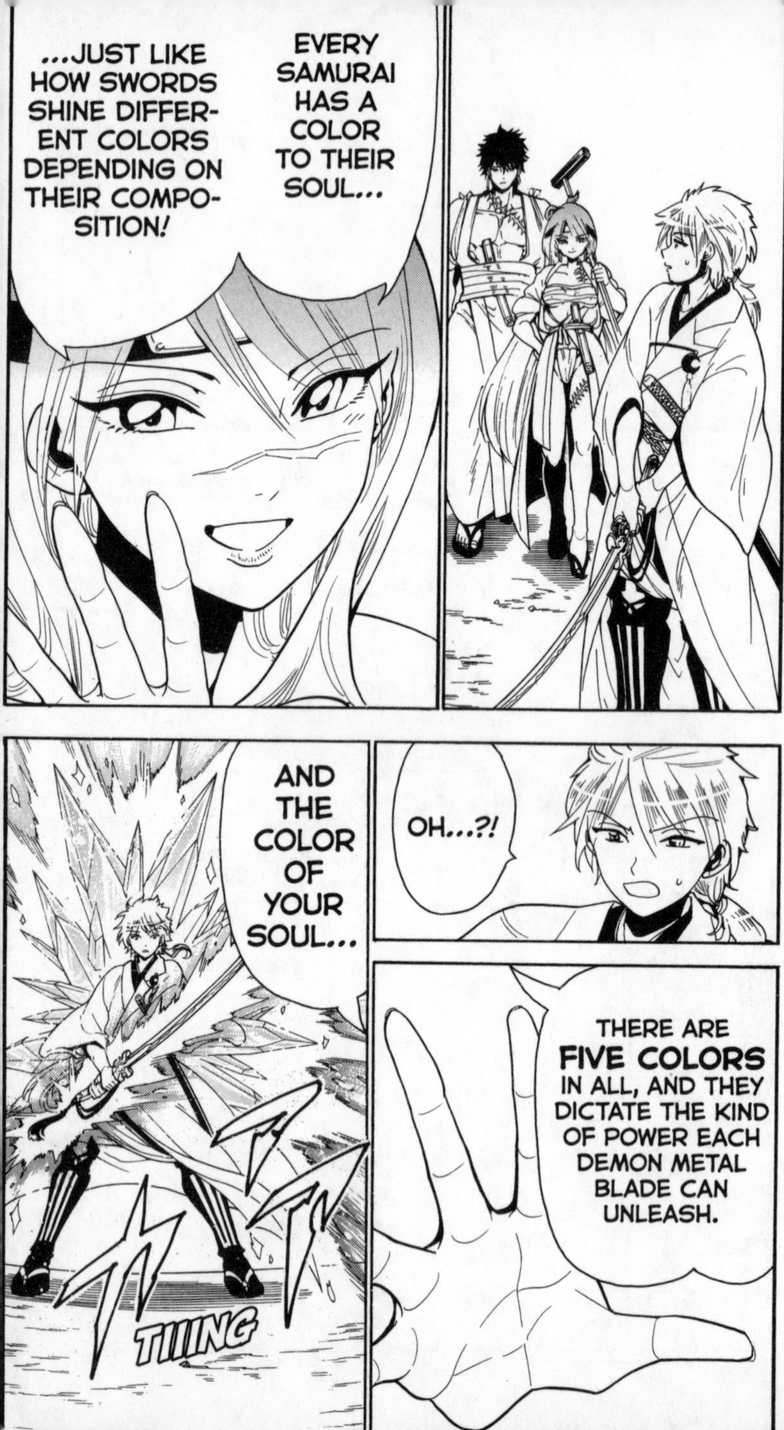
EVERY SAMURAI HAS A COLOR TO THEIR SOUL...
...JUST LIKE HOW SWORDS SHINE DIFFER-ENT COLORS DEPENDING ON THEIR COMPO-SITION!
OH...?!
THERE ARE **FIVE COLORS** IN ALL, AND THEY DICTATE THE KIND OF POWER EACH DEMON METAL BLADE CAN UNLEASH.
AND THE COLOR OF YOUR SOUL...
TIIING

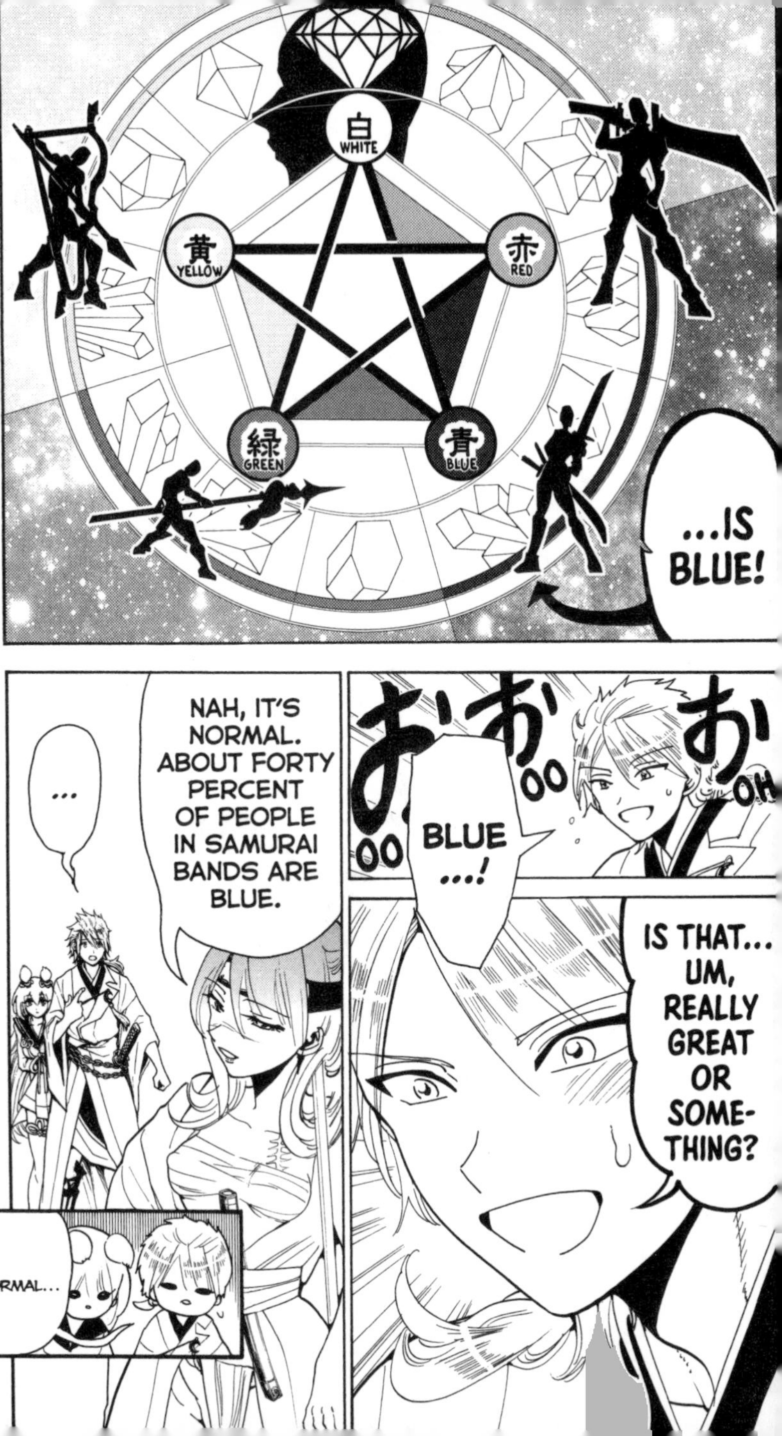
白
WHITE
赤
RED
黄
YELLOW
青
BLUE
緑
GREEN
...IS BLUE!
おおOO
おOH
BLUE ...!
IS THAT... UM, REALLY GREAT OR SOME-THING?
NAH, IT'S NORMAL. ABOUT FORTY PERCENT OF PEOPLE IN SAMURAI BANDS ARE BLUE.
...
NORMAL...

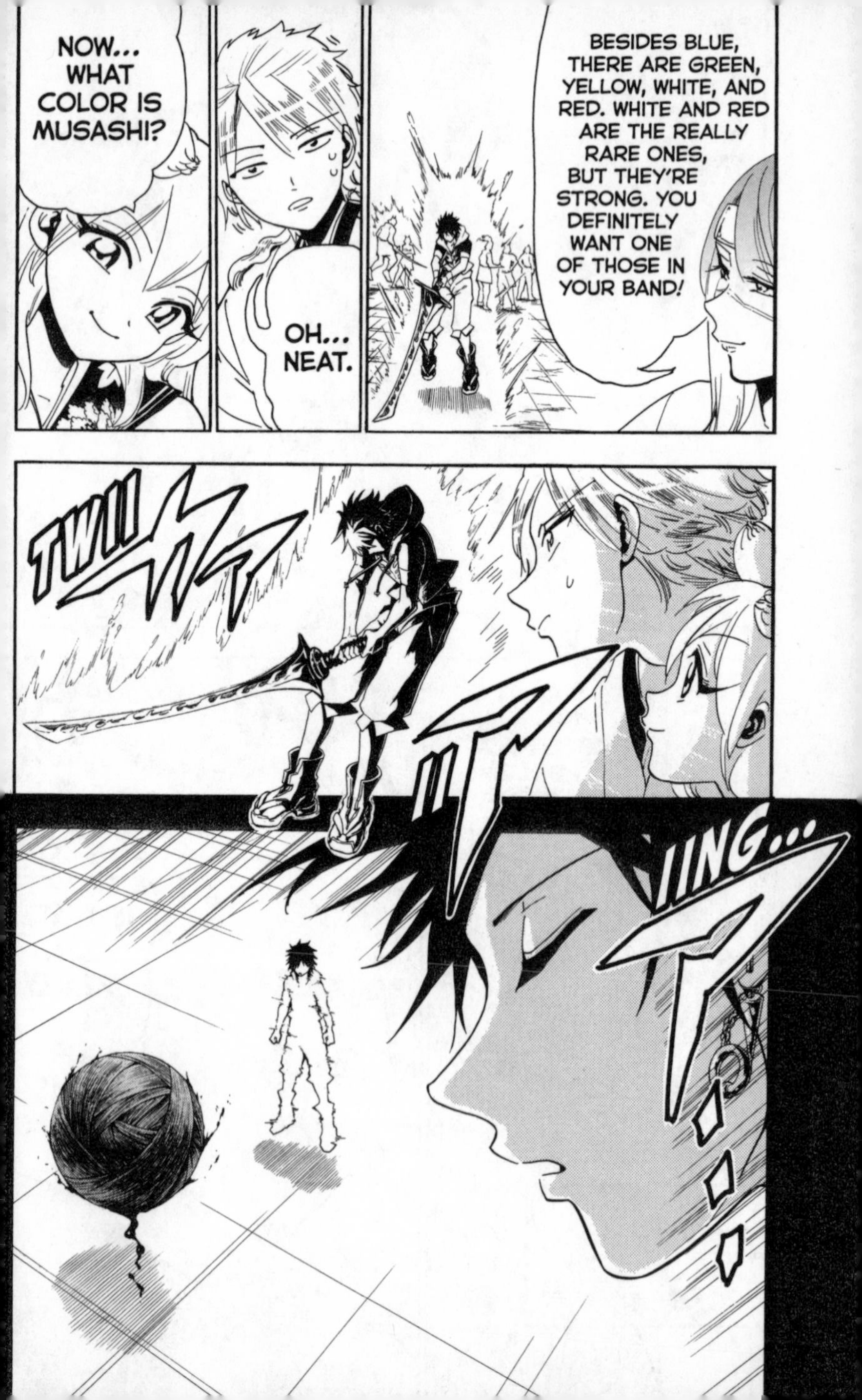
BESIDES BLUE, THERE ARE GREEN, YELLOW, WHITE, AND RED. WHITE AND RED ARE THE REALLY RARE ONES, BUT THEY'RE STRONG. YOU DEFINITELY WANT ONE OF THOSE IN YOUR BAND!
OH... NEAT.
NOW... WHAT COLOR IS MUSASHI?
TWII
IING...

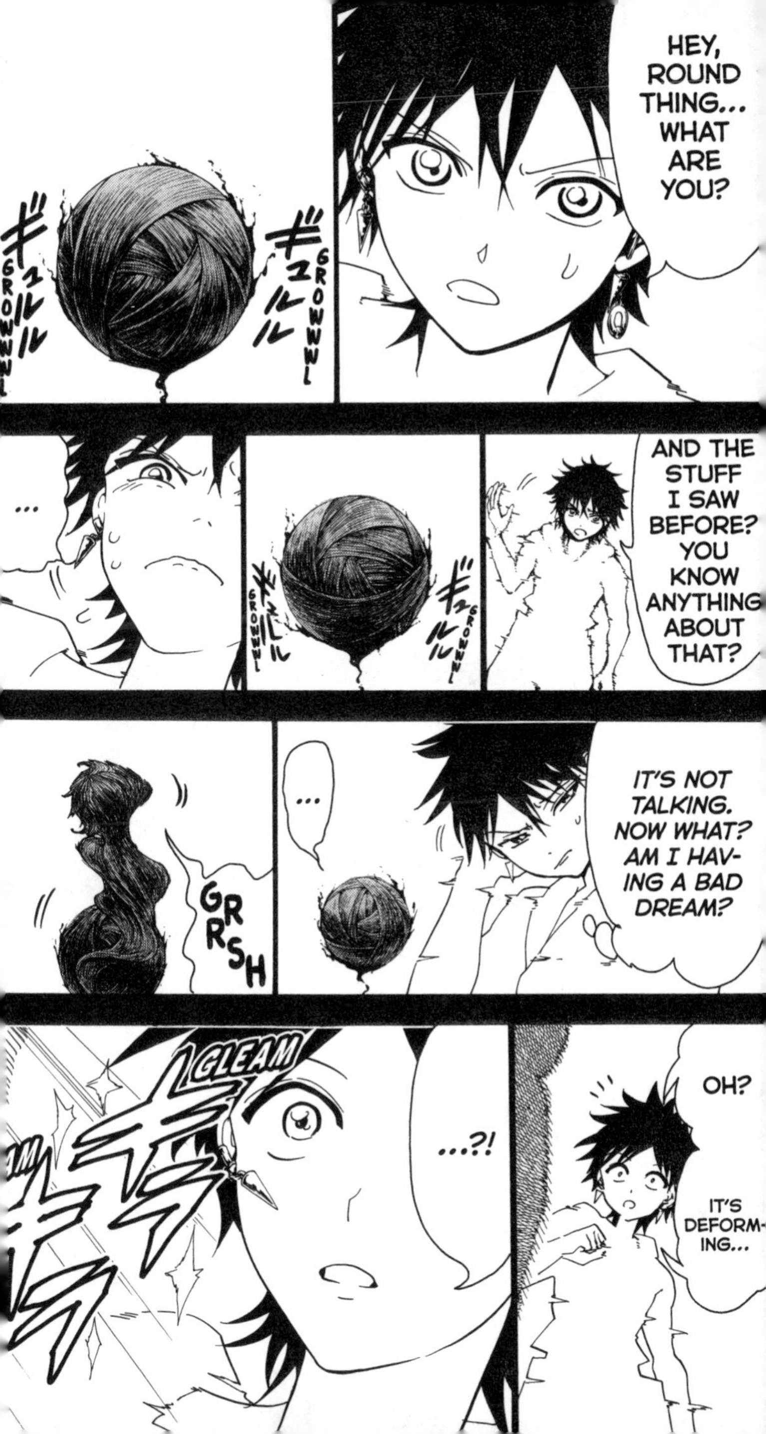
HEY, ROUND THING... WHAT ARE YOU?
GROWWWL
GROWWWL
AND THE STUFF I SAW BEFORE? YOU KNOW ANYTHING ABOUT THAT?
GROWWWL
GROWWWL
...
IT'S NOT TALKING. NOW WHAT? AM I HAV-ING A BAD DREAM?
...
GRRSH
OH?
IT'S DEFORM-ING...
...?!
GLEAM

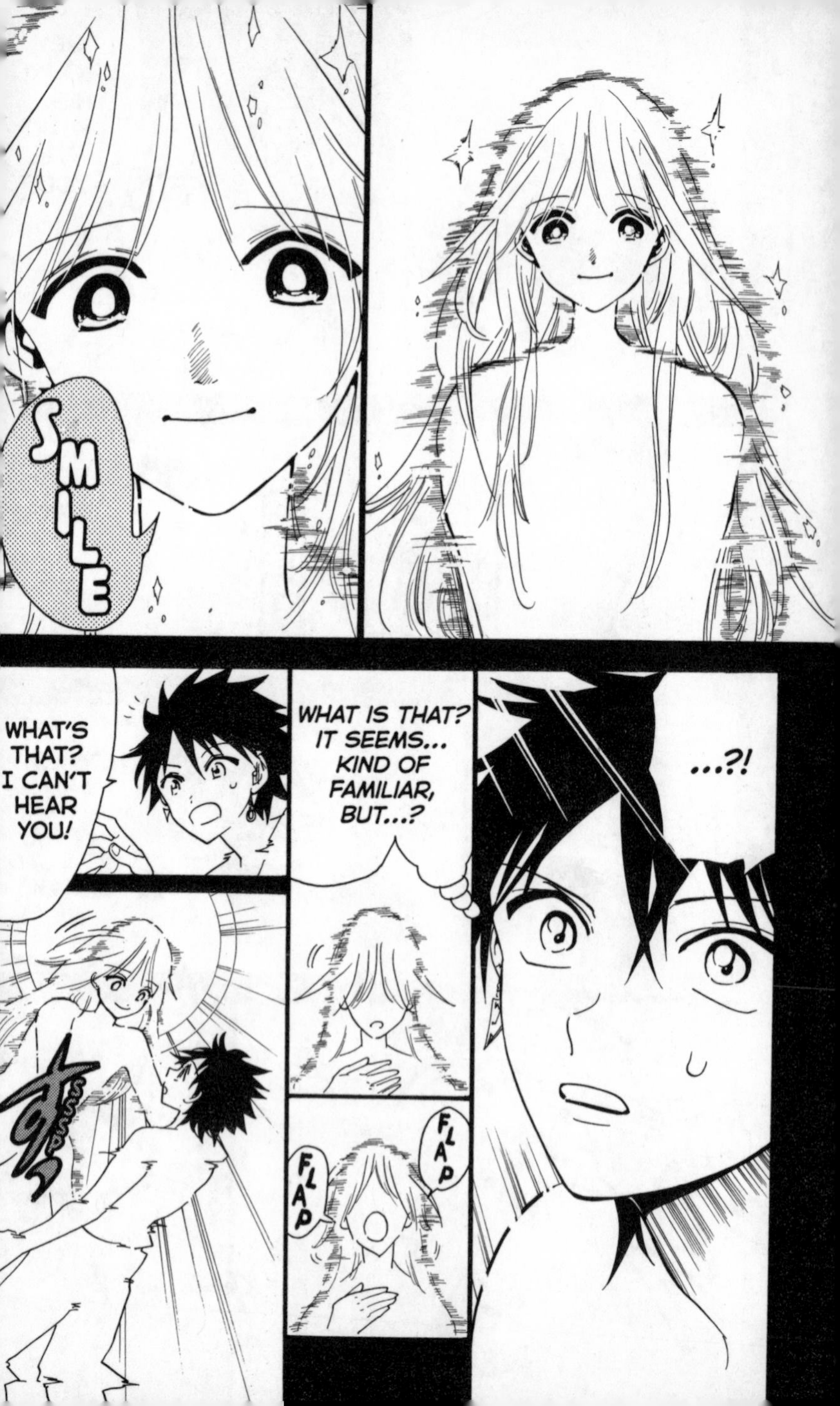
SMILE
...?!
WHAT IS THAT? IT SEEMS... KIND OF FAMILIAR, BUT...?
FLAP
FLAP
WHAT'S THAT? I CAN'T HEAR YOU!

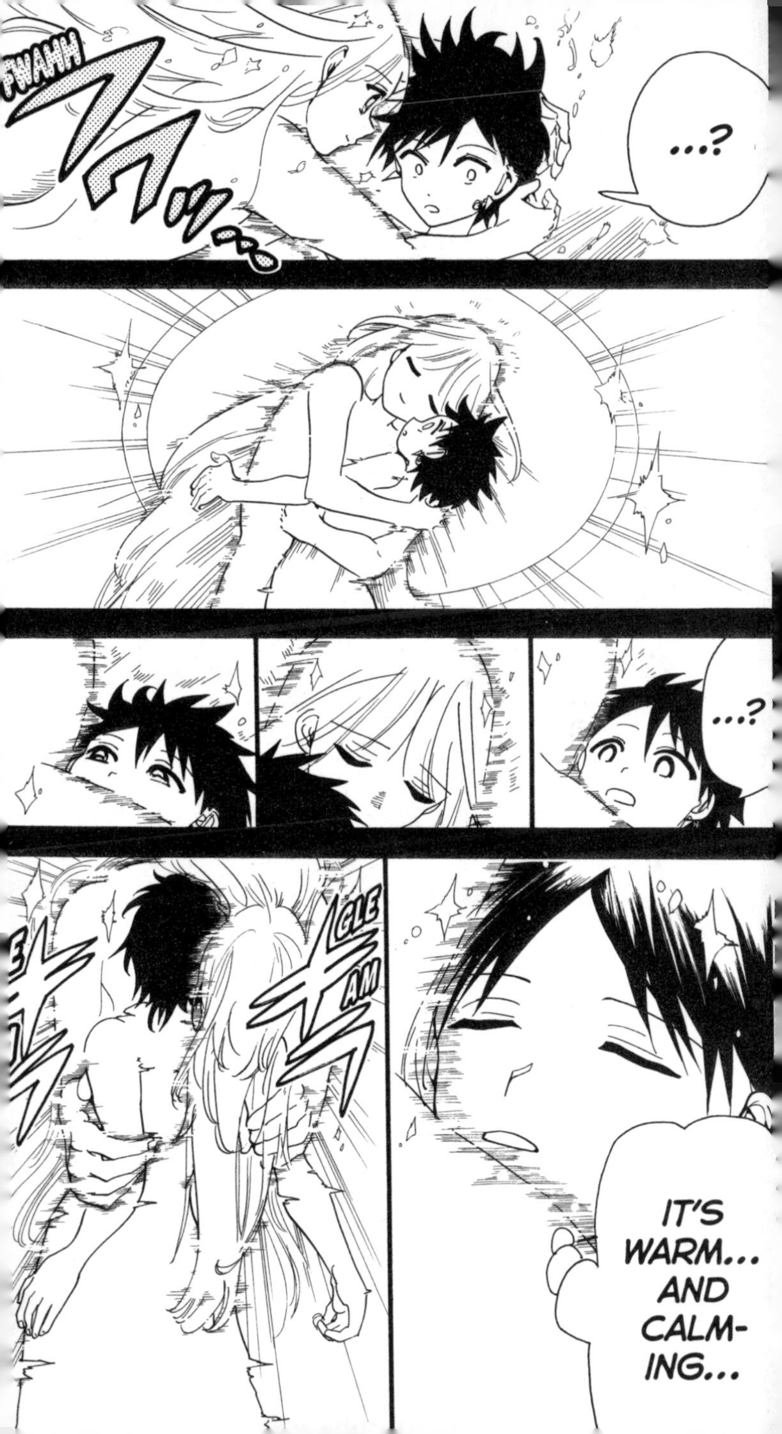
...?
FWAHH
...?
IT'S WARM... AND CALMING...
GLE
AM

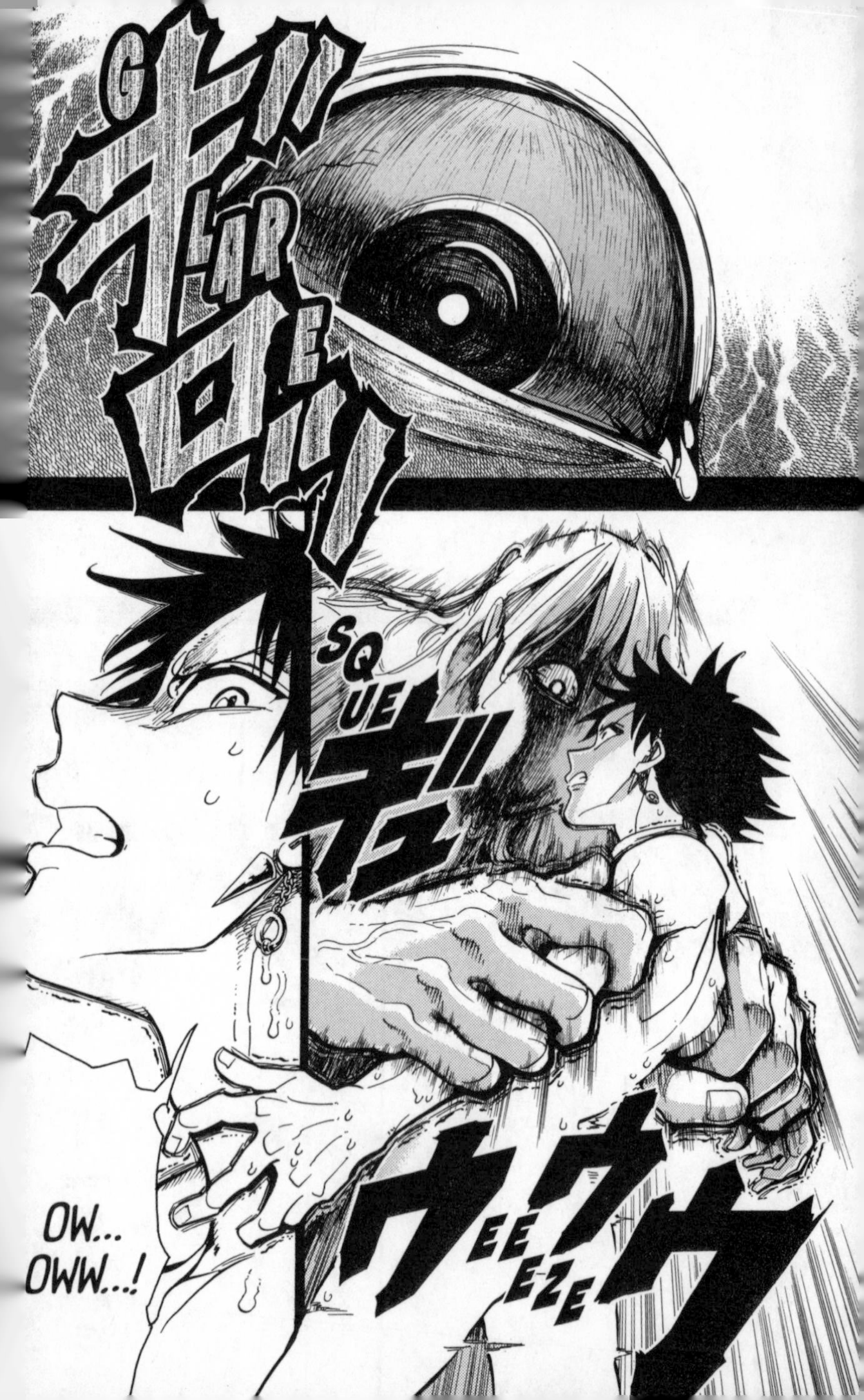
GLARE
SQUEEEE-ZE
OW... OWW...!

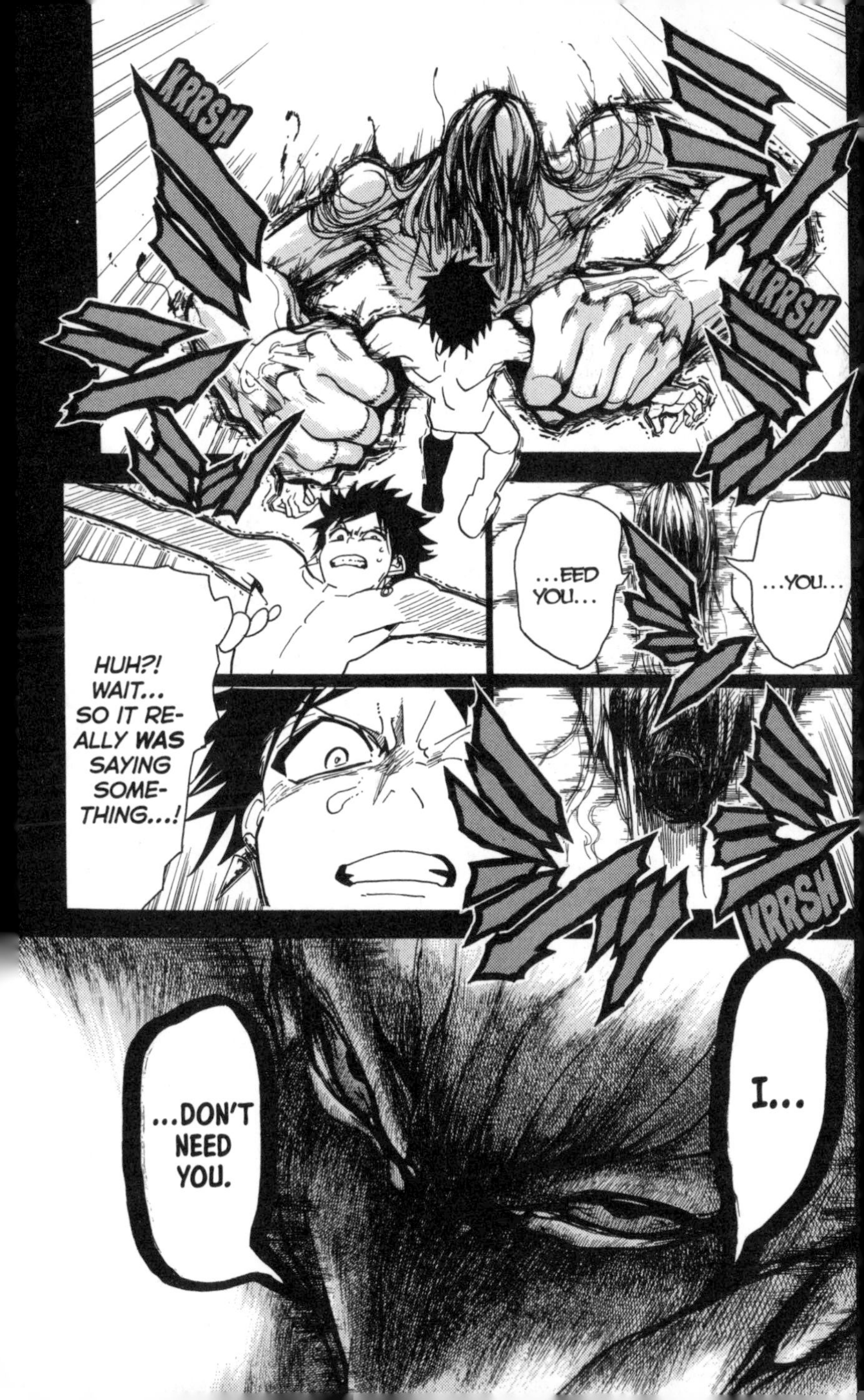
KRRSH
KRRSH
...YOU...
...EED YOU...
KRRSH
HUH?! WAIT... SO IT REALLY WAS SAYING SOMETHING...!
I...
...DON'T NEED YOU.

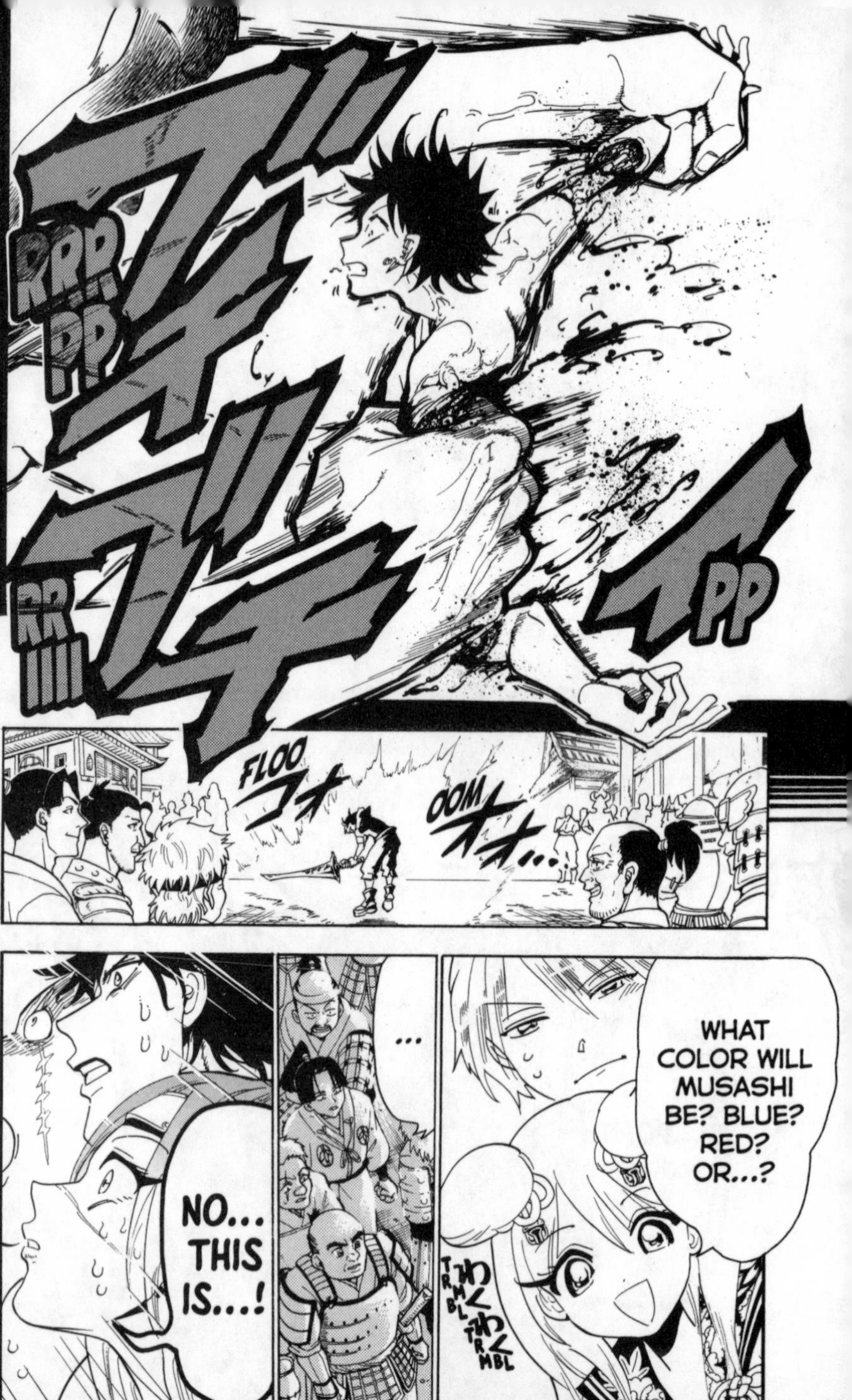

RRR PP
RR IIII
PP
FLOO
OOM...
WHAT COLOR WILL MUSASHI BE? BLUE? RED? OR...?
TRMBL TRMBL
...
NO... THIS IS...!

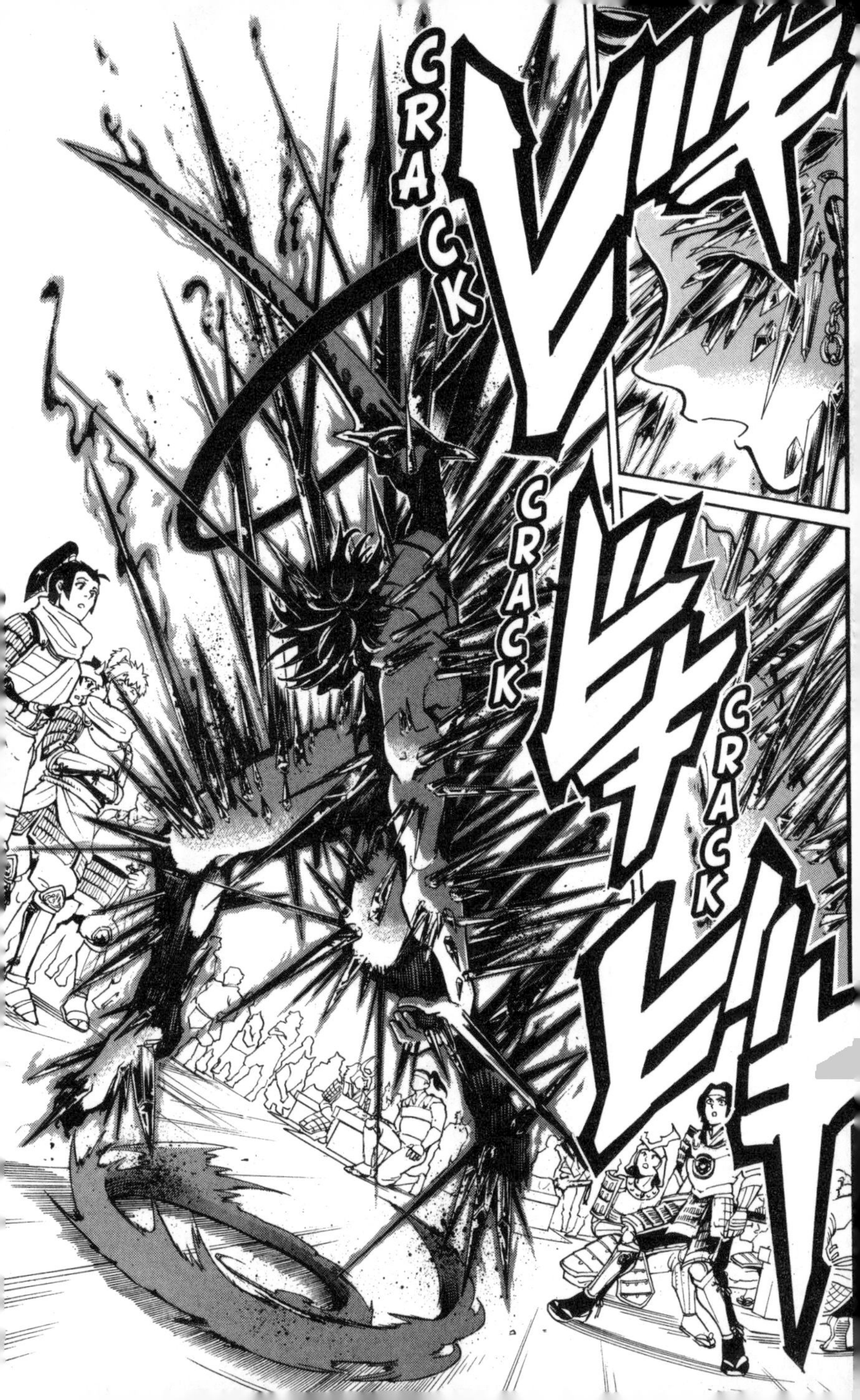
CRACK
CRACK
CRACK

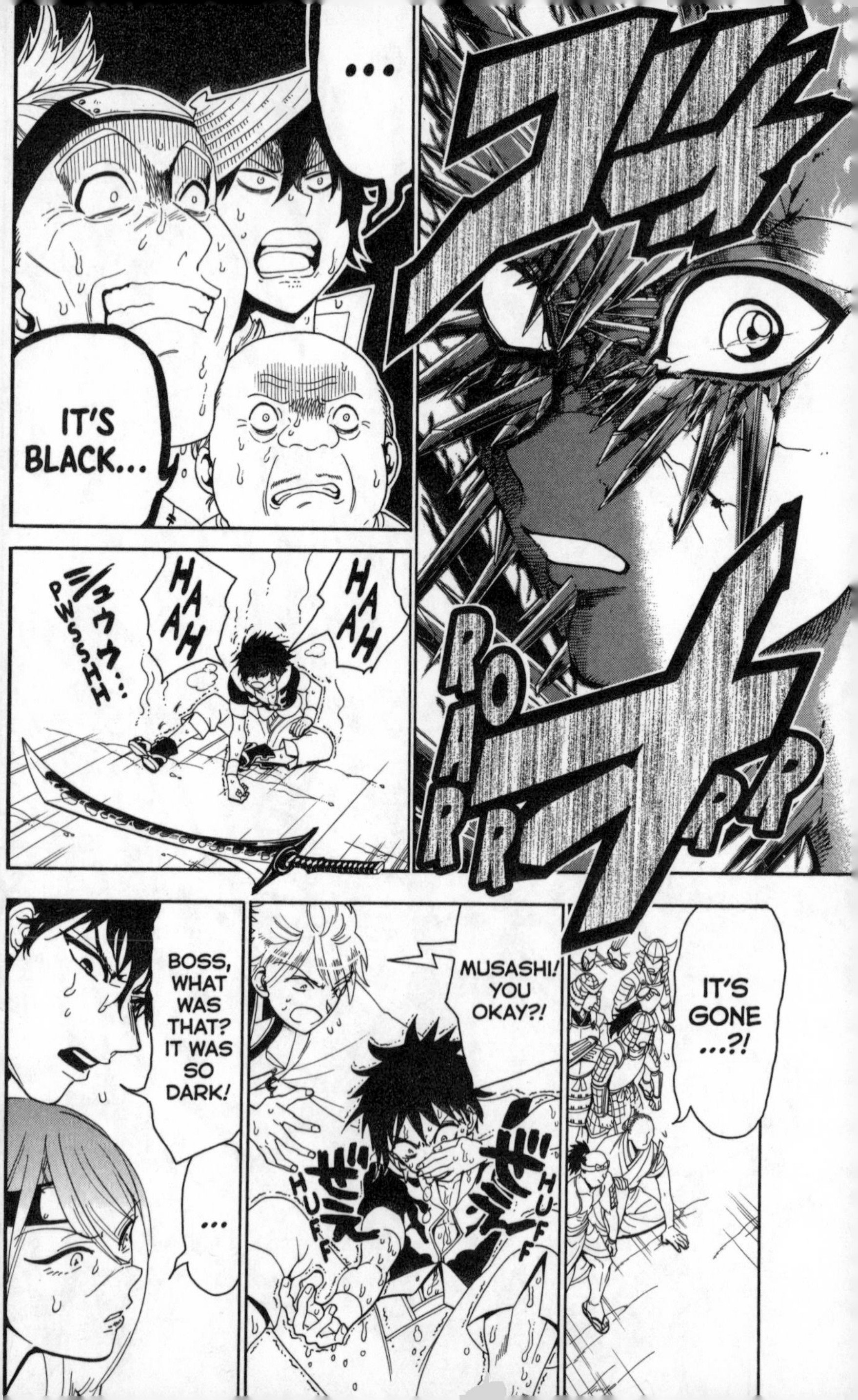
ROARRPP
...
IT'S BLACK...
HAAH
HAAH
PWSSHH
IT'S GONE ...?!
MUSASHI! YOU OKAY?!
HUFF
HUFF
BOSS, WHAT WAS THAT? IT WAS SO DARK!
...

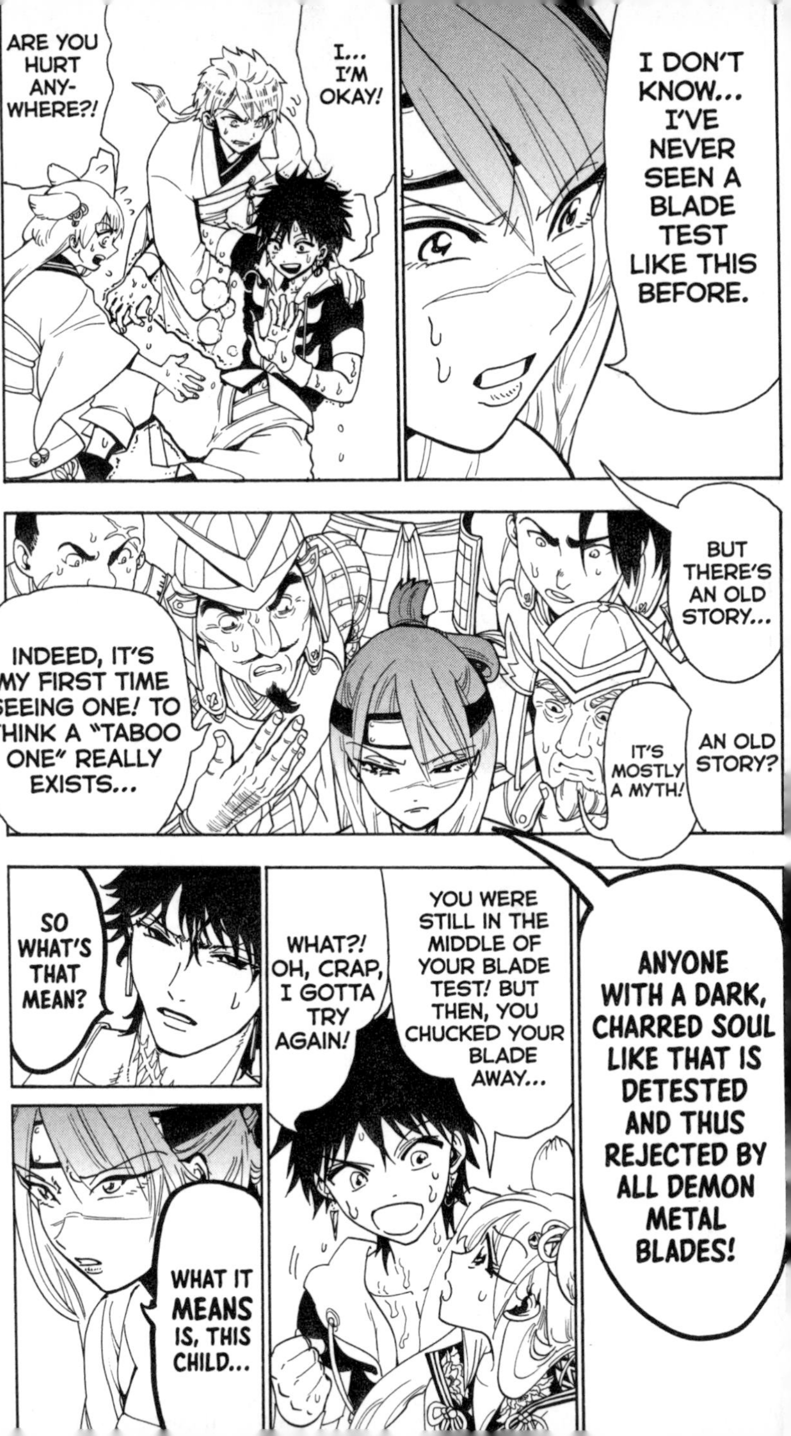
I DON'T KNOW... I'VE NEVER SEEN A BLADE TEST LIKE THIS BEFORE.
I... I'M OKAY!
ARE YOU HURT ANY-WHERE?!
BUT THERE'S AN OLD STORY...
AN OLD STORY?
IT'S MOSTLY A MYTH!
INDEED, IT'S MY FIRST TIME SEEING ONE! TO THINK A "TABOO ONE" REALLY EXISTS...
ANYONE WITH A DARK, CHARRED SOUL LIKE THAT IS DETESTED AND THUS REJECTED BY ALL DEMON METAL BLADES!
YOU WERE STILL IN THE MIDDLE OF YOUR BLADE TEST! BUT THEN, YOU CHUCKED YOUR BLADE AWAY...
WHAT?! OH, CRAP, I GOTTA TRY AGAIN!
SO WHAT'S THAT MEAN?
WHAT IT MEANS IS, THIS CHILD...

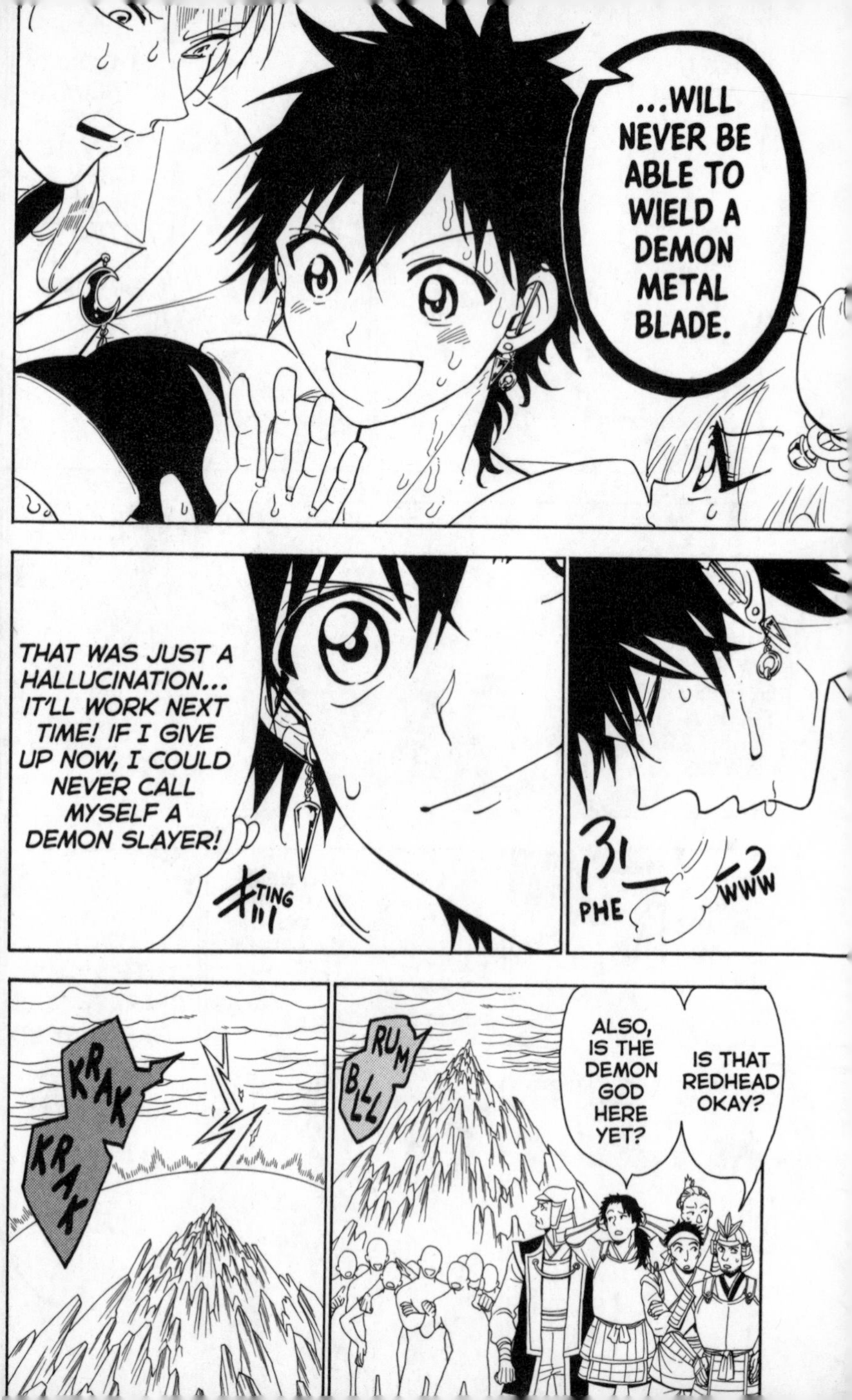
...WILL NEVER BE ABLE TO WIELD A DEMON METAL BLADE.
PHEWWW
THAT WAS JUST A HALLUCINATION... IT'LL WORK NEXT TIME! IF I GIVE UP NOW, I COULD NEVER CALL MYSELF A DEMON SLAYER!
TING
RUMBLL
IS THAT REDHEAD OKAY?
ALSO, IS THE DEMON GOD HERE YET?
KRAK KRAK

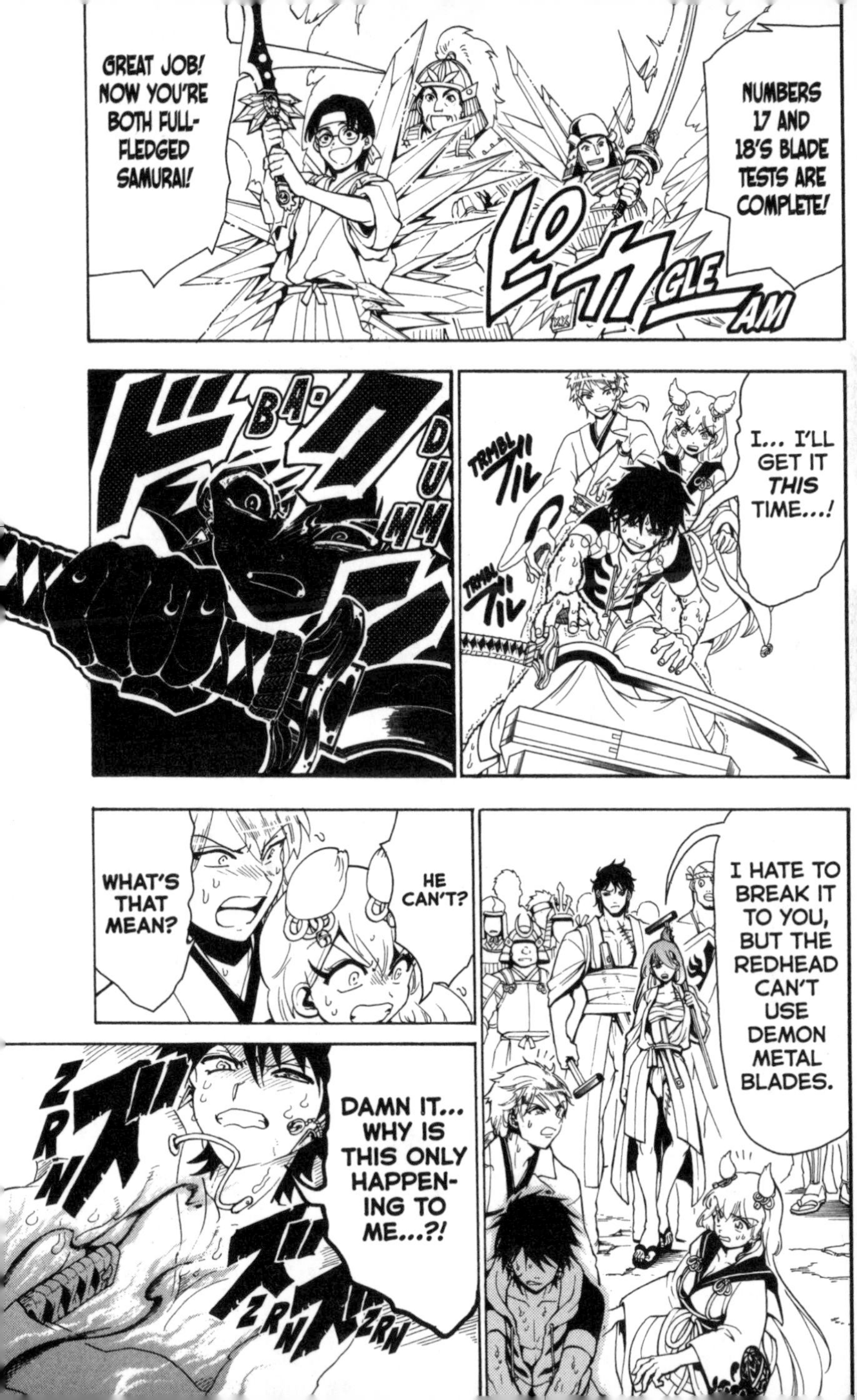
NUMBERS 17 AND 18'S BLADE TESTS ARE COMPLETE!
GREAT JOB! NOW YOU'RE BOTH FULL-FLEDGED SAMURAI!
GLEAM
I... I'LL GET IT THIS TIME...!
TRMBL
TRMBL
BA-DUMMM
I HATE TO BREAK IT TO YOU, BUT THE REDHEAD CAN'T USE DEMON METAL BLADES.
HE CAN'T?
WHAT'S THAT MEAN?
DAMN IT... WHY IS THIS ONLY HAPPENING TO ME...?!
ZRN
ZRN
ZRN

CHAPTER 24: YOU CAN'T BREATHE UNDERWATER

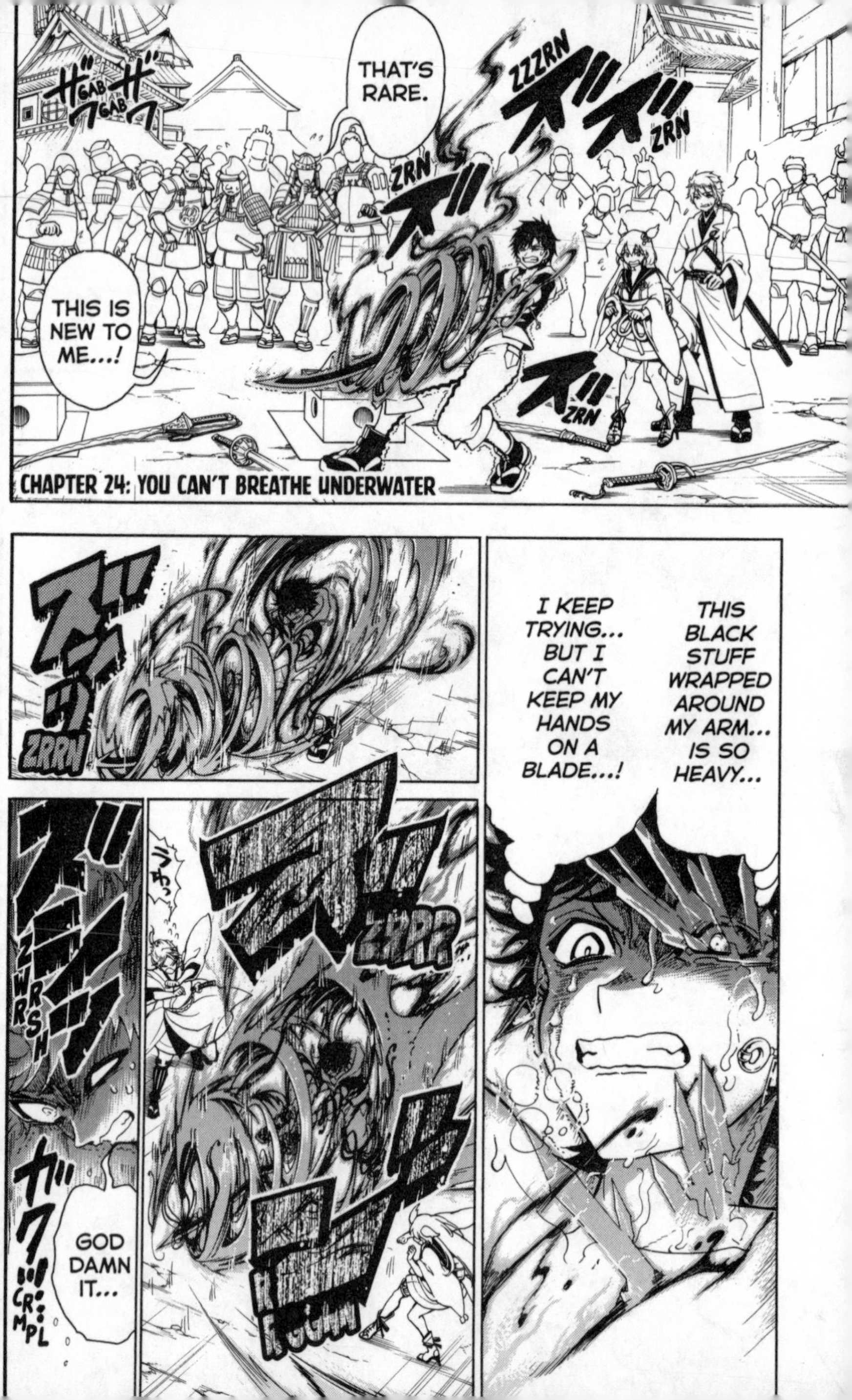
ZZZRN
ZRN
GAB GAB
THAT'S RARE.
ZRN
THIS IS NEW TO ME...!
ZRN
THIS BLACK STUFF WRAPPED AROUND MY ARM... IS SO HEAVY...
I KEEP TRYING... BUT I CAN'T KEEP MY HANDS ON A BLADE...!
ZRRN
ZRRR
ZWRRSH
GOD DAMN IT...
CRMPL

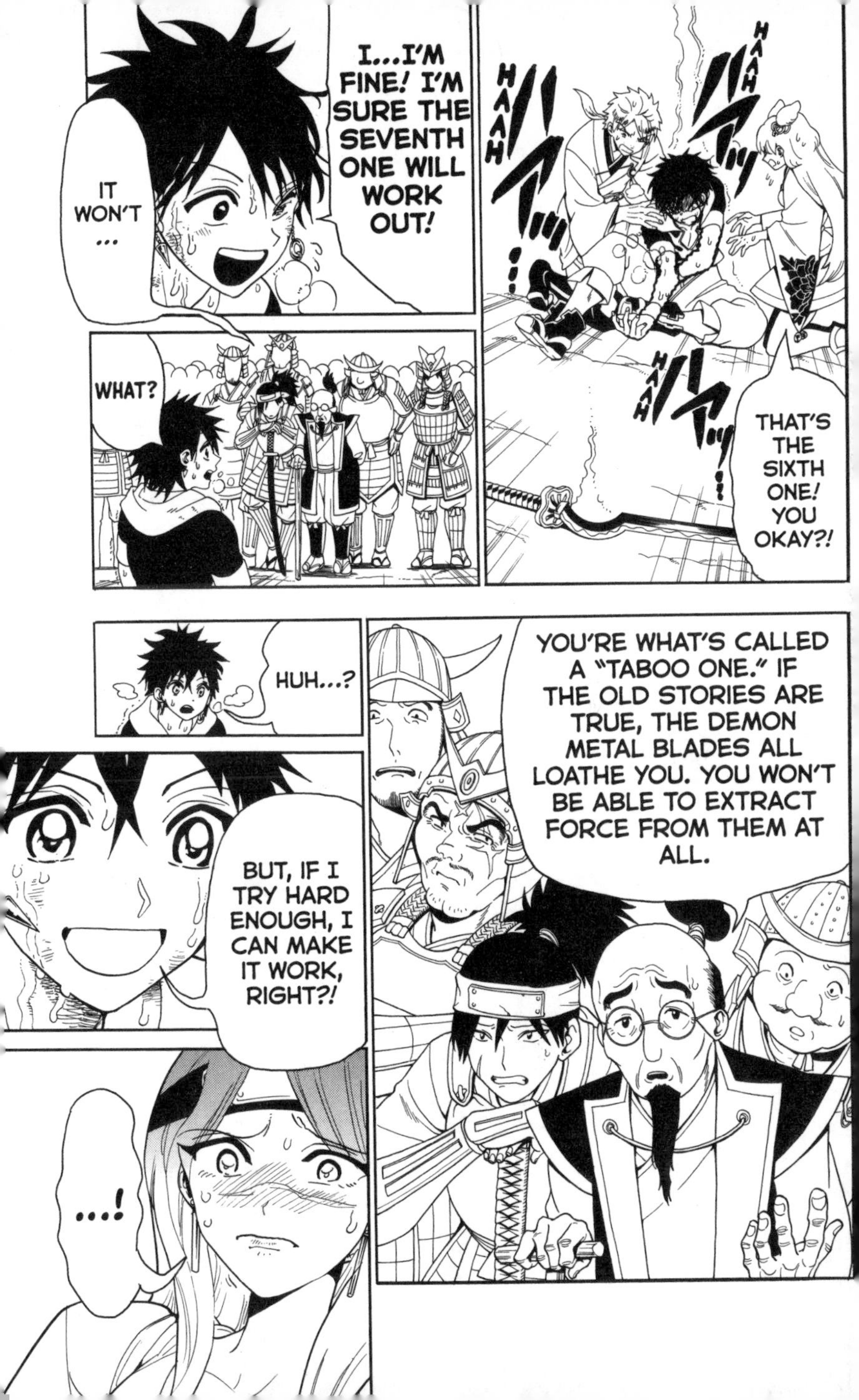
HAAAH
HAAAH
THAT'S THE SIXTH ONE! YOU OKAY?!
HAAAH
I...I'M FINE! I'M SURE THE SEVENTH ONE WILL WORK OUT!
IT WON'T ...
WHAT?
YOU'RE WHAT'S CALLED A "TABOO ONE." IF THE OLD STORIES ARE TRUE, THE DEMON METAL BLADES ALL LOATHE YOU. YOU WON'T BE ABLE TO EXTRACT FORCE FROM THEM AT ALL.
HUH...?
BUT, IF I TRY HARD ENOUGH, I CAN MAKE IT WORK, RIGHT?!
...!

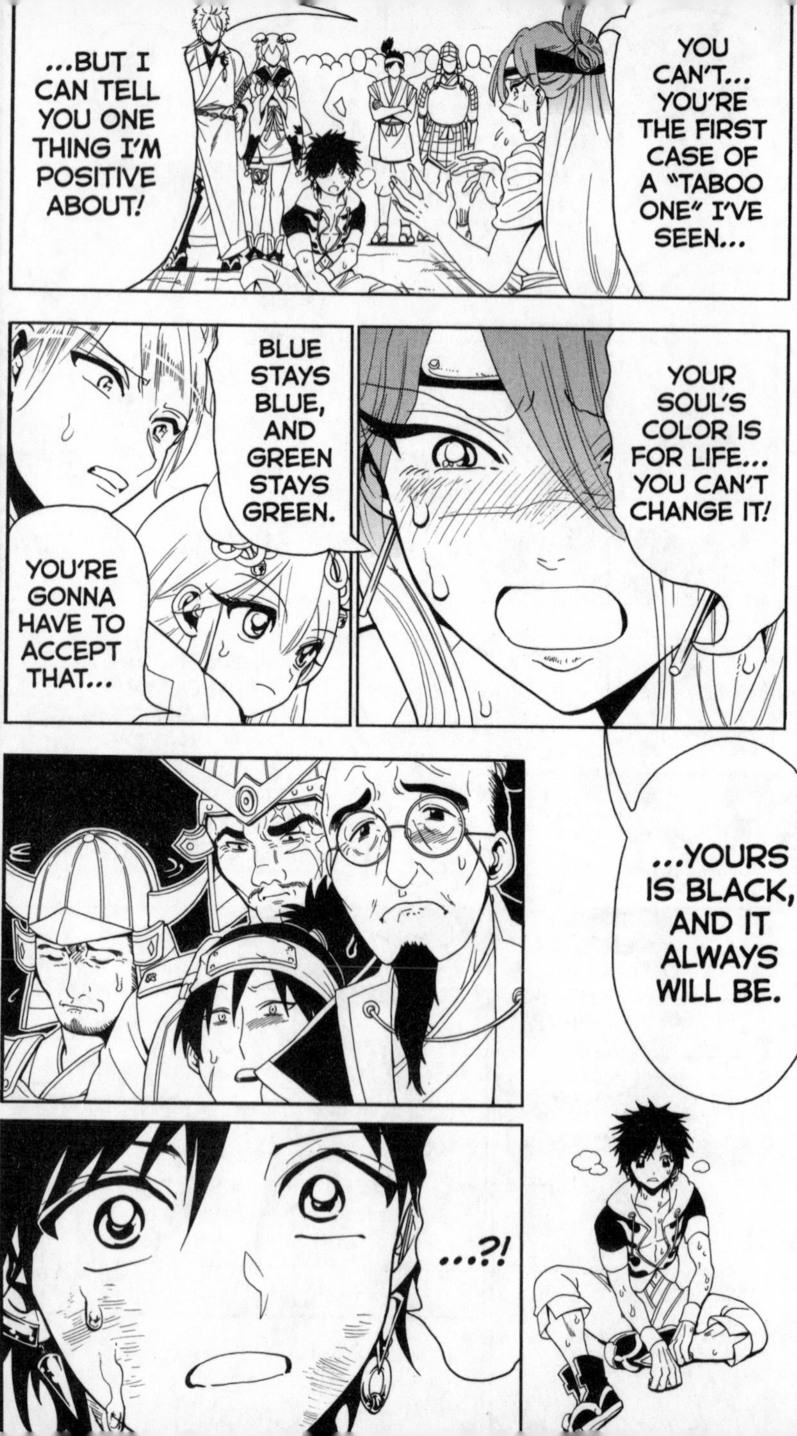
YOU CAN'T... YOU'RE THE FIRST CASE OF A "TABOO ONE" I'VE SEEN...
...BUT I CAN TELL YOU ONE THING I'M POSITIVE ABOUT!
YOUR SOUL'S COLOR IS FOR LIFE... YOU CAN'T CHANGE IT!
BLUE STAYS BLUE, AND GREEN STAYS GREEN.
YOU'RE GONNA HAVE TO ACCEPT THAT...
...YOURS IS BLACK, AND IT ALWAYS WILL BE.
...?!

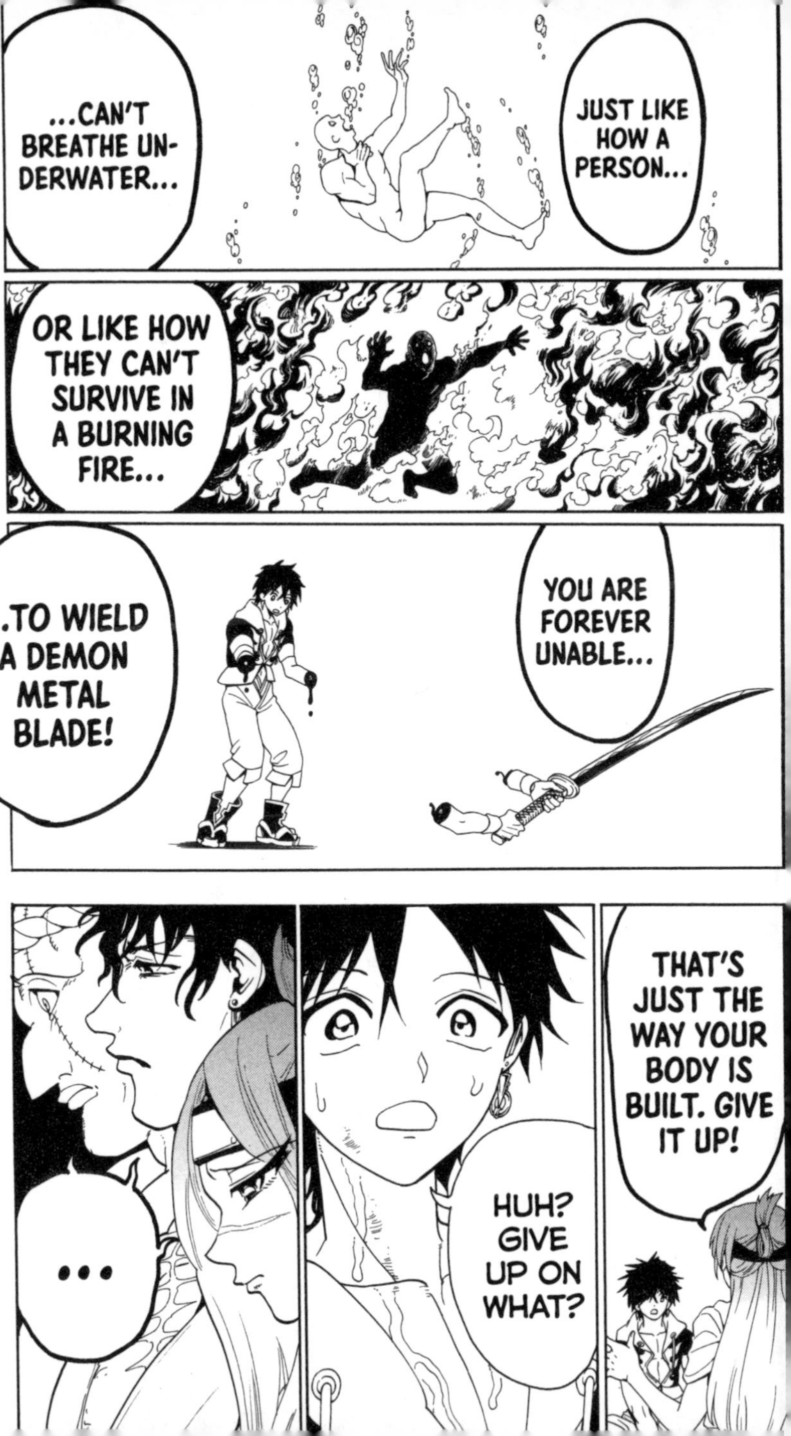
JUST LIKE HOW A PERSON...
...CAN'T BREATHE UNDERWATER...
OR LIKE HOW THEY CAN'T SURVIVE IN A BURNING FIRE...
YOU ARE FOREVER UNABLE...
...TO WIELD A DEMON METAL BLADE!
THAT'S JUST THE WAY YOUR BODY IS BUILT. GIVE IT UP!
HUH? GIVE UP ON WHAT?
...

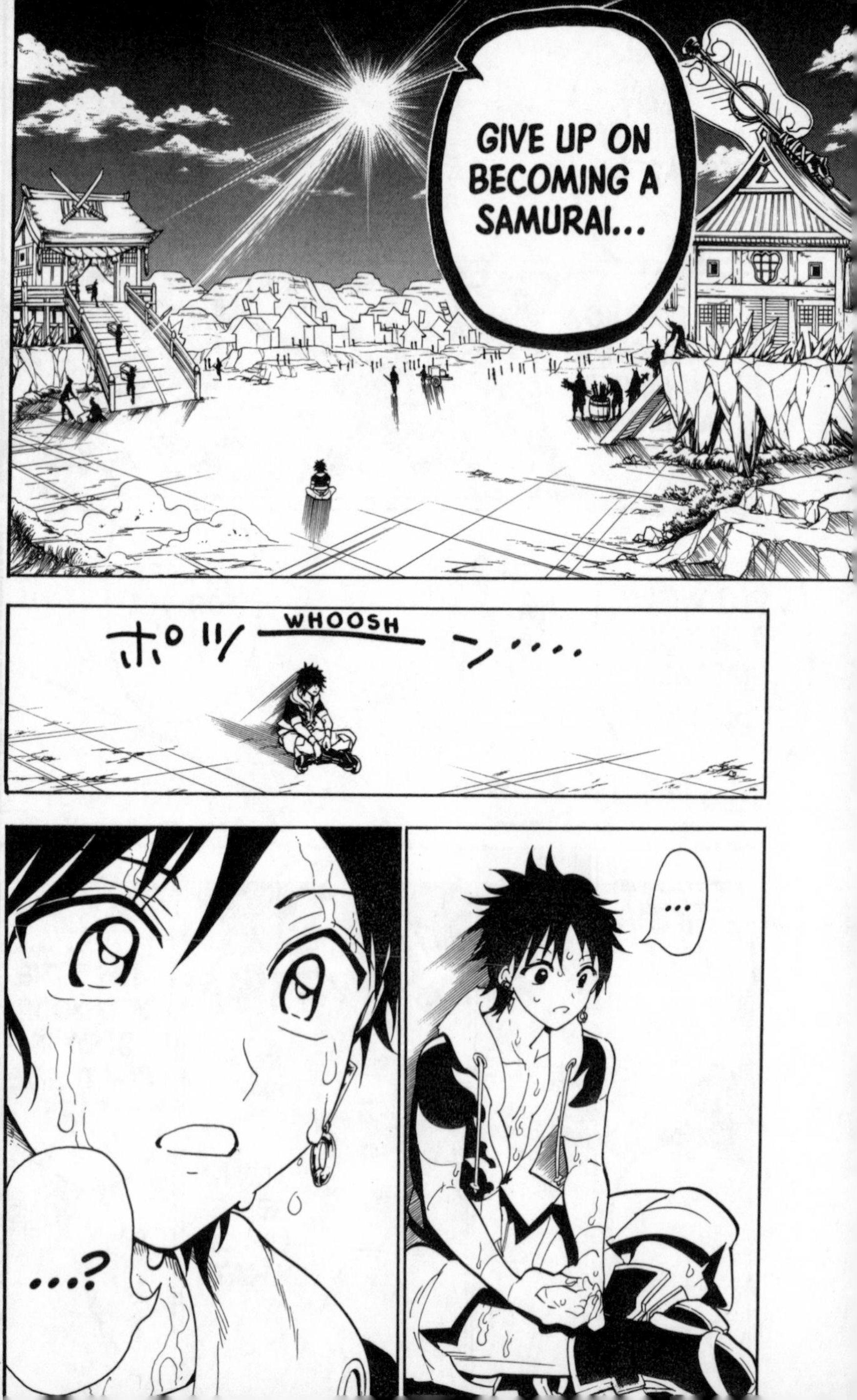
GIVE UP ON BECOMING A SAMURAI...
ポツ
WHOOSH
ン…
...
...?

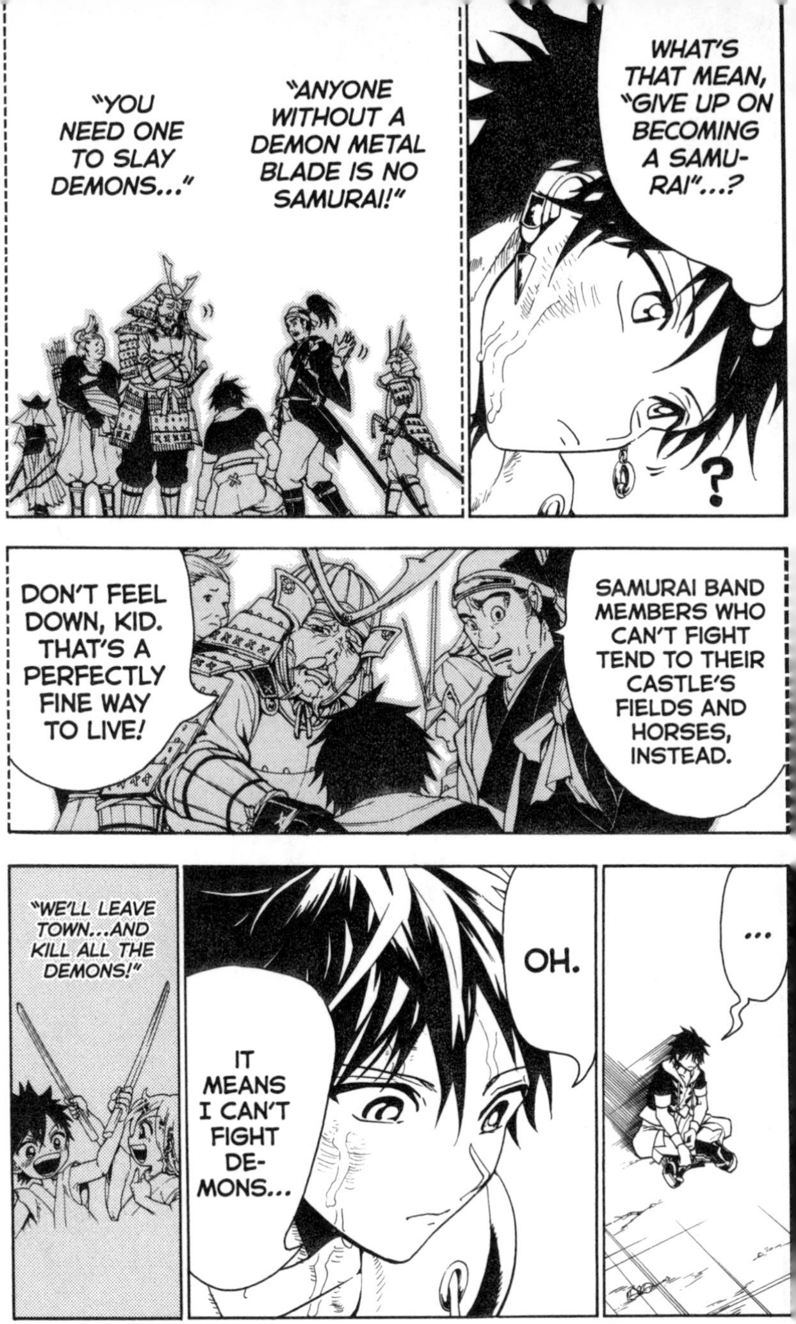
WHAT'S THAT MEAN, "GIVE UP ON BECOMING A SAMU-RAI"...?
?
"ANYONE WITHOUT A DEMON METAL BLADE IS NO SAMURAI!"
"YOU NEED ONE TO SLAY DEMONS..."
SAMURAI BAND MEMBERS WHO CAN'T FIGHT TEND TO THEIR CASTLE'S FIELDS AND HORSES, INSTEAD.
DON'T FEEL DOWN, KID. THAT'S A PERFECTLY FINE WAY TO LIVE!
...
OH.
IT MEANS I CAN'T FIGHT DE-MONS...
"WE'LL LEAVE TOWN...AND KILL ALL THE DEMONS!"

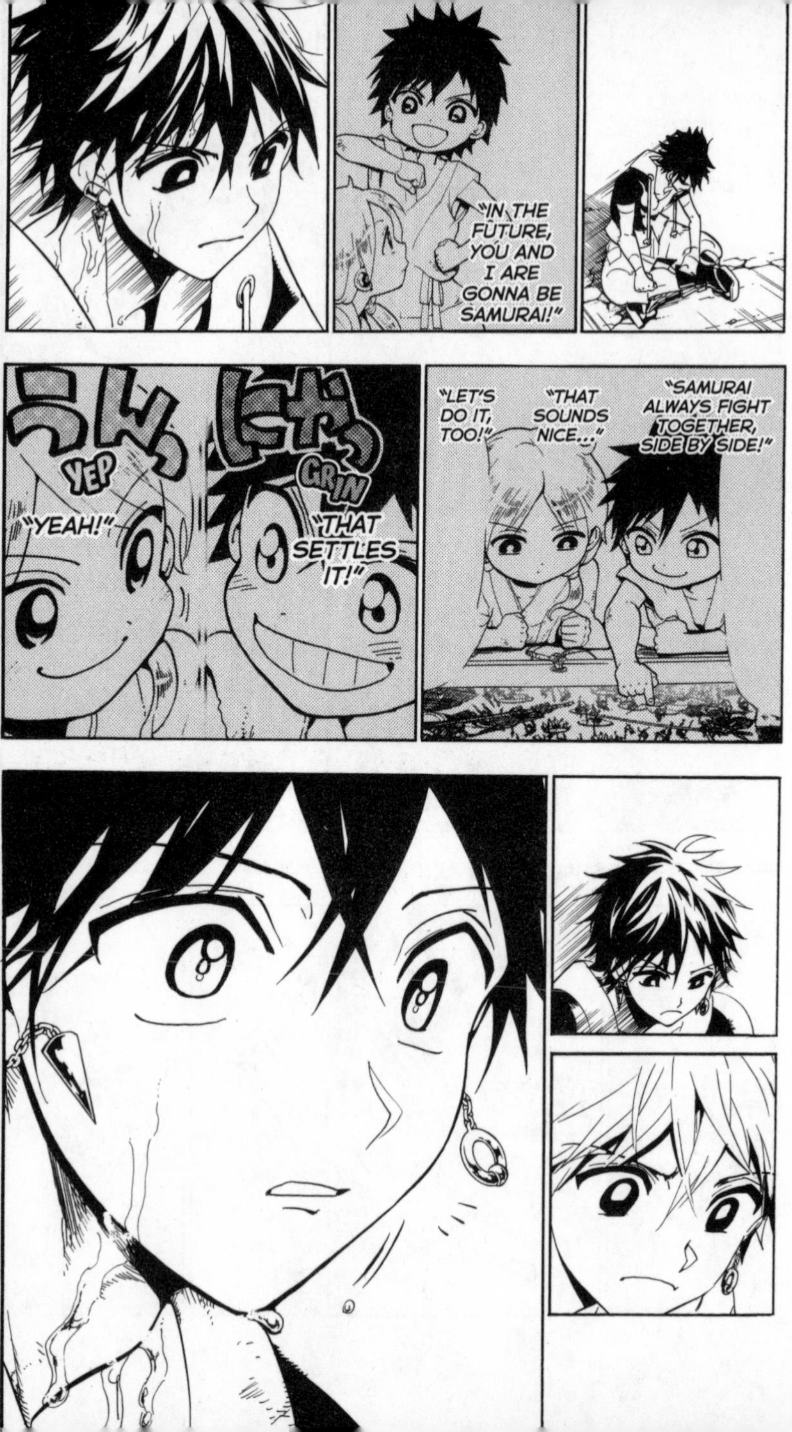
"IN THE FUTURE, YOU AND I ARE GONNA BE SAMURAI!"
"SAMURAI ALWAYS FIGHT TOGETHER, SIDE BY SIDE!"
"THAT SOUNDS NICE..."
"LET'S DO IT, TOO!"
にかっ
GRIN
"THAT SETTLES IT!"
うんっ
YEP
"YEAH!"

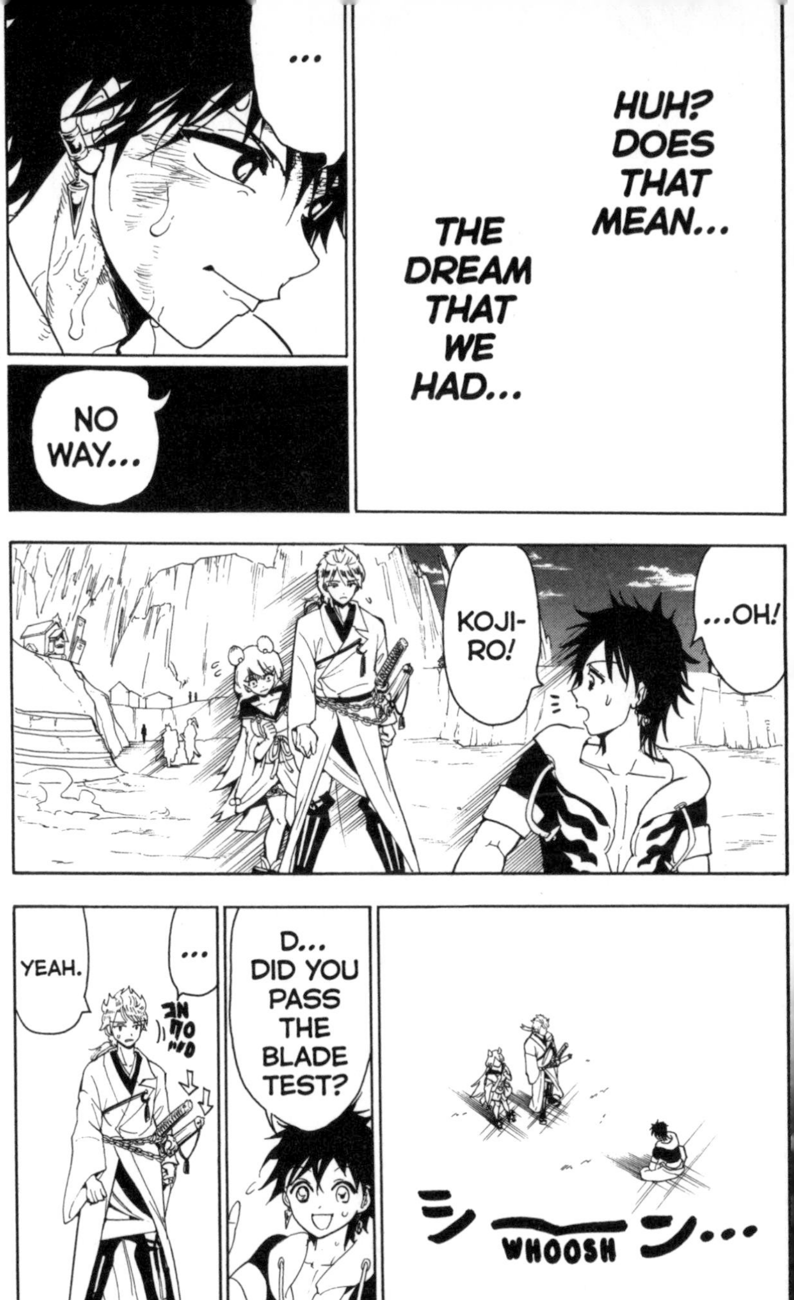
HUH? DOES THAT MEAN...
THE DREAM THAT WE HAD...
...
NO WAY...
...OH!
KOJI-RO!
WHOOSH
D... DID YOU PASS THE BLADE TEST?
...
YEAH.

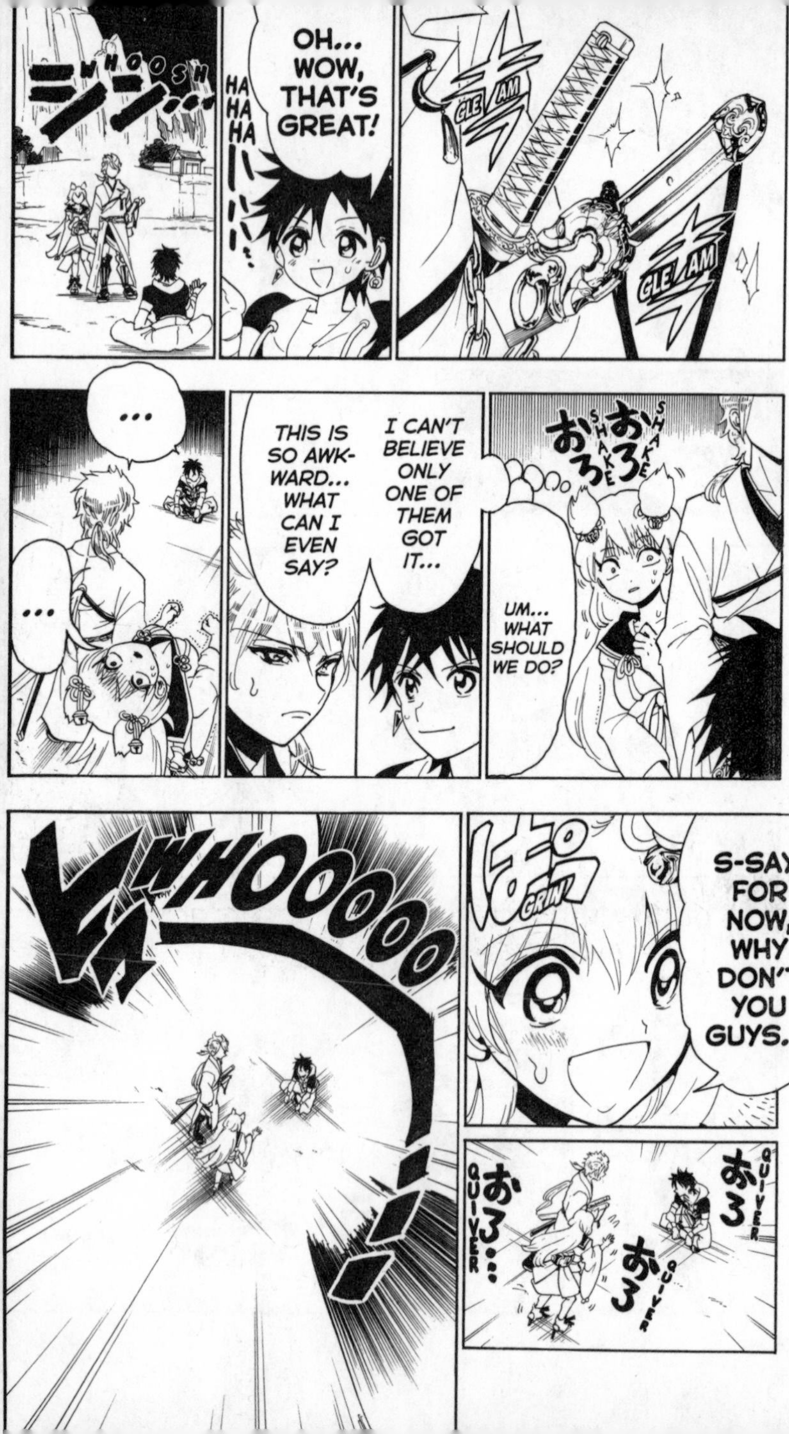
GLEAM
GLEAM
OH... WOW, THAT'S GREAT!
HA HA HA
WHOOSH
SHAKE おろ SHAKE おろ
UM... WHAT SHOULD WE DO?
I CAN'T BELIEVE ONLY ONE OF THEM GOT IT...
THIS IS SO AWK-WARD... WHAT CAN I EVEN SAY?
...
...
GRIN
S-SAY! FOR NOW, WHY DON'T YOU GUYS...
QUIVER おろ
QUIVER おろ
QUIVER おろ...
WHOOOOOO

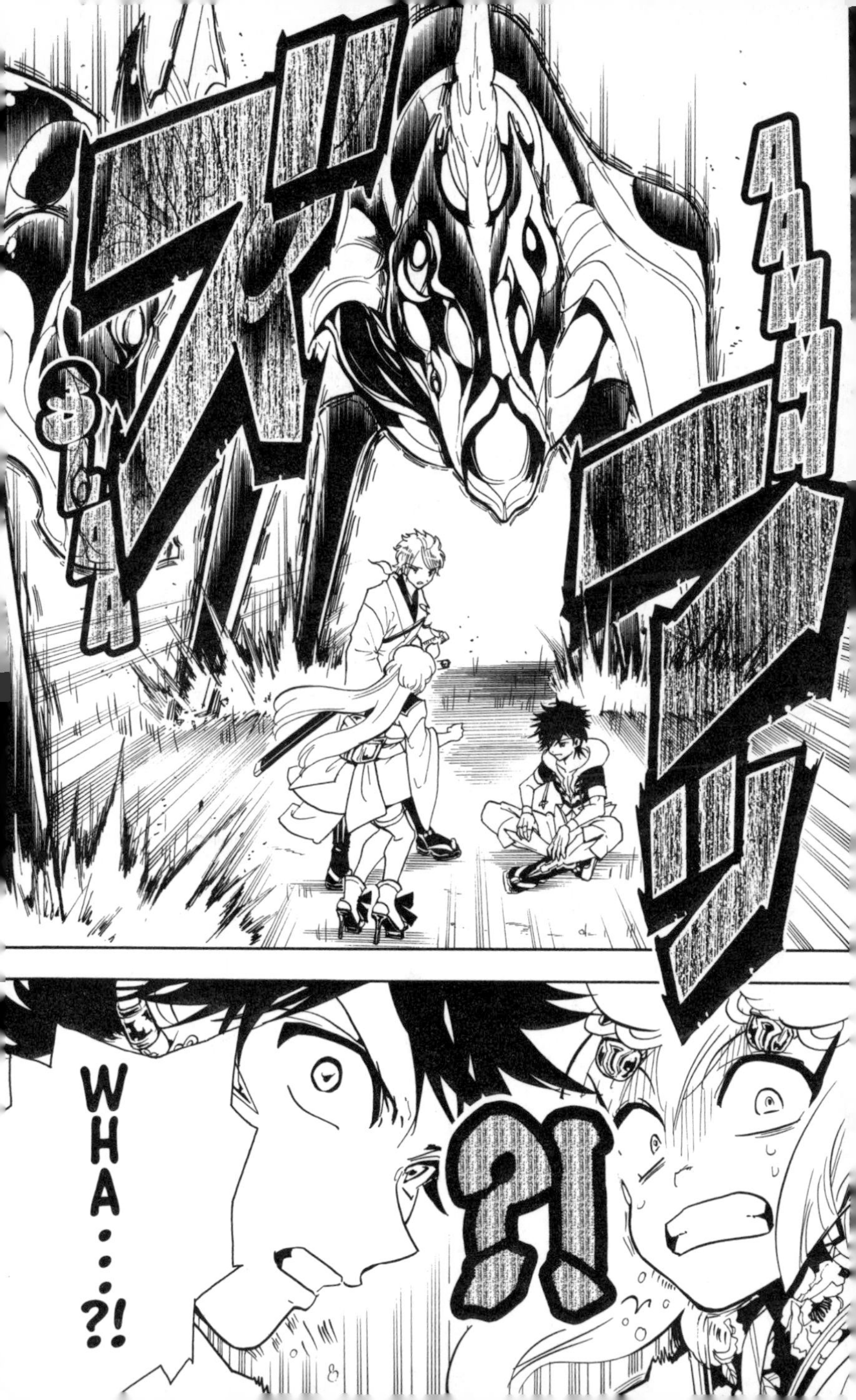
AAMMM
WHA...?!
?!

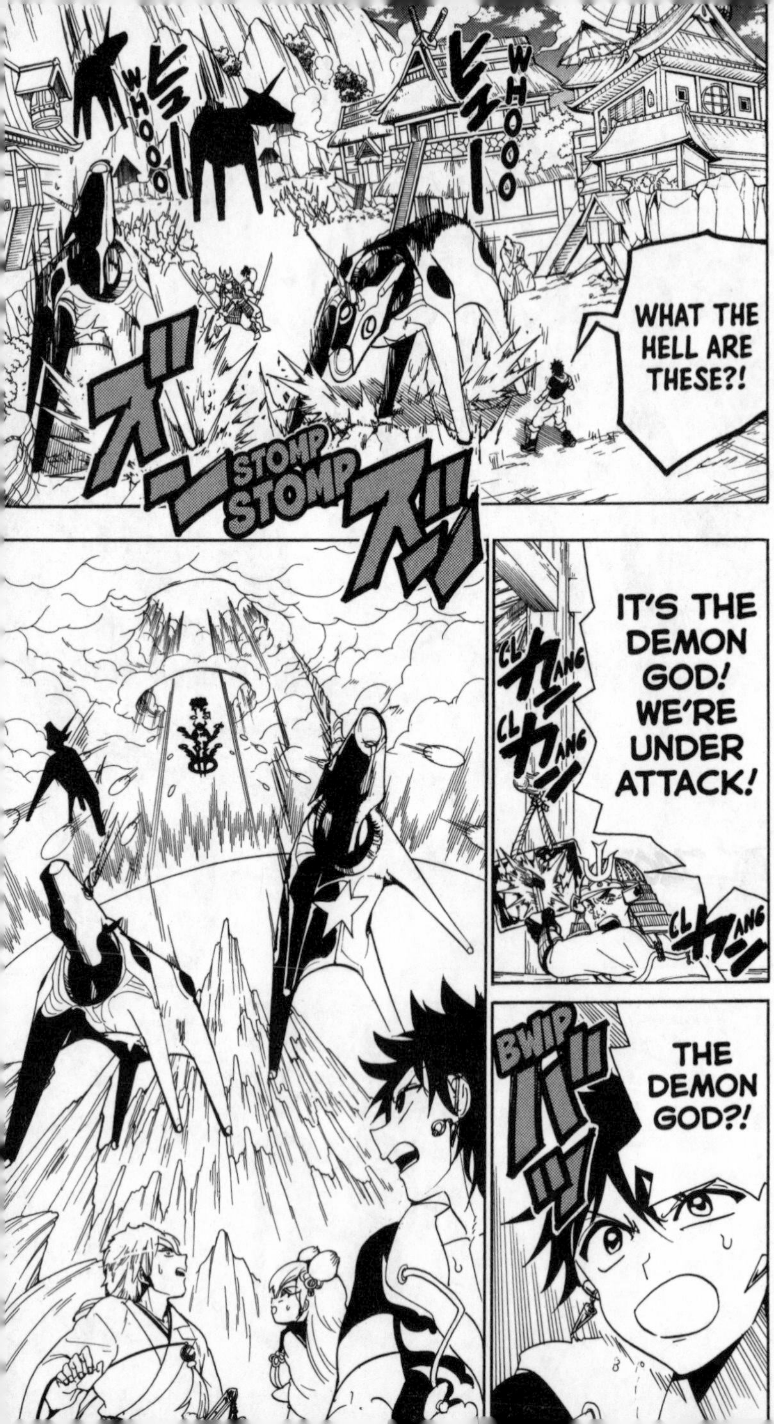
WHOOOO
WHAT THE HELL ARE THESE?!
WHOOOO
STOMP STOMP
CLANG
CLANG
IT'S THE DEMON GOD! WE'RE UNDER ATTACK!
CLANG
BWIP
THE DEMON GOD?!

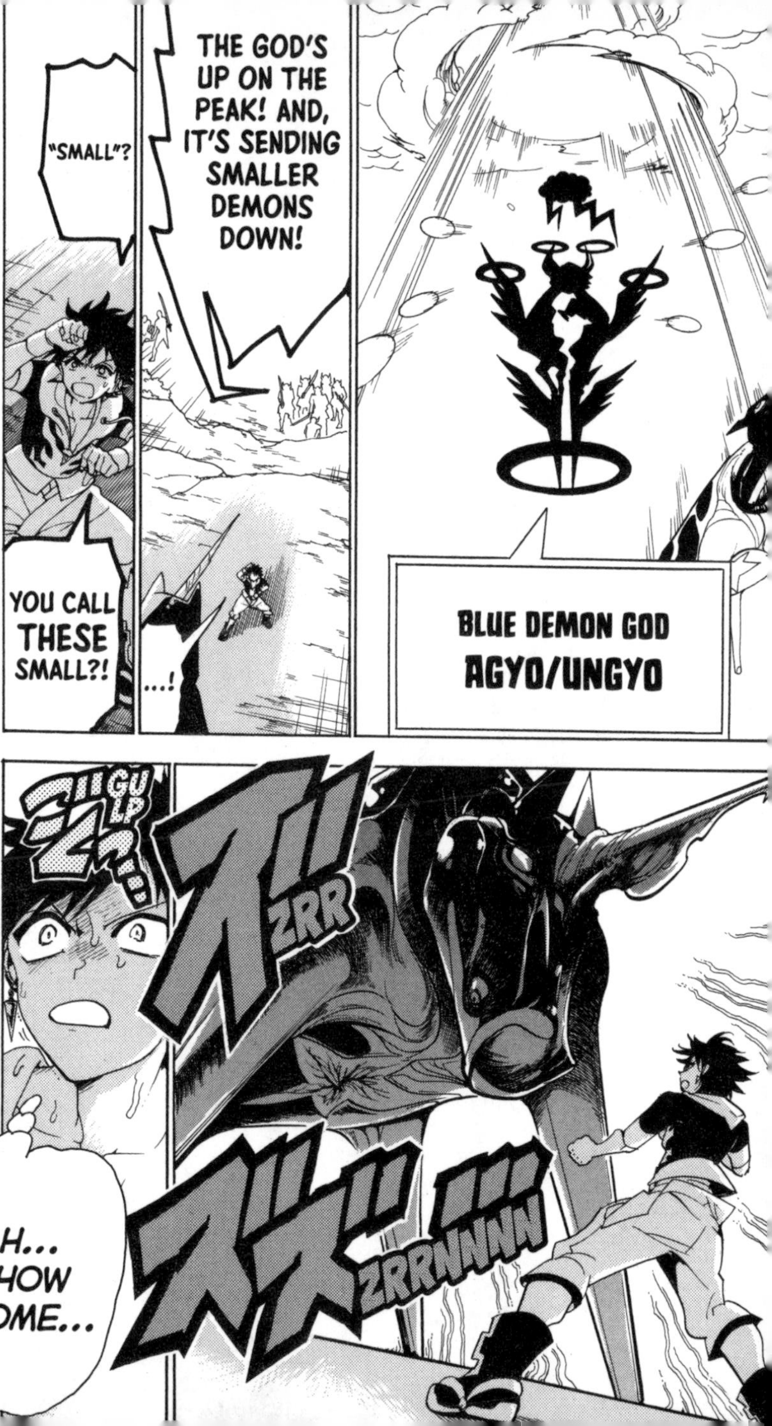
BLUE DEMON GOD
AGYO/UNGYO
THE GOD'S UP ON THE PEAK! AND, IT'S SENDING SMALLER DEMONS DOWN!
...!
"SMALL"?
YOU CALL THESE SMALL?!
ZRR
ZRRNNNNN
GULP
H... HOW COME...

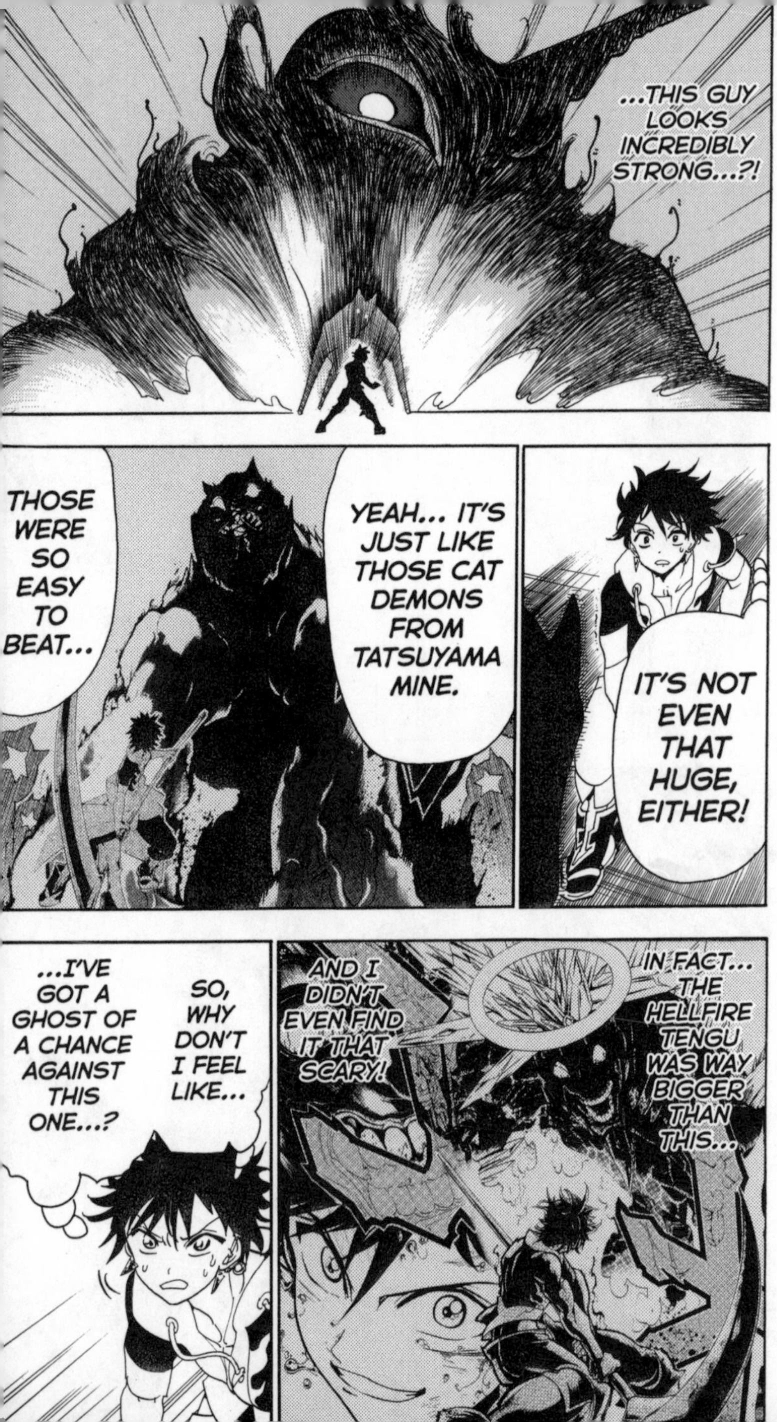
...THIS GUY LOOKS INCREDIBLY STRONG...?!
IT'S NOT EVEN THAT HUGE, EITHER!
YEAH... IT'S JUST LIKE THOSE CAT DEMONS FROM TATSUYAMA MINE.
THOSE WERE SO EASY TO BEAT...
IN FACT... THE HELLFIRE TENGU WAS WAY BIGGER THAN THIS...
AND I DIDN'T EVEN FIND IT THAT SCARY!
SO, WHY DON'T I FEEL LIKE...
...I'VE GOT A GHOST OF A CHANCE AGAINST THIS ONE...?

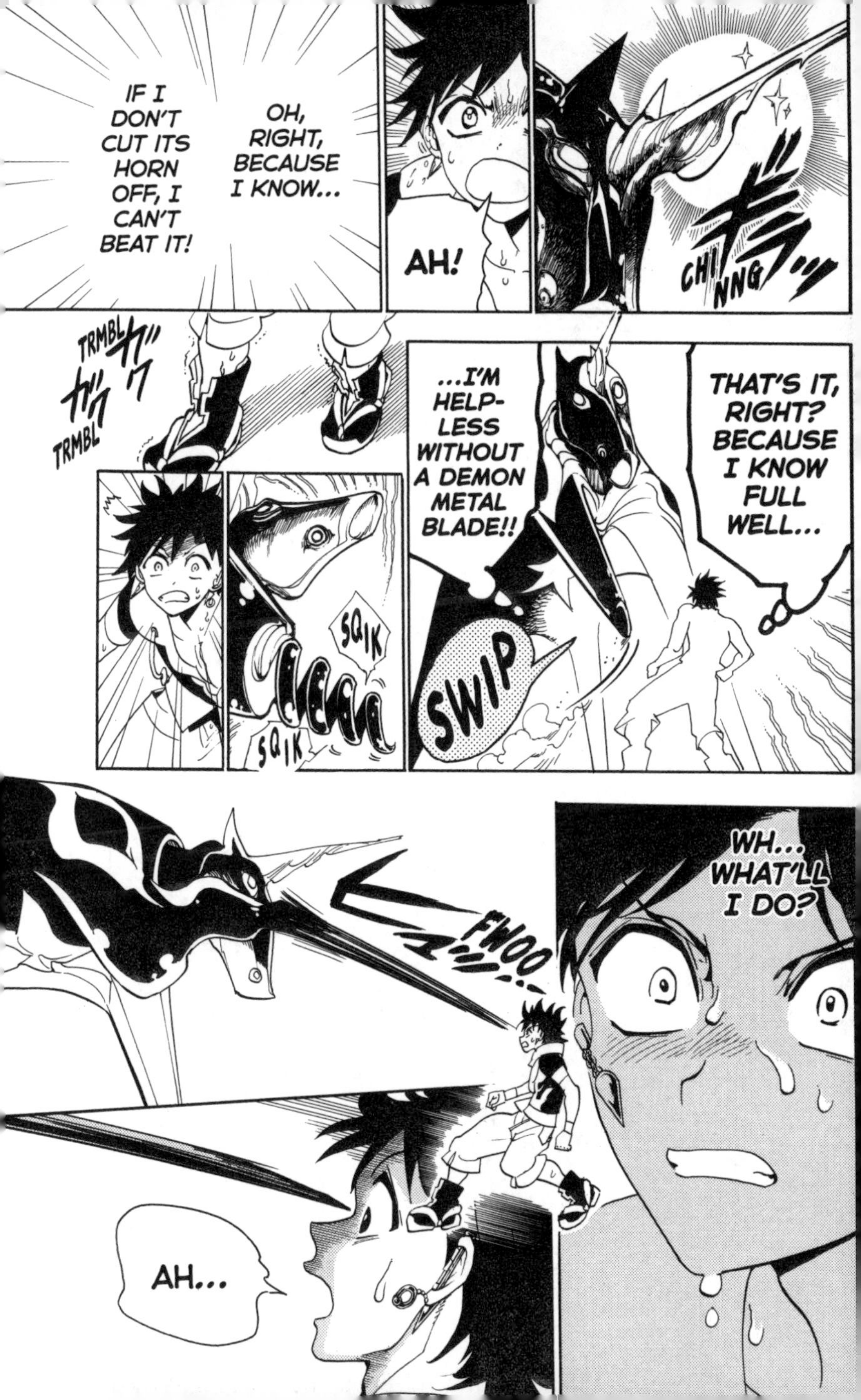
CHINNG
AH!
OH, RIGHT, BECAUSE I KNOW...
IF I DON'T CUT ITS HORN OFF, I CAN'T BEAT IT!
THAT'S IT, RIGHT? BECAUSE I KNOW FULL WELL...
...I'M HELP-LESS WITHOUT A DEMON METAL BLADE!!
SWIP
SQIK
SQIK
TRMBL
TRMBL
WH... WHAT'LL I DO?
FWOO
AH...

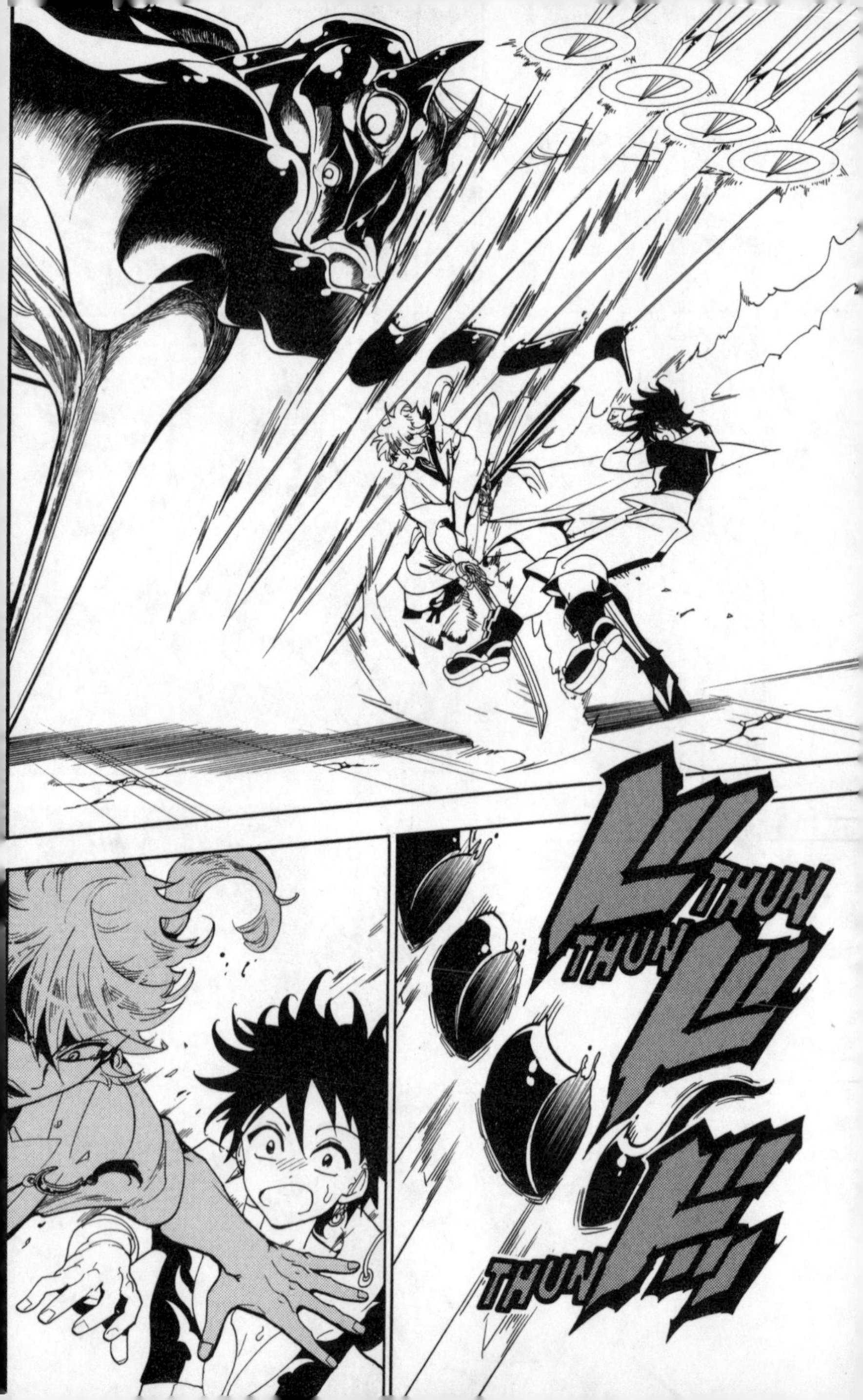
THUN
THUN
THUN

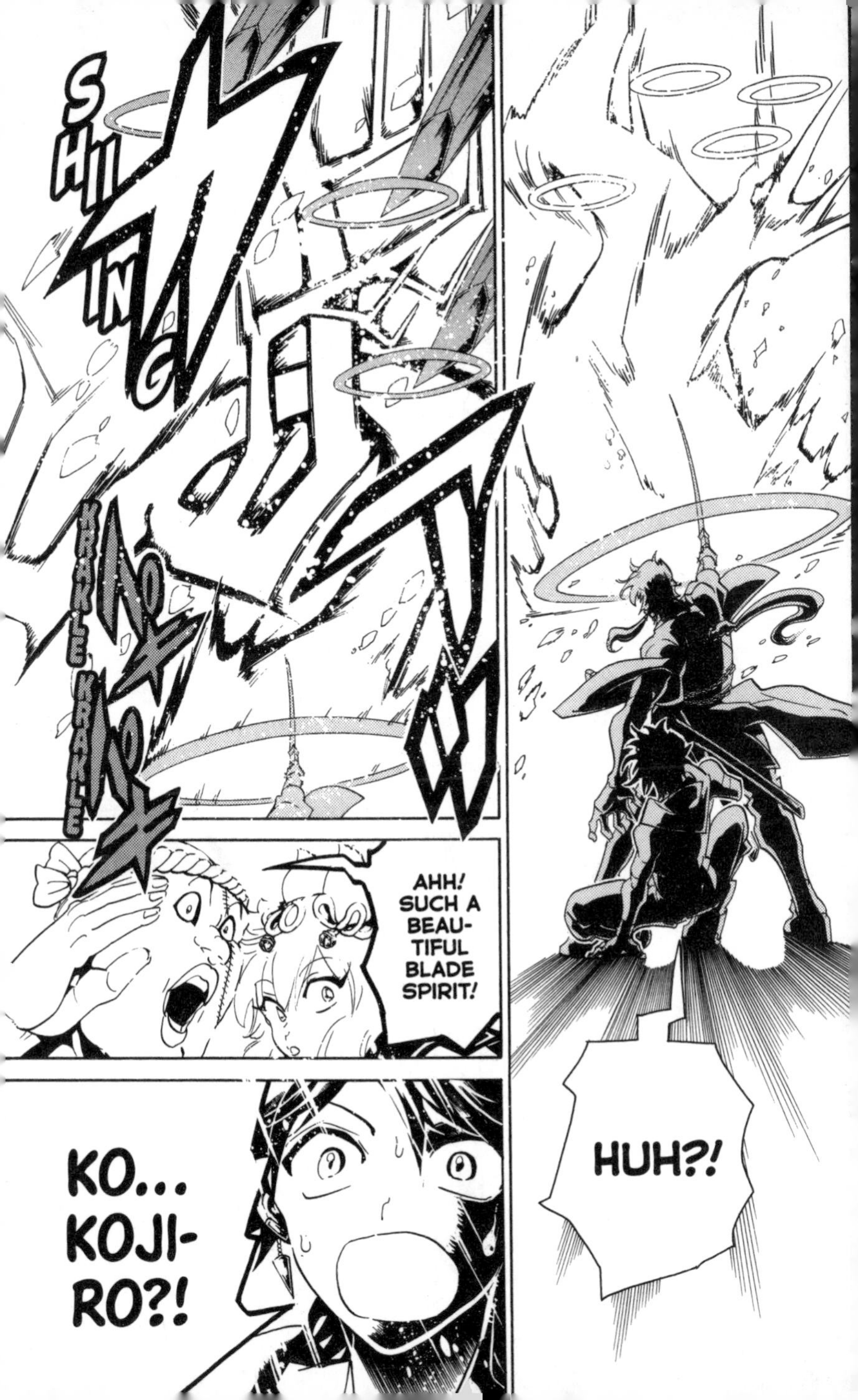
HUH?!
SHIING
KRAKLE KRAKLE
AHH! SUCH A BEAU-TIFUL BLADE SPIRIT!
KO... KOJI-RO?!

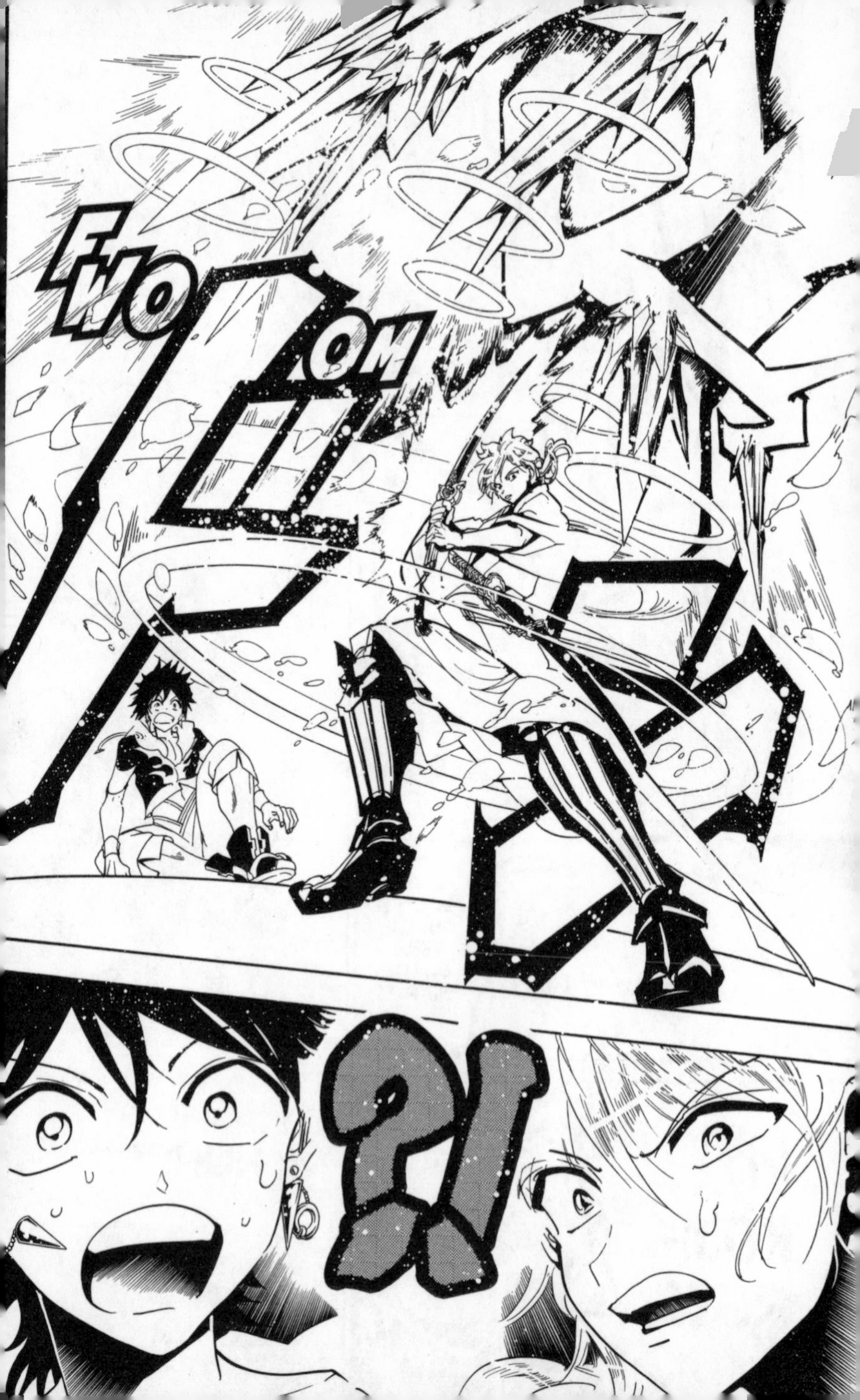

FWOOM
?!

CHAPTER 25: REKKU YAE-ZAKURA

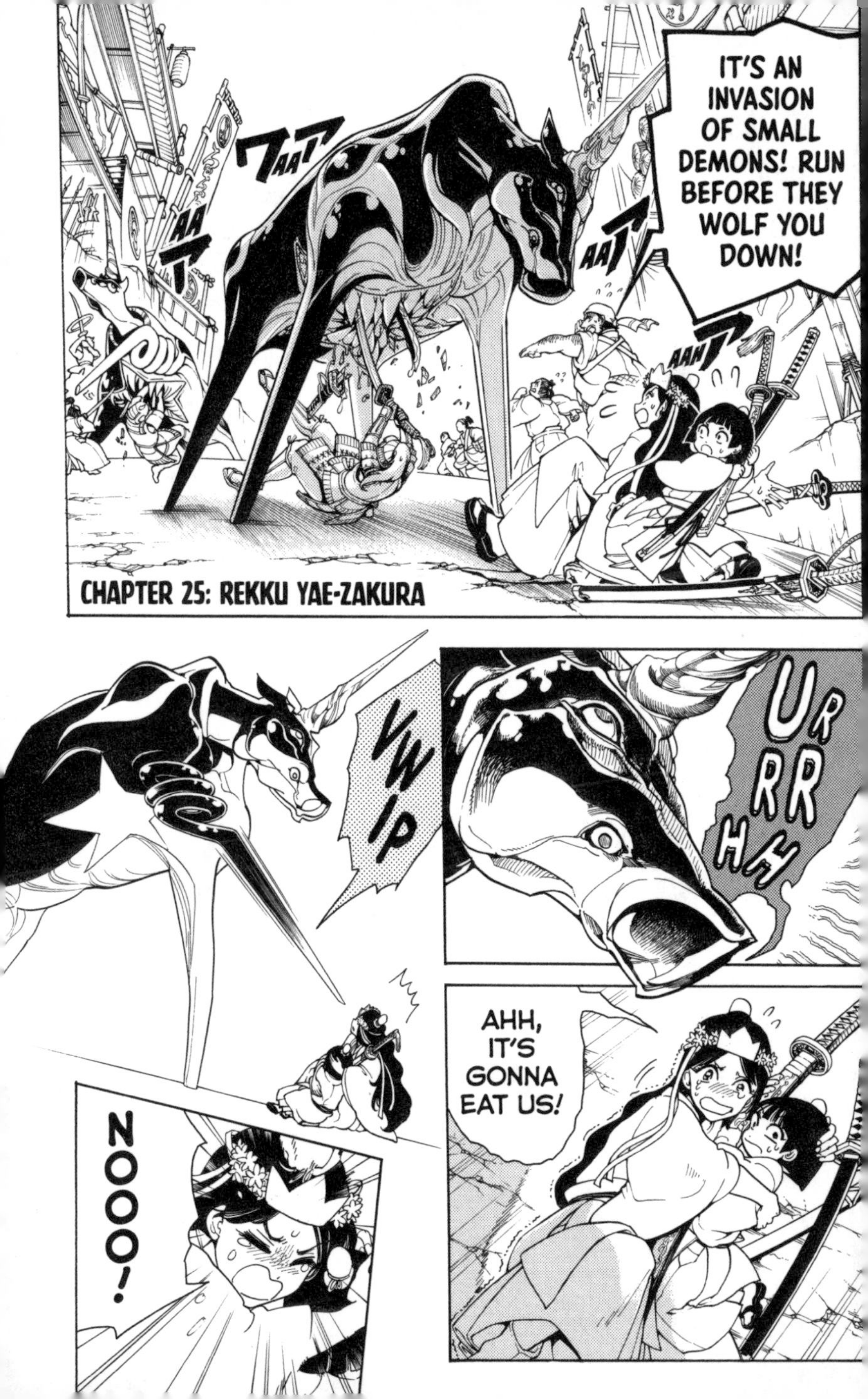
IT'S AN INVASION OF SMALL DEMONS! RUN BEFORE THEY WOLF YOU DOWN!
AAH
URRRHH
VWIP
AHH, IT'S GONNA EAT US!
NOOOO!

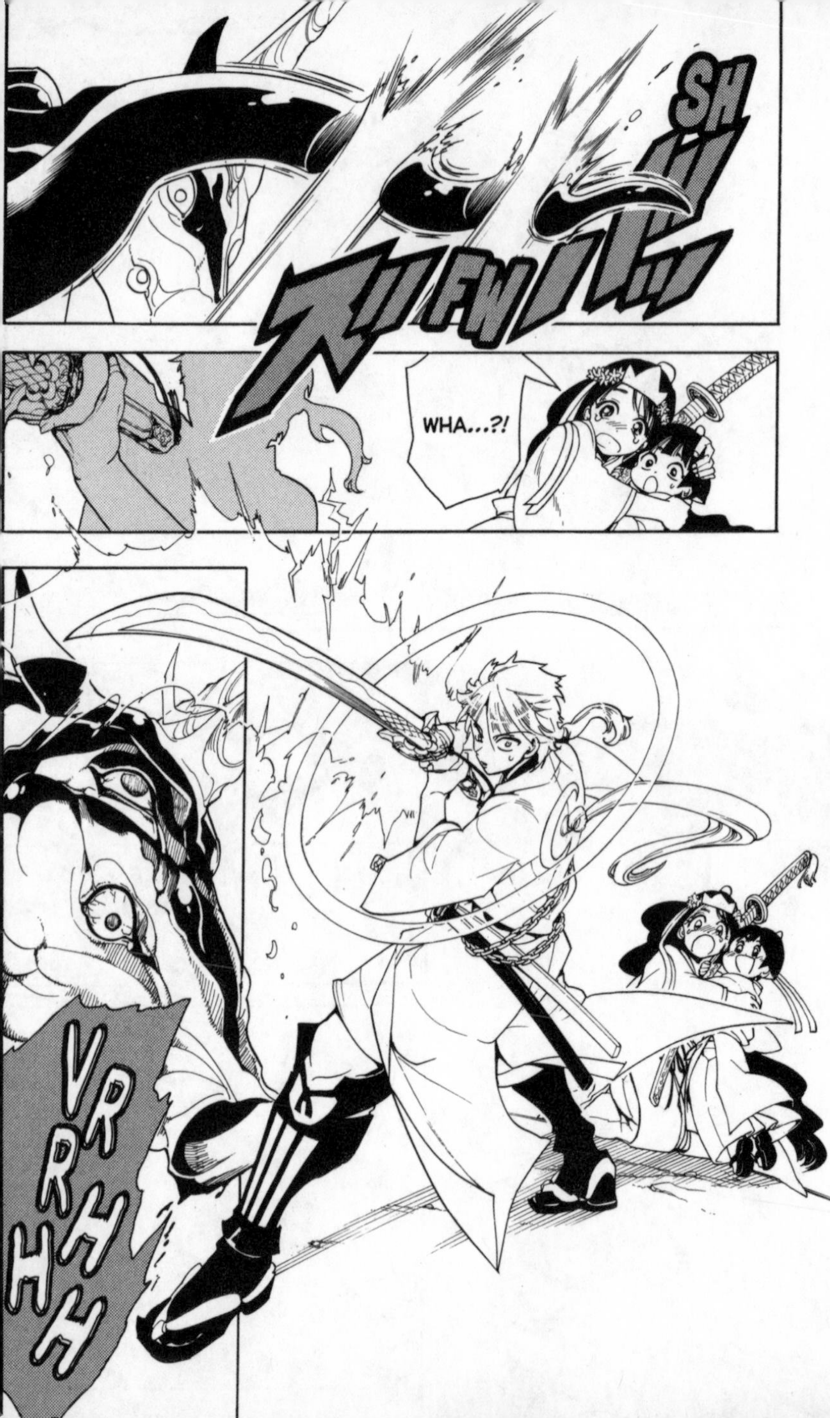

SH
FW
WHA...?!
VRRHHHH

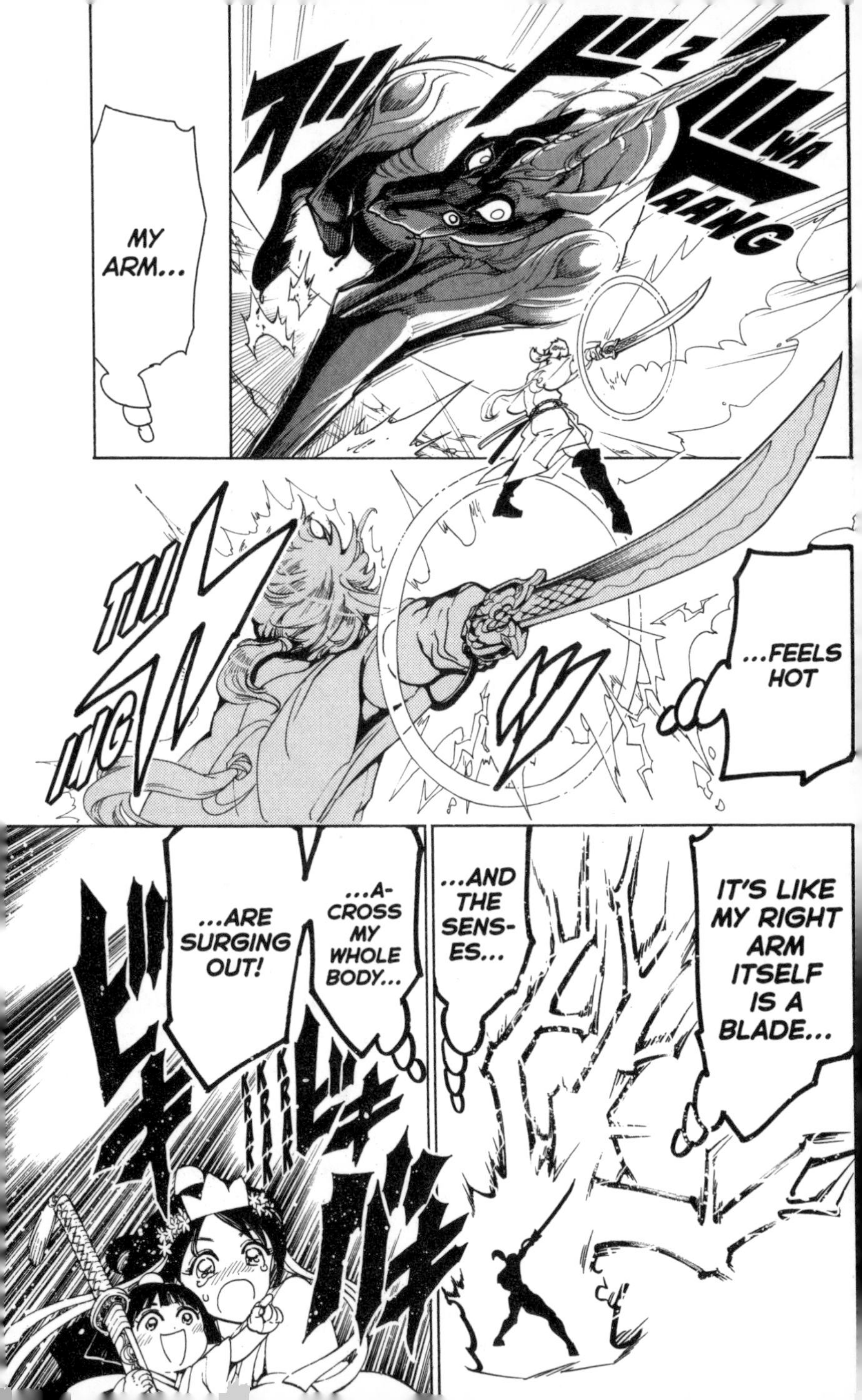
WA
AANG
MY ARM...
...FEELS HOT
TWING
IT'S LIKE MY RIGHT ARM ITSELF IS A BLADE...
...AND THE SENS-ES...
...A-CROSS MY WHOLE BODY...
...ARE SURGING OUT!
KRAK KRAK KRAK

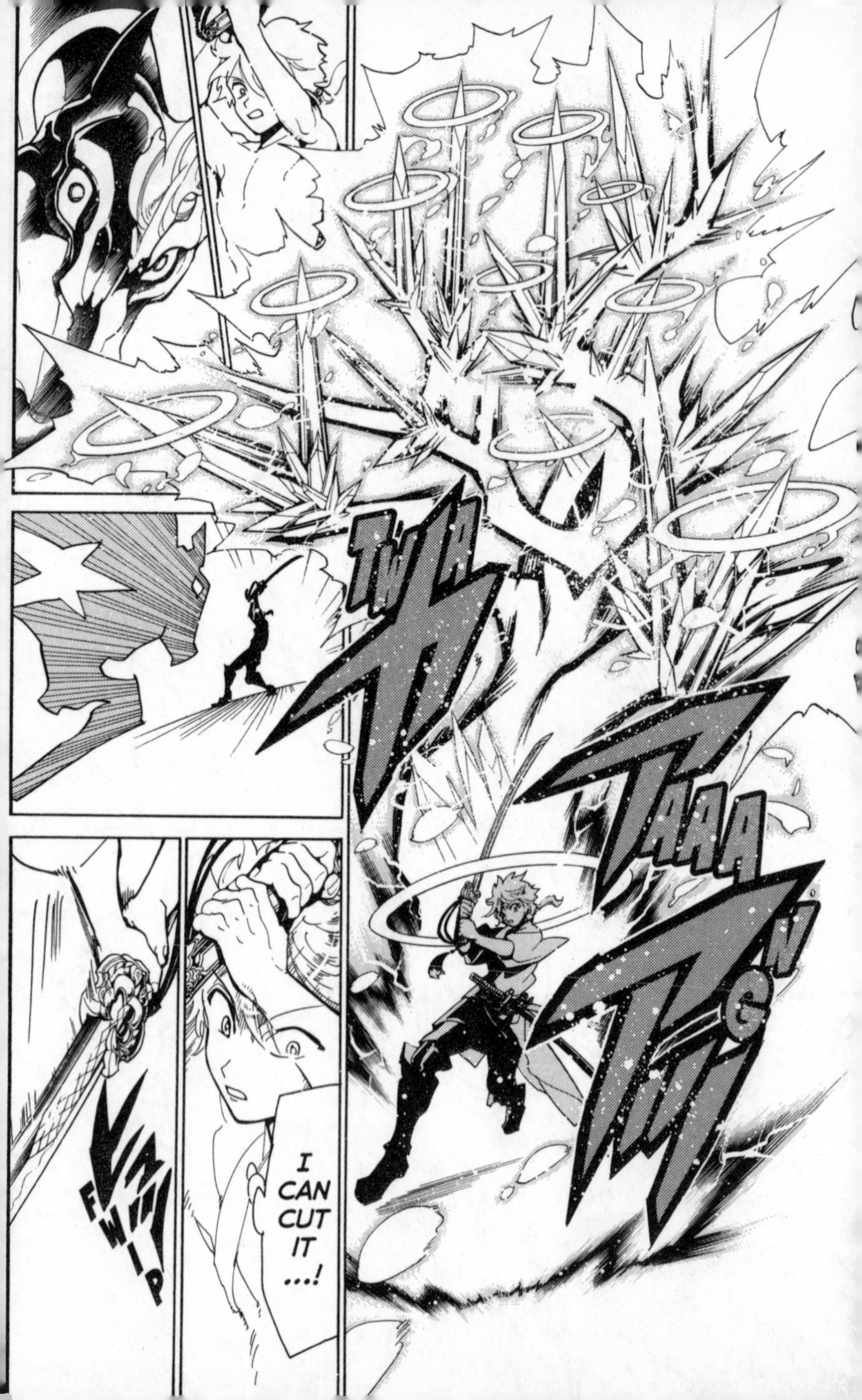
TWAAAANG
I CAN CUT IT ...!
FWIP

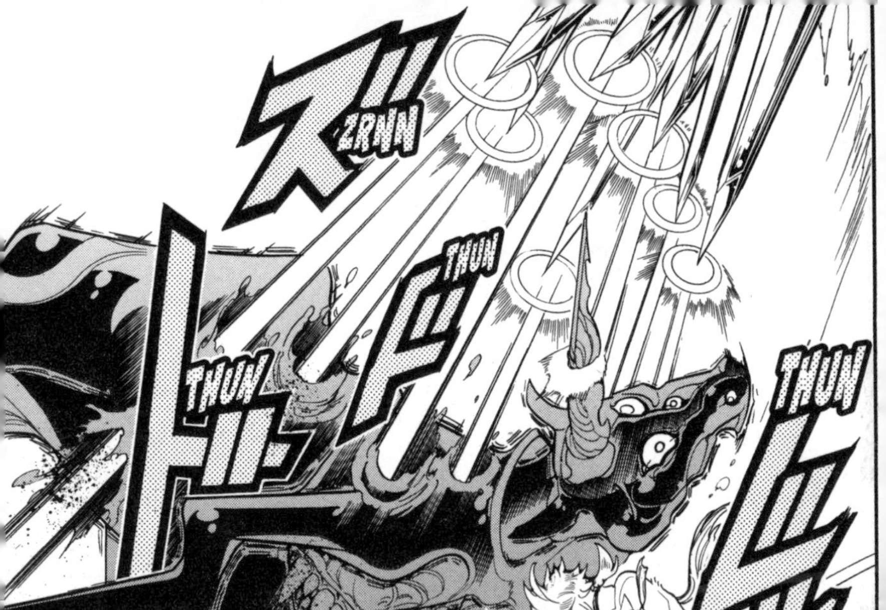
ZRNN
THUN
THUN
THUN
THUN
THUN
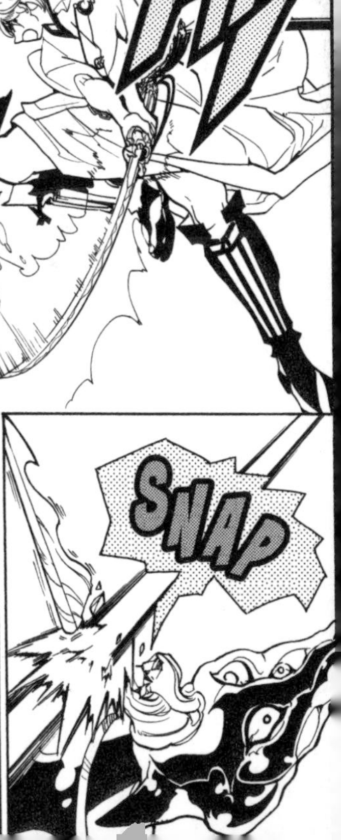
SNAP
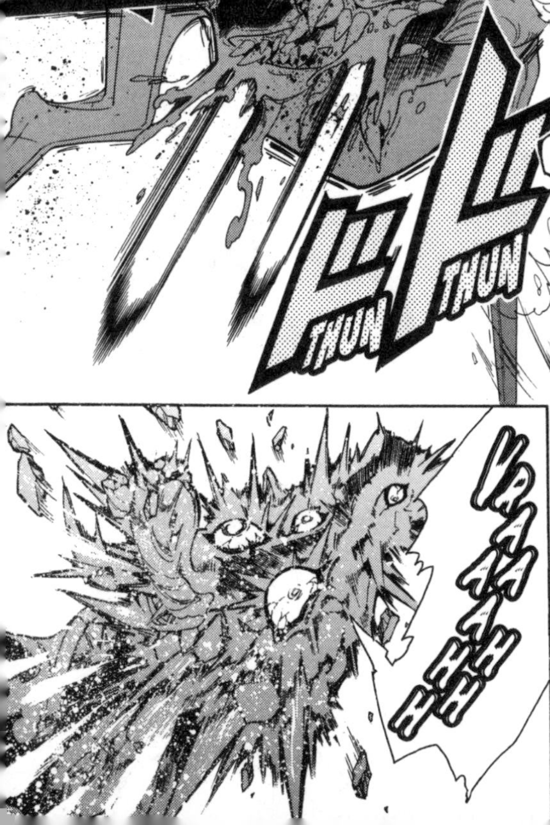

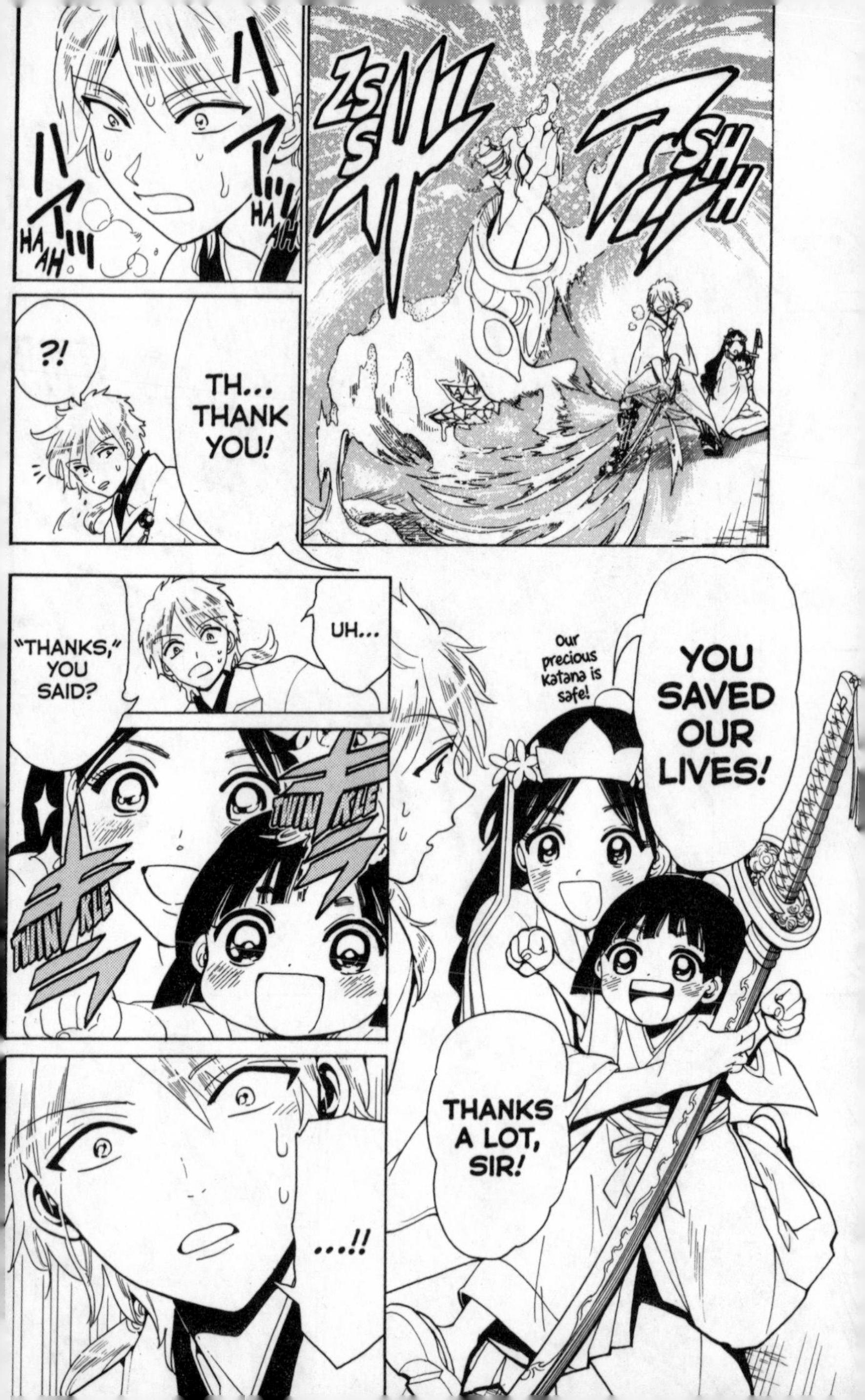
ZSSH
TSHH
HA AH!!
HA AH!!
?!
TH... THANK YOU!
YOU SAVED OUR LIVES!
Our precious Katana is safe!
THANKS A LOT, SIR!
UH...
"THANKS," YOU SAID?
TWINKLE
TWINKLE
...!!

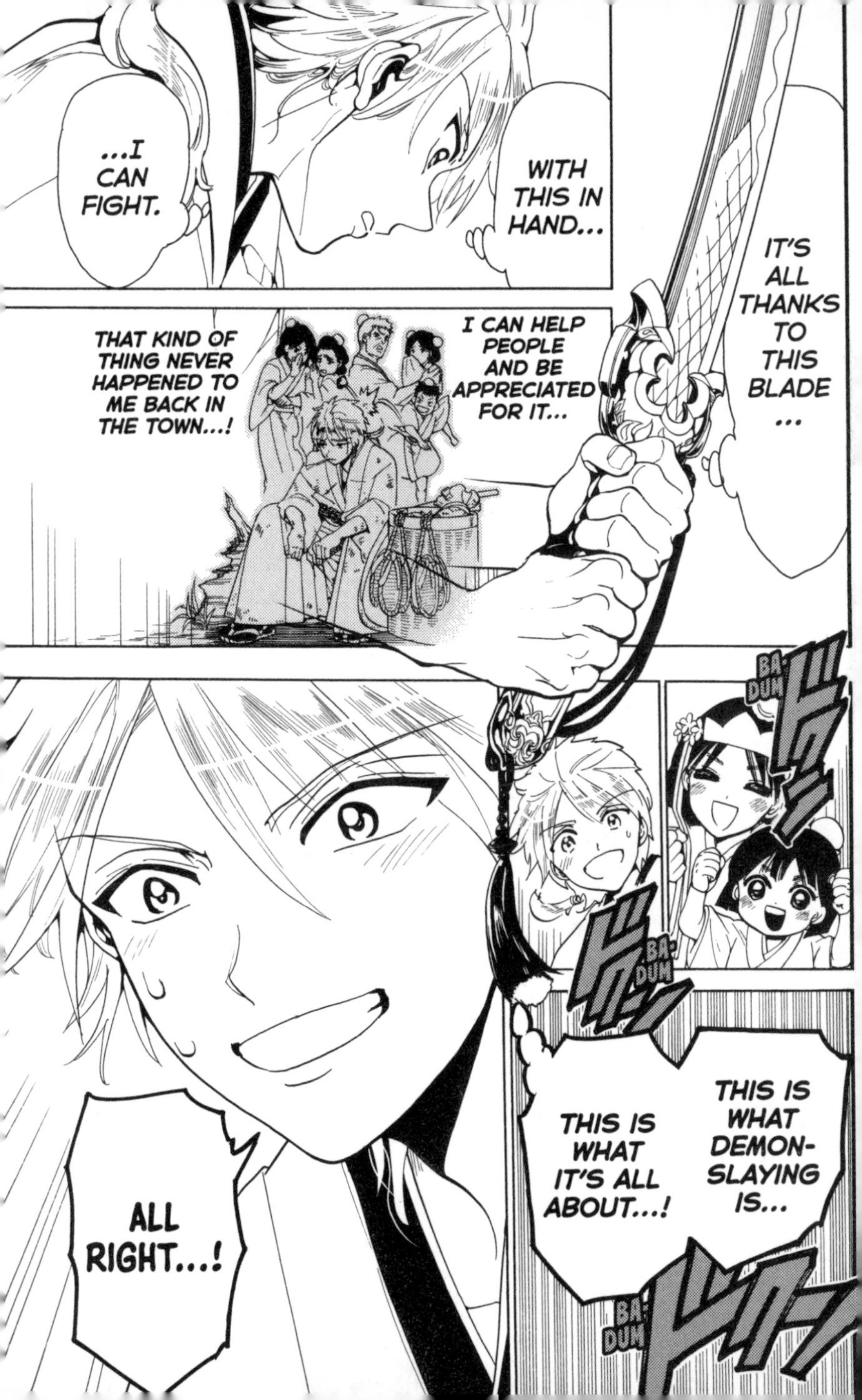
WITH THIS IN HAND...
...I CAN FIGHT.
IT'S ALL THANKS TO THIS BLADE...
I CAN HELP PEOPLE AND BE APPRECIATED FOR IT...
THAT KIND OF THING NEVER HAPPENED TO ME BACK IN THE TOWN...!
BA-DUM
BA-DUM
THIS IS WHAT DEMON-SLAYING IS...
THIS IS WHAT IT'S ALL ABOUT...!
BA-DUM
ALL RIGHT...!

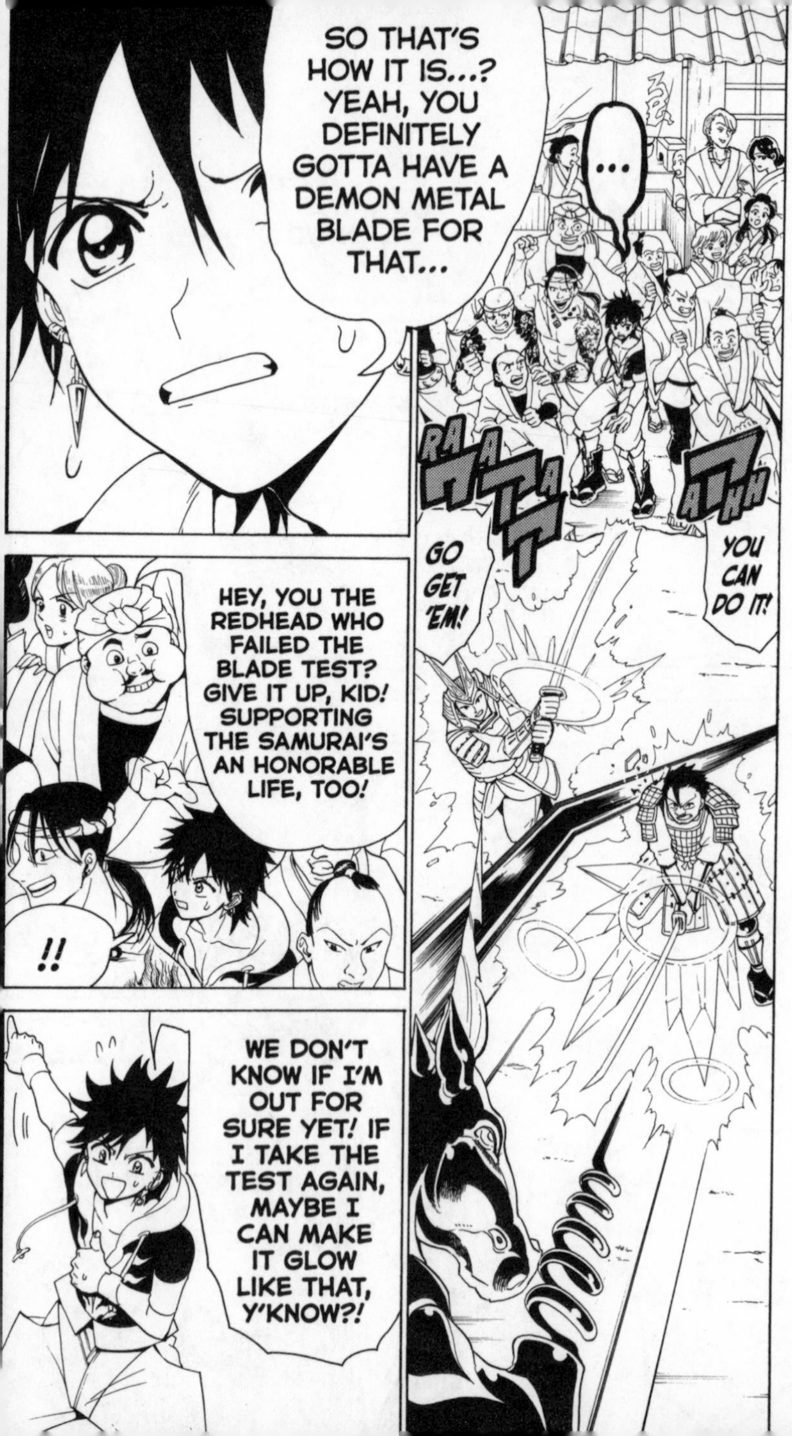
...
RAAAAAHH
YOU CAN DO IT!
GO GET 'EM!
SO THAT'S HOW IT IS...? YEAH, YOU DEFINITELY GOTTA HAVE A DEMON METAL BLADE FOR THAT...
HEY, YOU THE REDHEAD WHO FAILED THE BLADE TEST? GIVE IT UP, KID! SUPPORTING THE SAMURAI'S AN HONORABLE LIFE, TOO!
!!
WE DON'T KNOW IF I'M OUT FOR SURE YET! IF I TAKE THE TEST AGAIN, MAYBE I CAN MAKE IT GLOW LIKE THAT, Y'KNOW?!

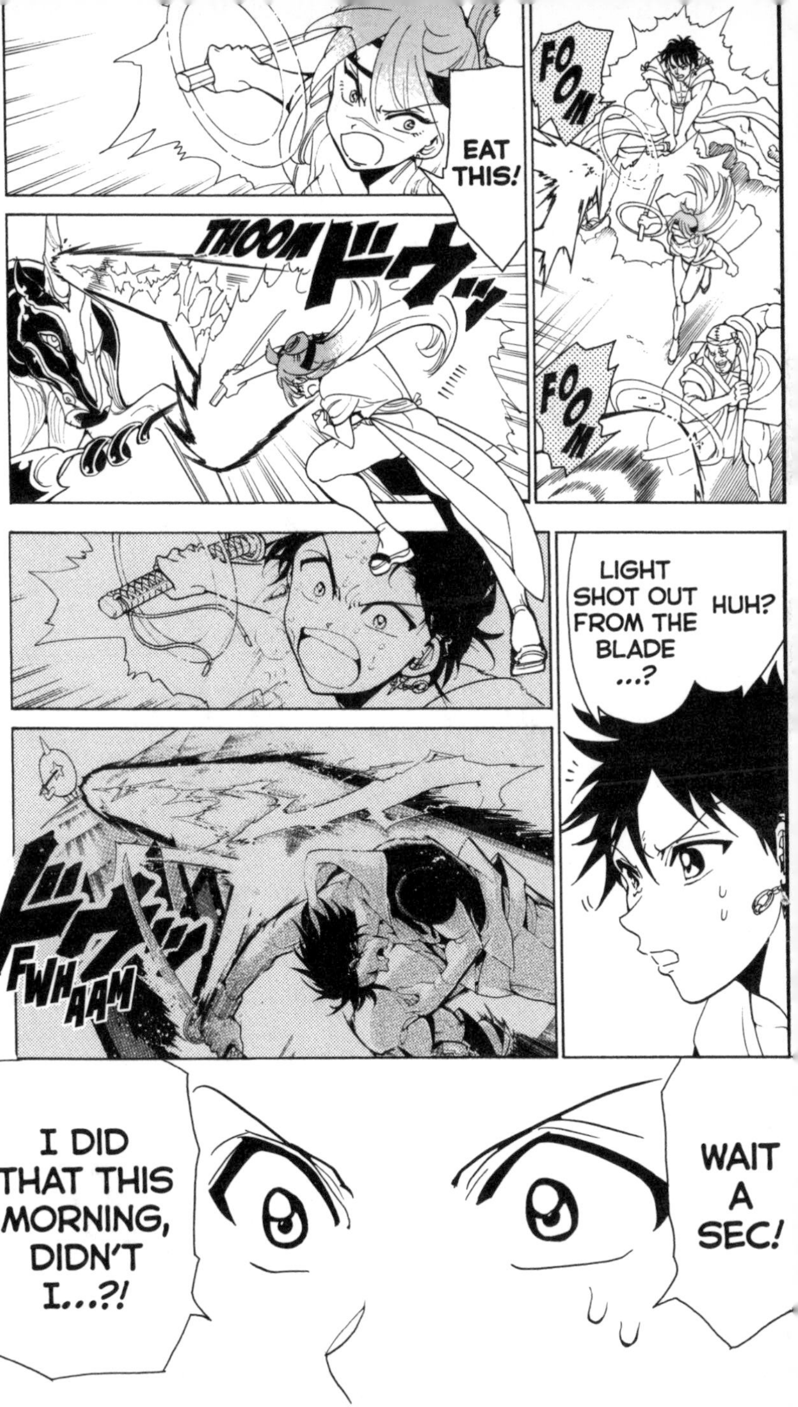

FOOM
FOOM
EAT THIS!
THOOM
ドゥッ
HUH?
LIGHT SHOT OUT FROM THE BLADE ...?
ドゥッ
FWHAAM
WAIT A SEC!
I DID THAT THIS MORNING, DIDN'T I...?!

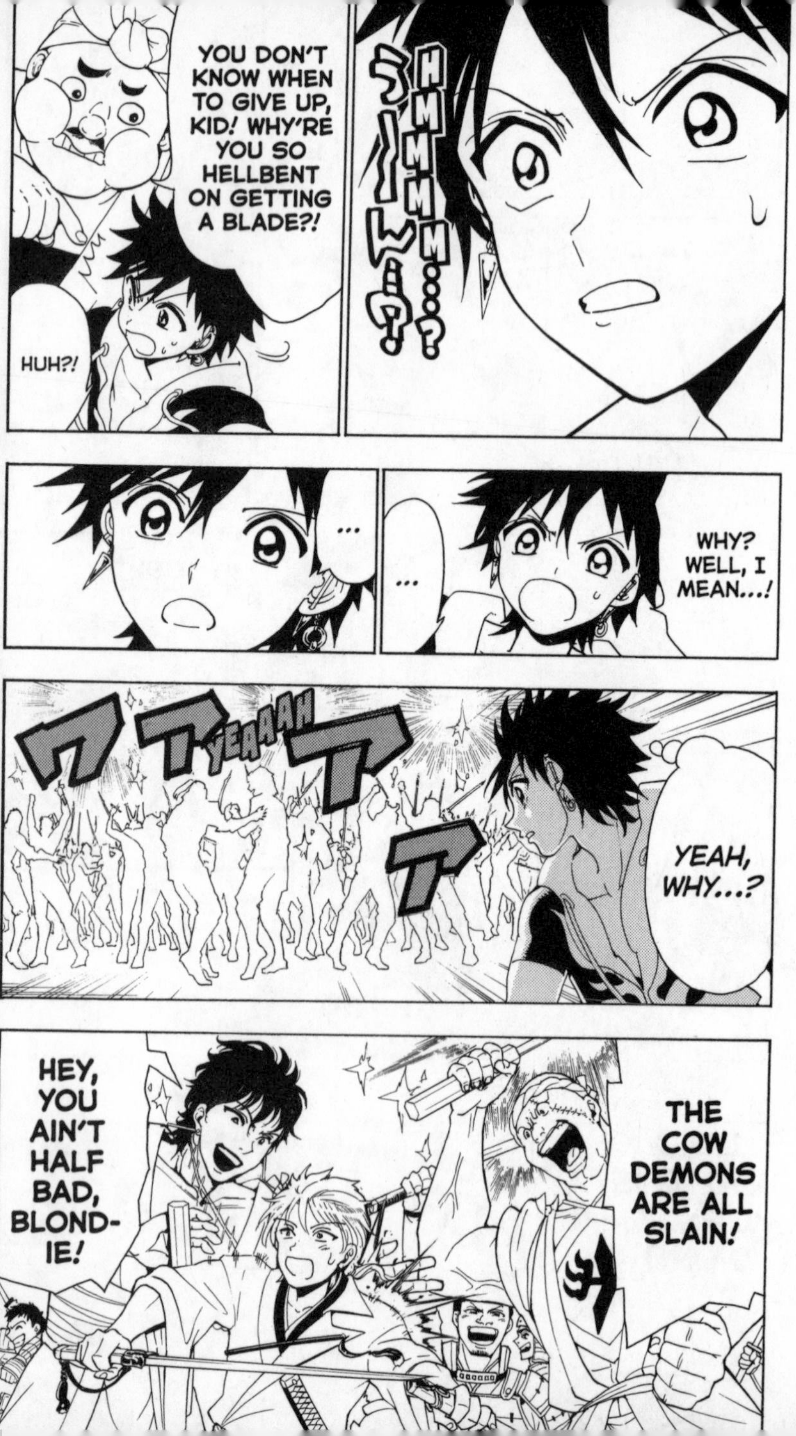
HMMMMM...?
うーーん…?
YOU DON'T KNOW WHEN TO GIVE UP, KID! WHY'RE YOU SO HELLBENT ON GETTING A BLADE?!
HUH?!
WHY? WELL, I MEAN...!
...
...
YEAH, WHY...?
ワアアアア
YEAAAAH
THE COW DEMONS ARE ALL SLAIN!
HEY, YOU AIN'T HALF BAD, BLOND-IE!

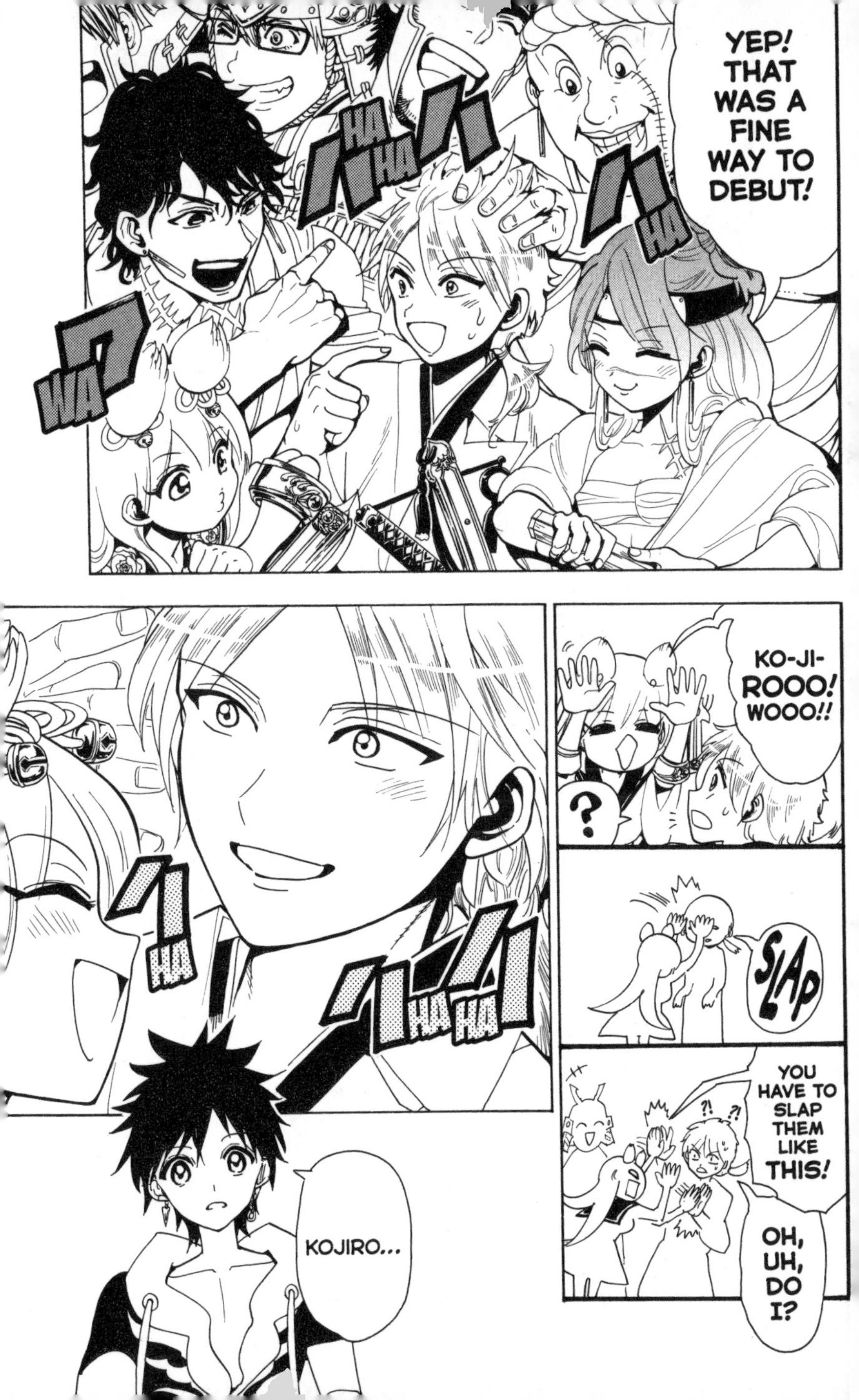
YEP! THAT WAS A FINE WAY TO DEBUT!
HA
HA HA
WA
KO-JI-ROOO! WOOO!!
?
SLAP
YOU HAVE TO SLAP THEM LIKE THIS!
?! ?!
OH, UH, DO I?
HA
HA HA
KOJIRO...

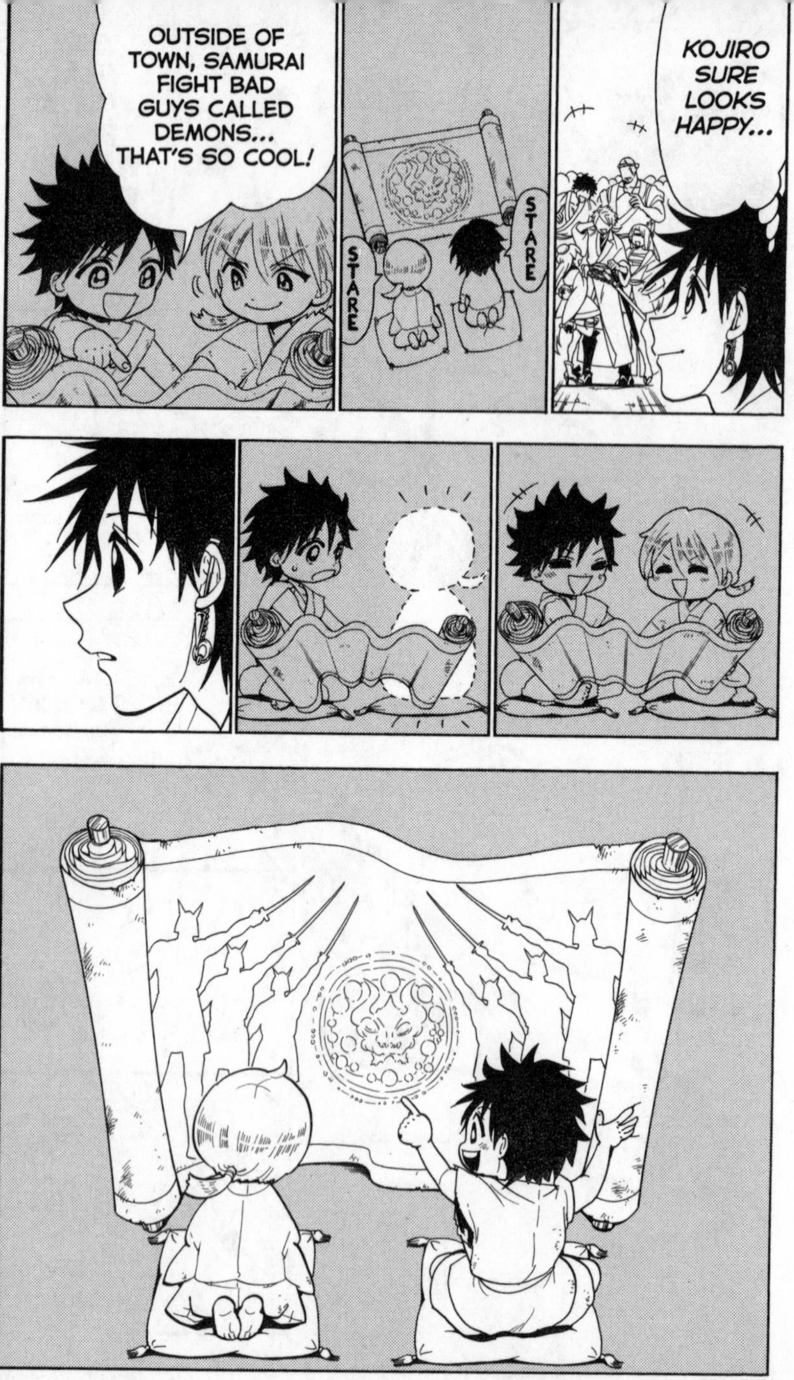
KOJIRO SURE LOOKS HAPPY...
STARE
STARE
OUTSIDE OF TOWN, SAMURAI FIGHT BAD GUYS CALLED DEMONS... THAT'S SO COOL!

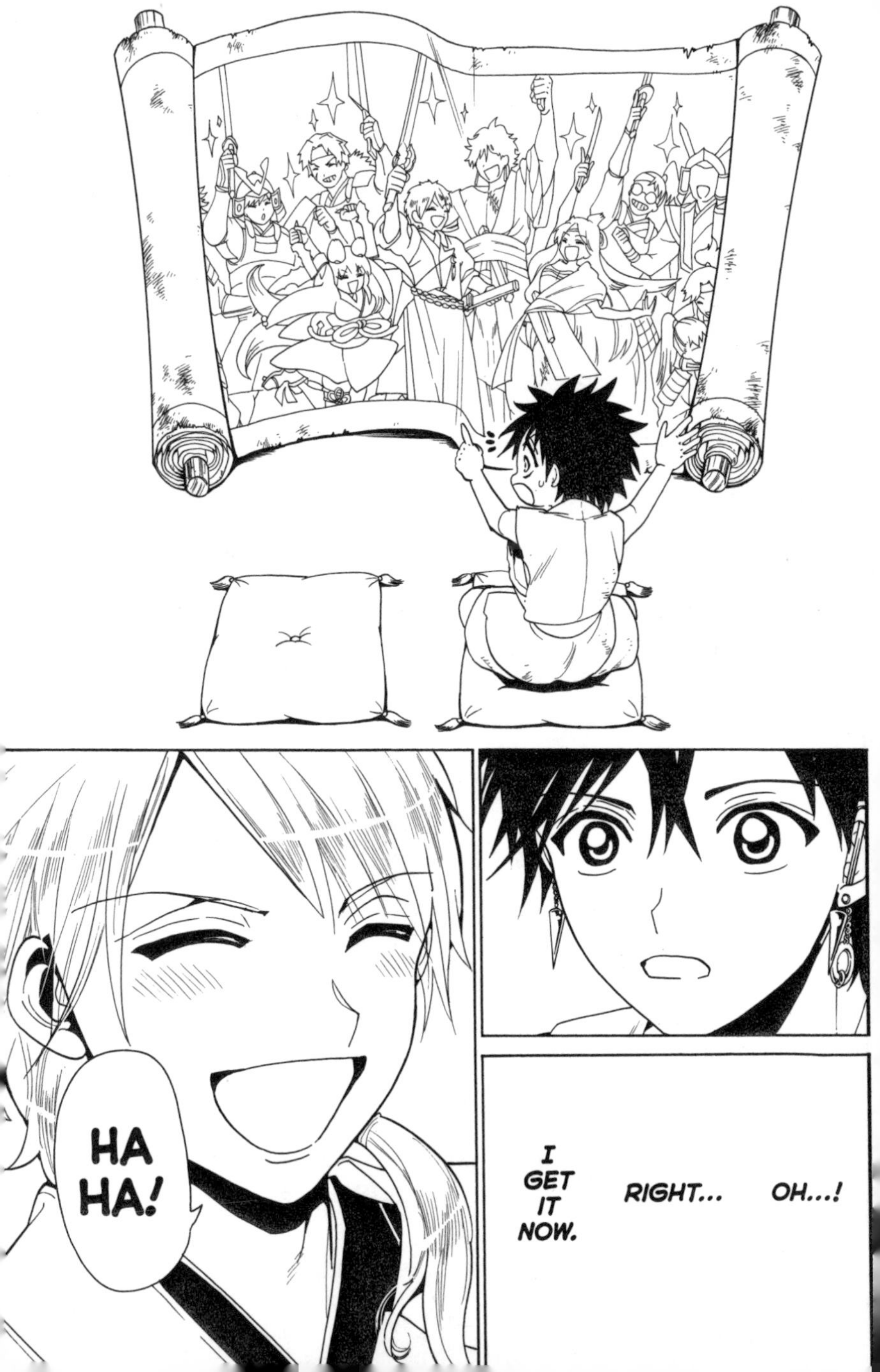
OH...!
RIGHT...
I GET IT NOW.
HA HA!

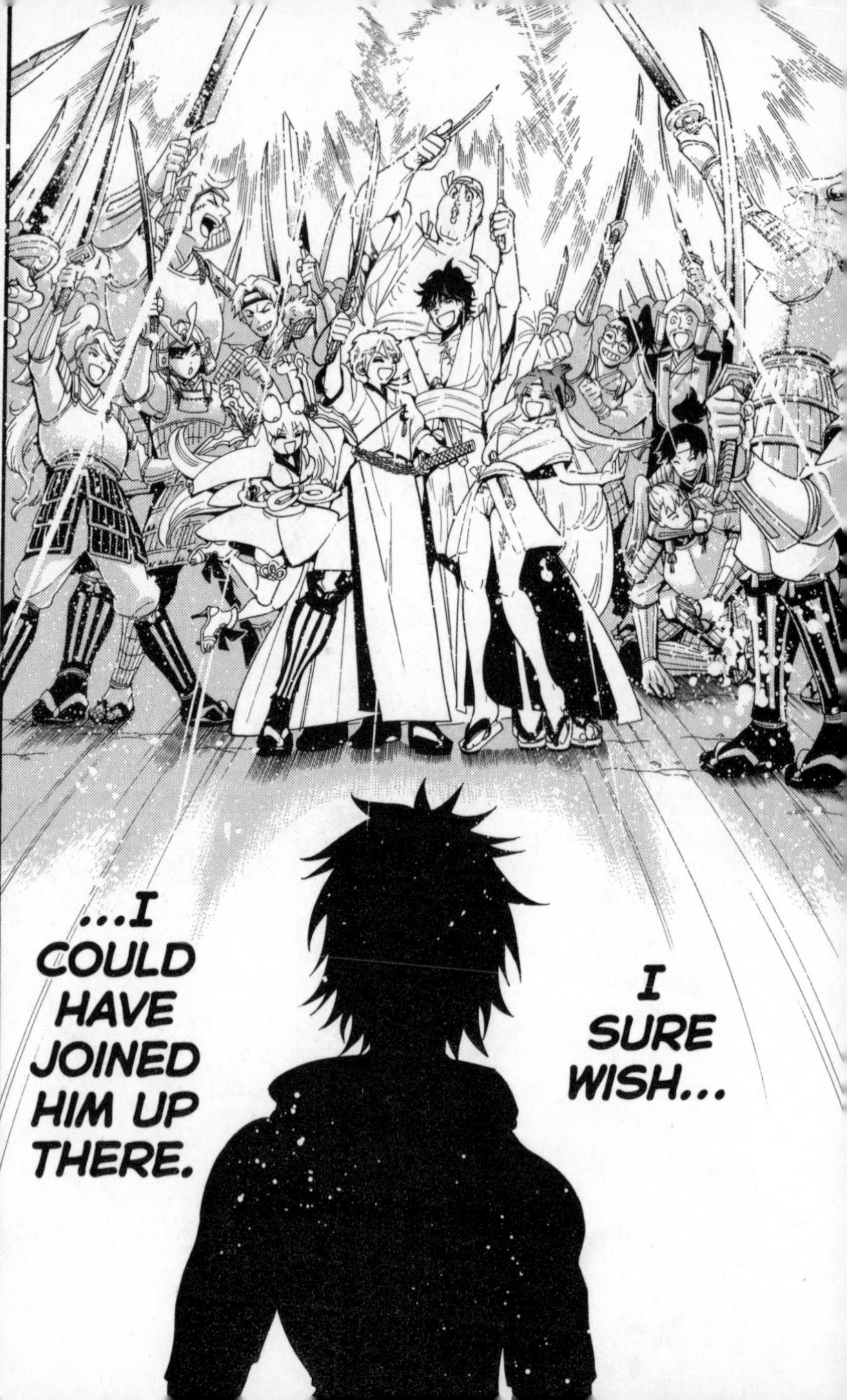
I SURE WISH...
...I COULD HAVE JOINED HIM UP THERE.

BUT IF I CAN'T USE A DEMON METAL BLADE, I CAN'T FIGHT.

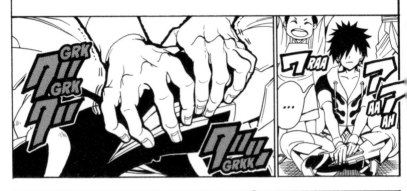

RAA ...

GRK GRK GRII GRKK AAT AAH

ROAAR

THUN THUN THUN

WE'RE SCALING THE PEAK! IF YOU GOT A BLADE, LET'S GO SLAY THE GOD!

RAA AAT TAH

KOJI-RO!

YEAH... MU-SASHI!

GASP

WE NEED TO JOIN THEM!

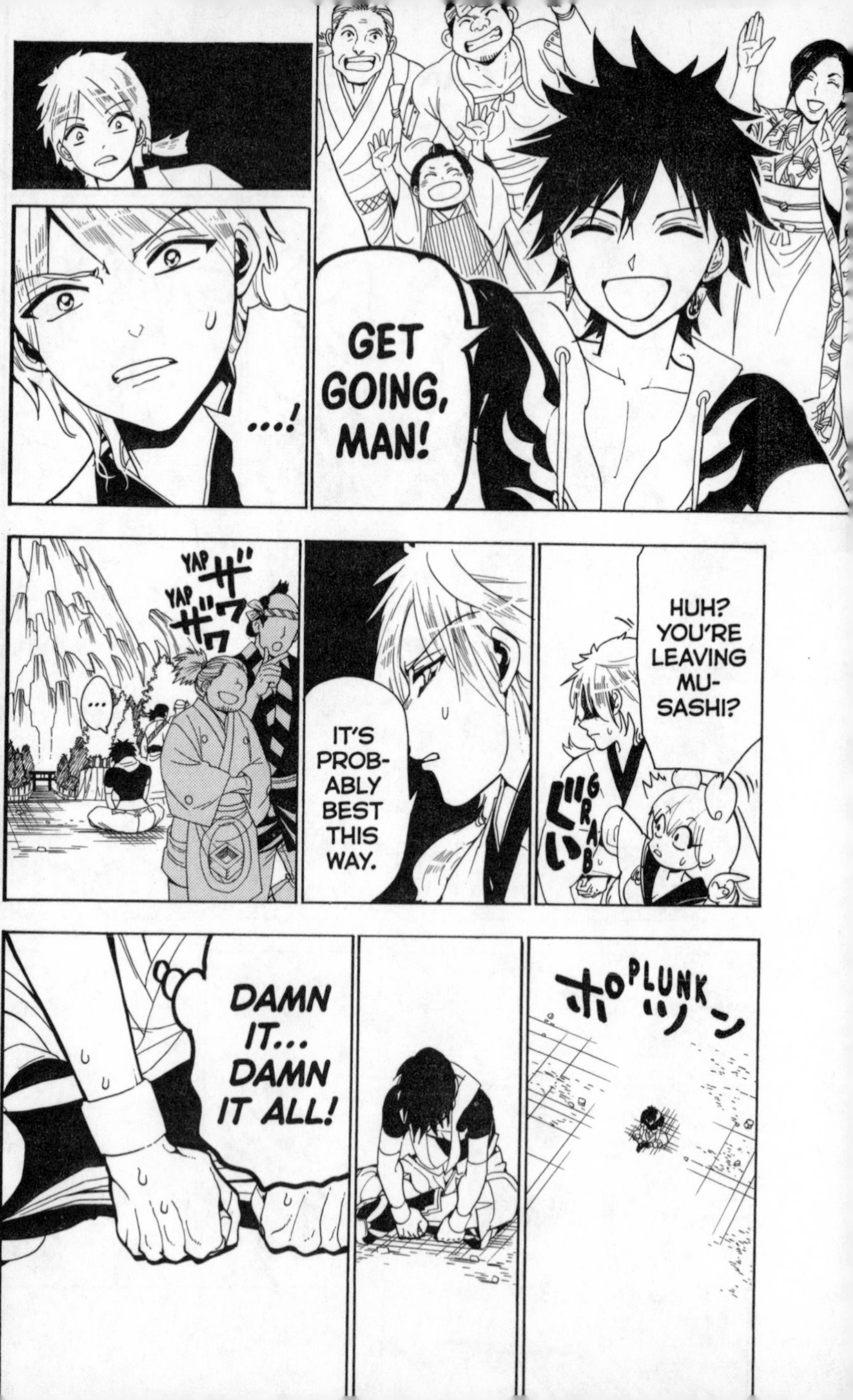

GET GOING, MAN!
...!
HUH? YOU'RE LEAVING MU-SASHI?
GRAB
ぐい
IT'S PROB-ABLY BEST THIS WAY.
YAP ザワ
YAP ザワ
...
PLUNK
ポツン
DAMN IT... DAMN IT ALL!

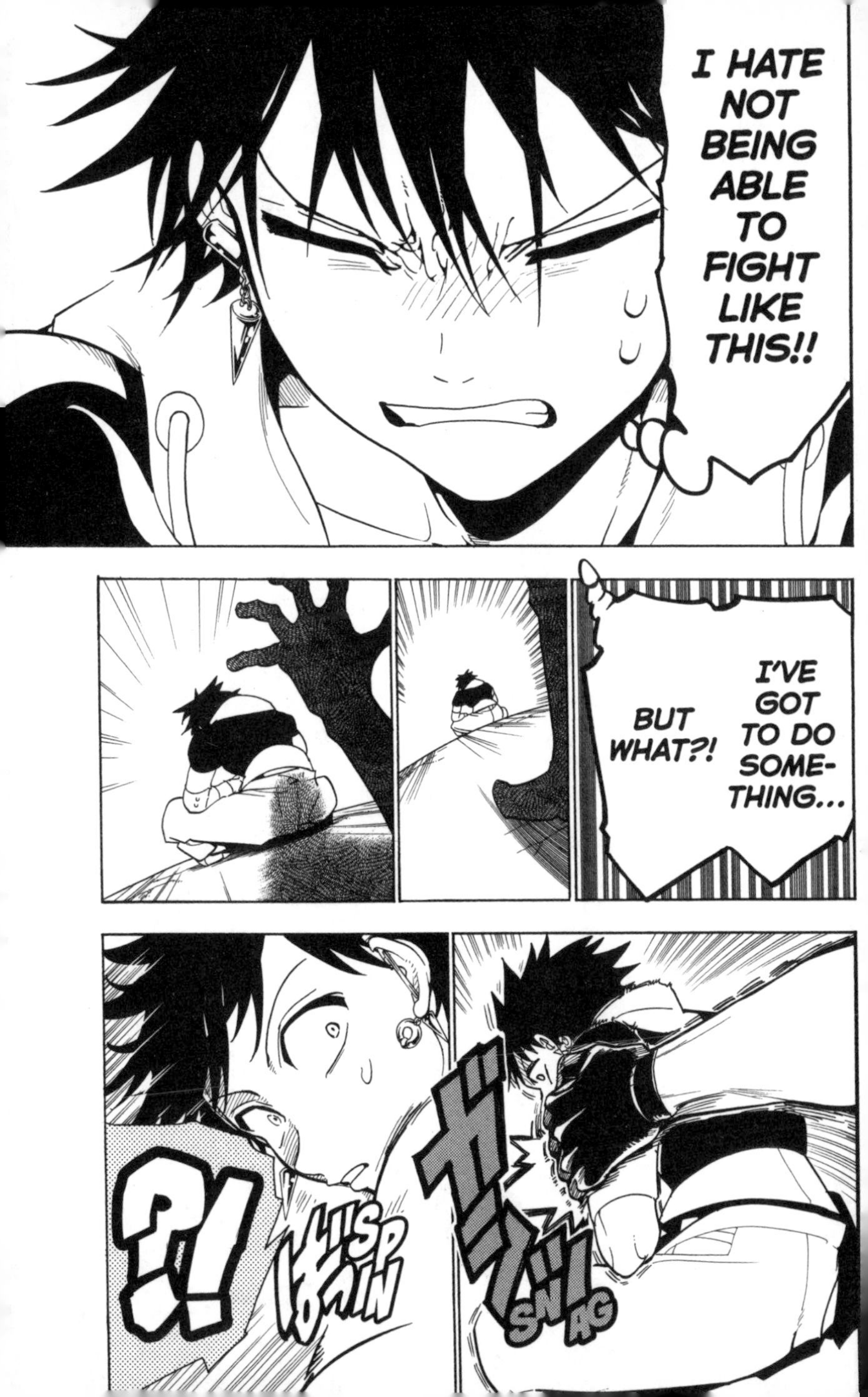
I HATE NOT BEING ABLE TO FIGHT LIKE THIS!!
I'VE GOT TO DO SOMETHING...
BUT WHAT?!
SNAG
?!
SPIN

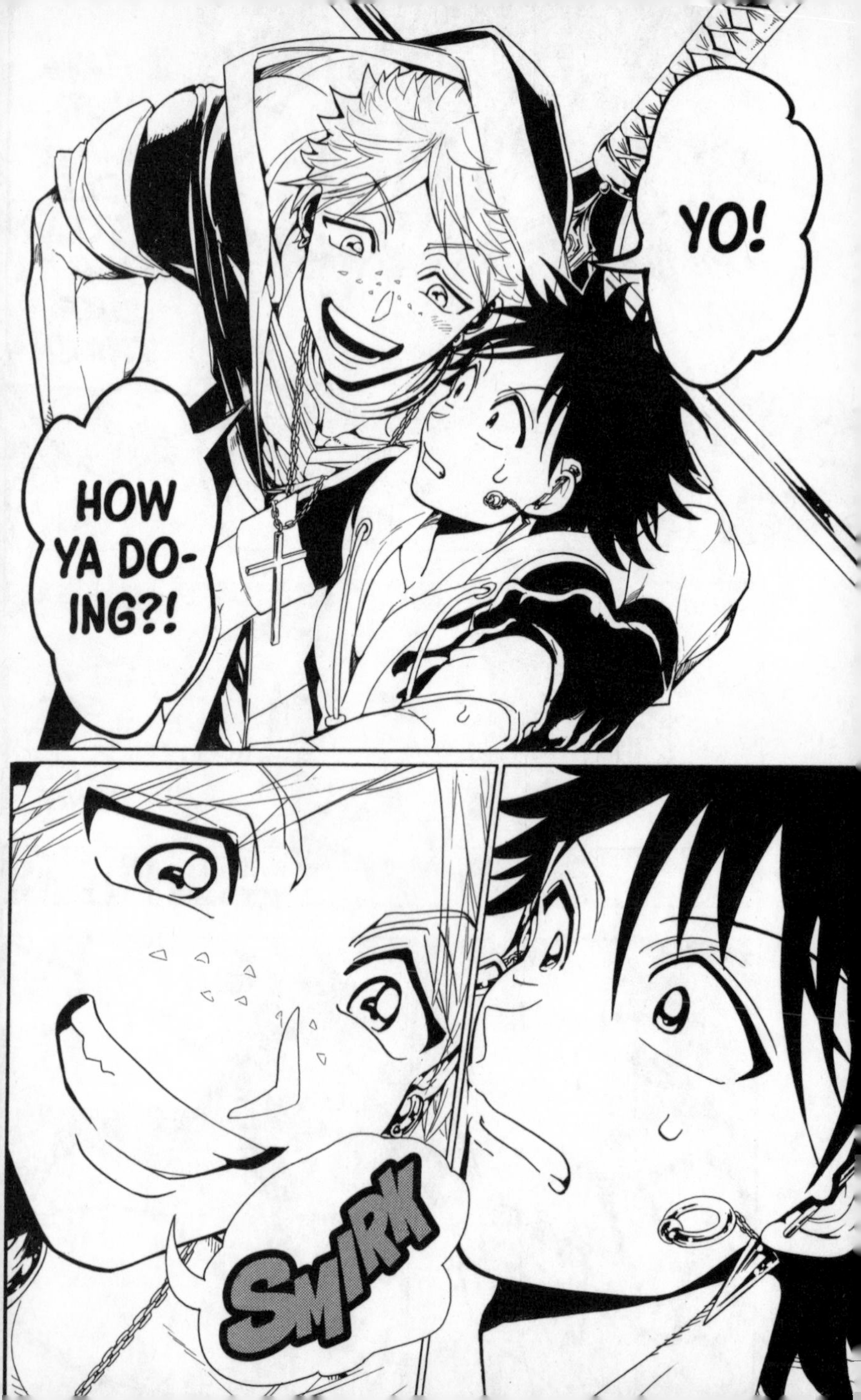
YO!
HOW YA DO-ING?!
SMIRK

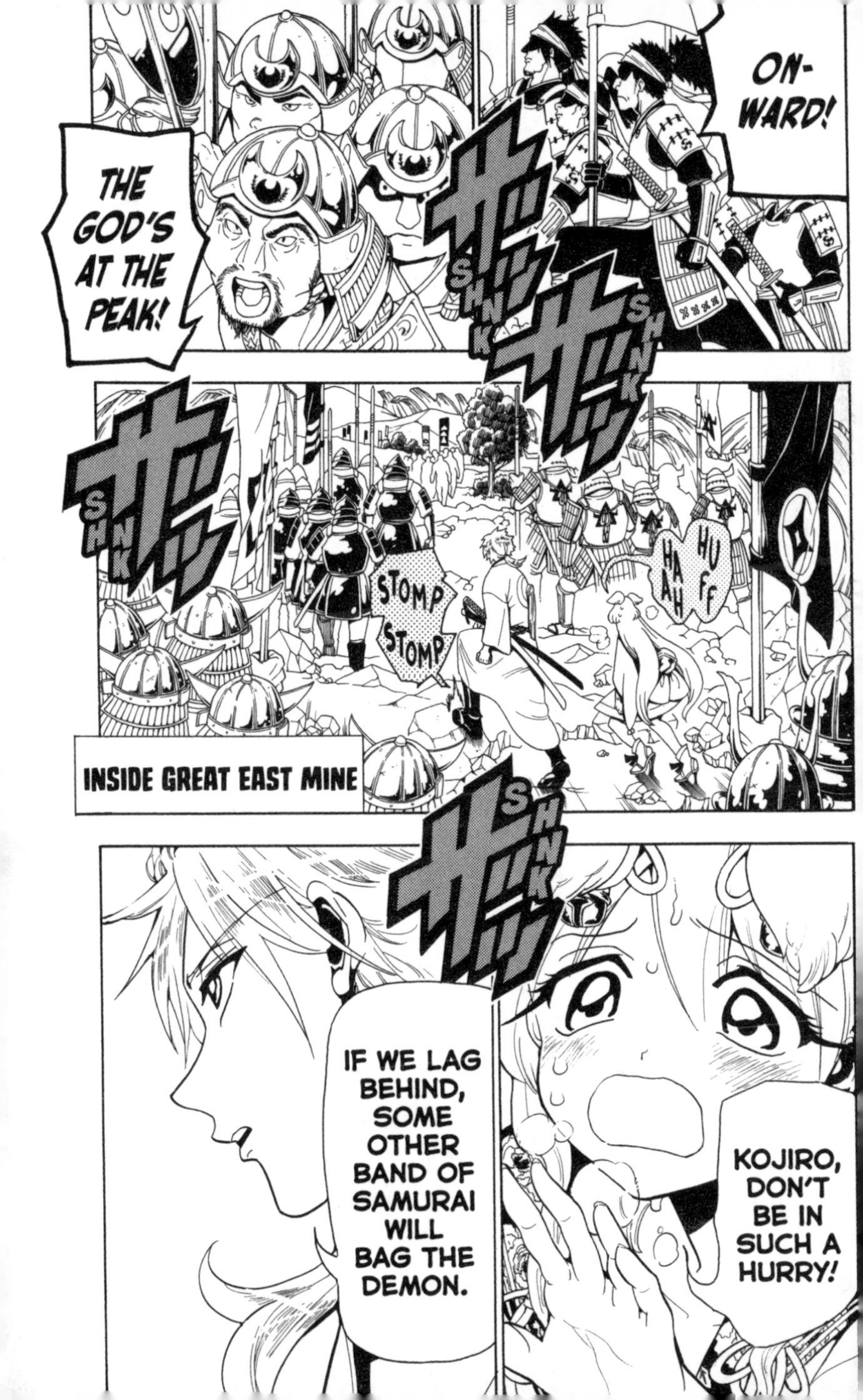
ON-WARD!
SHNK
SHNK
THE GOD'S AT THE PEAK!
HUFF
HAAH
STOMP STOMP
SHNK
INSIDE GREAT EAST MINE
SHNK
KOJIRO, DON'T BE IN SUCH A HURRY!
IF WE LAG BEHIND, SOME OTHER BAND OF SAMURAI WILL BAG THE DEMON.

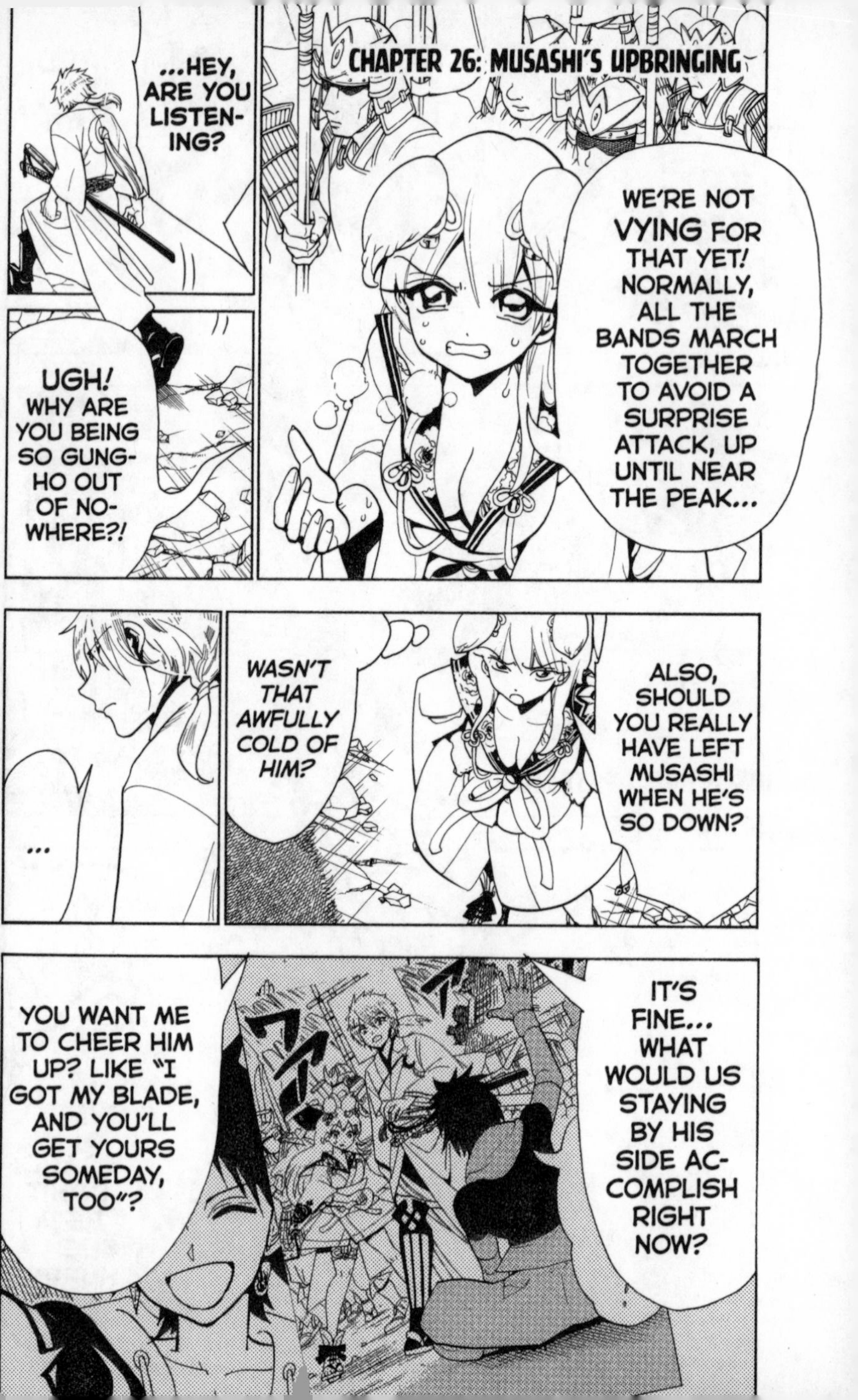
CHAPTER 26: MUSASHI'S UPBRINGING
WE'RE NOT VYING FOR THAT YET! NORMALLY, ALL THE BANDS MARCH TOGETHER TO AVOID A SURPRISE ATTACK, UP UNTIL NEAR THE PEAK...
...HEY, ARE YOU LISTEN-ING?
UGH! WHY ARE YOU BEING SO GUNG-HO OUT OF NO-WHERE?!
ALSO, SHOULD YOU REALLY HAVE LEFT MUSASHI WHEN HE'S SO DOWN?
WASN'T THAT AWFULLY COLD OF HIM?
...
IT'S FINE... WHAT WOULD US STAYING BY HIS SIDE AC-COMPLISH RIGHT NOW?
YOU WANT ME TO CHEER HIM UP? LIKE "I GOT MY BLADE, AND YOU'LL GET YOURS SOMEDAY, TOO"?

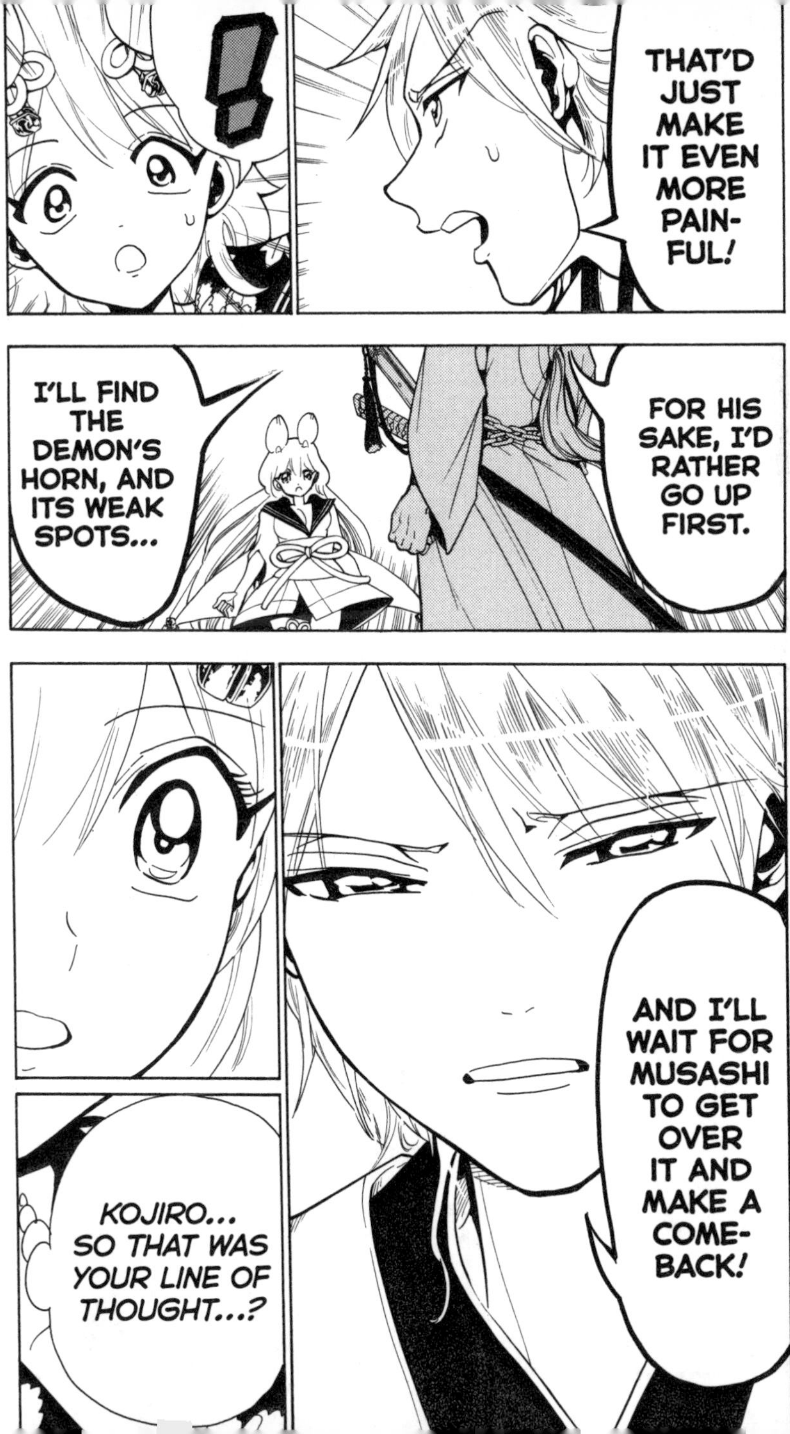
THAT'D JUST MAKE IT EVEN MORE PAIN-FUL!
!
FOR HIS SAKE, I'D RATHER GO UP FIRST.
I'LL FIND THE DEMON'S HORN, AND ITS WEAK SPOTS...
AND I'LL WAIT FOR MUSASHI TO GET OVER IT AND MAKE A COME-BACK!
KOJIRO... SO THAT WAS YOUR LINE OF THOUGHT...?

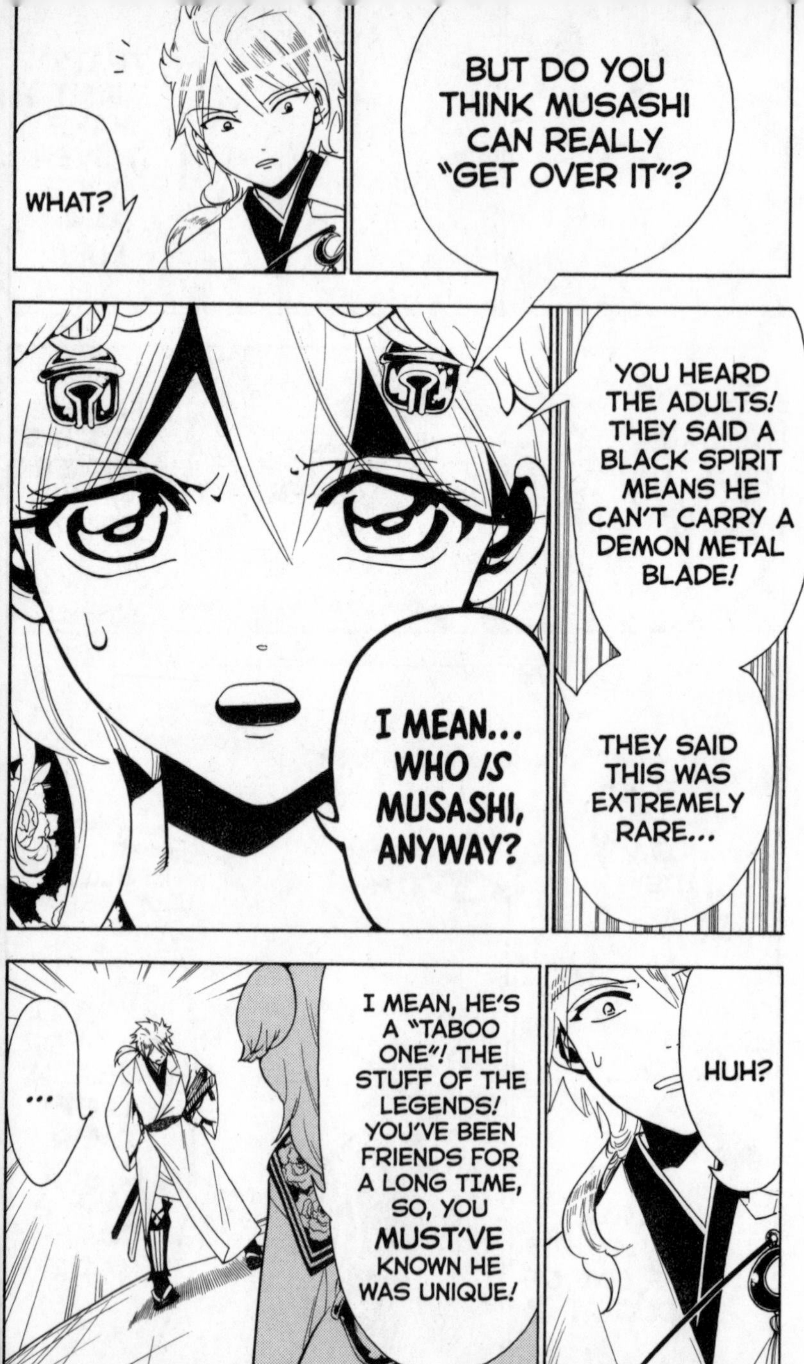
BUT DO YOU THINK MUSASHI CAN REALLY "GET OVER IT"?
WHAT?
YOU HEARD THE ADULTS! THEY SAID A BLACK SPIRIT MEANS HE CAN'T CARRY A DEMON METAL BLADE!
THEY SAID THIS WAS EXTREMELY RARE...
I MEAN... WHO IS MUSASHI, ANYWAY?
HUH?
I MEAN, HE'S A "TABOO ONE"! THE STUFF OF THE LEGENDS! YOU'VE BEEN FRIENDS FOR A LONG TIME, SO, YOU MUST'VE KNOWN HE WAS UNIQUE!
...

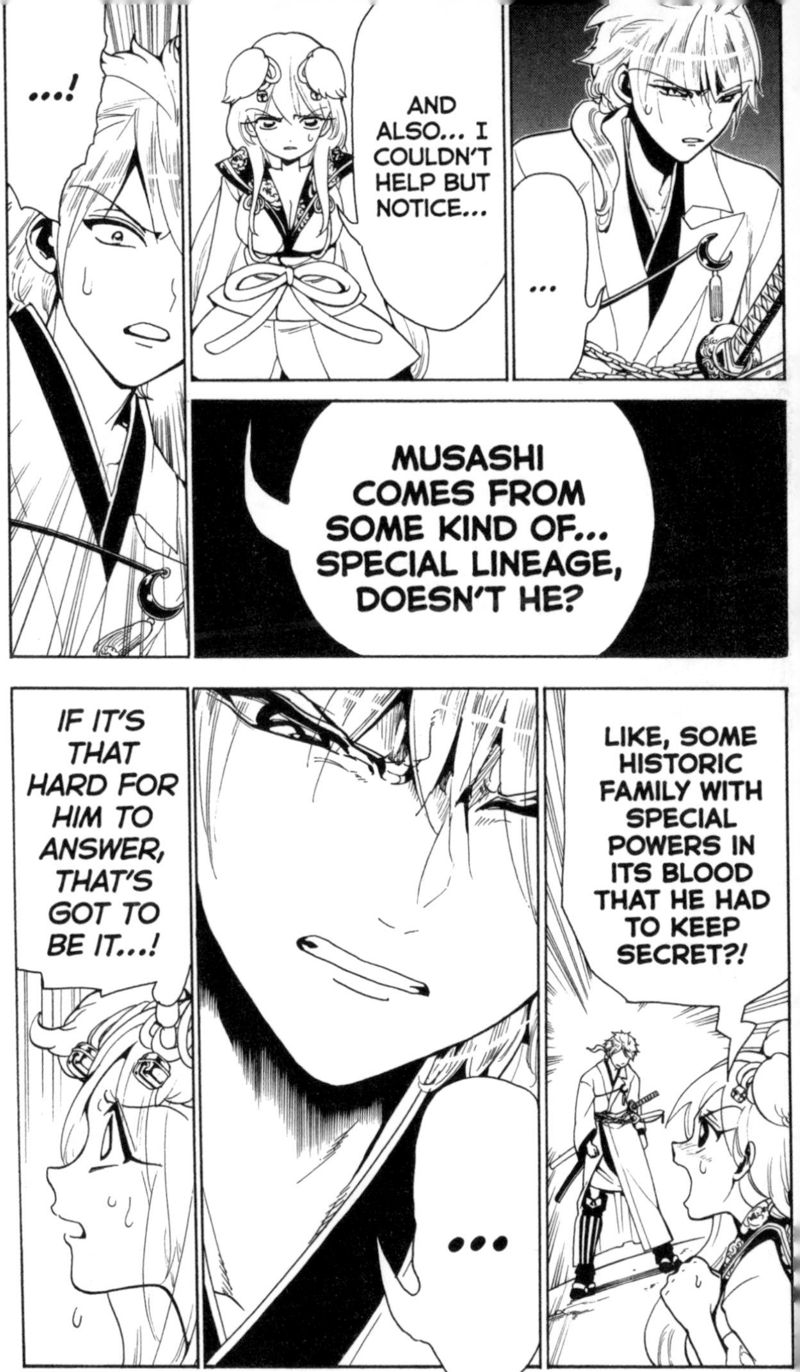
...
AND ALSO... I COULDN'T HELP BUT NOTICE...
MUSASHI COMES FROM SOME KIND OF... SPECIAL LINEAGE, DOESN'T HE?
...!
LIKE, SOME HISTORIC FAMILY WITH SPECIAL POWERS IN ITS BLOOD THAT HE HAD TO KEEP SECRET?!
...
IF IT'S THAT HARD FOR HIM TO ANSWER, THAT'S GOT TO BE IT...!

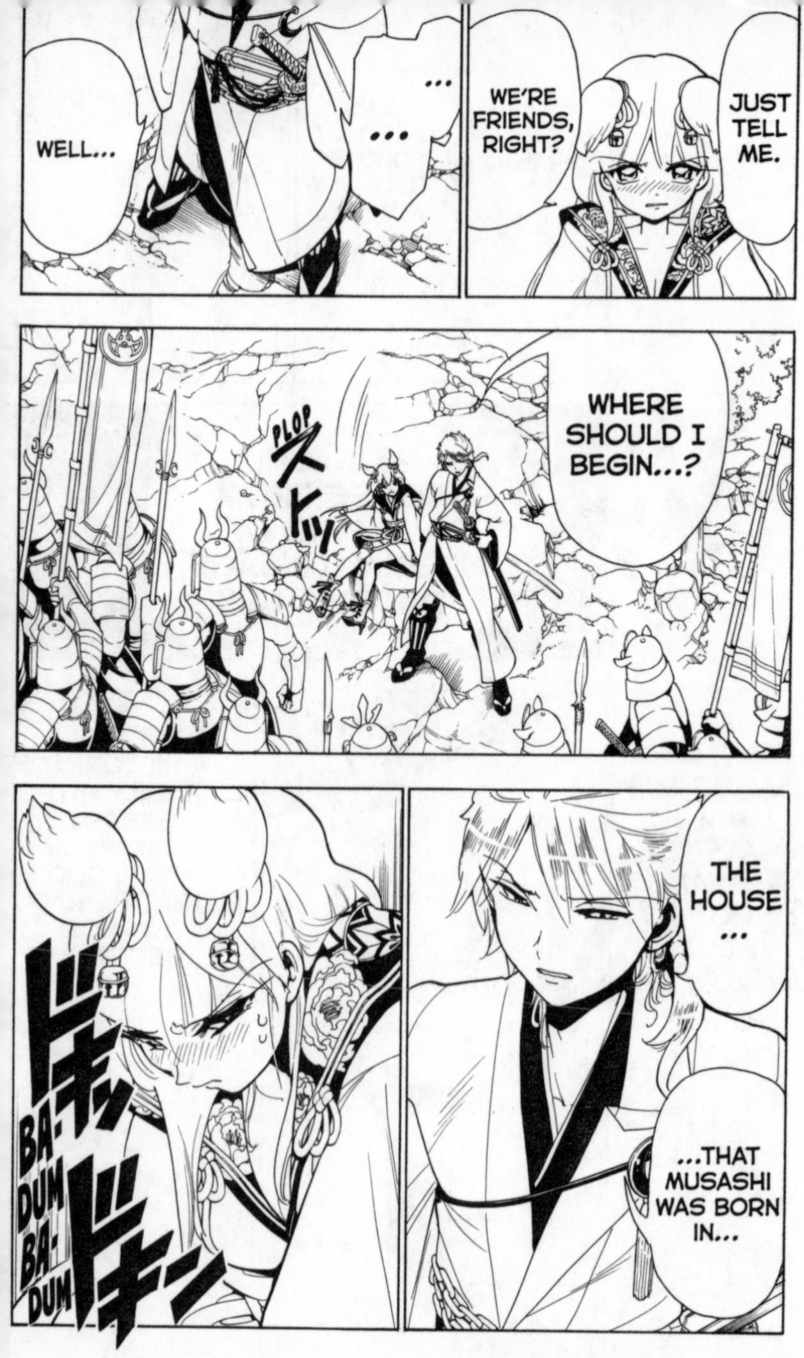
JUST TELL ME.
WE'RE FRIENDS, RIGHT?
...
...
WELL...
WHERE SHOULD I BEGIN...?
PLOP
THE HOUSE ...
...THAT MUSASHI WAS BORN IN...
BA-DUM BA-DUM

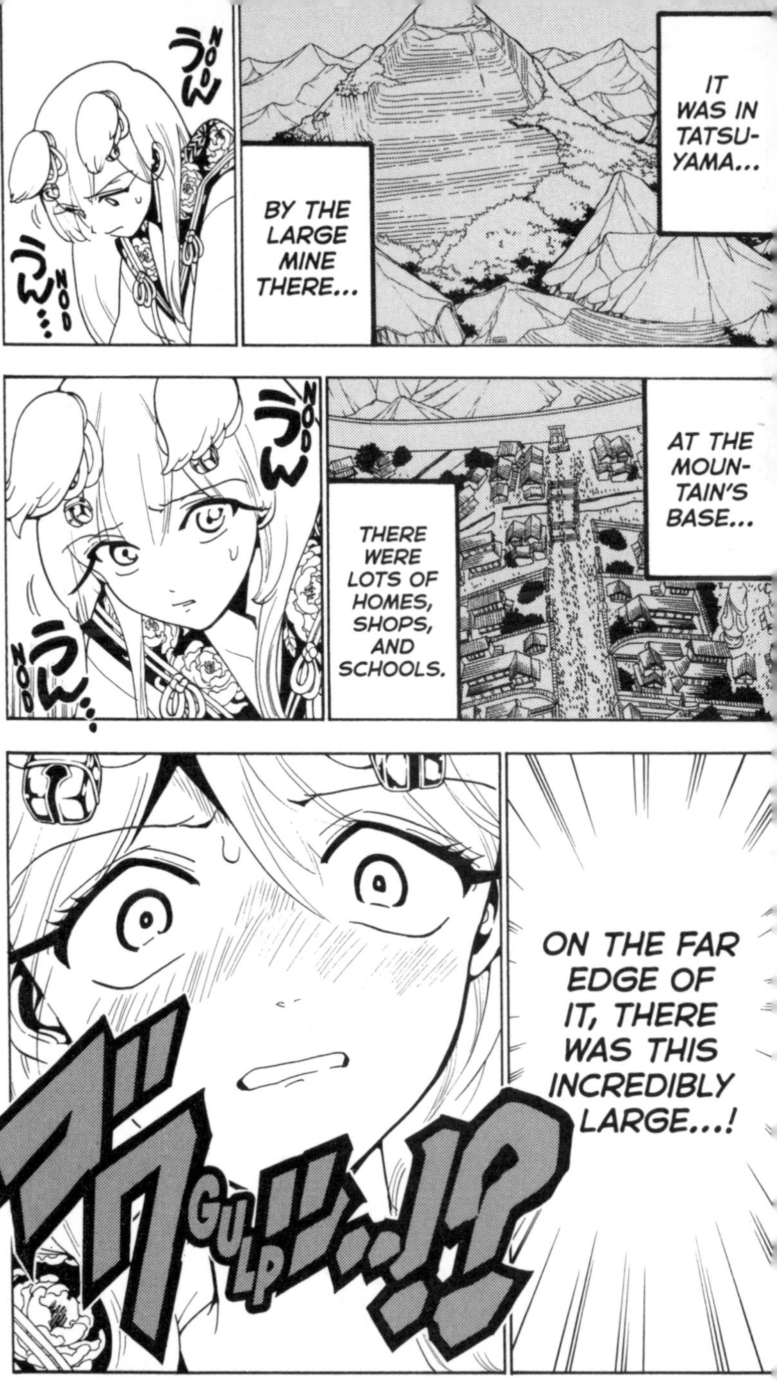
IT WAS IN TATSU-YAMA...
BY THE LARGE MINE THERE...
うん NOD
うん... NOD
AT THE MOUN-TAIN'S BASE...
THERE WERE LOTS OF HOMES, SHOPS, AND SCHOOLS.
うん NOD
うん... NOD
ON THE FAR EDGE OF IT, THERE WAS THIS INCREDIBLY LARGE...!
GULP!!...!?

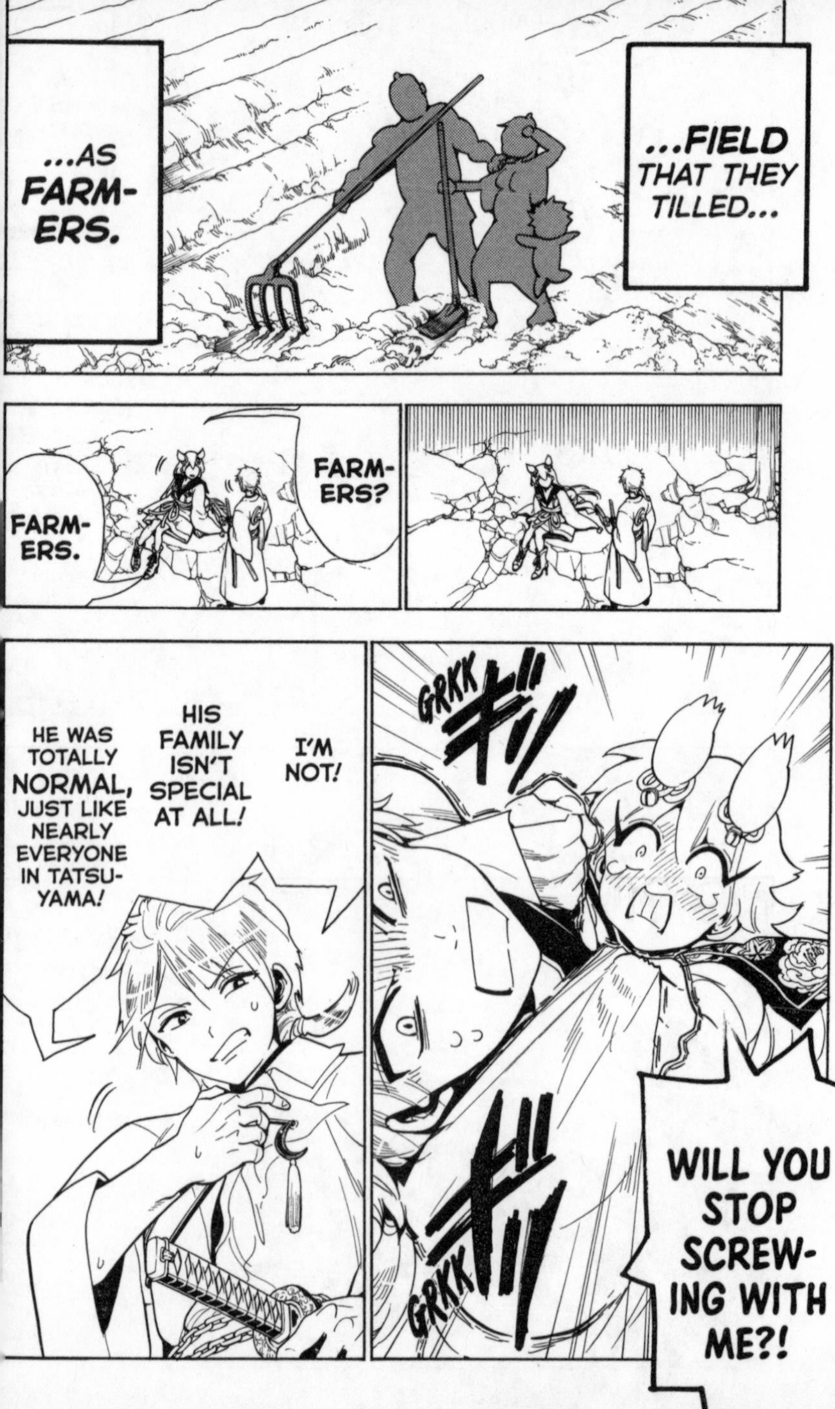
...FIELD THAT THEY TILLED...
...AS FARMERS.
FARMERS?
FARMERS.
GRKK
WILL YOU STOP SCREWING WITH ME?!
GRKK
I'M NOT!
HIS FAMILY ISN'T SPECIAL AT ALL!
HE WAS TOTALLY NORMAL, JUST LIKE NEARLY EVERYONE IN TATSUYAMA!

WOW, WHAT A LET-DOWN...

...OH, BUT WAIT.

WOULD A FARMER BE CONSIDERED "NORMAL"?

IN TATSU-YAMA, SURE. THE TOWN WAS KEPT FED ON ALL THE CROPS THAT WERE GROWN AND DELIVERED FROM THE FIELDS.

HUGE NUMBERS OF PEOPLE DEVOTED THEIR LIVES TO WORKING THAT SOIL.

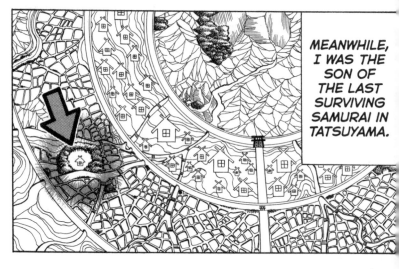

MEANWHILE, I WAS THE SON OF THE LAST SURVIVING SAMURAI IN TATSUYAMA.

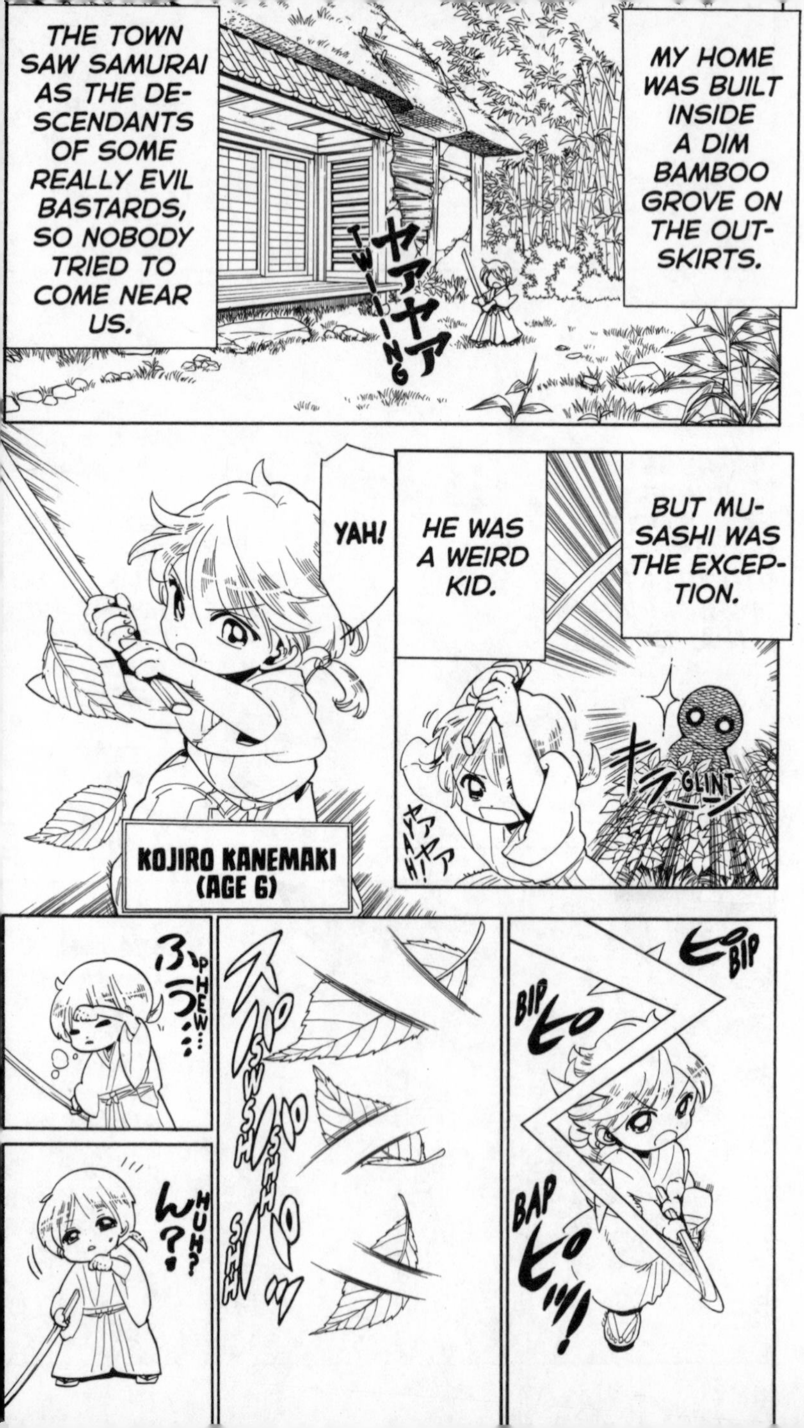

MY HOME WAS BUILT INSIDE A DIM BAMBOO GROVE ON THE OUT-SKIRTS.
ヤアヤア
TWI-I-I-NG
THE TOWN SAW SAMURAI AS THE DE-SCENDANTS OF SOME REALLY EVIL BASTARDS, SO NOBODY TRIED TO COME NEAR US.
BUT MU-SASHI WAS THE EXCEP-TION.
HE WAS A WEIRD KID.
キラーン
GLINT
ヤアヤア
YAH!
YAH!
KOJIRO KANEMAKI (AGE 6)
ヒ
BIP
ヒ
BIP
ヒッ!
BAP
スパパパ!!
SWISH
SHH
SHH
ふう…
PHEW...
ん?
HUH?

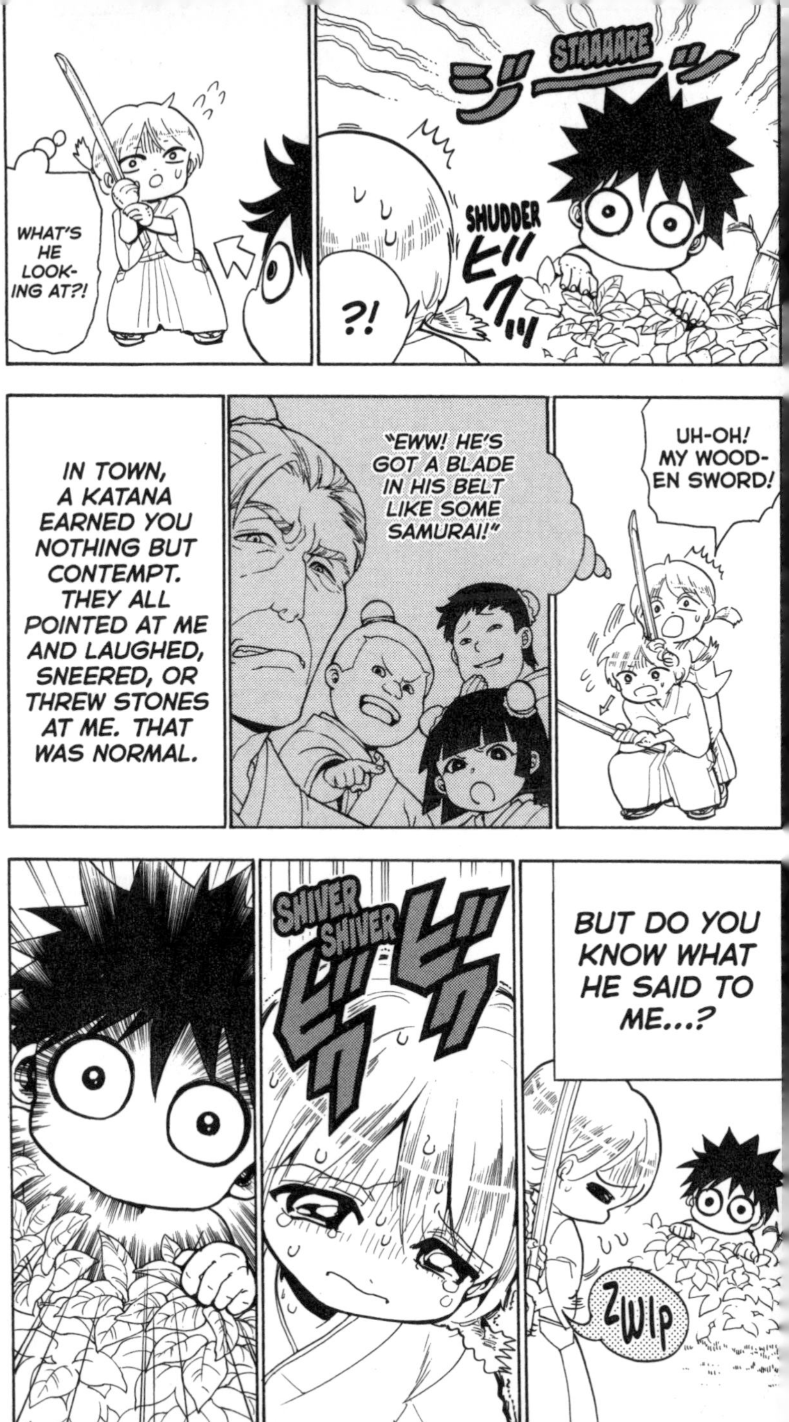
STAAAARE
SHUDDER
?!
WHAT'S HE LOOK-ING AT?!
UH-OH! MY WOOD-EN SWORD!
"EWW! HE'S GOT A BLADE IN HIS BELT LIKE SOME SAMURAI!"
IN TOWN, A KATANA EARNED YOU NOTHING BUT CONTEMPT. THEY ALL POINTED AT ME AND LAUGHED, SNEERED, OR THREW STONES AT ME. THAT WAS NORMAL.
BUT DO YOU KNOW WHAT HE SAID TO ME...?
ZWIP
SHIVER SHIVER

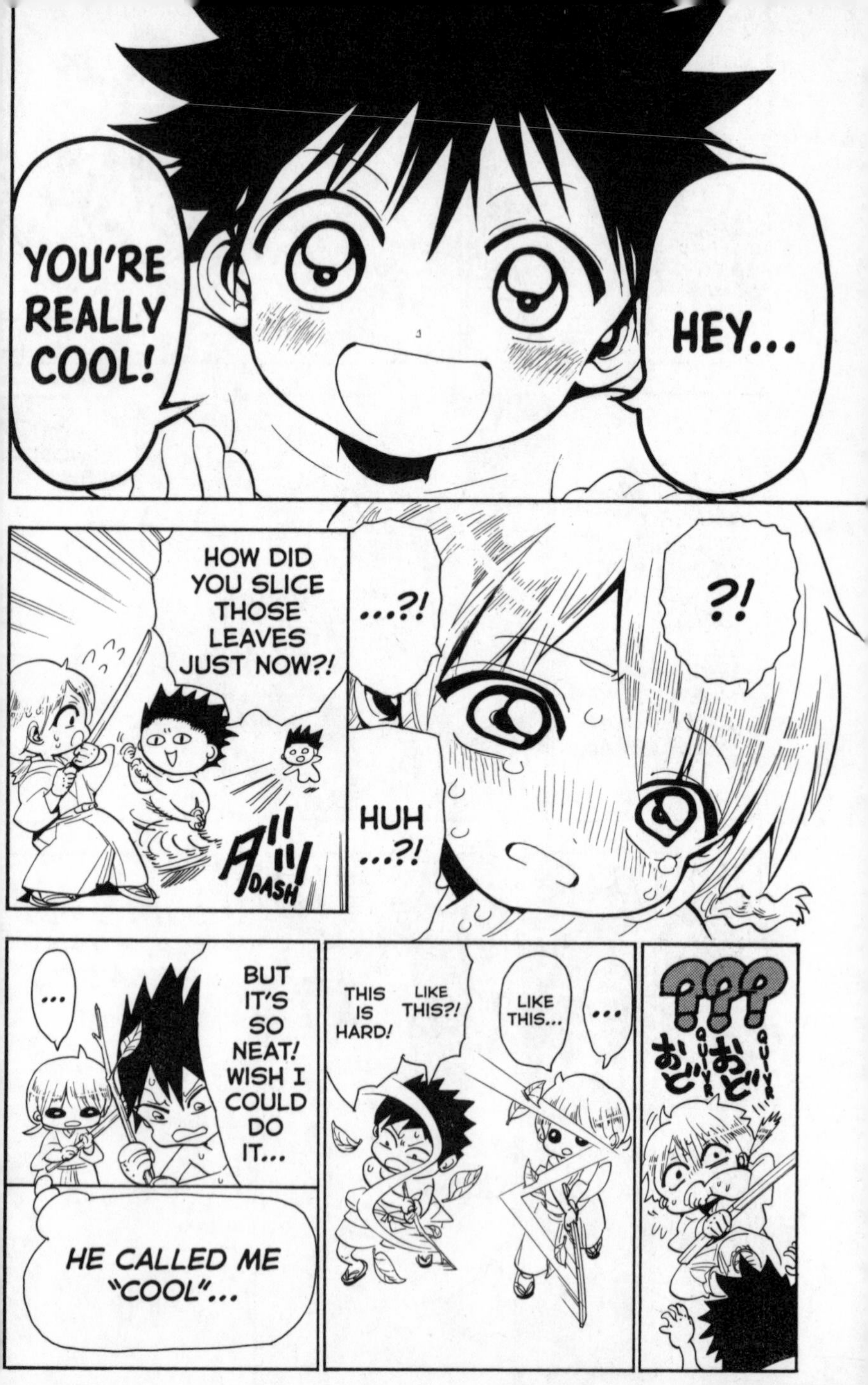
HEY...
YOU'RE REALLY COOL!
?!
...?!
HUH ...?!
HOW DID YOU SLICE THOSE LEAVES JUST NOW?!
DASH
???
おど QUIVER
おど QUIVER
...
LIKE THIS...
LIKE THIS?!
THIS IS HARD!
BUT IT'S SO NEAT! WISH I COULD DO IT...
...
HE CALLED ME "COOL"...

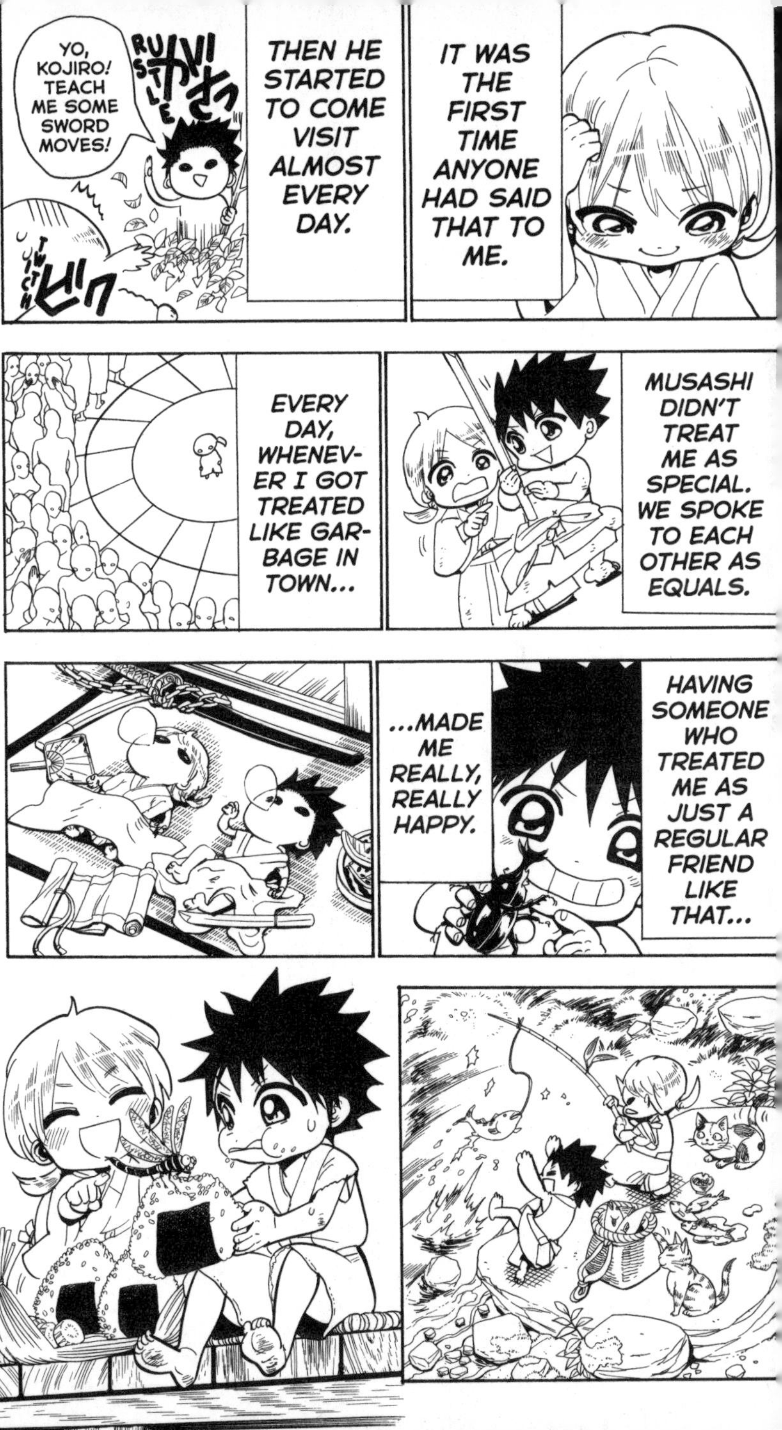
IT WAS THE FIRST TIME ANYONE HAD SAID THAT TO ME.
THEN HE STARTED TO COME VISIT ALMOST EVERY DAY.
RUSTLE
YO, KOJIRO! TEACH ME SOME SWORD MOVES!
TWITCH
MUSASHI DIDN'T TREAT ME AS SPECIAL. WE SPOKE TO EACH OTHER AS EQUALS.
EVERY DAY, WHENEVER I GOT TREATED LIKE GARBAGE IN TOWN...
HAVING SOMEONE WHO TREATED ME AS JUST A REGULAR FRIEND LIKE THAT...
...MADE ME REALLY, REALLY HAPPY.

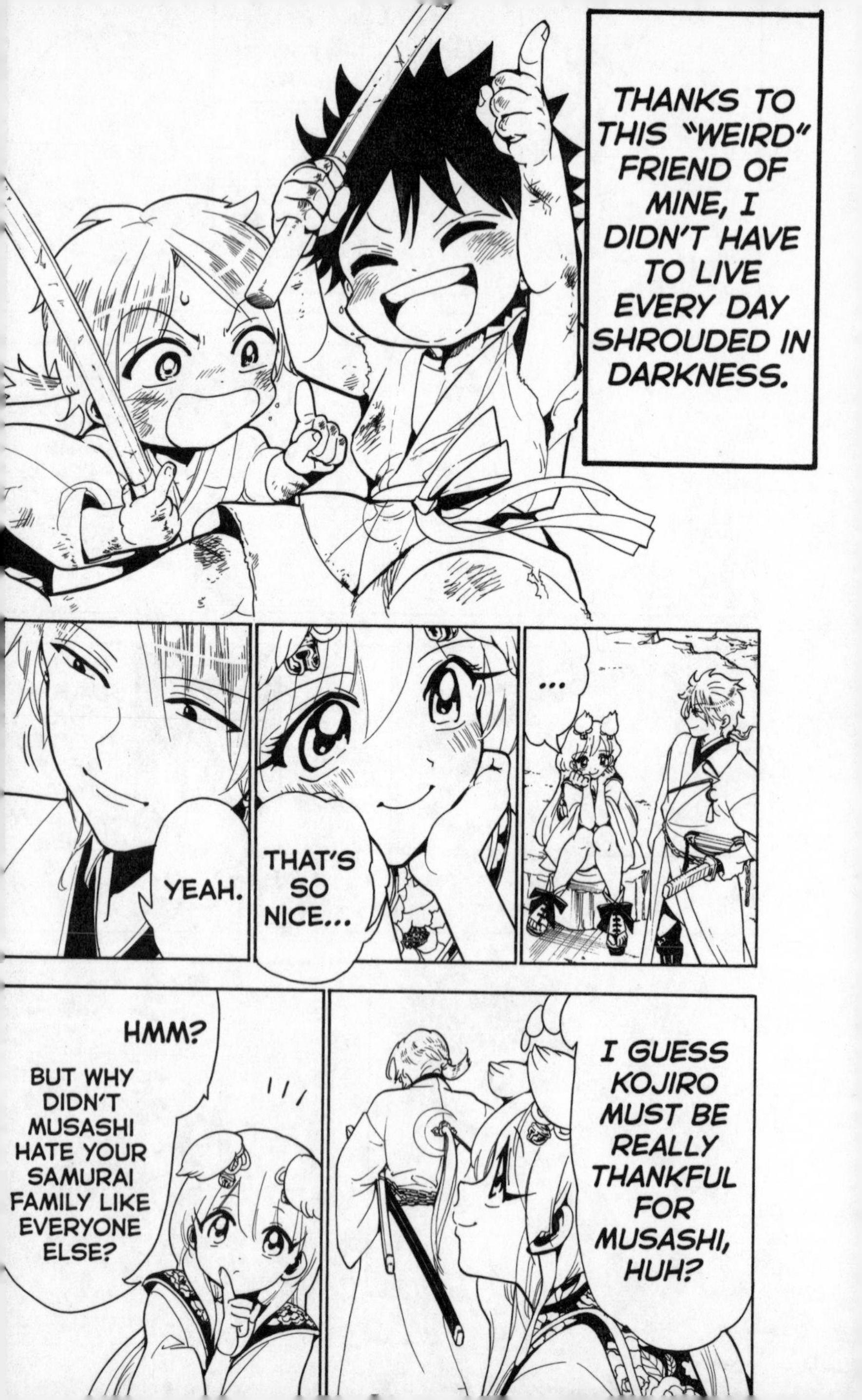
THANKS TO THIS "WEIRD" FRIEND OF MINE, I DIDN'T HAVE TO LIVE EVERY DAY SHROUDED IN DARKNESS.
...
THAT'S SO NICE...
YEAH.
I GUESS KOJIRO MUST BE REALLY THANKFUL FOR MUSASHI, HUH?
HMM?
BUT WHY DIDN'T MUSASHI HATE YOUR SAMURAI FAMILY LIKE EVERYONE ELSE?

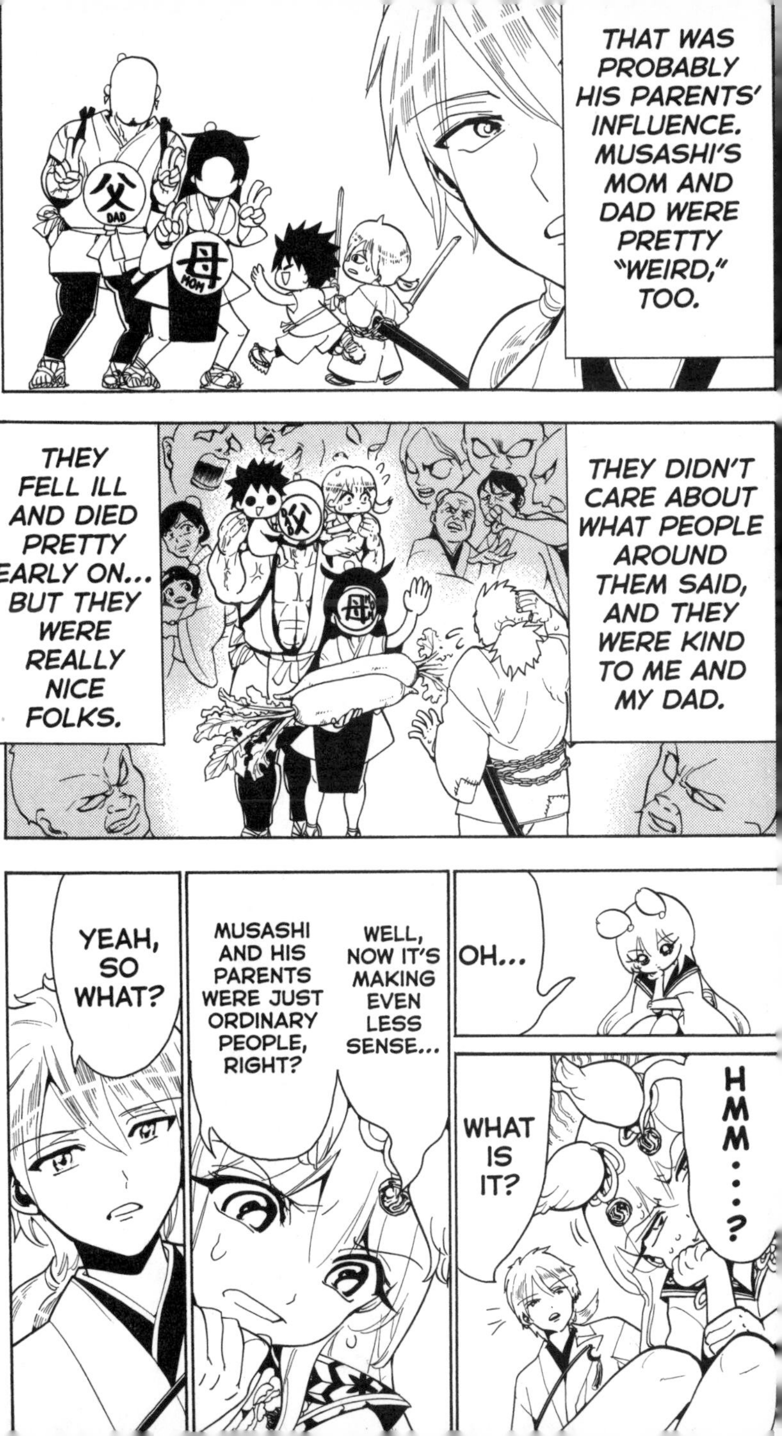
THAT WAS PROBABLY HIS PARENTS' INFLUENCE. MUSASHI'S MOM AND DAD WERE PRETTY "WEIRD," TOO.
父
DAD
母
MOM
THEY DIDN'T CARE ABOUT WHAT PEOPLE AROUND THEM SAID, AND THEY WERE KIND TO ME AND MY DAD.
THEY FELL ILL AND DIED PRETTY EARLY ON... BUT THEY WERE REALLY NICE FOLKS.
OH...
HMM...?
WHAT IS IT?
WELL, NOW IT'S MAKING EVEN LESS SENSE...
MUSASHI AND HIS PARENTS WERE JUST ORDINARY PEOPLE, RIGHT?
YEAH, SO WHAT?

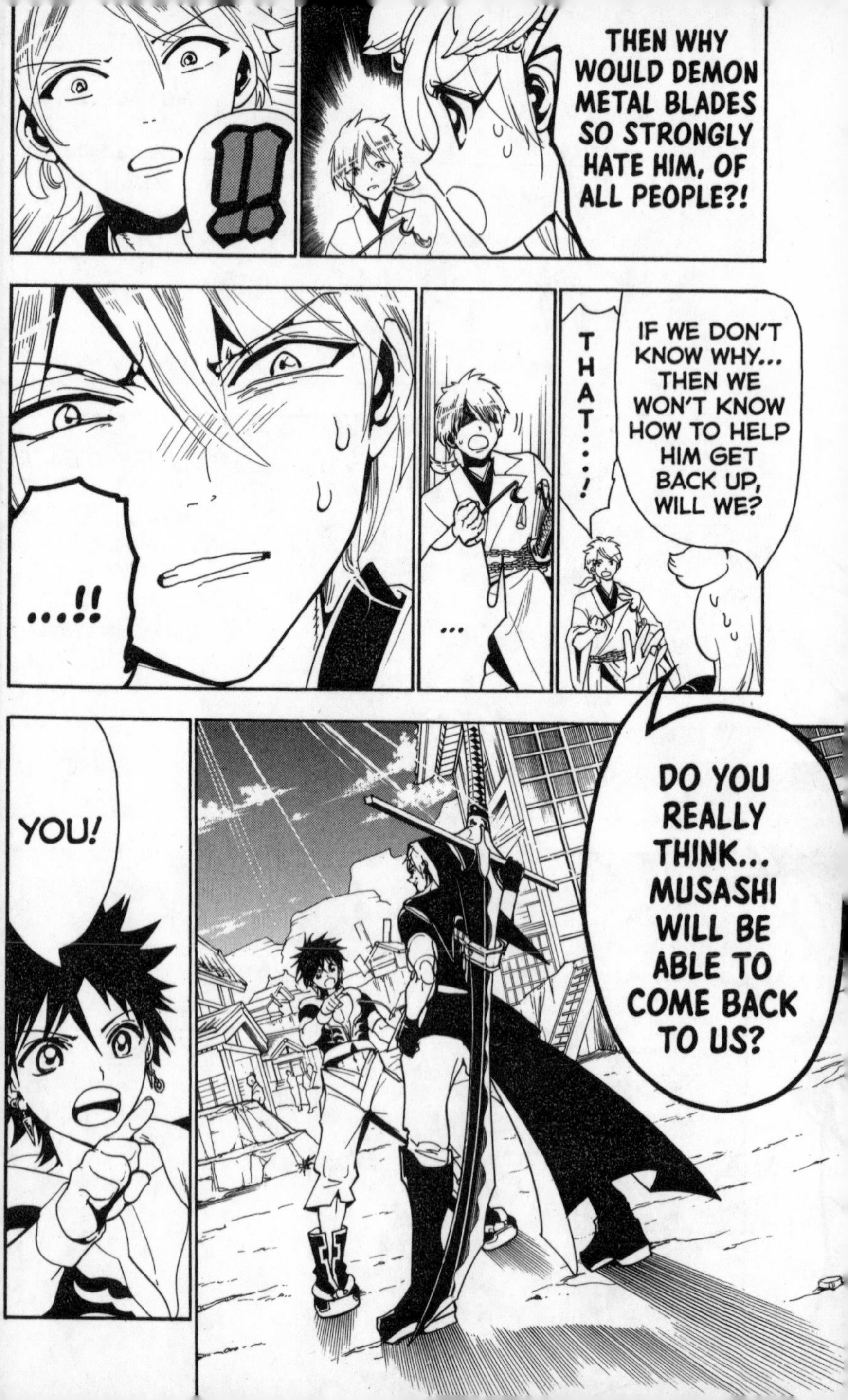
THEN WHY WOULD DEMON METAL BLADES SO STRONGLY HATE HIM, OF ALL PEOPLE?!
IF WE DON'T KNOW WHY... THEN WE WON'T KNOW HOW TO HELP HIM GET BACK UP, WILL WE?
THAT...!
...
...!!
DO YOU REALLY THINK... MUSASHI WILL BE ABLE TO COME BACK TO US?
YOU!

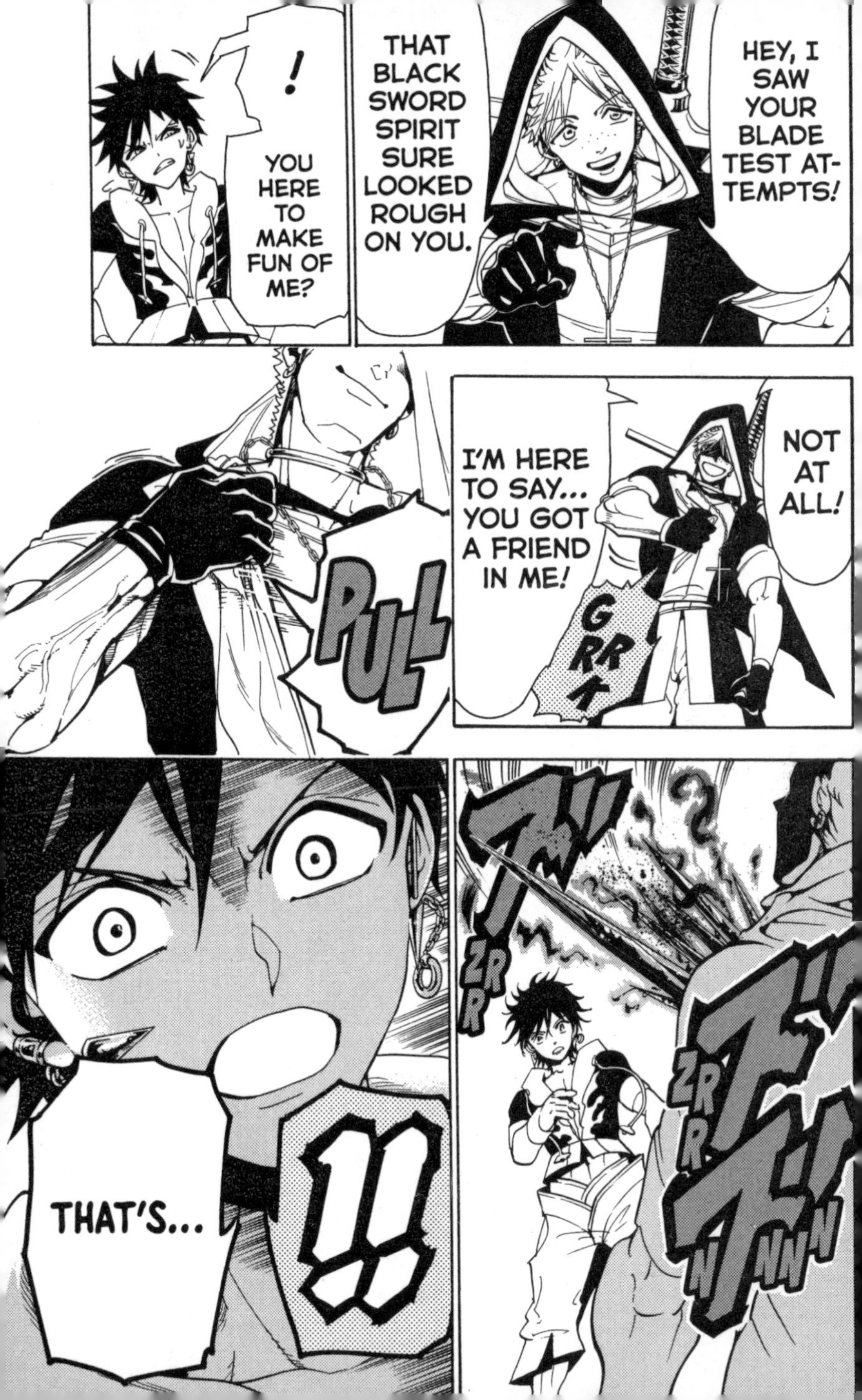
HEY, I SAW YOUR BLADE TEST AT-TEMPTS!
THAT BLACK SWORD SPIRIT SURE LOOKED ROUGH ON YOU.
!
YOU HERE TO MAKE FUN OF ME?
NOT AT ALL!
I'M HERE TO SAY... YOU GOT A FRIEND IN ME!
GRRK
PULL
ZRR
ZRR
NNNNN
!!
THAT'S...

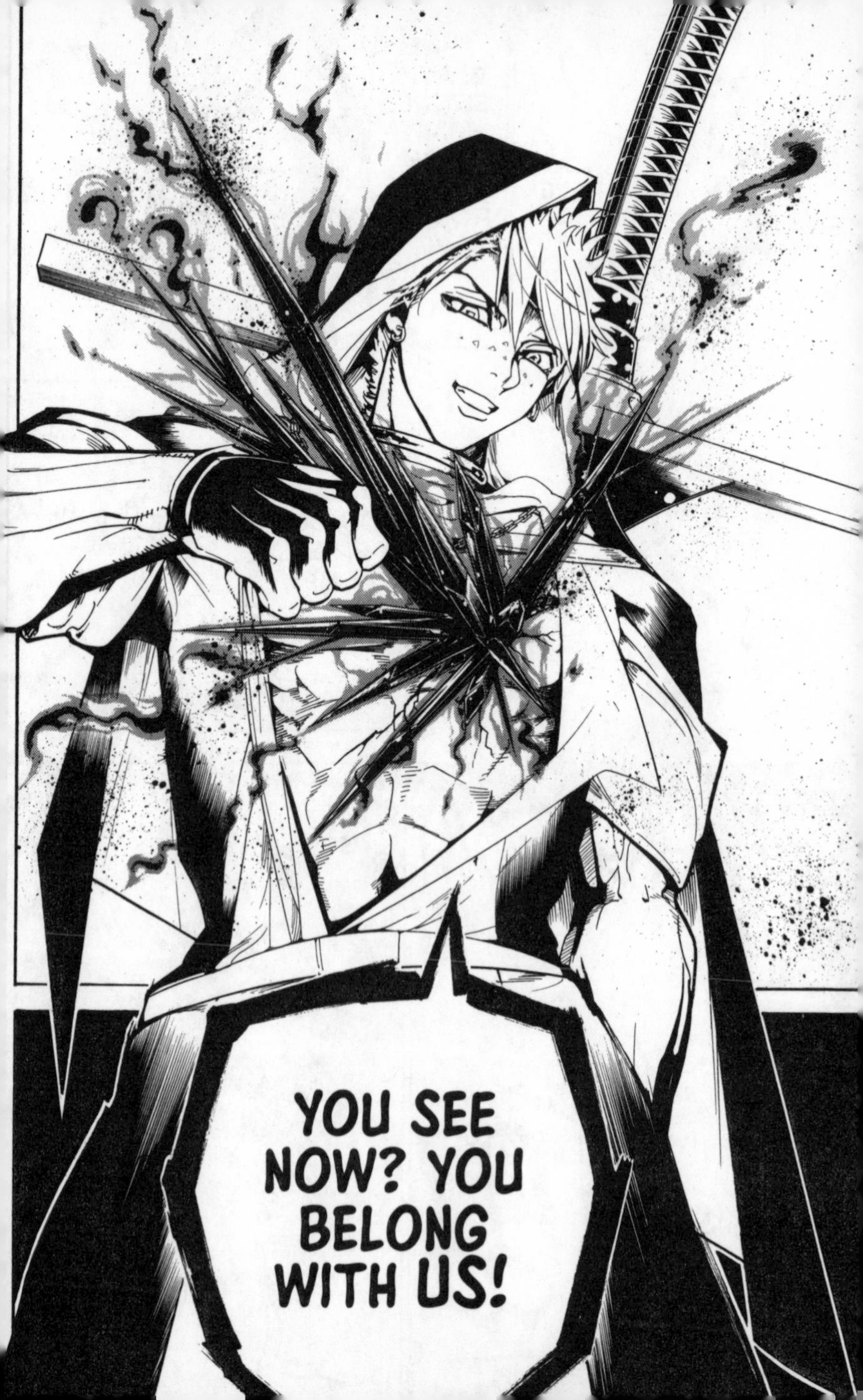
YOU SEE NOW? YOU BELONG WITH US!

CHAPTER 27: WE FINALLY MEET

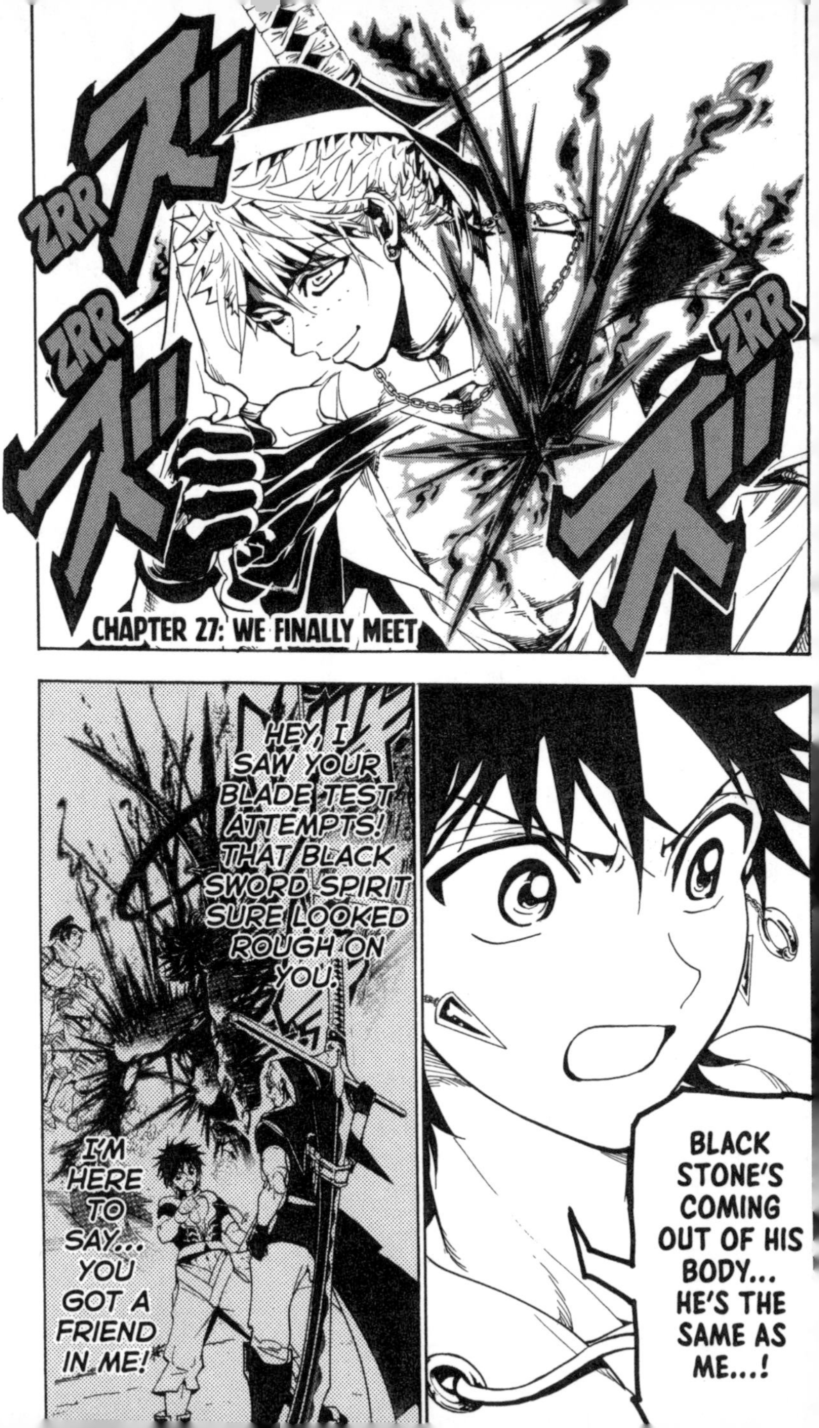
ZRR
ズ
ZRR
ズ
ZRR
ズ
BLACK STONE'S COMING OUT OF HIS BODY... HE'S THE SAME AS ME...!
HEY, I SAW YOUR BLADE TEST ATTEMPTS! THAT BLACK SWORD SPIRIT SURE LOOKED ROUGH ON YOU.
I'M HERE TO SAY... YOU GOT A FRIEND IN ME!

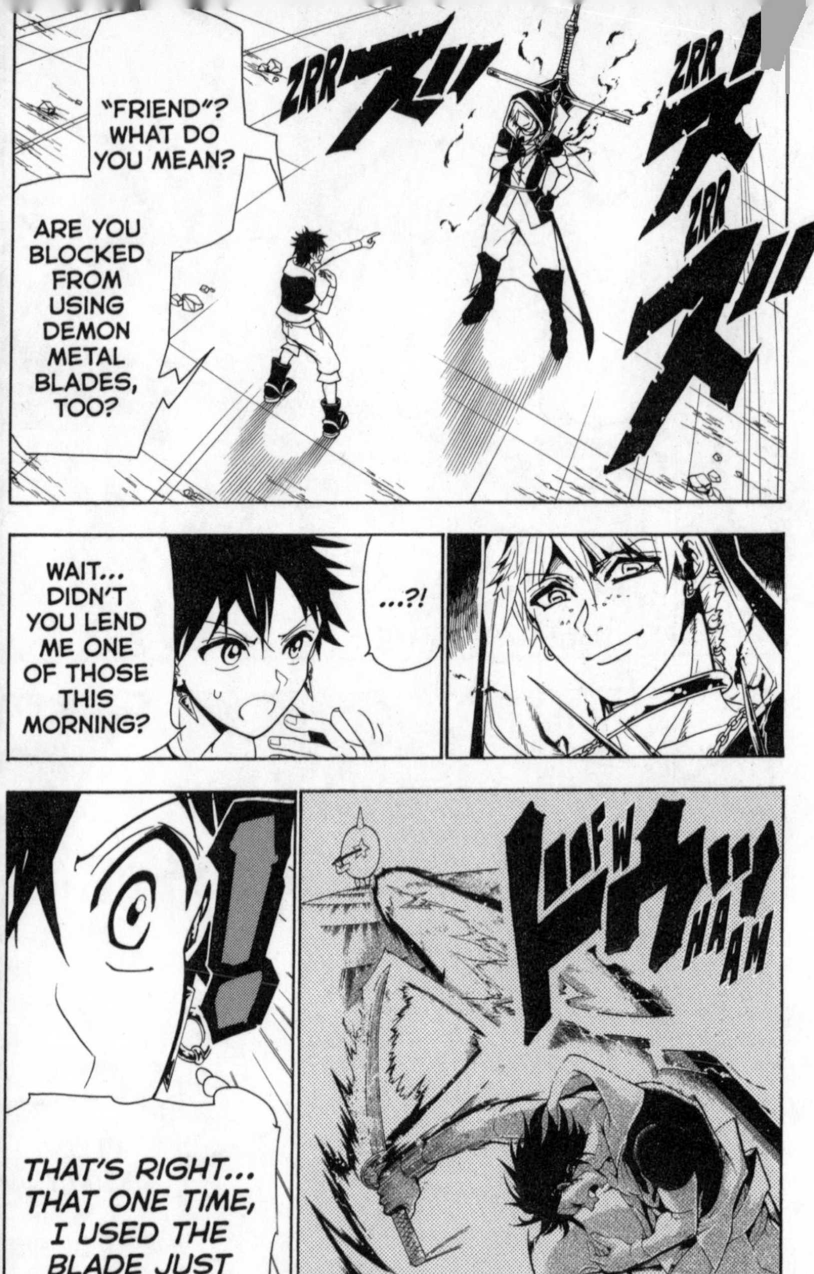
ZRR
ZRR
ZRR
"FRIEND"? WHAT DO YOU MEAN?
ARE YOU BLOCKED FROM USING DEMON METAL BLADES, TOO?
...?!
WAIT... DIDN'T YOU LEND ME ONE OF THOSE THIS MORNING?
WHAAM
THAT'S RIGHT... THAT ONE TIME, I USED THE BLADE JUST FINE!

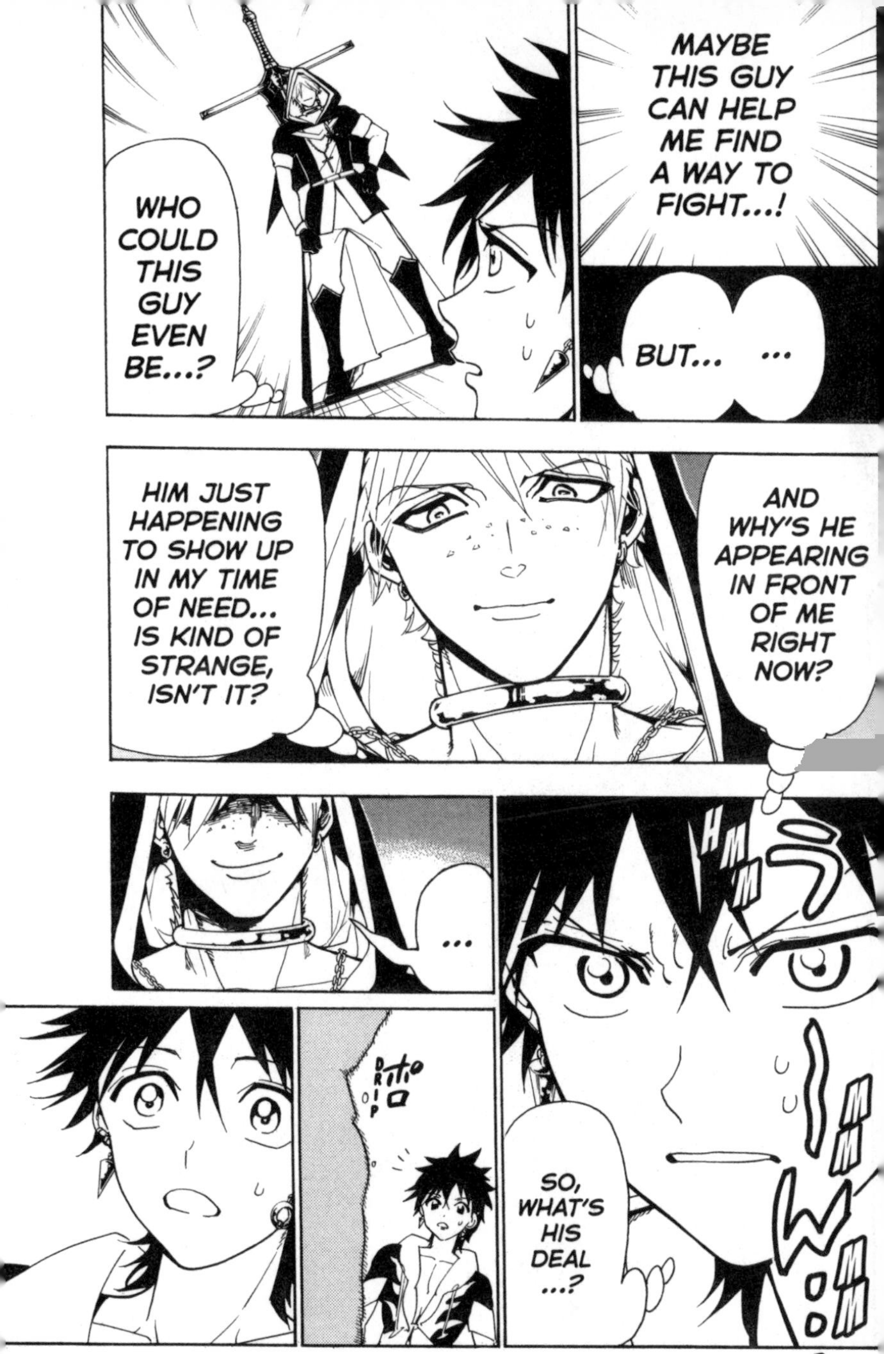
MAYBE THIS GUY CAN HELP ME FIND A WAY TO FIGHT...!
BUT... ...
WHO COULD THIS GUY EVEN BE...?
AND WHY'S HE APPEARING IN FRONT OF ME RIGHT NOW?
HIM JUST HAPPENING TO SHOW UP IN MY TIME OF NEED... IS KIND OF STRANGE, ISN'T IT?
HMMM
SO, WHAT'S HIS DEAL ...?
...
DRIP

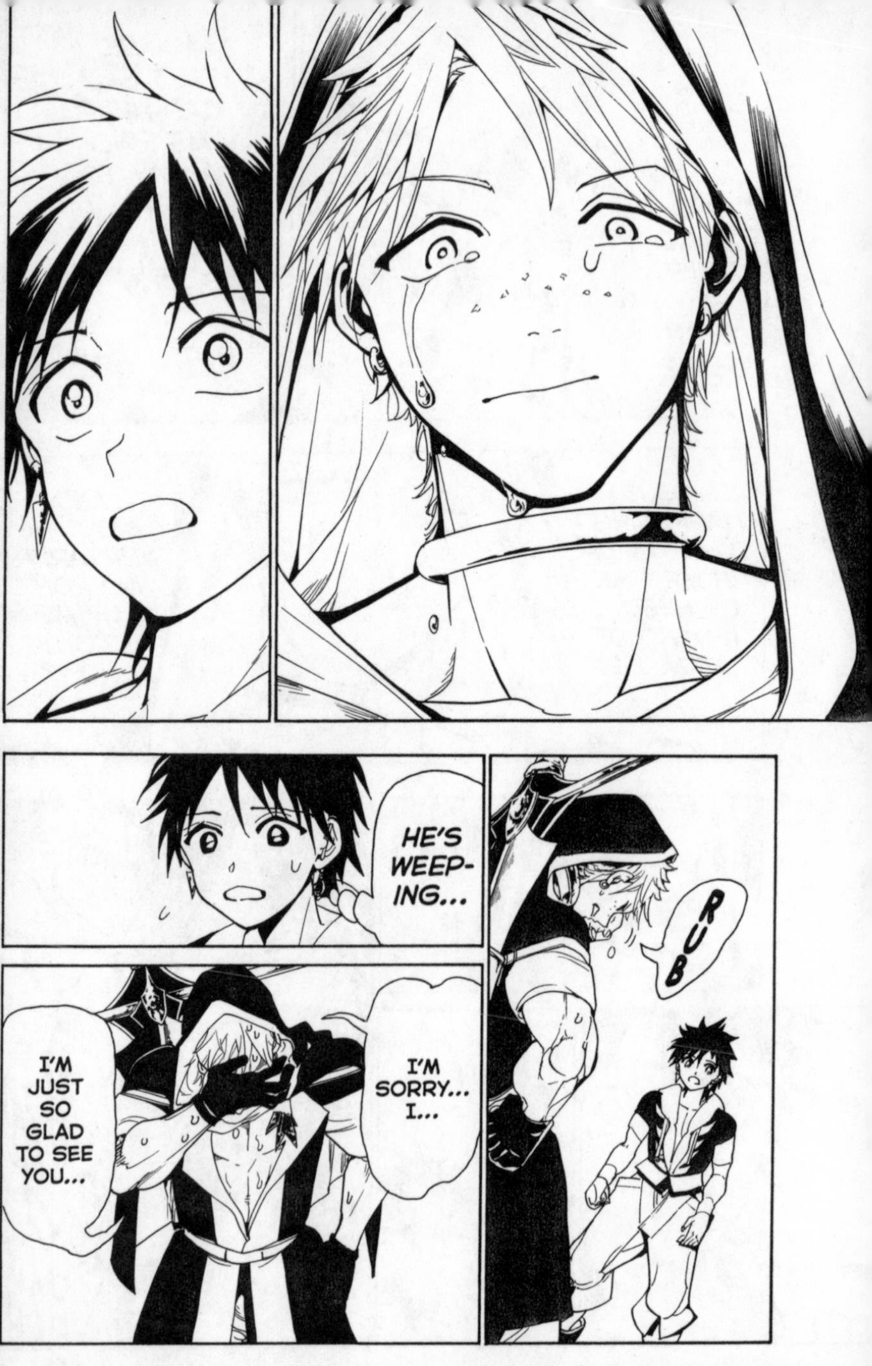
RUB
HE'S WEEP-ING...
I'M SORRY... I...
I'M JUST SO GLAD TO SEE YOU...

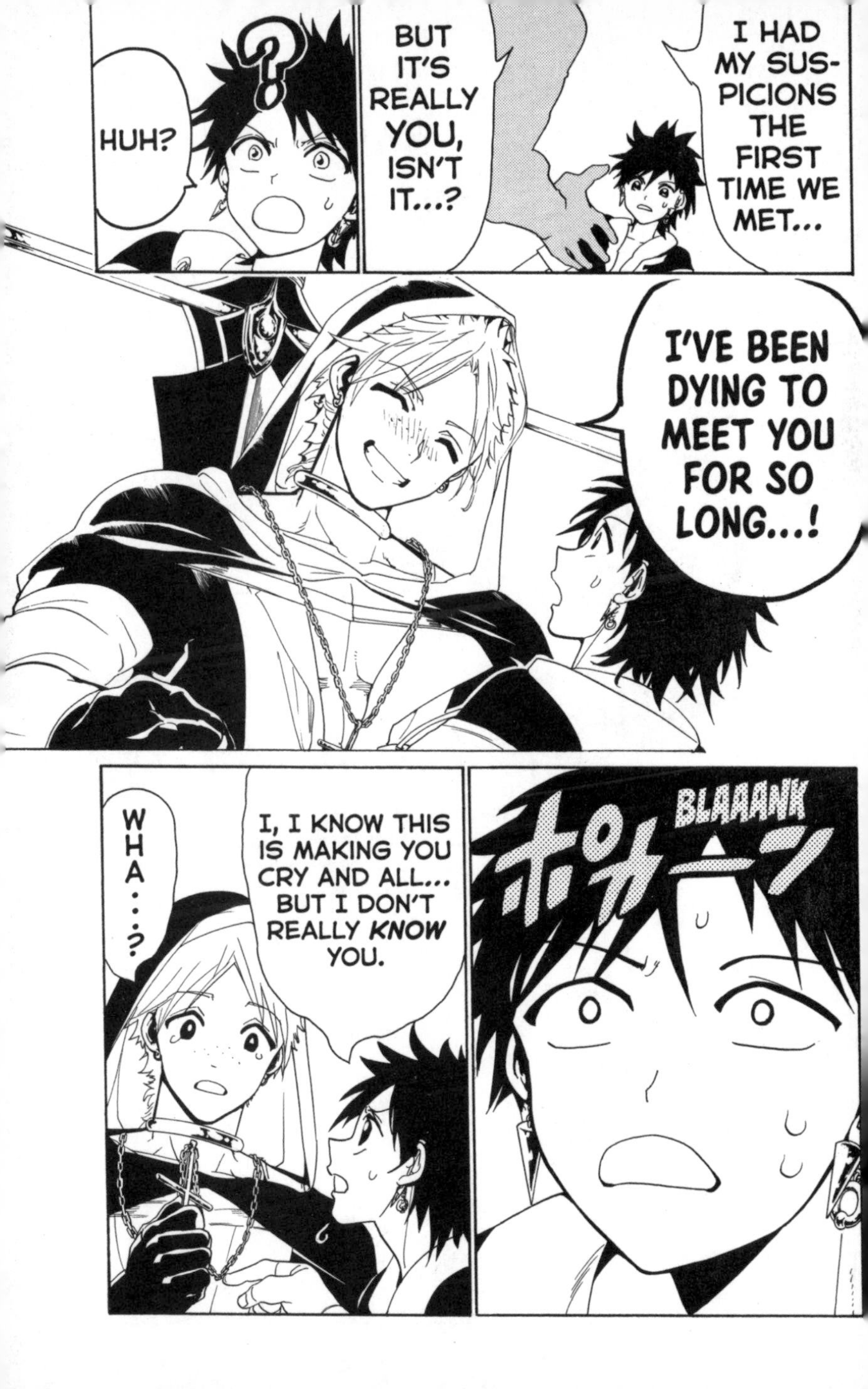
I HAD MY SUS-PICIONS THE FIRST TIME WE MET...
BUT IT'S REALLY YOU, ISN'T IT...?
HUH?
I'VE BEEN DYING TO MEET YOU FOR SO LONG...!
ポカーン
BLAAANK
I, I KNOW THIS IS MAKING YOU CRY AND ALL... BUT I DON'T REALLY *KNOW* YOU.
WHA...?

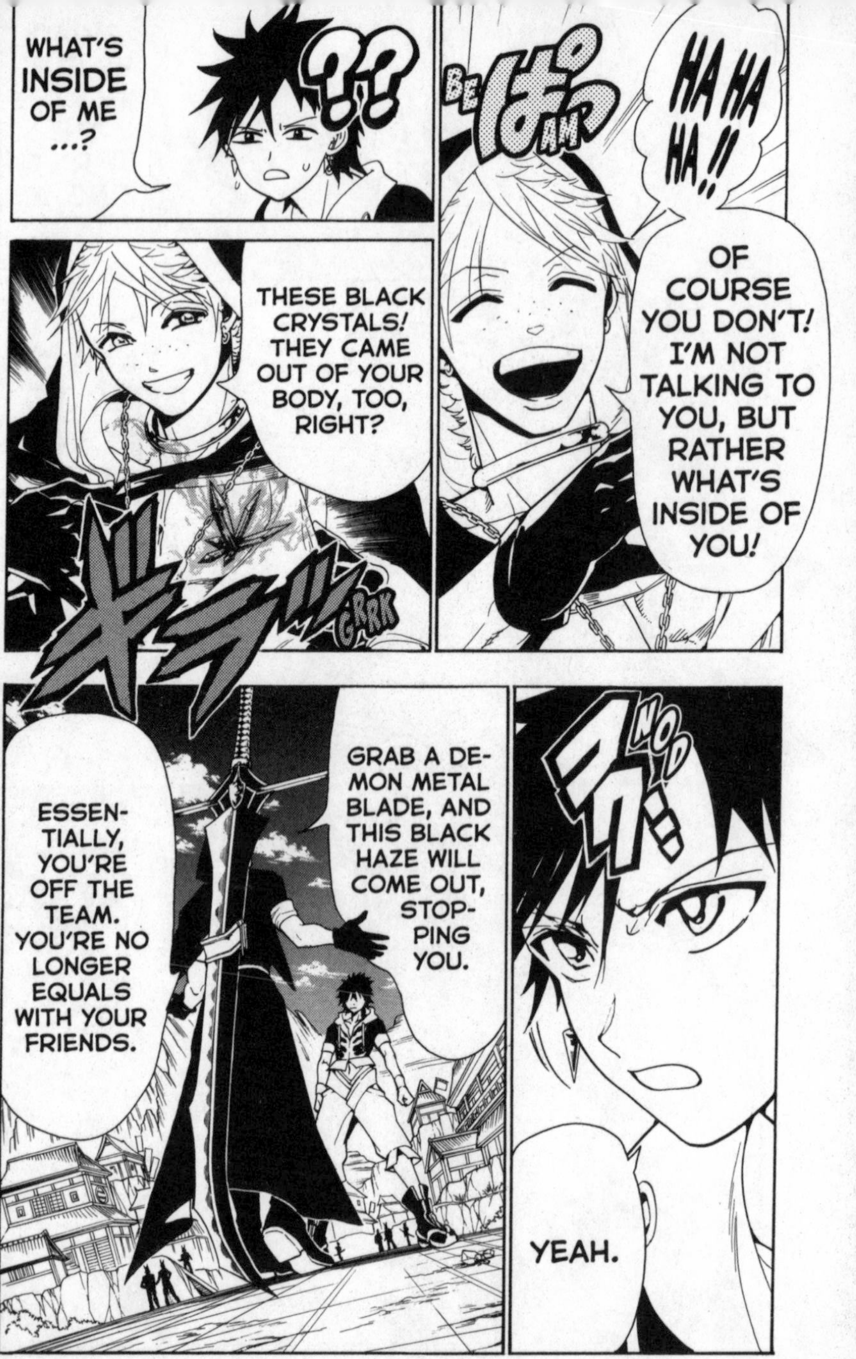
BE
AMP
HA HA HA!!
OF COURSE YOU DON'T! I'M NOT TALKING TO YOU, BUT RATHER WHAT'S INSIDE OF YOU!
WHAT'S INSIDE OF ME ...?
??
THESE BLACK CRYSTALS! THEY CAME OUT OF YOUR BODY, TOO, RIGHT?
GRRK
NOD
YEAH.
GRAB A DEMON METAL BLADE, AND THIS BLACK HAZE WILL COME OUT, STOPPING YOU.
ESSENTIALLY, YOU'RE OFF THE TEAM. YOU'RE NO LONGER EQUALS WITH YOUR FRIENDS.

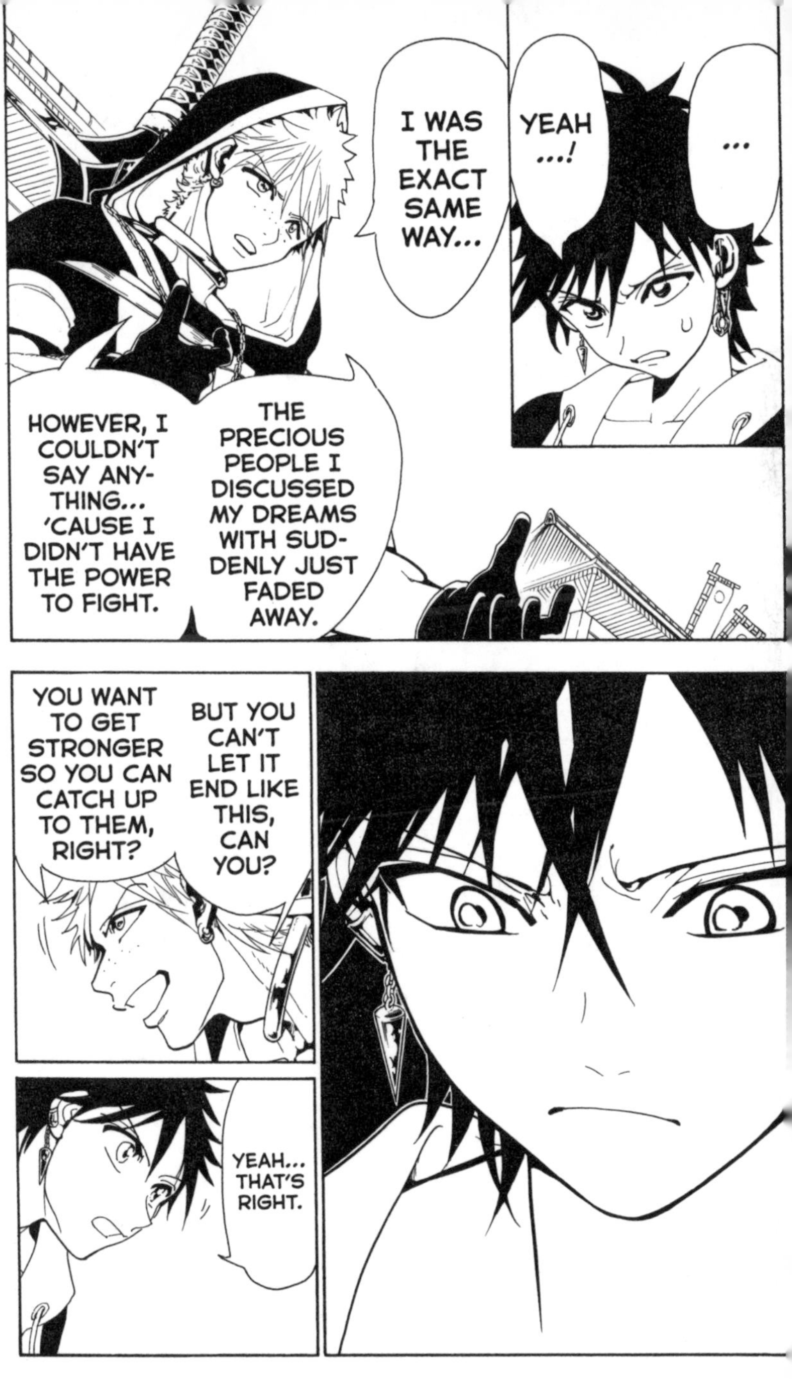
...
YEAH ...!
I WAS THE EXACT SAME WAY...
THE PRECIOUS PEOPLE I DISCUSSED MY DREAMS WITH SUDDENLY JUST FADED AWAY.
HOWEVER, I COULDN'T SAY ANYTHING... 'CAUSE I DIDN'T HAVE THE POWER TO FIGHT.
BUT YOU CAN'T LET IT END LIKE THIS, CAN YOU?
YOU WANT TO GET STRONGER SO YOU CAN CATCH UP TO THEM, RIGHT?
YEAH... THAT'S RIGHT.

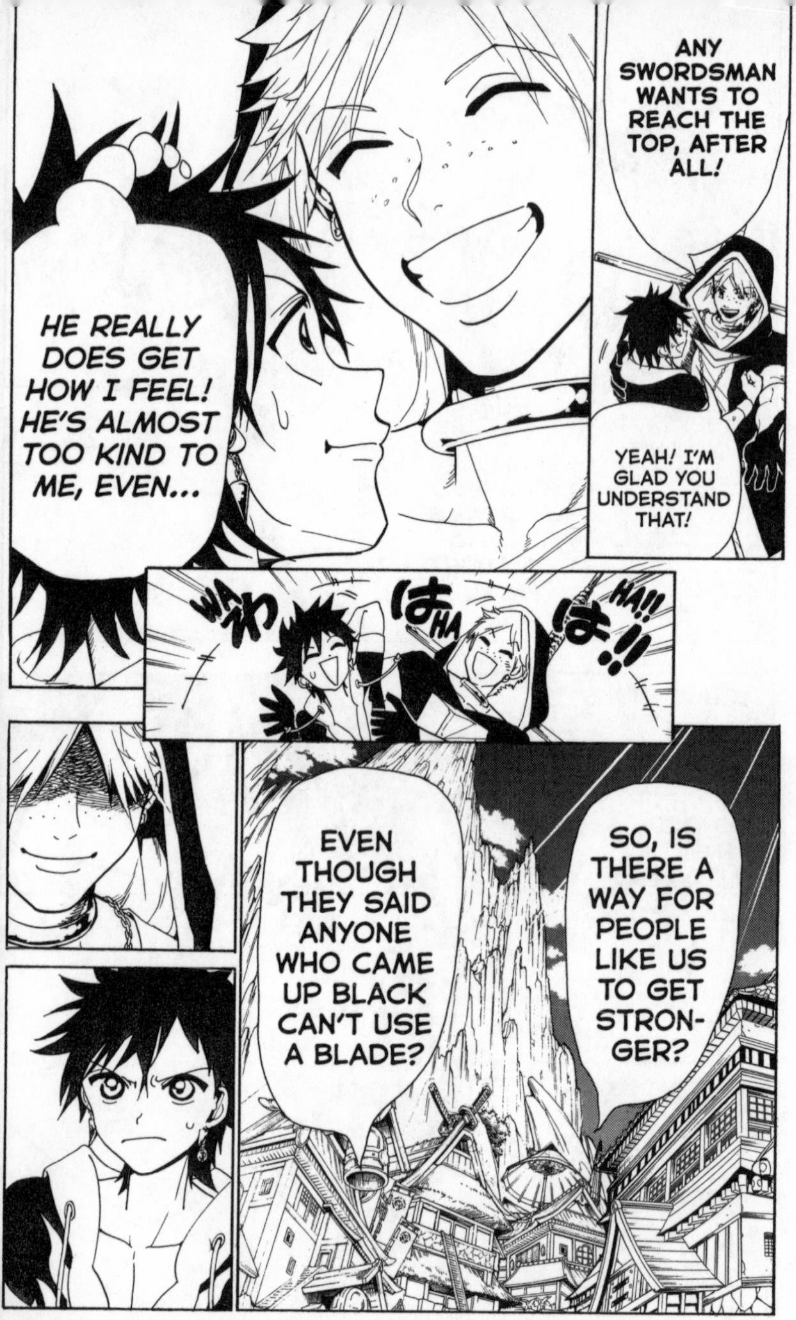
ANY SWORDSMAN WANTS TO REACH THE TOP, AFTER ALL!
YEAH! I'M GLAD YOU UNDERSTAND THAT!
HE REALLY DOES GET HOW I FEEL! HE'S ALMOST TOO KIND TO ME, EVEN...
わはは!! WA HA HA!!
SO, IS THERE A WAY FOR PEOPLE LIKE US TO GET STRON-GER?
EVEN THOUGH THEY SAID ANYONE WHO CAME UP BLACK CAN'T USE A BLADE?

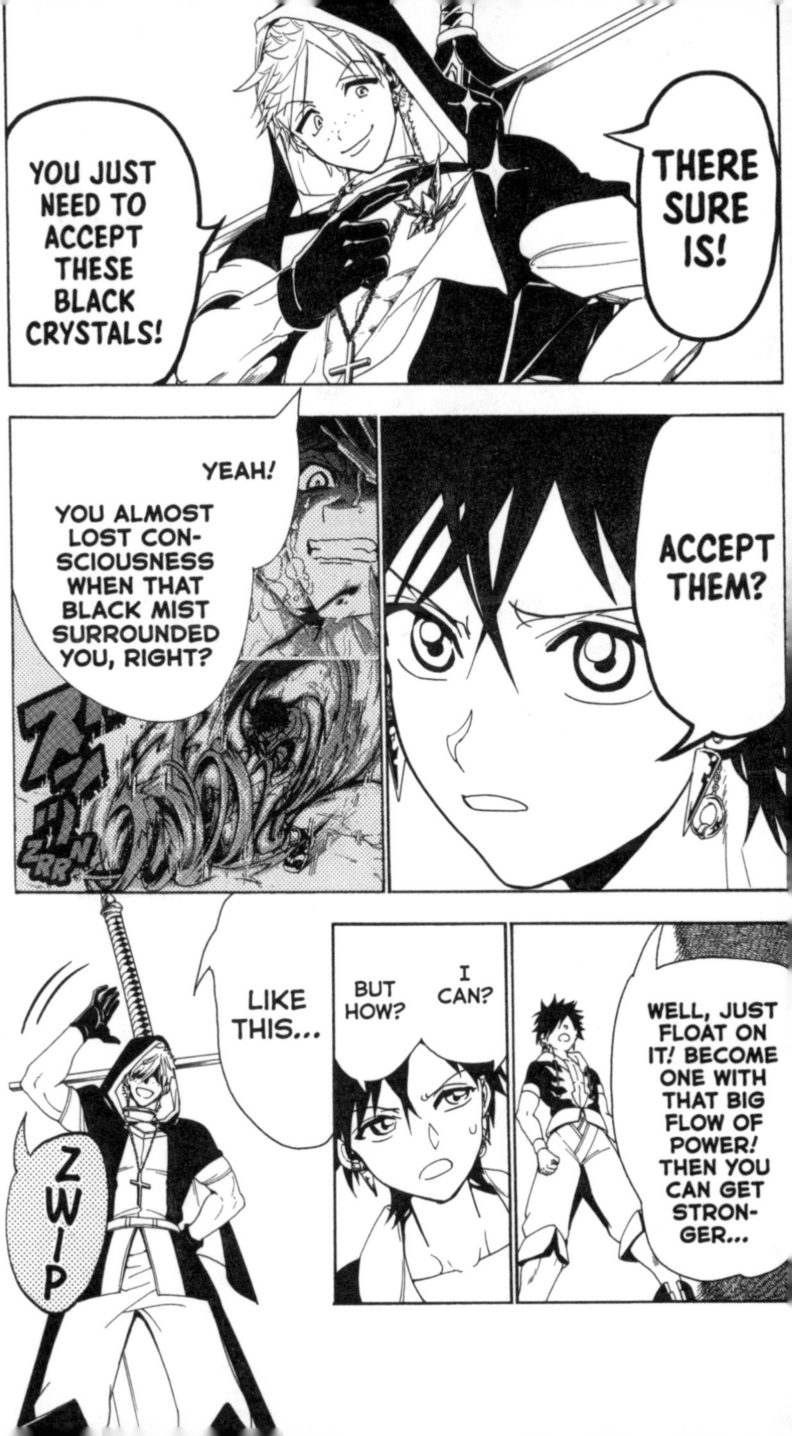
THERE SURE IS!
YOU JUST NEED TO ACCEPT THESE BLACK CRYSTALS!
ACCEPT THEM?
YEAH!
YOU ALMOST LOST CON-SCIOUSNESS WHEN THAT BLACK MIST SURROUNDED YOU, RIGHT?
WELL, JUST FLOAT ON IT! BECOME ONE WITH THAT BIG FLOW OF POWER! THEN YOU CAN GET STRON-GER...
I CAN?
BUT HOW?
LIKE THIS...
ZWIP

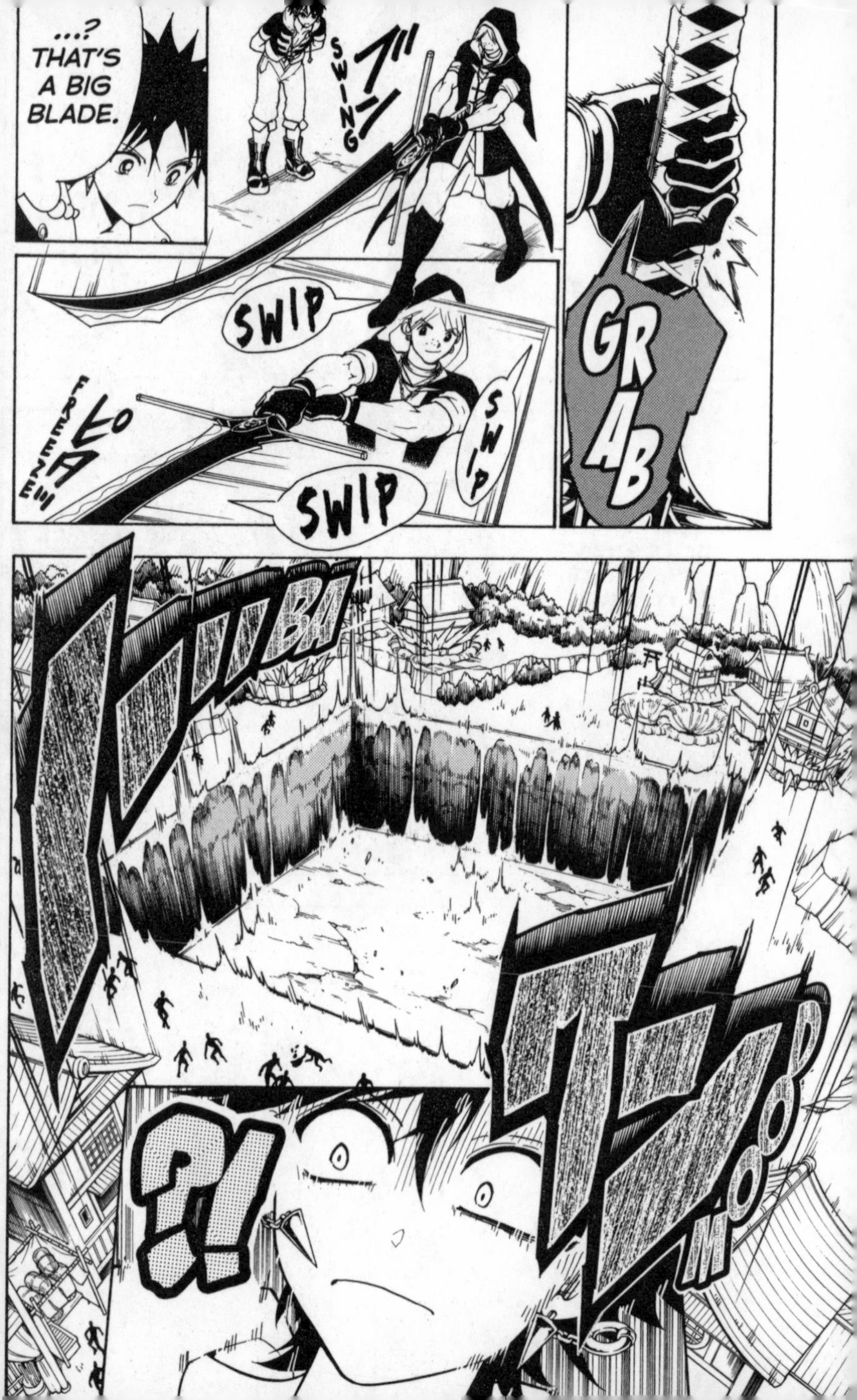
GRAB
SWING
...? THAT'S A BIG BLADE.
SWIP
SWIP
SWIP
FREEZE!!
BA
DOOOM
?!

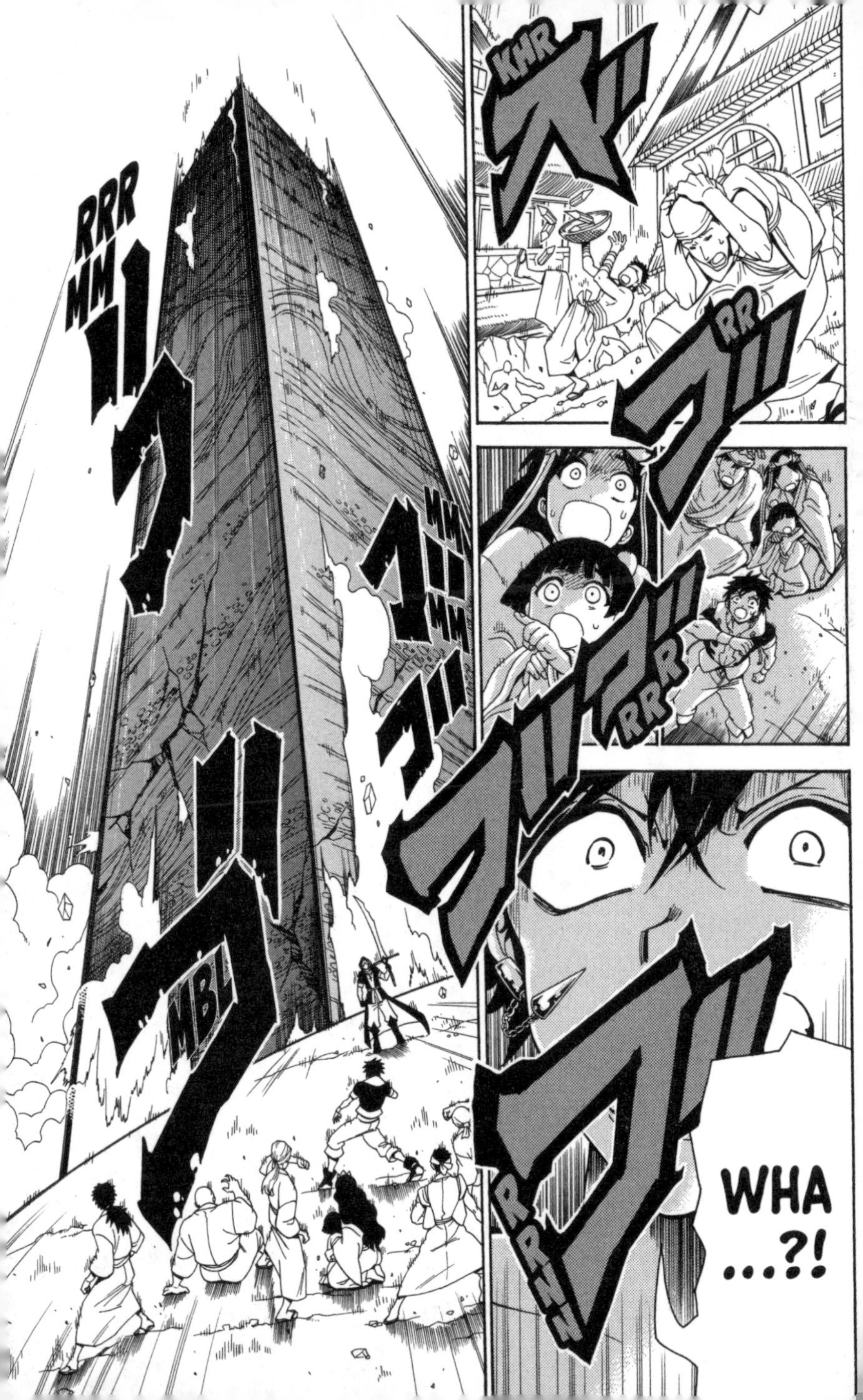
KHR
RR
RRR
WHA ...?!
RRRNN
RRR
MM
MM
MM
MBL

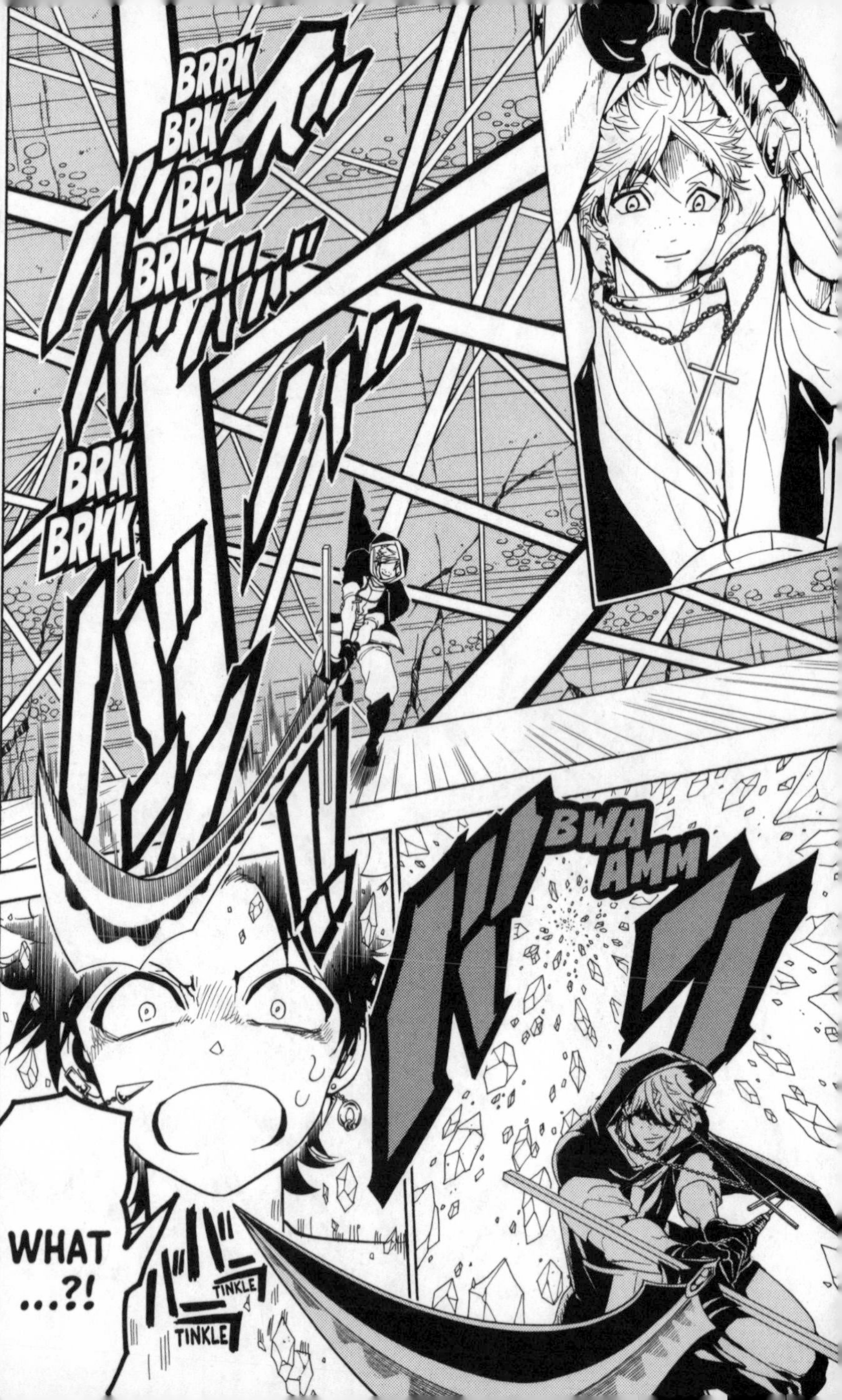
BRRK
BRK
BRK
BRK
BRK
BRKK
BWA
AMM
WHAT
...?!
TINKLE
TINKLE

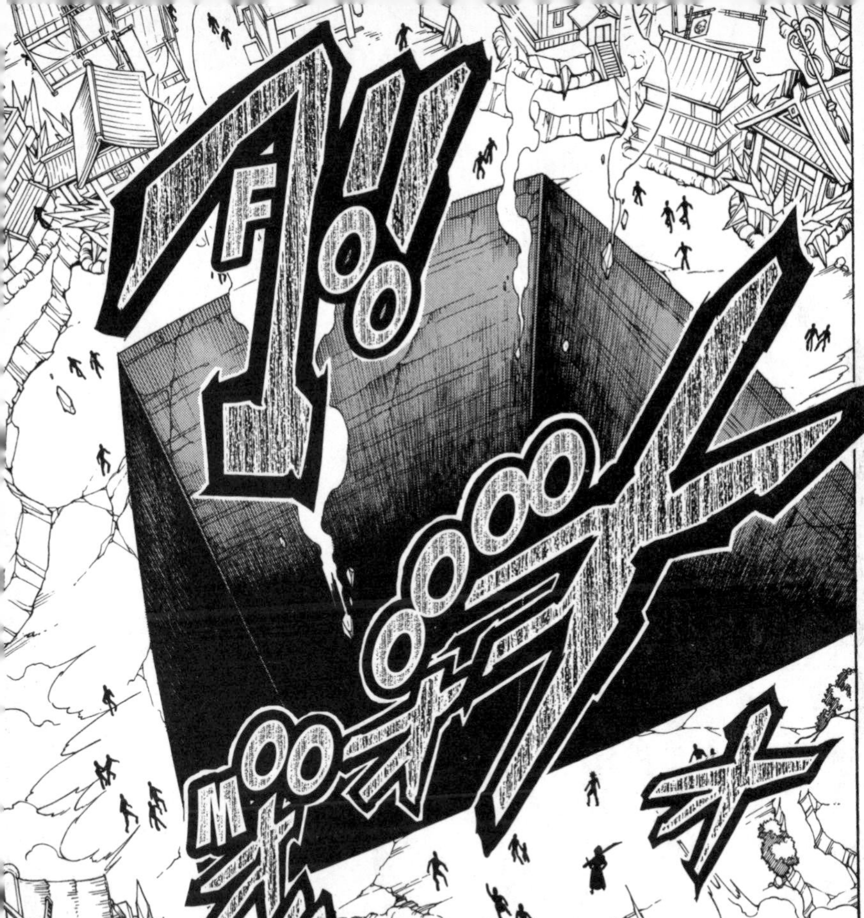
FOOOOOOOOOOM
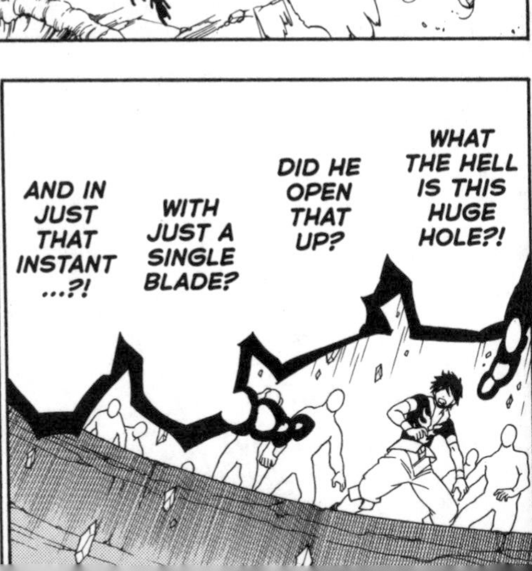
WHAT THE HELL IS THIS HUGE HOLE?!
DID HE OPEN THAT UP?
WITH JUST A SINGLE BLADE?
AND IN JUST THAT INSTANT ...?!
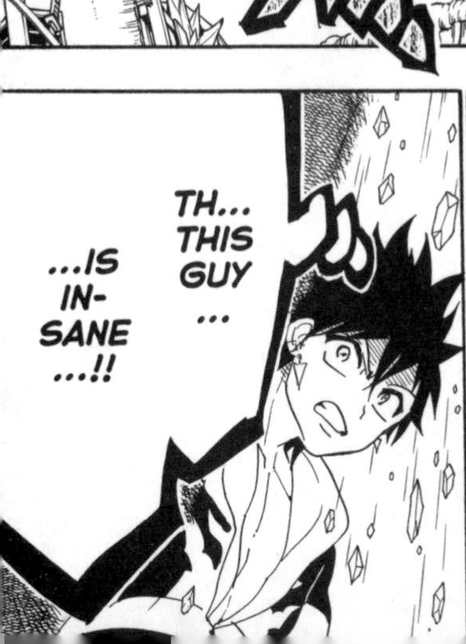
TH... THIS GUY ...
...IS IN-SANE ...!!

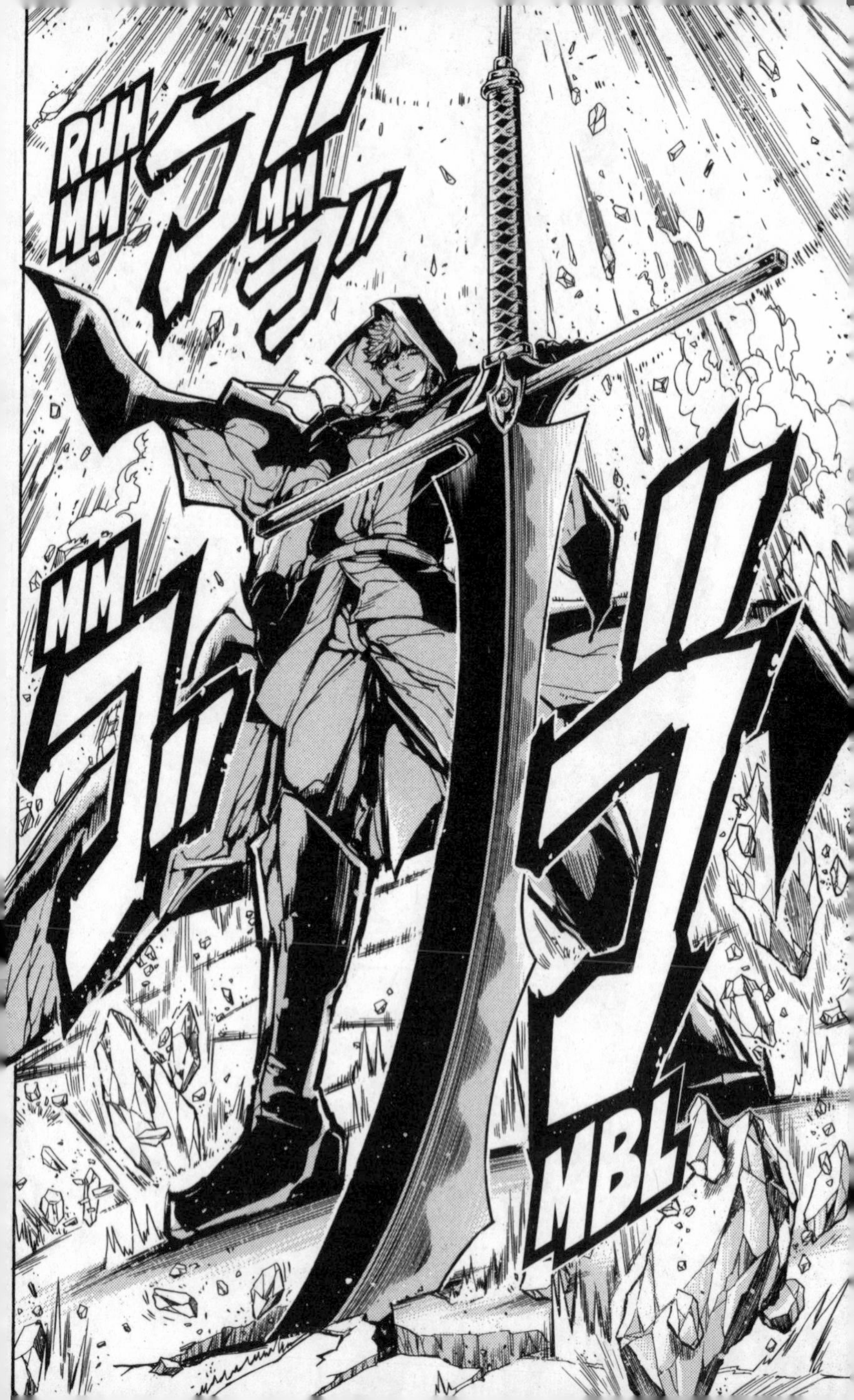
RHH
MM
MM
MM
MBL

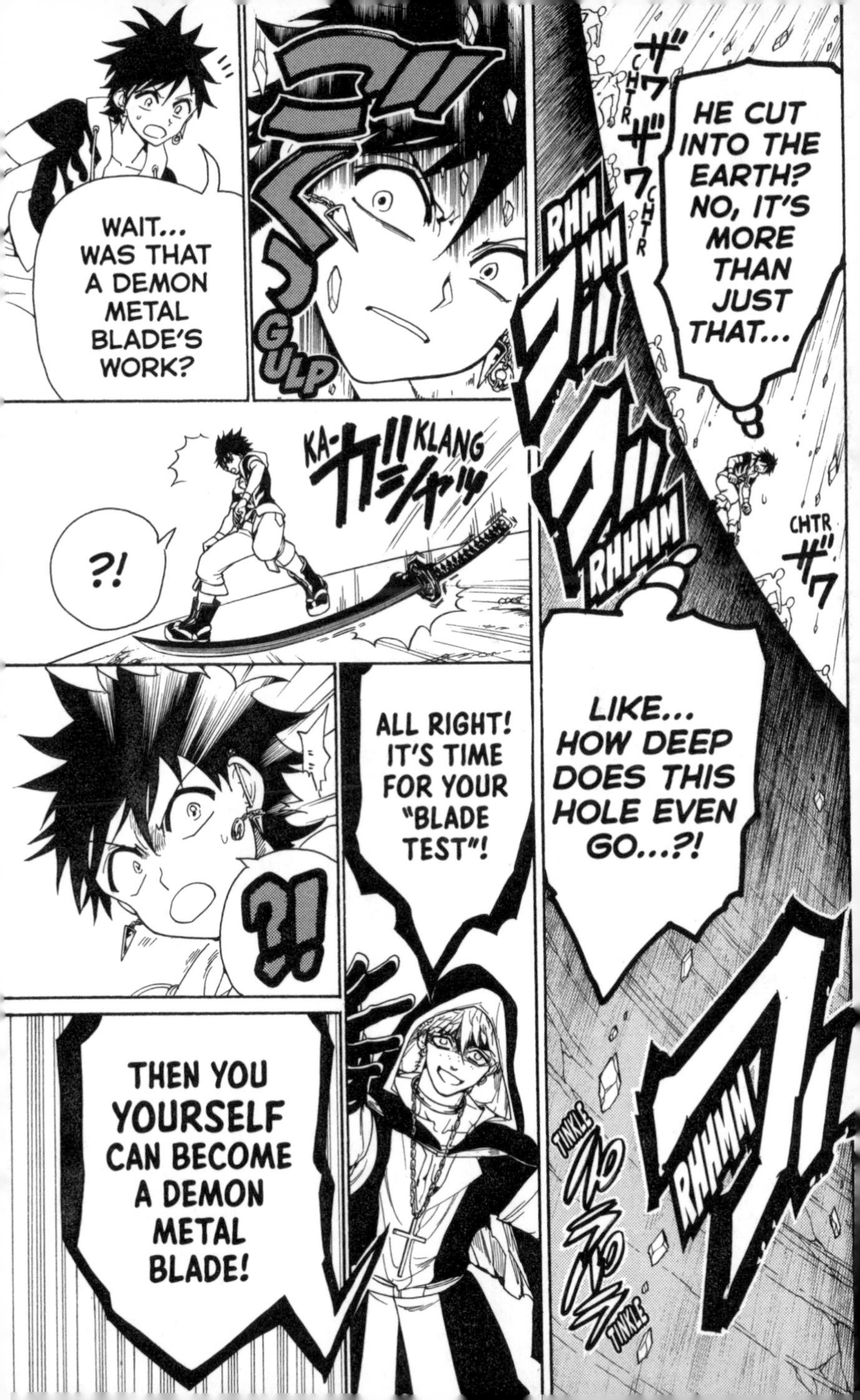
CHTR
CHTR
HE CUT INTO THE EARTH? NO, IT'S MORE THAN JUST THAT...
RHHMM
RHHMM
CHTR
LIKE... HOW DEEP DOES THIS HOLE EVEN GO...?!
RHHMM
TINKLE
TINKLE
GULP
WAIT... WAS THAT A DEMON METAL BLADE'S WORK?
KA-KLANG
?!
ALL RIGHT! IT'S TIME FOR YOUR "BLADE TEST"!
?!
THEN YOU YOURSELF CAN BECOME A DEMON METAL BLADE!

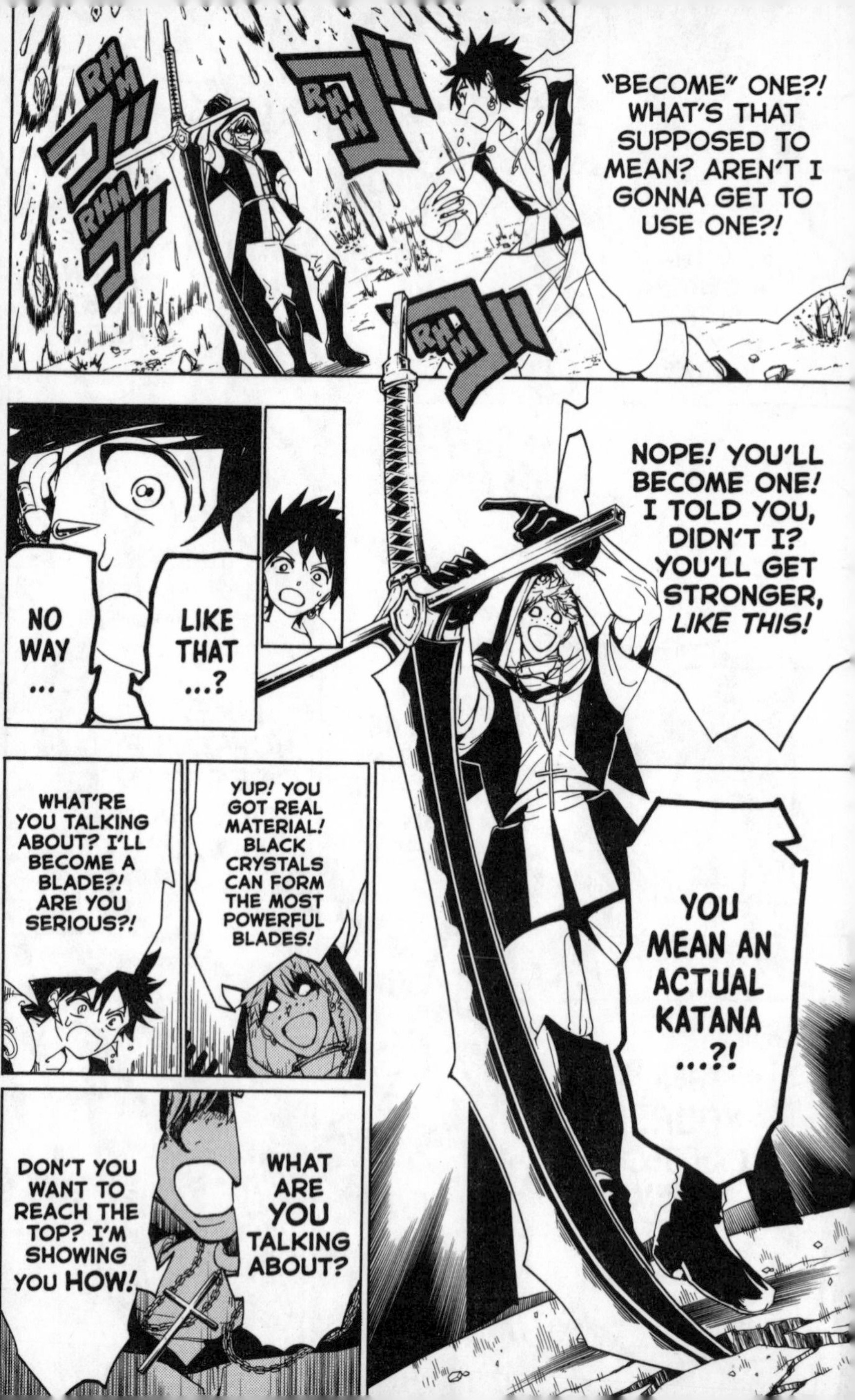
"BECOME" ONE?! WHAT'S THAT SUPPOSED TO MEAN? AREN'T I GONNA GET TO USE ONE?!
RHM
RHM
RHM
RHM
NOPE! YOU'LL BECOME ONE! I TOLD YOU, DIDN'T I? YOU'LL GET STRONGER, LIKE THIS!
YOU MEAN AN ACTUAL KATANA ...?!
LIKE THAT ...?
NO WAY ...
YUP! YOU GOT REAL MATERIAL! BLACK CRYSTALS CAN FORM THE MOST POWERFUL BLADES!
WHAT'RE YOU TALKING ABOUT? I'LL BECOME A BLADE?! ARE YOU SERIOUS?!
WHAT ARE YOU TALKING ABOUT?
DON'T YOU WANT TO REACH THE TOP? I'M SHOWING YOU HOW!

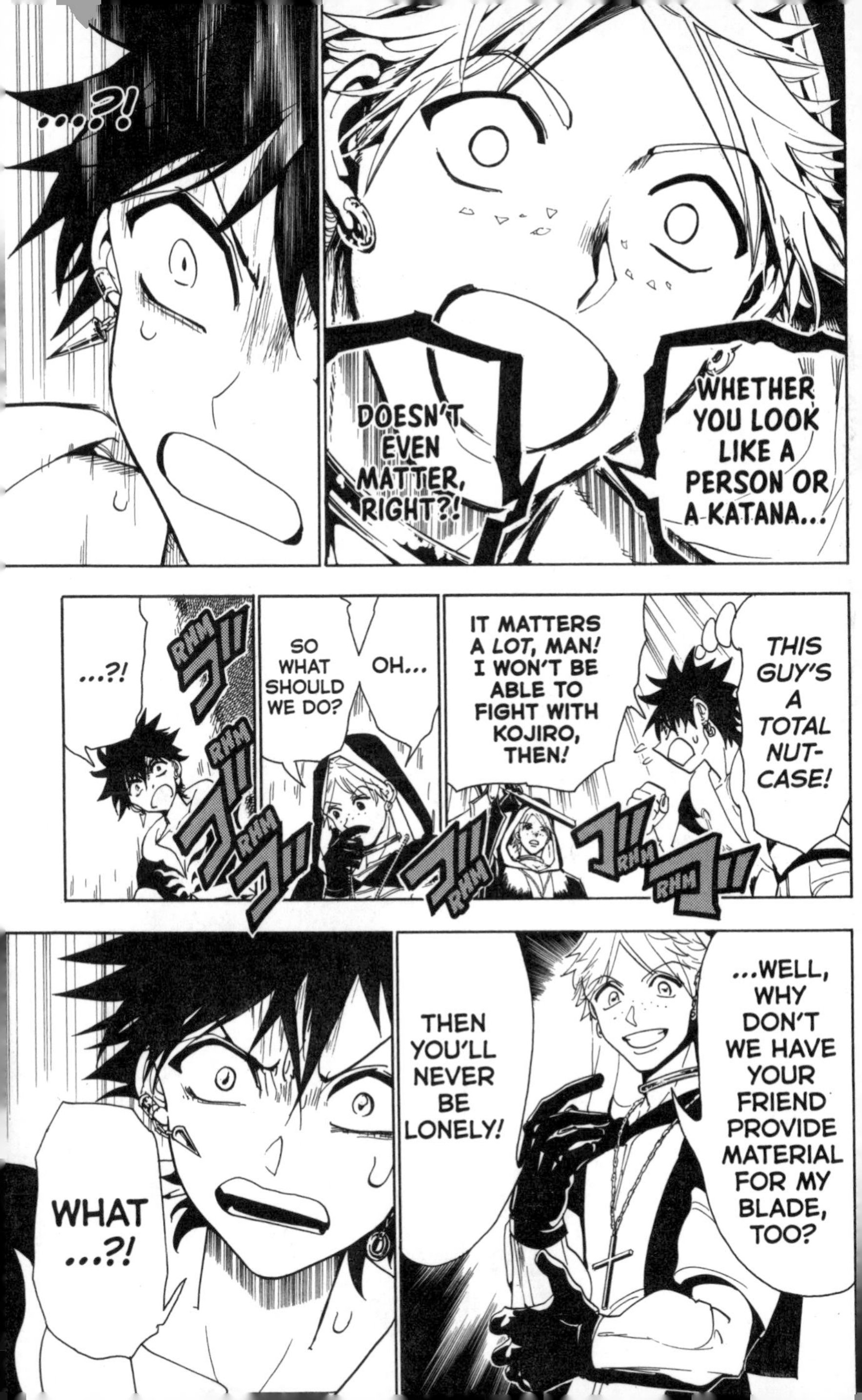
WHETHER YOU LOOK LIKE A PERSON OR A-KATANA...
DOESN'T EVEN MATTER, RIGHT?!
...?!
THIS GUY'S A TOTAL NUT-CASE!
IT MATTERS A *LOT*, MAN! I WON'T BE ABLE TO FIGHT WITH KOJIRO, THEN!
RHM RHM RHM
OH...
SO WHAT SHOULD WE DO?
RHM RHM
...?!
RHM RHM RHM
...WELL, WHY DON'T WE HAVE YOUR FRIEND PROVIDE MATERIAL FOR MY BLADE, TOO?
THEN YOU'LL NEVER BE LONELY!
WHAT...?!

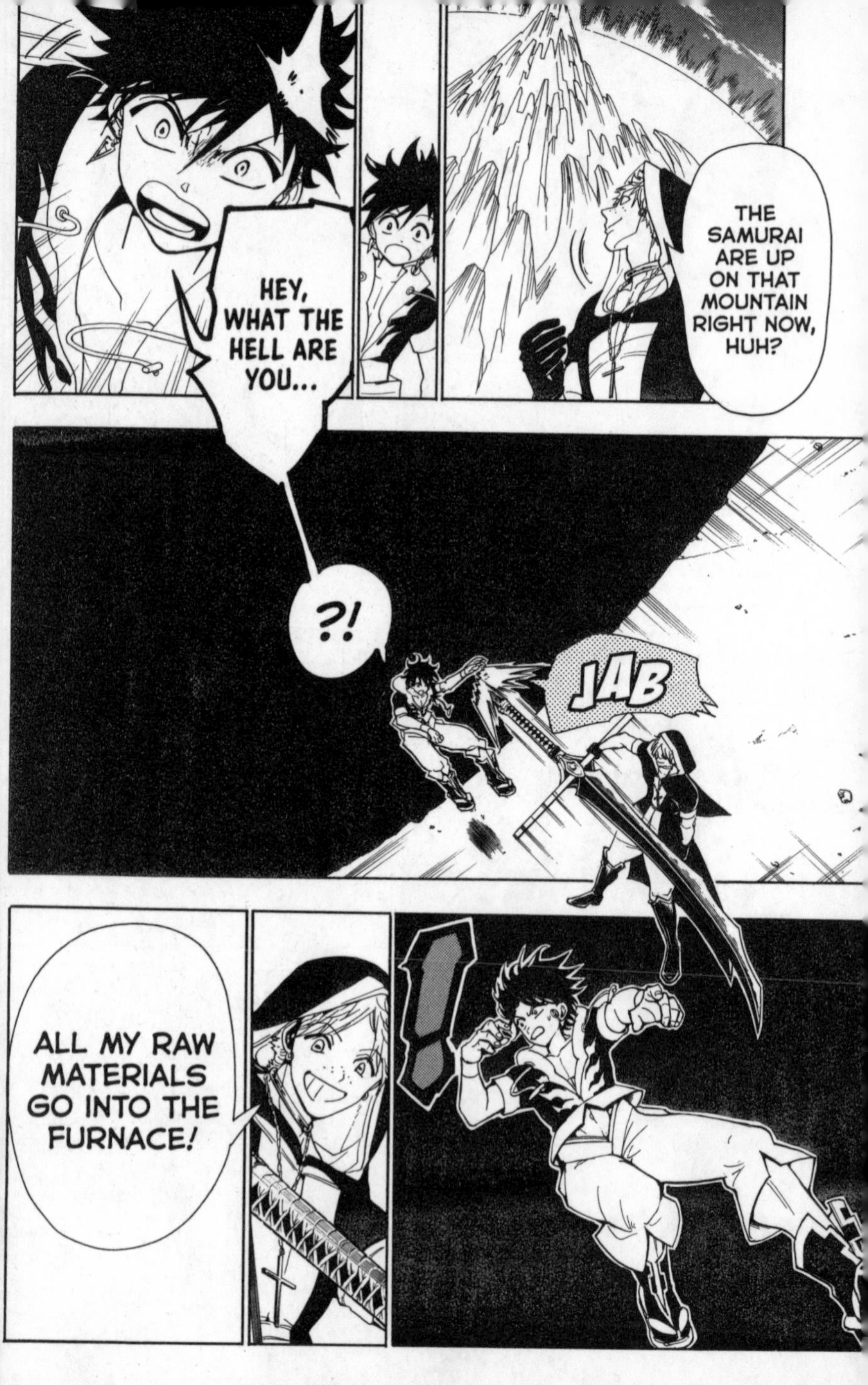
THE SAMURAI ARE UP ON THAT MOUNTAIN RIGHT NOW, HUH?
HEY, WHAT THE HELL ARE YOU...
?!
JAB
!
ALL MY RAW MATERIALS GO INTO THE FURNACE!

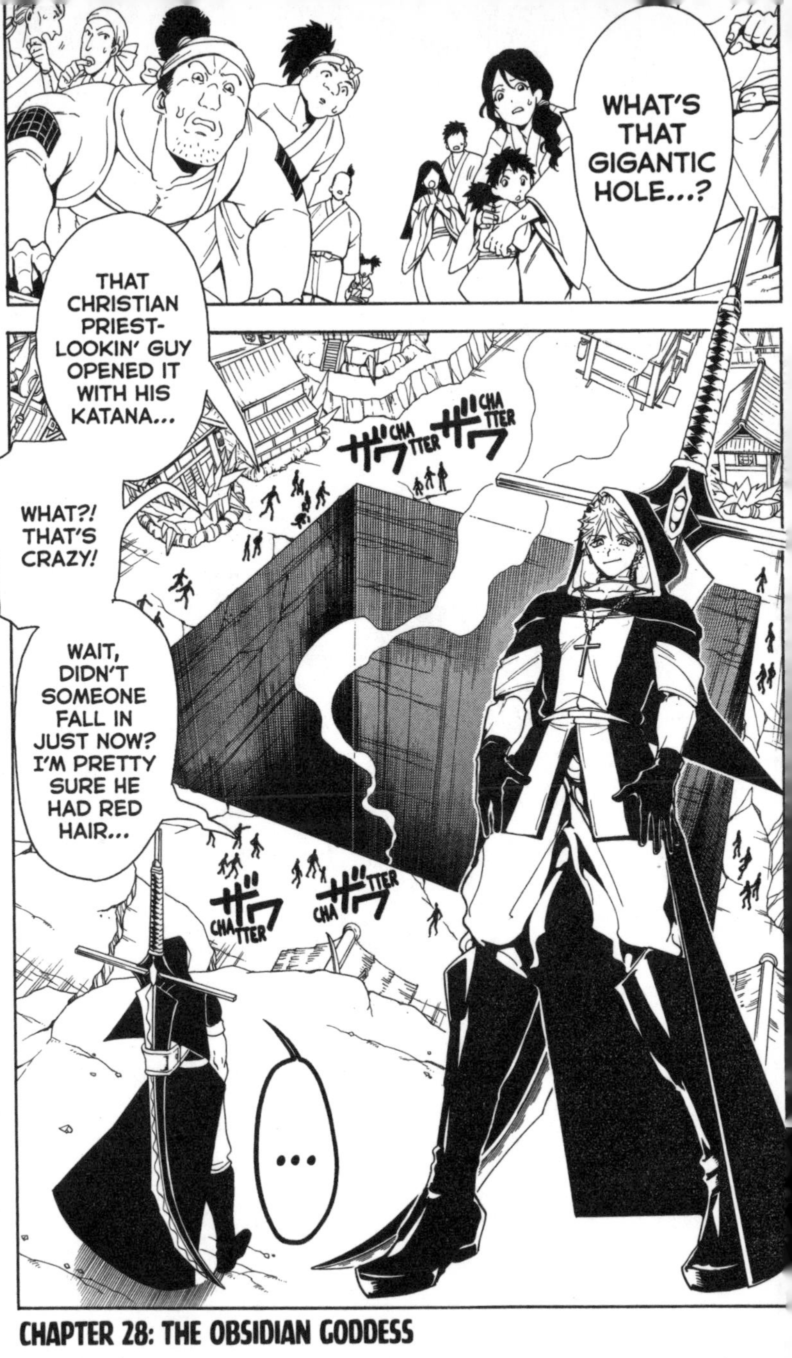
WHAT'S THAT GIGANTIC HOLE...?
THAT CHRISTIAN PRIEST-LOOKIN' GUY OPENED IT WITH HIS KATANA...
ザワ CHATTER ザワ CHATTER
WHAT?! THAT'S CRAZY!
WAIT, DIDN'T SOMEONE FALL IN JUST NOW? I'M PRETTY SURE HE HAD RED HAIR...
ザワ CHATTER ザワ CHATTER
...

CHAPTER 28: THE OBSIDIAN GODDESS

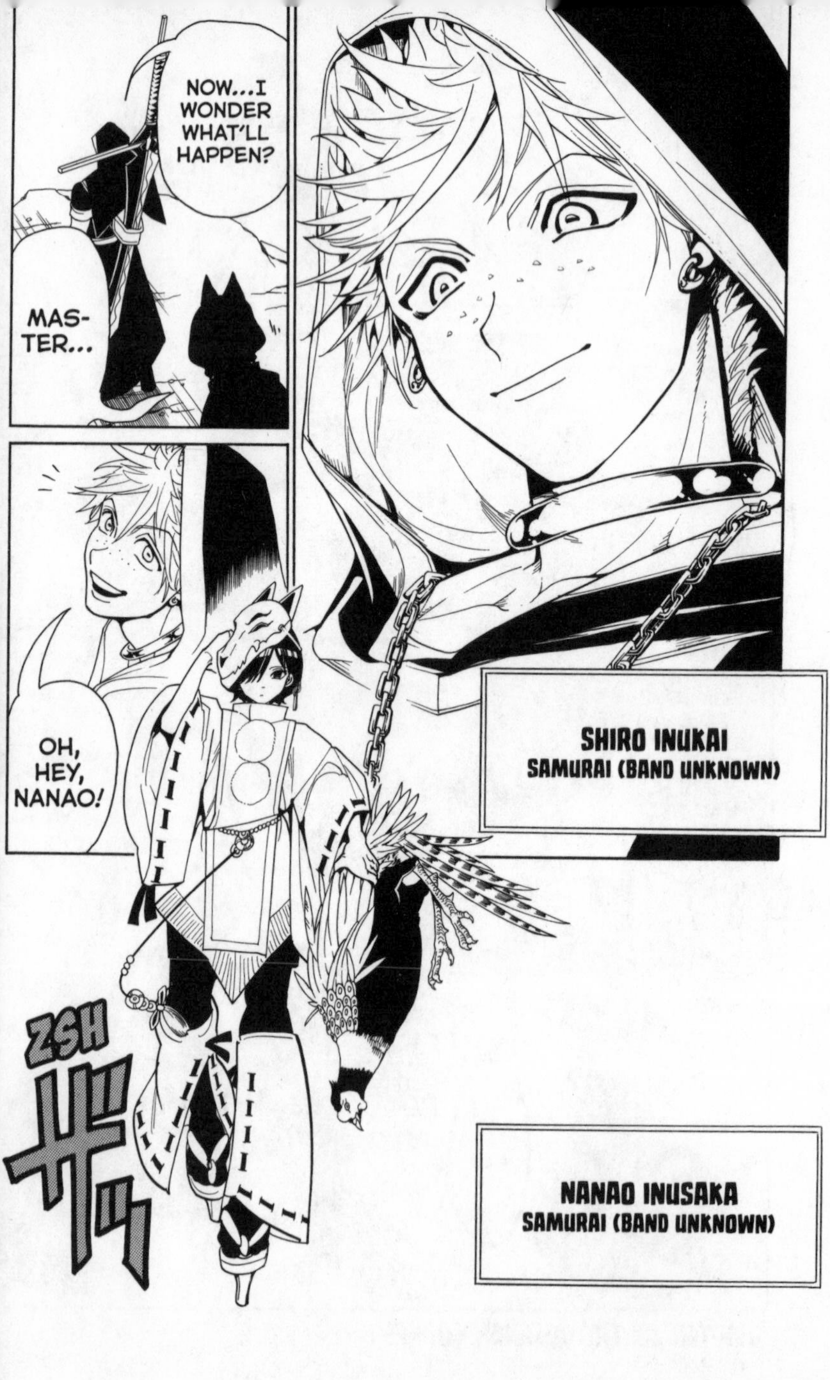
SHIRO INUKAI
SAMURAI (BAND UNKNOWN)
NOW...I WONDER WHAT'LL HAPPEN?
MASTER...
OH, HEY, NANAO!
ZSH
NANAO INUSAKA
SAMURAI (BAND UNKNOWN)

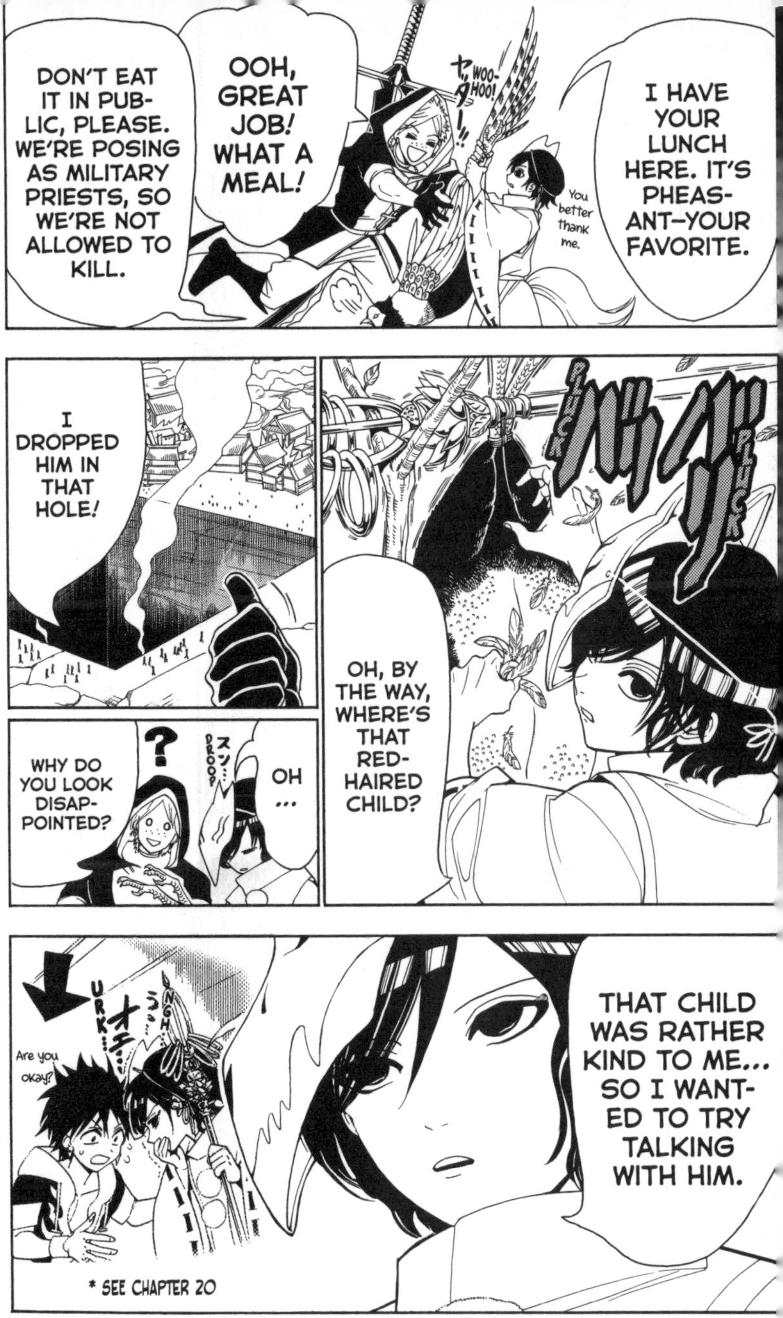

I HAVE YOUR LUNCH HERE. IT'S PHEASANT—YOUR FAVORITE.
You better thank me.
ヤッター!! WOO-HOO!
OOH, GREAT JOB! WHAT A MEAL!
DON'T EAT IT IN PUBLIC, PLEASE. WE'RE POSING AS MILITARY PRIESTS, SO WE'RE NOT ALLOWED TO KILL.
バッ バッ PLUCK PLUCK
OH, BY THE WAY, WHERE'S THAT RED-HAIRED CHILD?
I DROPPED HIM IN THAT HOLE!
OH ...
スン… DROOP
?
WHY DO YOU LOOK DISAPPOINTED?
THAT CHILD WAS RATHER KIND TO ME... SO I WANTED TO TRY TALKING WITH HIM.
うぅ… NGH...
オエ… URK...
Are you okay?
* SEE CHAPTER 20

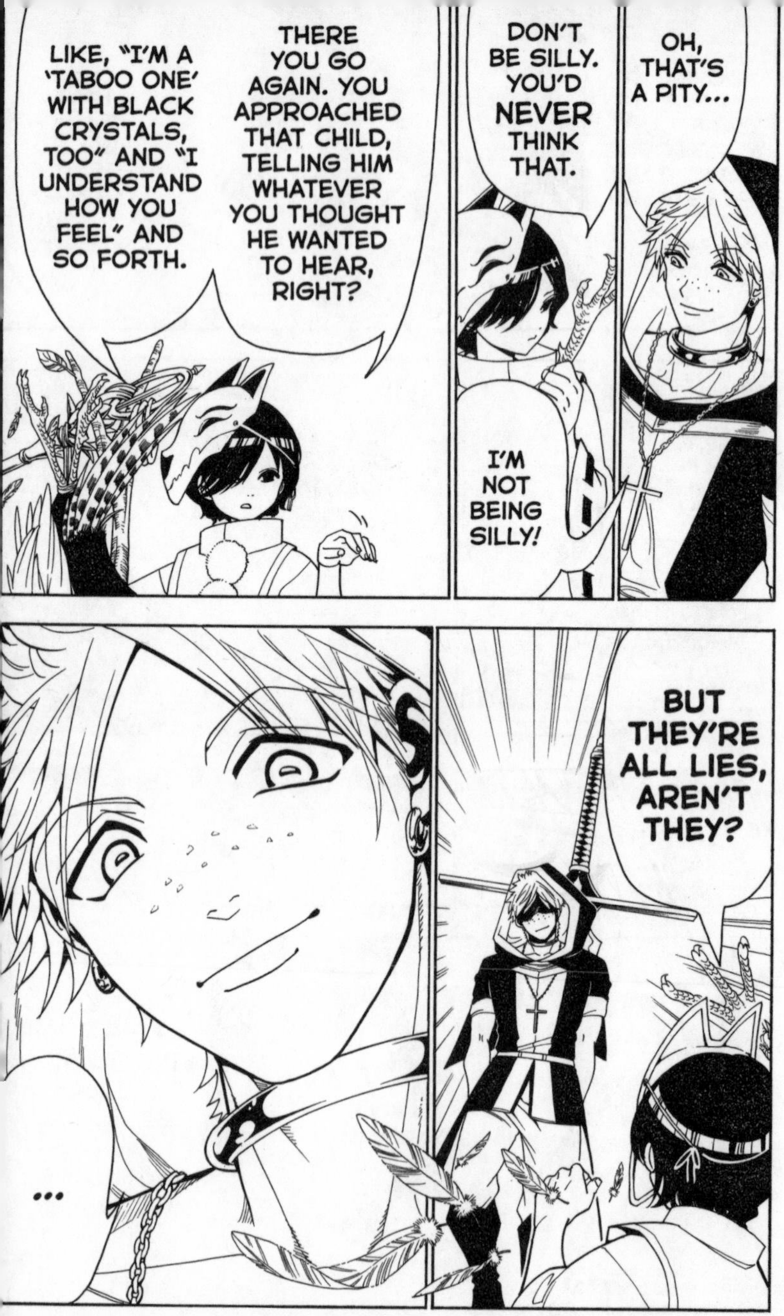
OH, THAT'S A PITY...
DON'T BE SILLY. YOU'D NEVER THINK THAT.
I'M NOT BEING SILLY!
THERE YOU GO AGAIN. YOU APPROACHED THAT CHILD, TELLING HIM WHATEVER YOU THOUGHT HE WANTED TO HEAR, RIGHT?
LIKE, "I'M A 'TABOO ONE' WITH BLACK CRYSTALS, TOO" AND "I UNDERSTAND HOW YOU FEEL" AND SO FORTH.
BUT THEY'RE ALL LIES, AREN'T THEY?
...

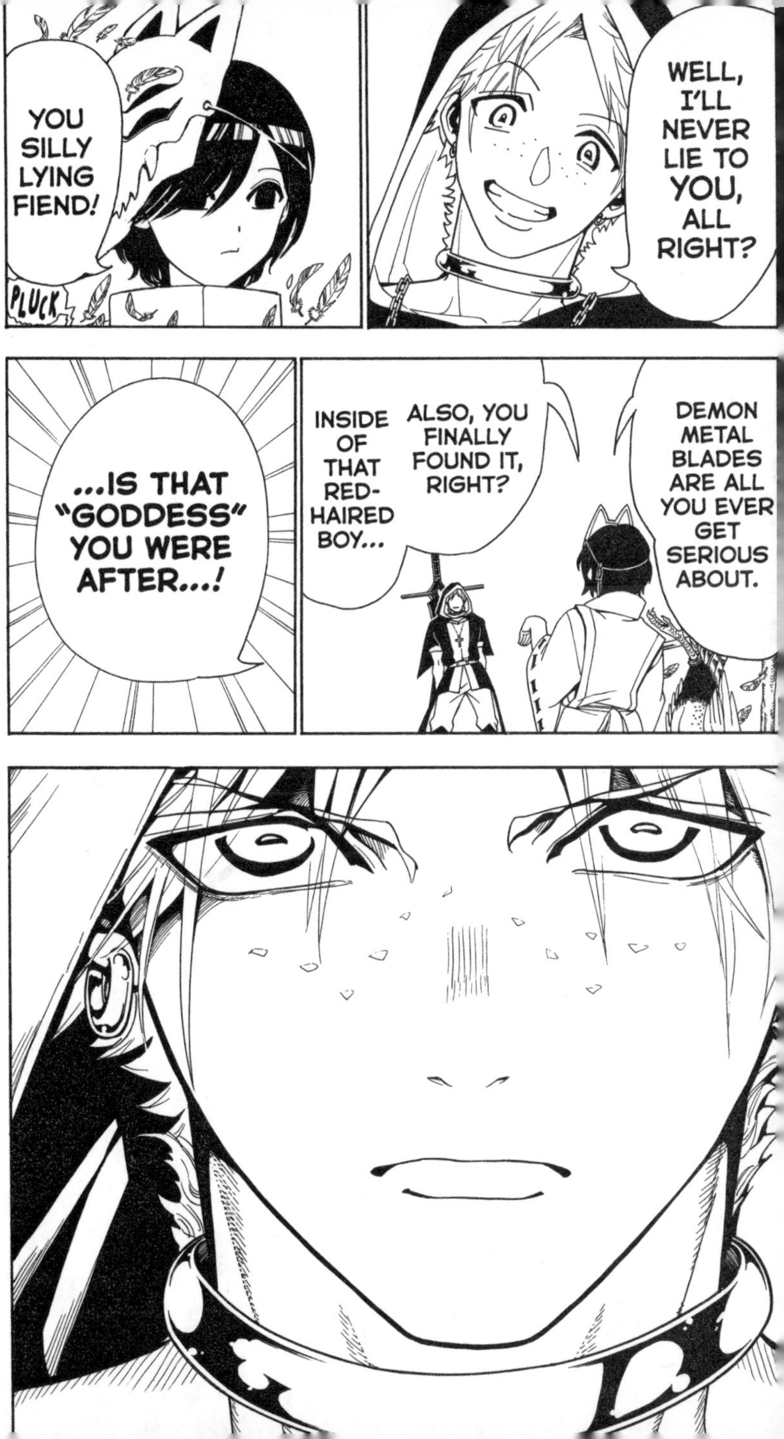
WELL, I'LL NEVER LIE TO YOU, ALL RIGHT?
YOU SILLY LYING FIEND!
PLUCK
DEMON METAL BLADES ARE ALL YOU EVER GET SERIOUS ABOUT.
ALSO, YOU FINALLY FOUND IT, RIGHT?
INSIDE OF THAT RED-HAIRED BOY...
...IS THAT "GODDESS" YOU WERE AFTER...!

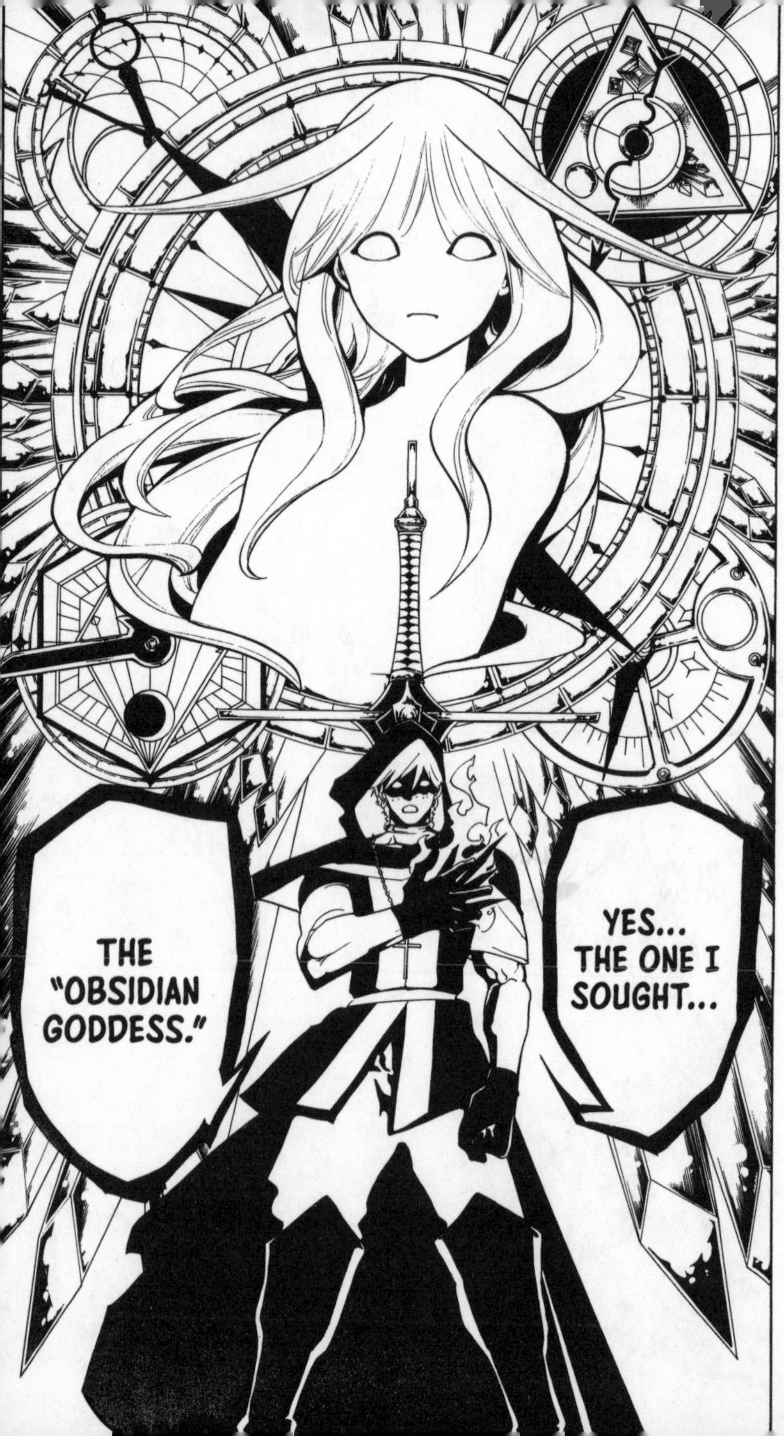
YES... THE ONE I SOUGHT...
THE "OBSIDIAN GODDESS."

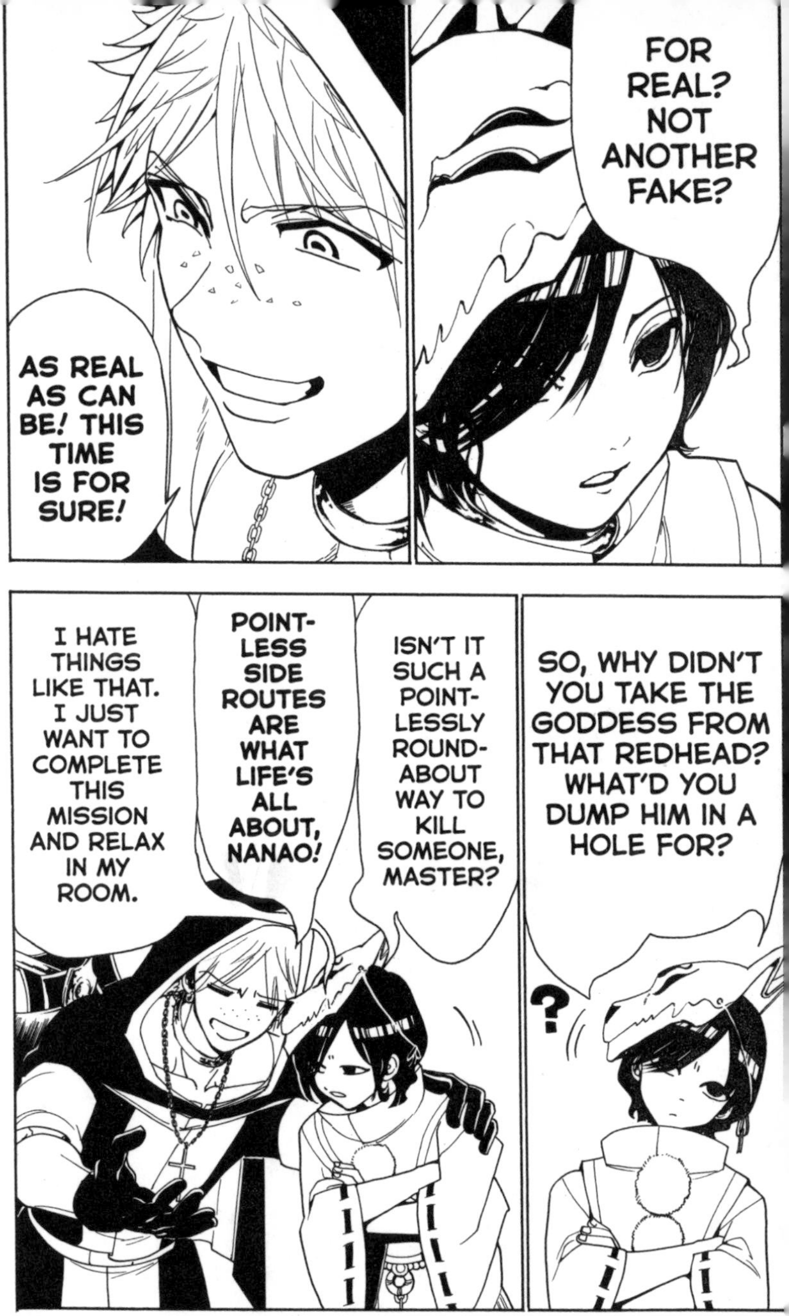
FOR REAL? NOT ANOTHER FAKE?
AS REAL AS CAN BE! THIS TIME IS FOR SURE!
SO, WHY DIDN'T YOU TAKE THE GODDESS FROM THAT REDHEAD? WHAT'D YOU DUMP HIM IN A HOLE FOR?
?
ISN'T IT SUCH A POINT-LESSLY ROUND-ABOUT WAY TO KILL SOMEONE, MASTER?
POINT-LESS SIDE ROUTES ARE WHAT LIFE'S ALL ABOUT, NANAO!
I HATE THINGS LIKE THAT. I JUST WANT TO COMPLETE THIS MISSION AND RELAX IN MY ROOM.

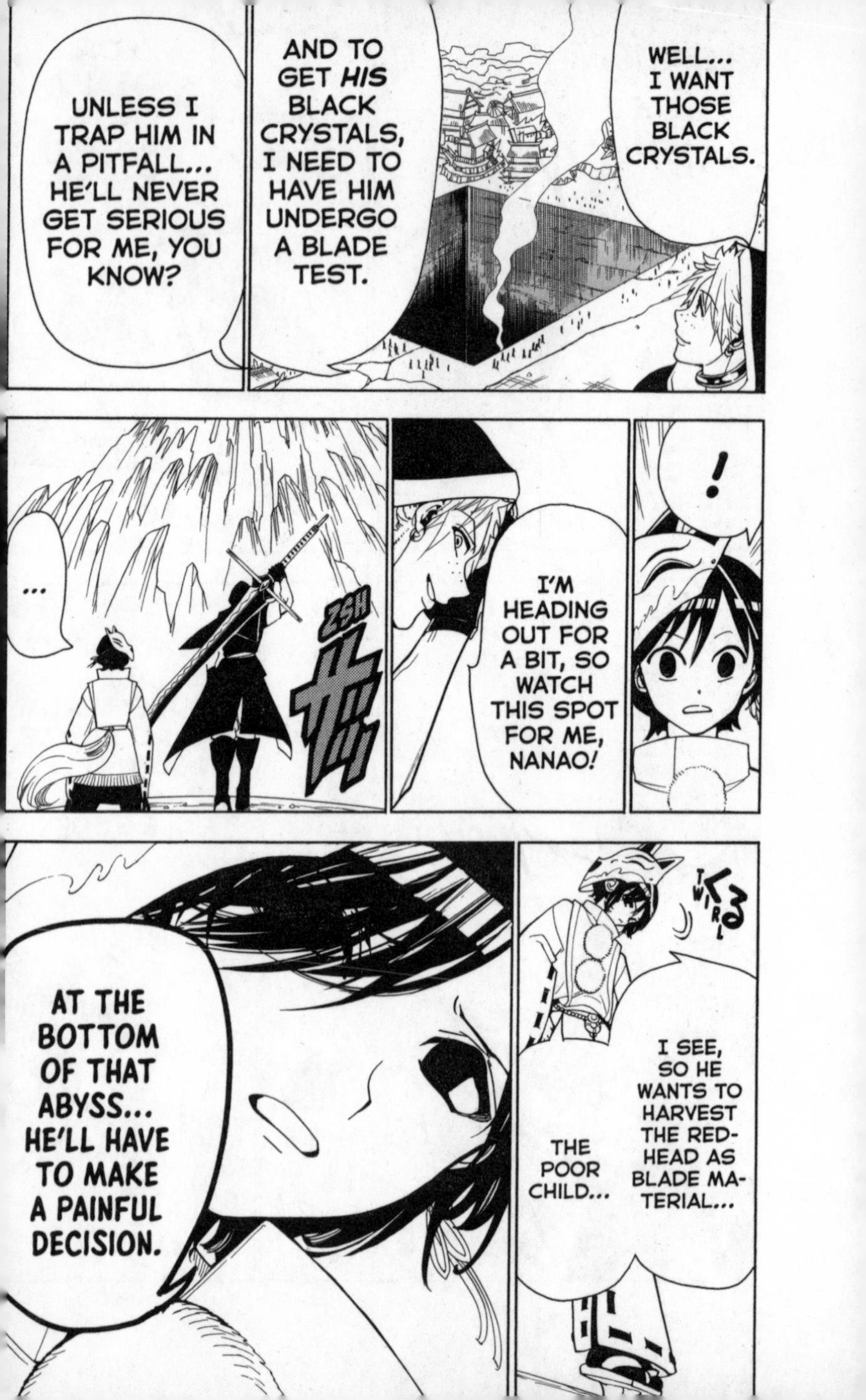

WELL... I WANT THOSE BLACK CRYSTALS.
AND TO GET *HIS* BLACK CRYSTALS, I NEED TO HAVE HIM UNDERGO A BLADE TEST.
UNLESS I TRAP HIM IN A PITFALL... HE'LL NEVER GET SERIOUS FOR ME, YOU KNOW?
!
I'M HEADING OUT FOR A BIT, SO WATCH THIS SPOT FOR ME, NANAO!
ZSH
...
TWIRL
I SEE, SO HE WANTS TO HARVEST THE RED-HEAD AS BLADE MA-TERIAL...
THE POOR CHILD...
AT THE BOTTOM OF THAT ABYSS... HE'LL HAVE TO MAKE A PAINFUL DECISION.

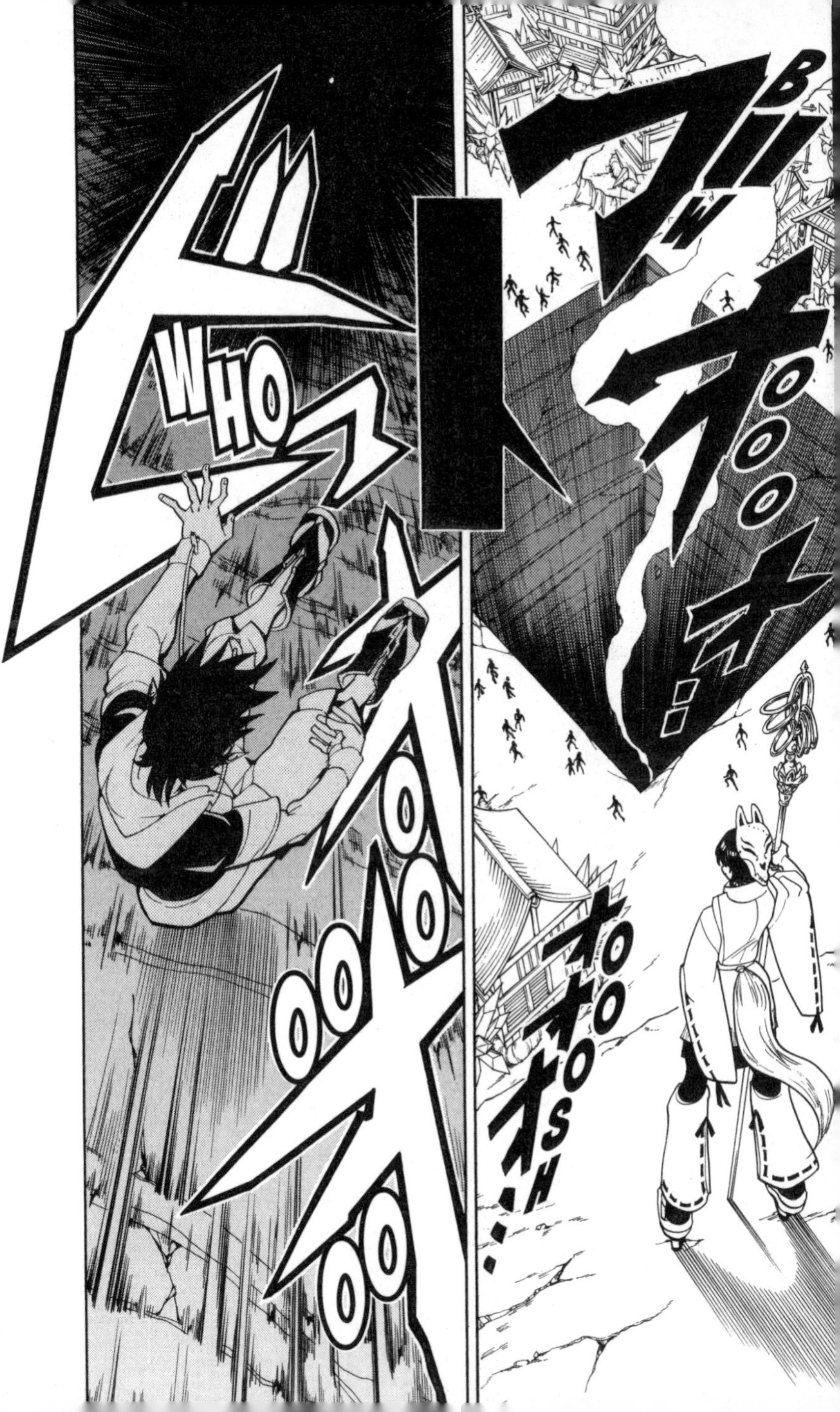
BWOOO...!!
WHOOSH...
WHOOOOOOOO

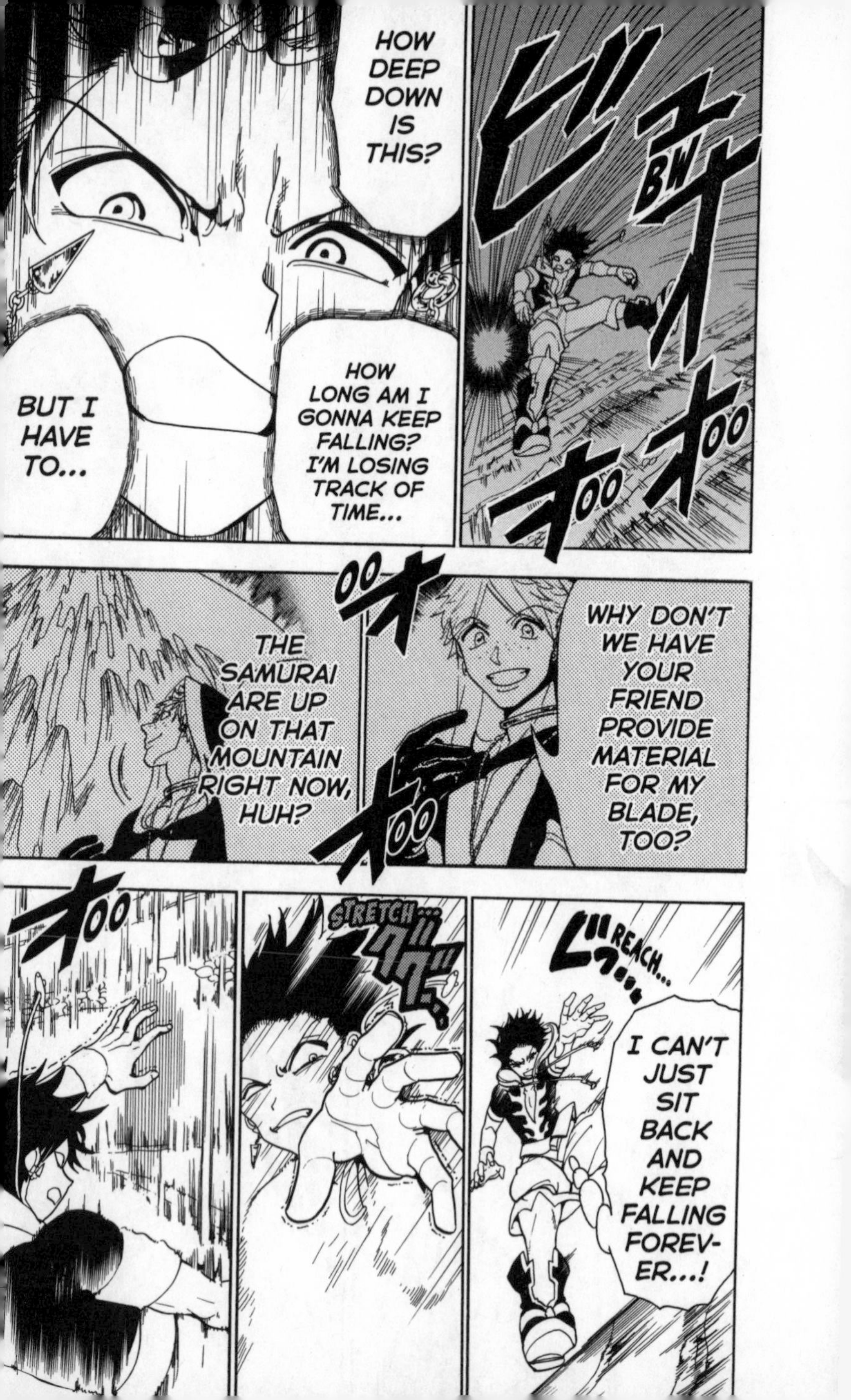
BW
OO
OO
HOW DEEP DOWN IS THIS?
HOW LONG AM I GONNA KEEP FALLING? I'M LOSING TRACK OF TIME...
BUT I HAVE TO...
OO
WHY DON'T WE HAVE YOUR FRIEND PROVIDE MATERIAL FOR MY BLADE, TOO?
OO
THE SAMURAI ARE UP ON THAT MOUNTAIN RIGHT NOW, HUH?
REACH...
I CAN'T JUST SIT BACK AND KEEP FALLING FOREVER...!
STRETCH...
OO

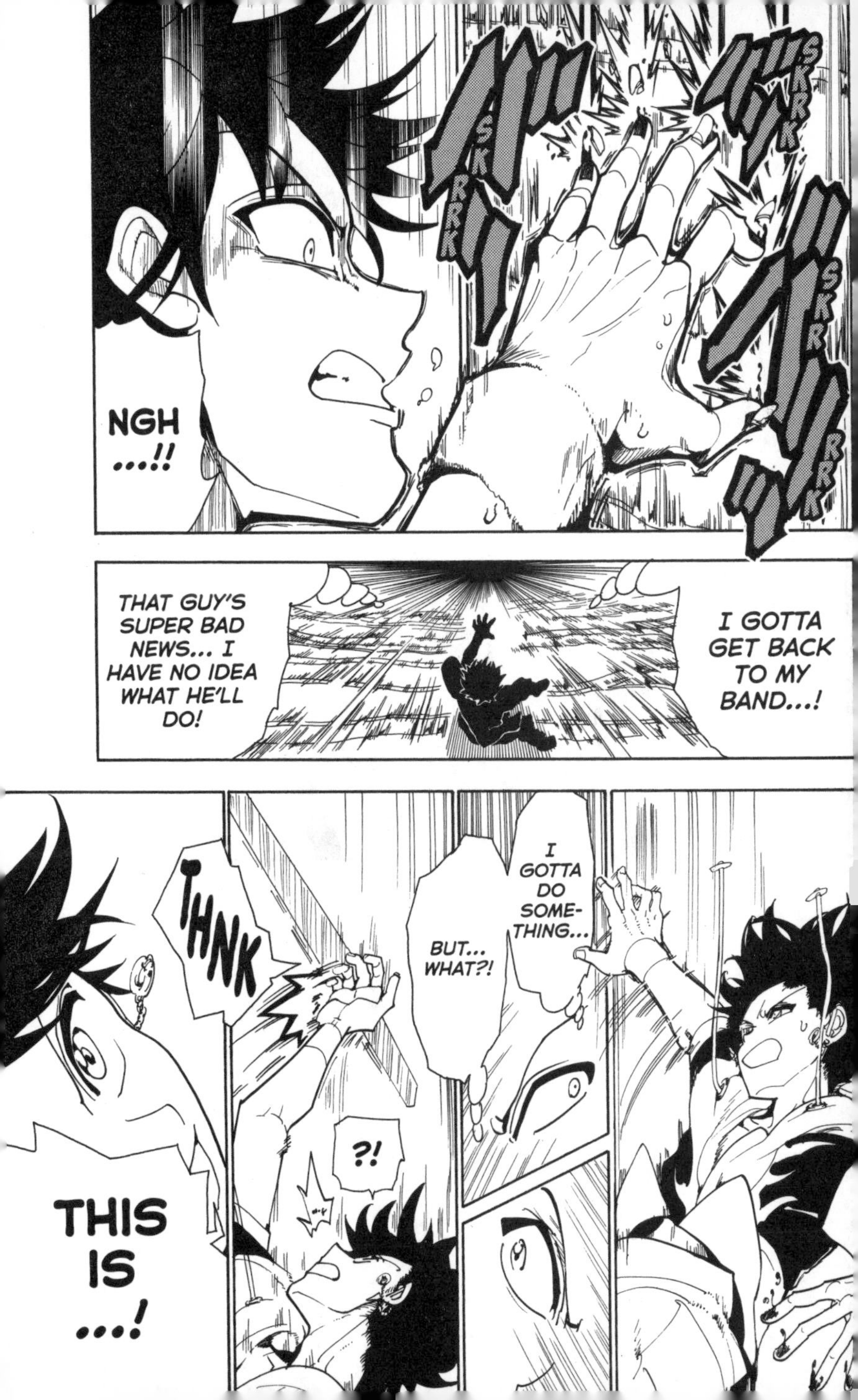
SKRK
SKRRK
SKRRK
NGH ...!!
I GOTTA GET BACK TO MY BAND...!
THAT GUY'S SUPER BAD NEWS... I HAVE NO IDEA WHAT HE'LL DO!
I GOTTA DO SOME-THING...
BUT... WHAT?!
?!
THNK
THIS IS ...!

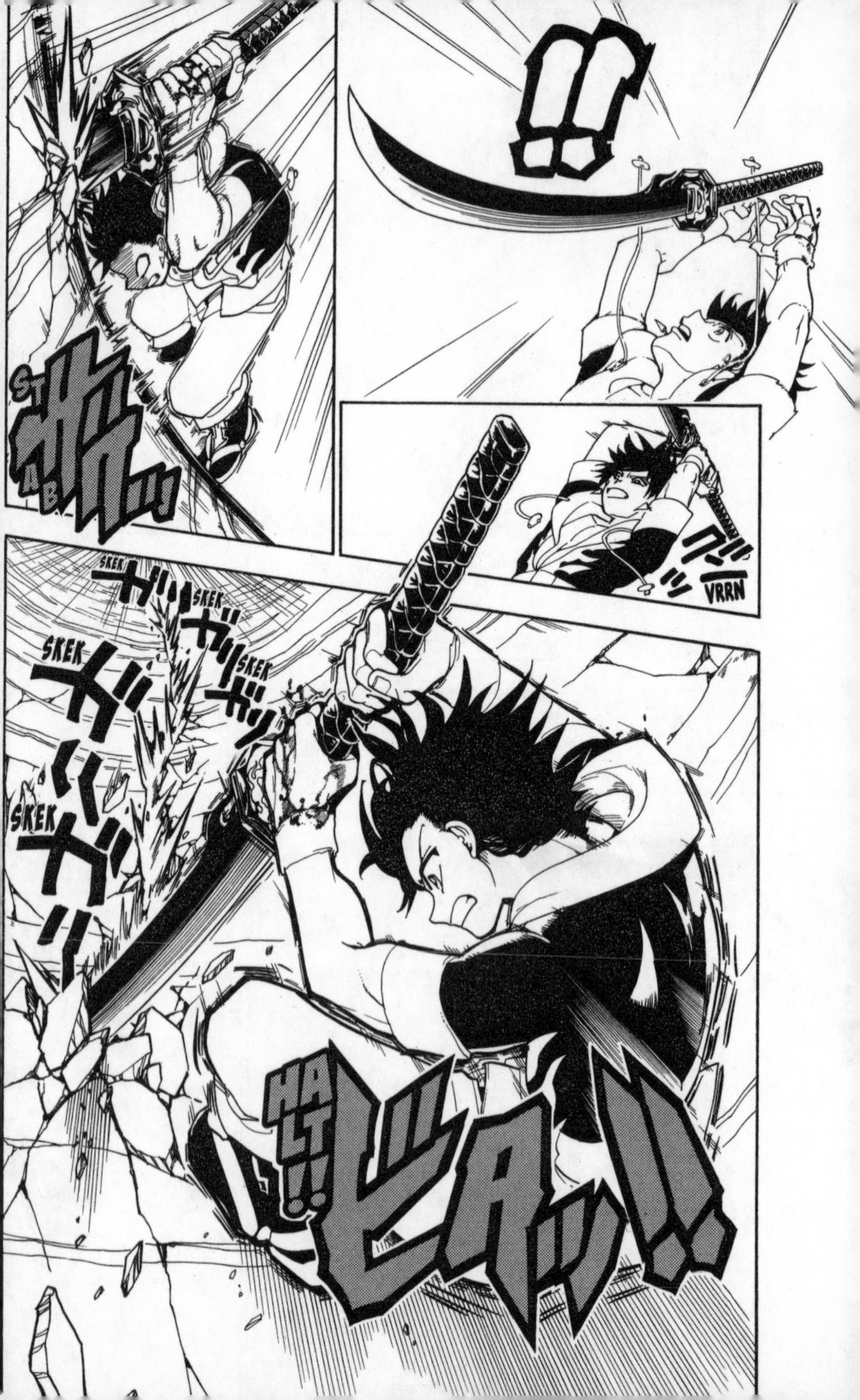
!!
VRRN
STAB
SKEK
SKEK
SKEK
SKEK
SKEK
HALT!!

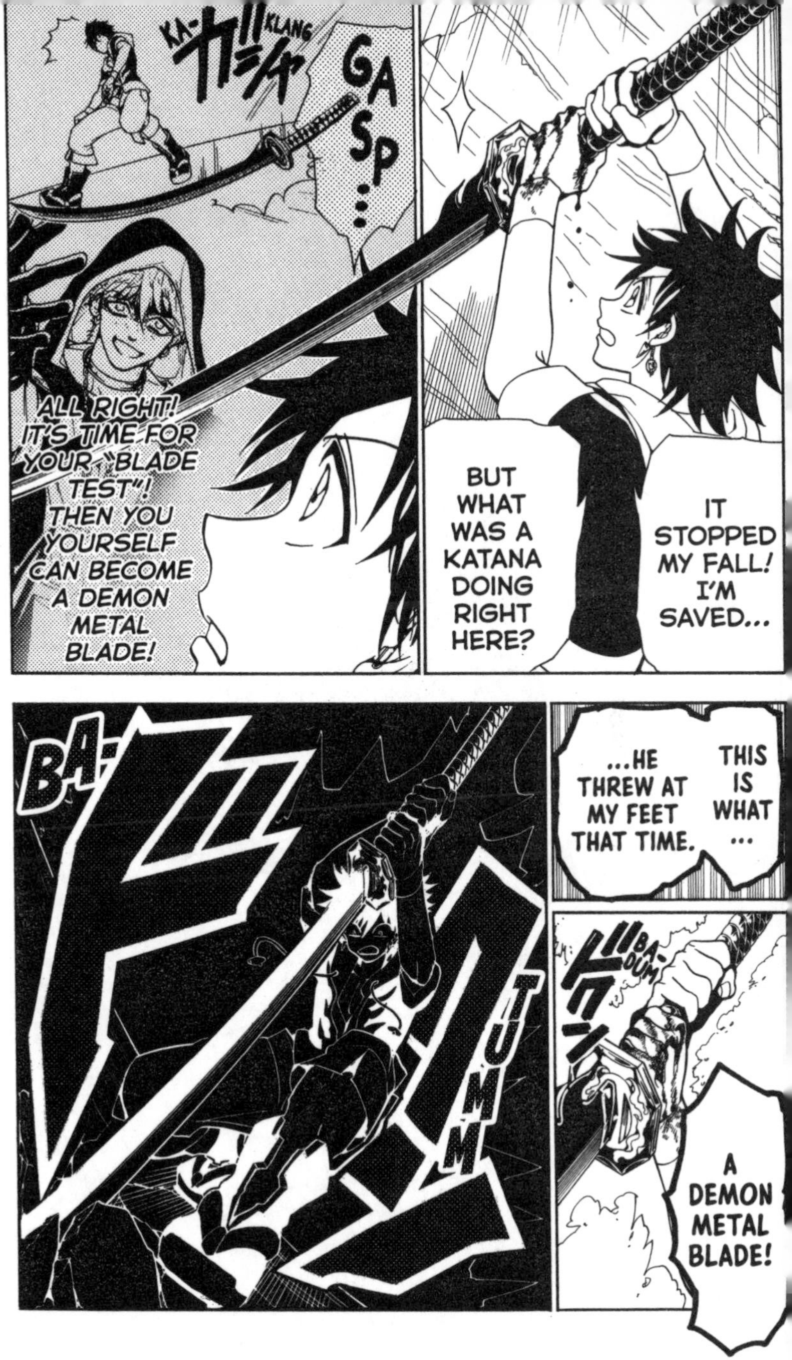
IT STOPPED MY FALL! I'M SAVED...
BUT WHAT WAS A KATANA DOING RIGHT HERE?
KA-KLANG
GASP...
ALL RIGHT! IT'S TIME FOR YOUR "BLADE TEST"! THEN YOU YOURSELF CAN BECOME A DEMON METAL BLADE!
THIS IS WHAT...
...HE THREW AT MY FEET THAT TIME.
BA-DUM
A DEMON METAL BLADE!
BA-
TUMMM

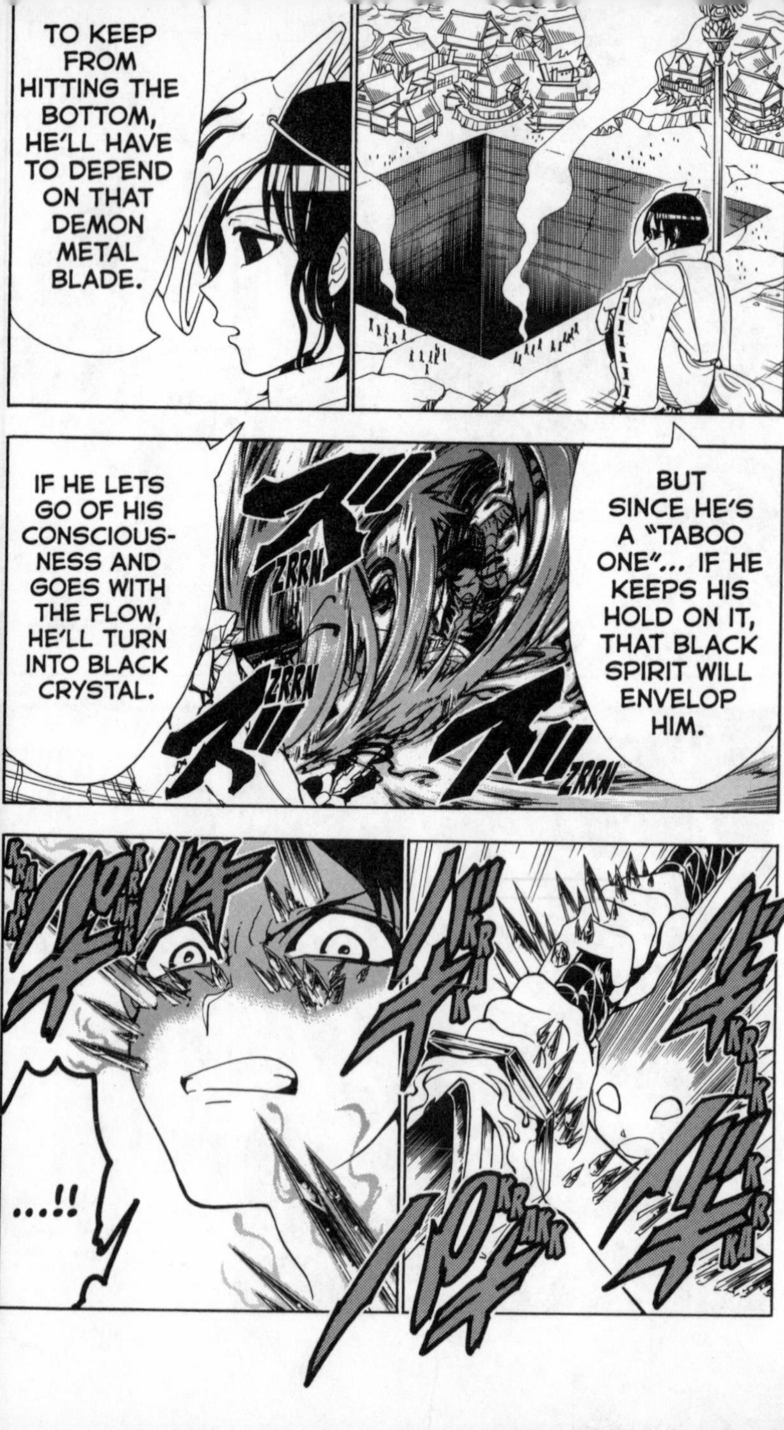
TO KEEP FROM HITTING THE BOTTOM, HE'LL HAVE TO DEPEND ON THAT DEMON METAL BLADE.
BUT SINCE HE'S A "TABOO ONE"... IF HE KEEPS HIS HOLD ON IT, THAT BLACK SPIRIT WILL ENVELOP HIM.
ZRRN
ZRRN
ZRRN
IF HE LETS GO OF HIS CONSCIOUS-NESS AND GOES WITH THE FLOW, HE'LL TURN INTO BLACK CRYSTAL.
KRAK
KRAK
KRAK
KRAK
...!!

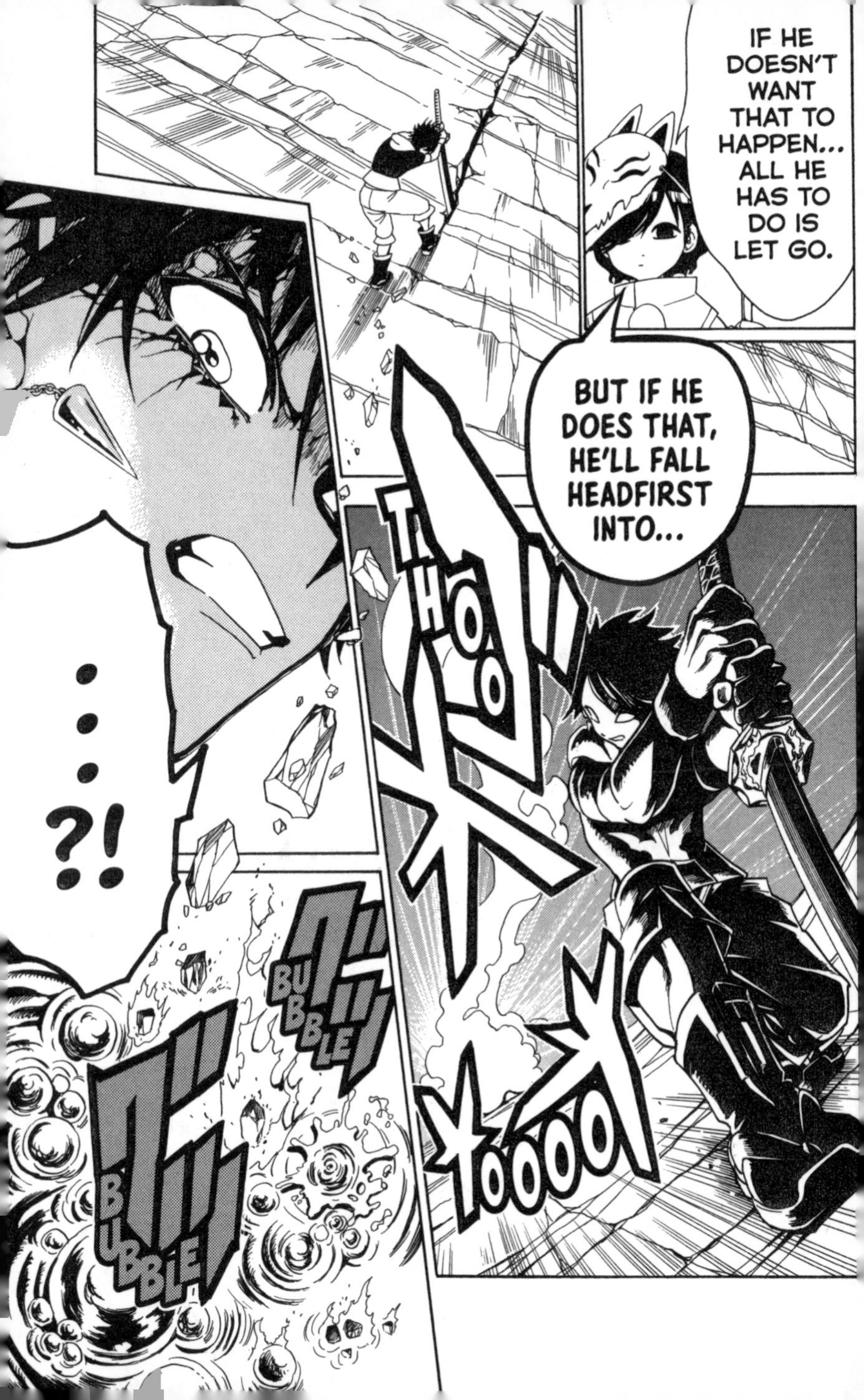
IF HE DOESN'T WANT THAT TO HAPPEN... ALL HE HAS TO DO IS LET GO.
BUT IF HE DOES THAT, HE'LL FALL HEADFIRST INTO...
THOOOOOO
...?!
BUBBLE
BUBBLE

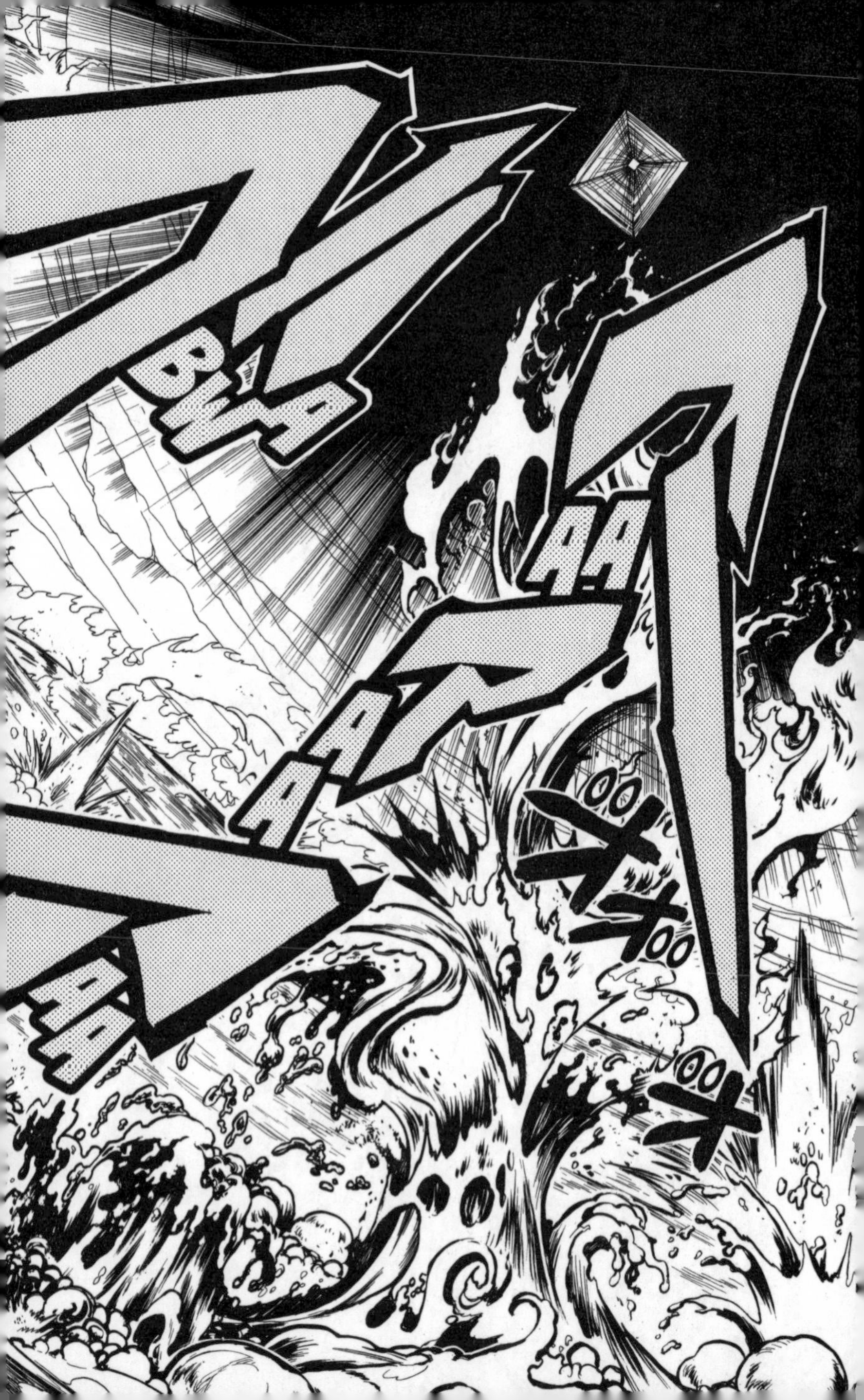

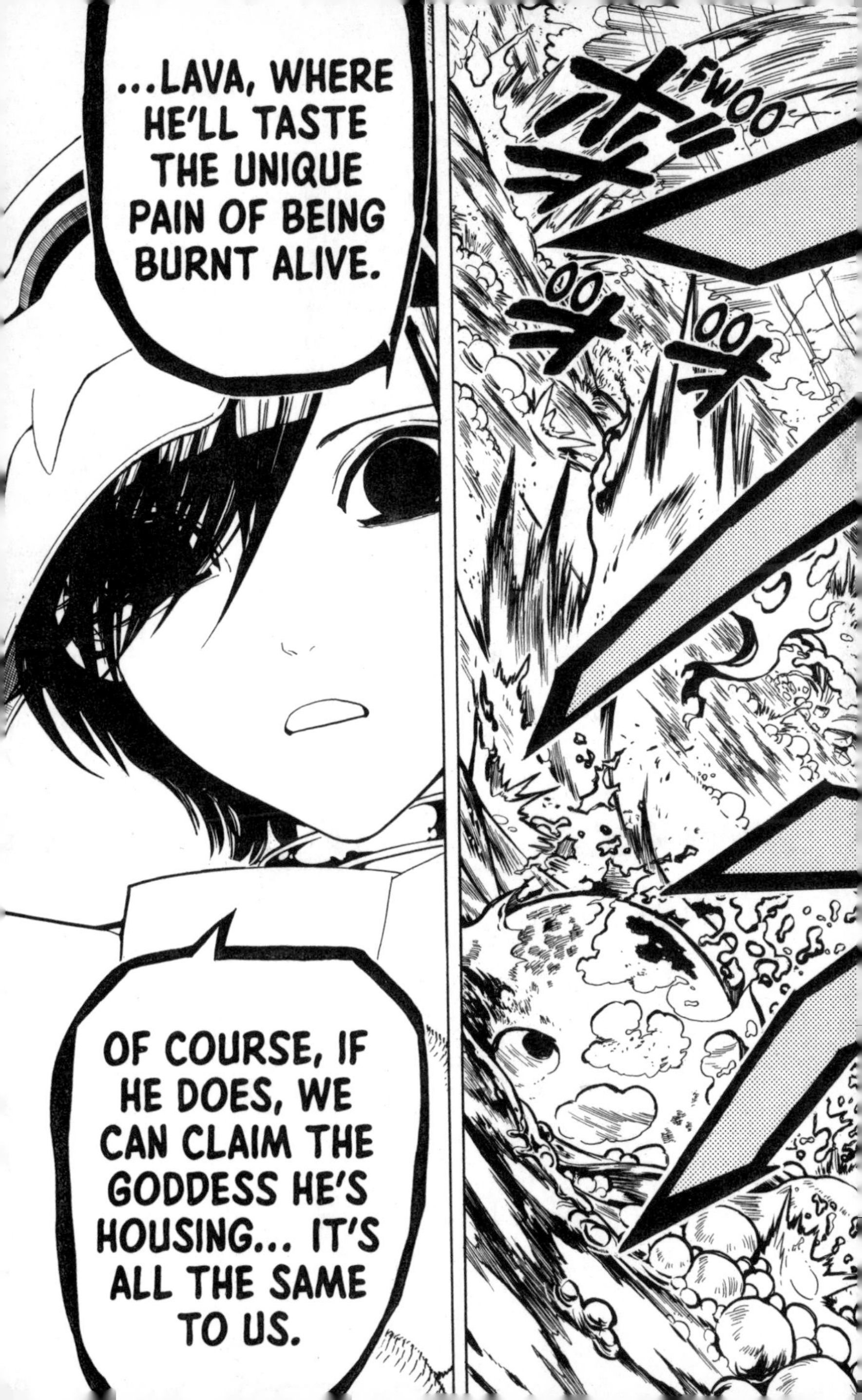
FWOO
OO
OO
...LAVA, WHERE HE'LL TASTE THE UNIQUE PAIN OF BEING BURNT ALIVE.
OF COURSE, IF HE DOES, WE CAN CLAIM THE GODDESS HE'S HOUSING... IT'S ALL THE SAME TO US.

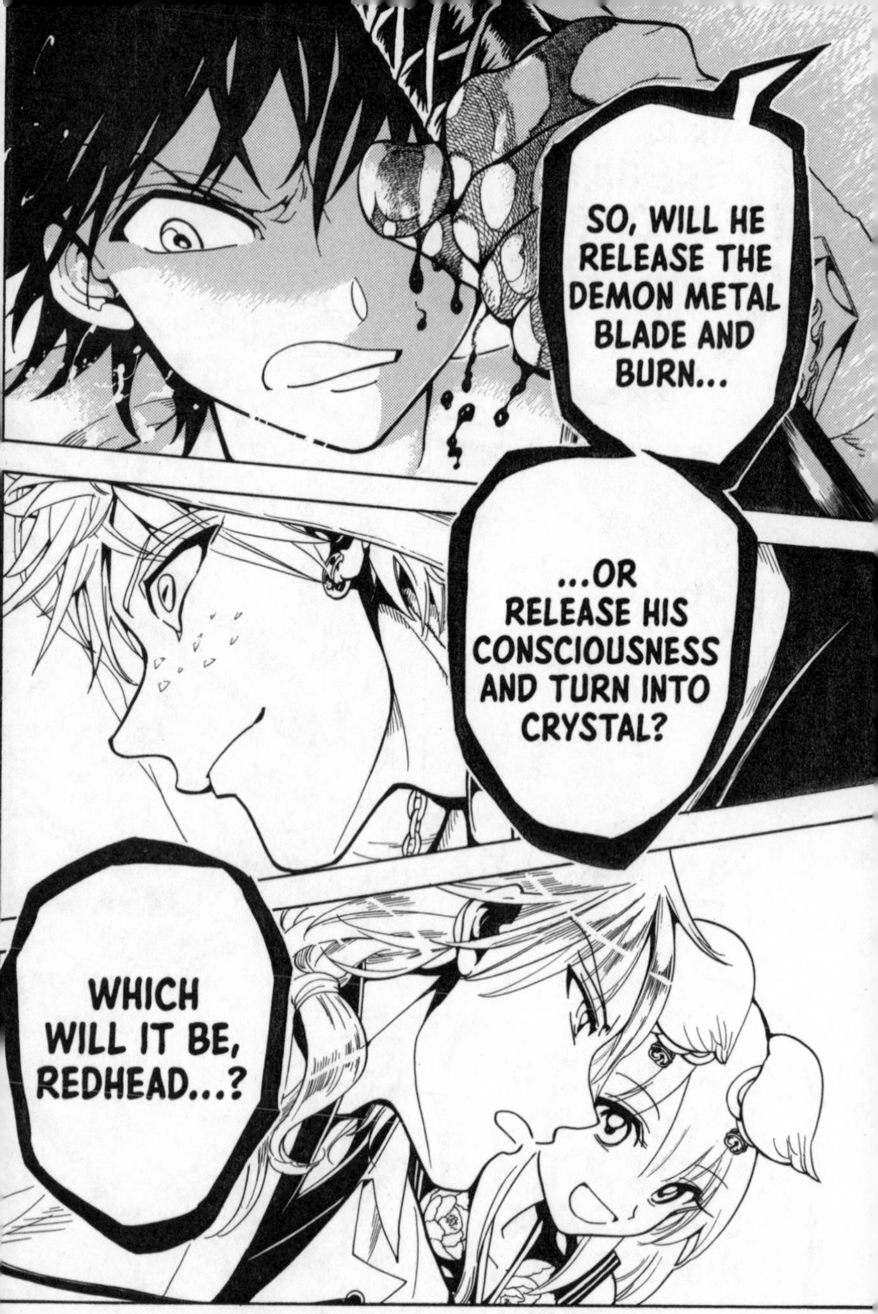
SO, WILL HE RELEASE THE DEMON METAL BLADE AND BURN...
...OR RELEASE HIS CONSCIOUSNESS AND TURN INTO CRYSTAL?
WHICH WILL IT BE, REDHEAD...?

CHAPTER 29: CONVERSING WITH THE GODDESS

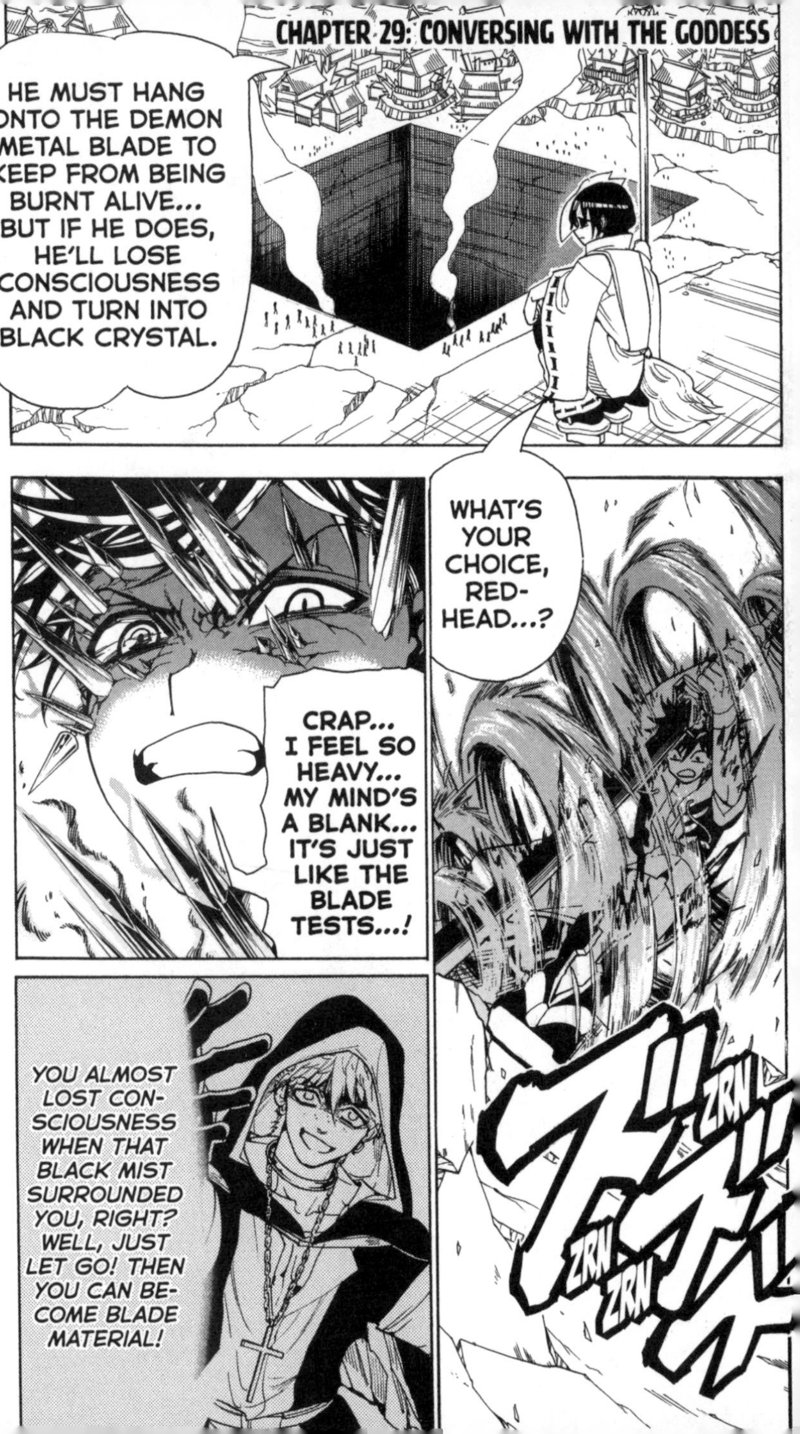

HE MUST HANG ONTO THE DEMON METAL BLADE TO KEEP FROM BEING BURNT ALIVE... BUT IF HE DOES, HE'LL LOSE CONSCIOUSNESS AND TURN INTO BLACK CRYSTAL.
WHAT'S YOUR CHOICE, RED-HEAD...?
ZRN
ZRN
ZRN
ZRN
CRAP... I FEEL SO HEAVY... MY MIND'S A BLANK... IT'S JUST LIKE THE BLADE TESTS...!
YOU ALMOST LOST CONSCIOUSNESS WHEN THAT BLACK MIST SURROUNDED YOU, RIGHT? WELL, JUST LET GO! THEN YOU CAN BECOME BLADE MATERIAL!

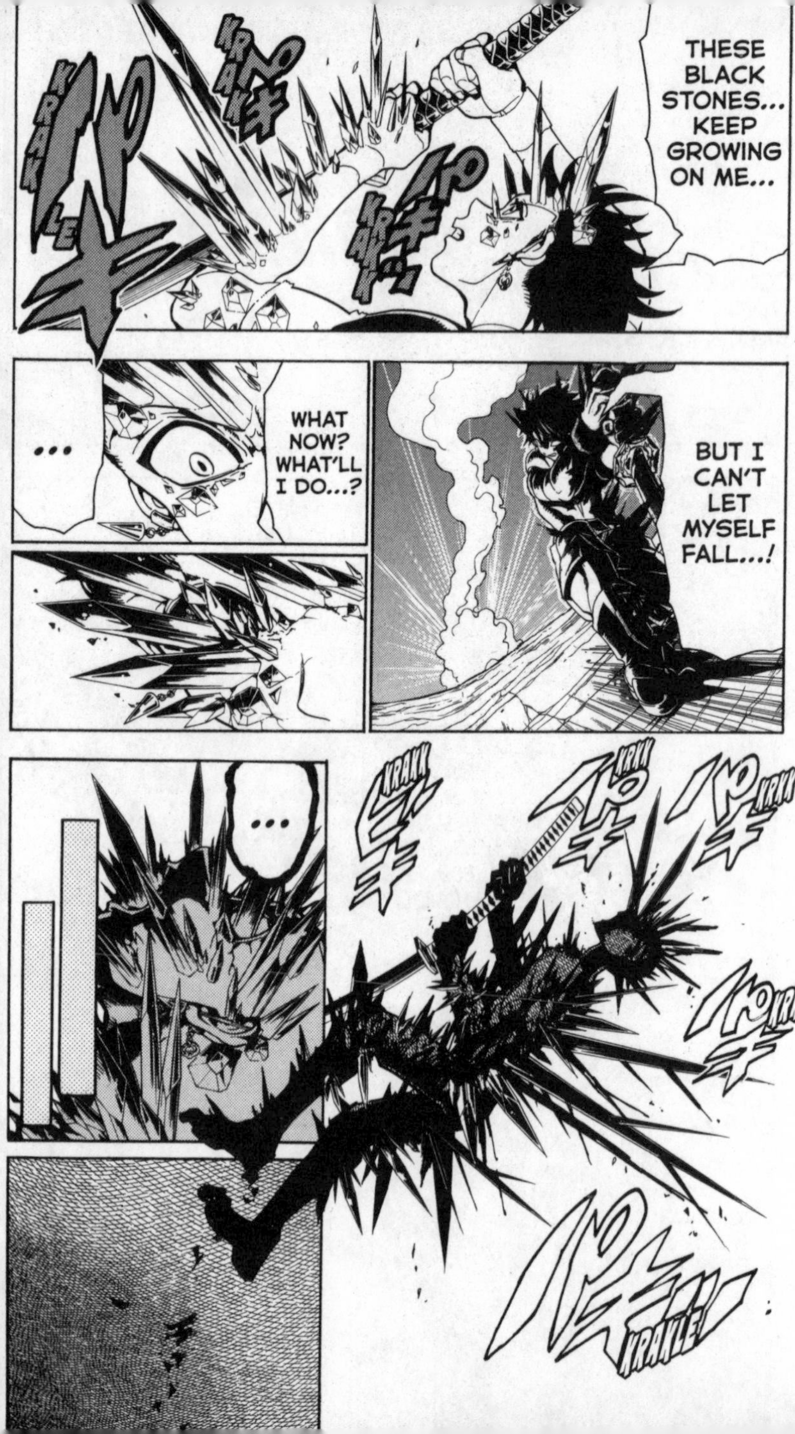
THESE BLACK STONES... KEEP GROWING ON ME...
KRAK
KRAKKLE
BUT I CAN'T LET MYSELF FALL...!
WHAT NOW? WHAT'LL I DO...?
...
KRKK
KRKK
KRAKK
KRKK
...
KRAKLE!

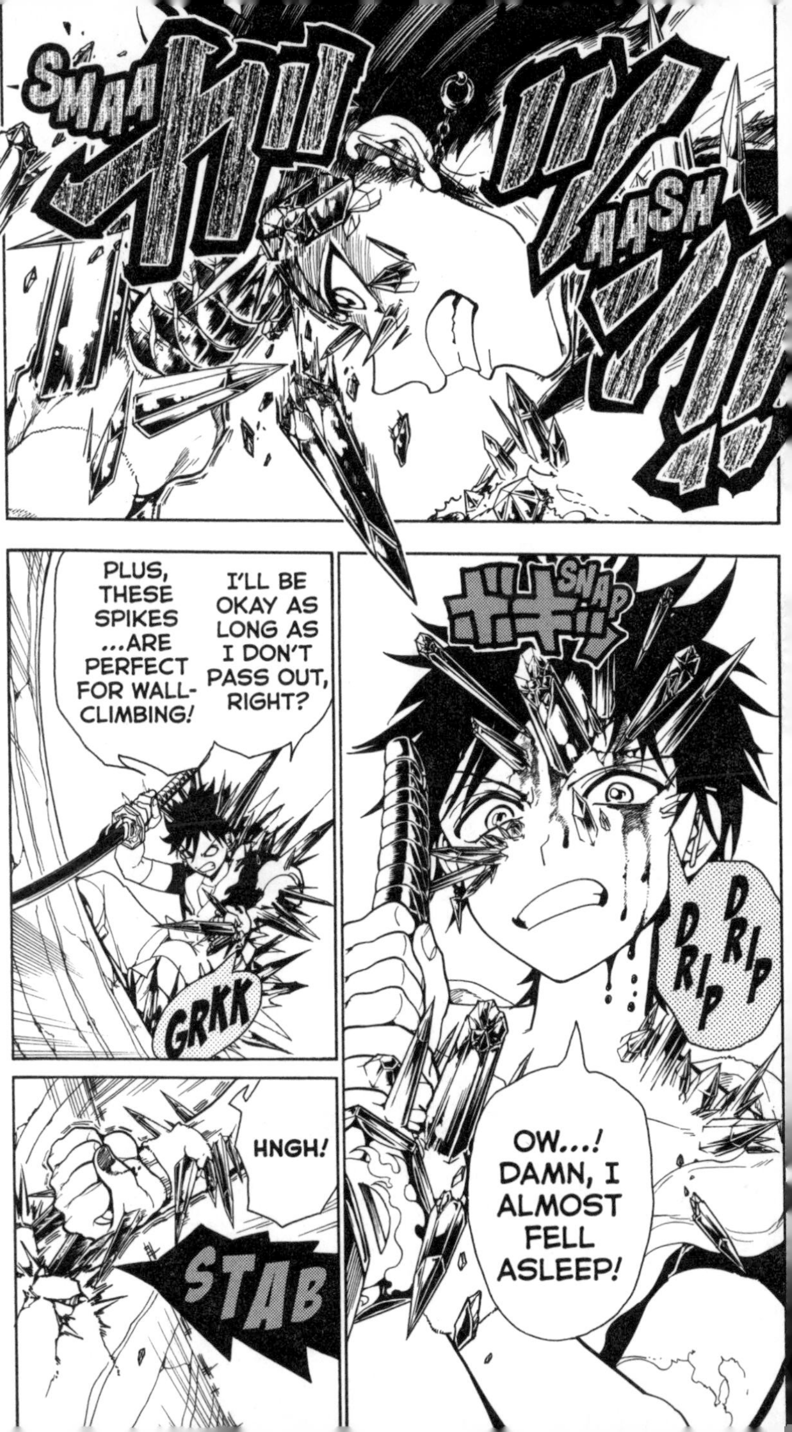
SMAA
AASH
SNAP
DRIP
DRIP
OW...! DAMN, I ALMOST FELL ASLEEP!
I'LL BE OKAY AS LONG AS I DON'T PASS OUT, RIGHT?
PLUS, THESE SPIKES ...ARE PERFECT FOR WALL-CLIMBING!
GRKK
HNGH!
STAB

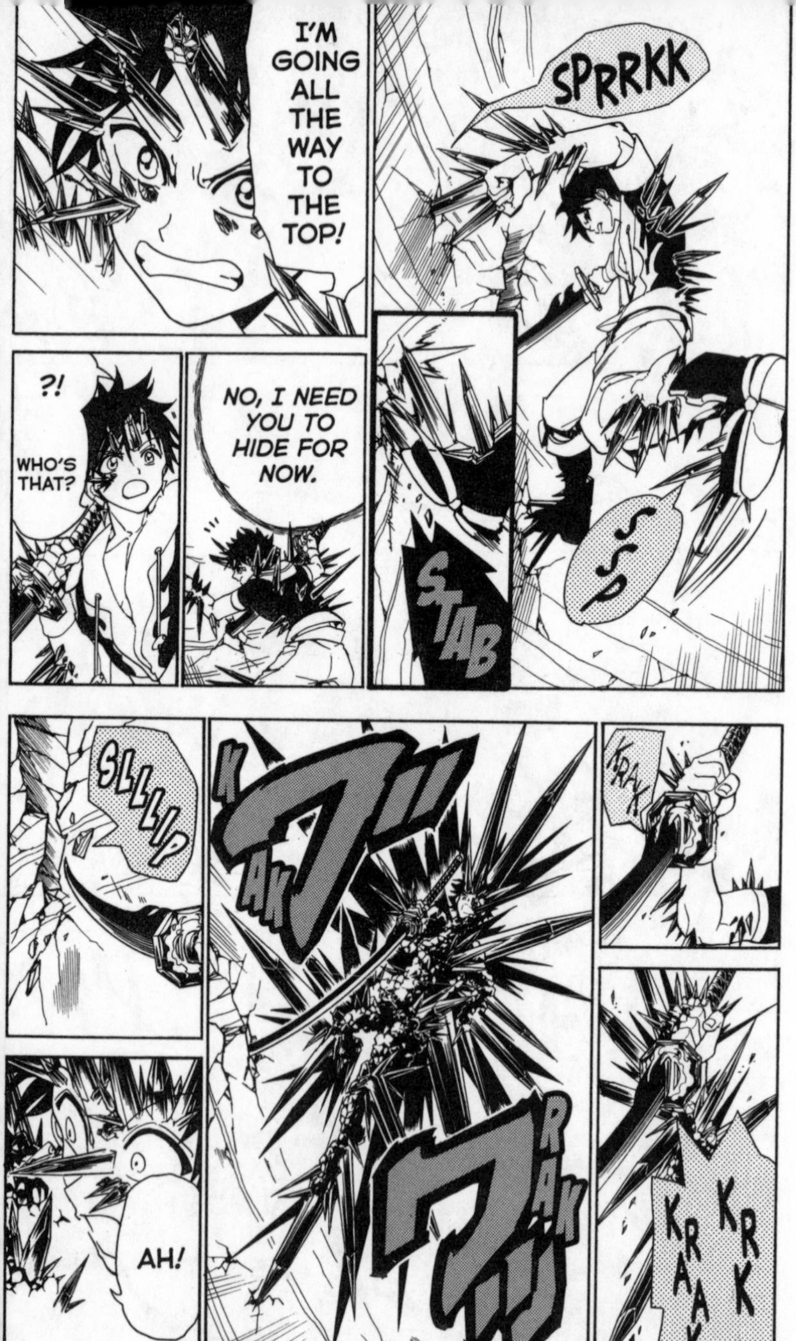
SPRRKK
I'M GOING ALL THE WAY TO THE TOP!
STAB
NO, I NEED YOU TO HIDE FOR NOW.
?!
WHO'S THAT?
KRAK
KRAK KRK
SLLLIP
AH!

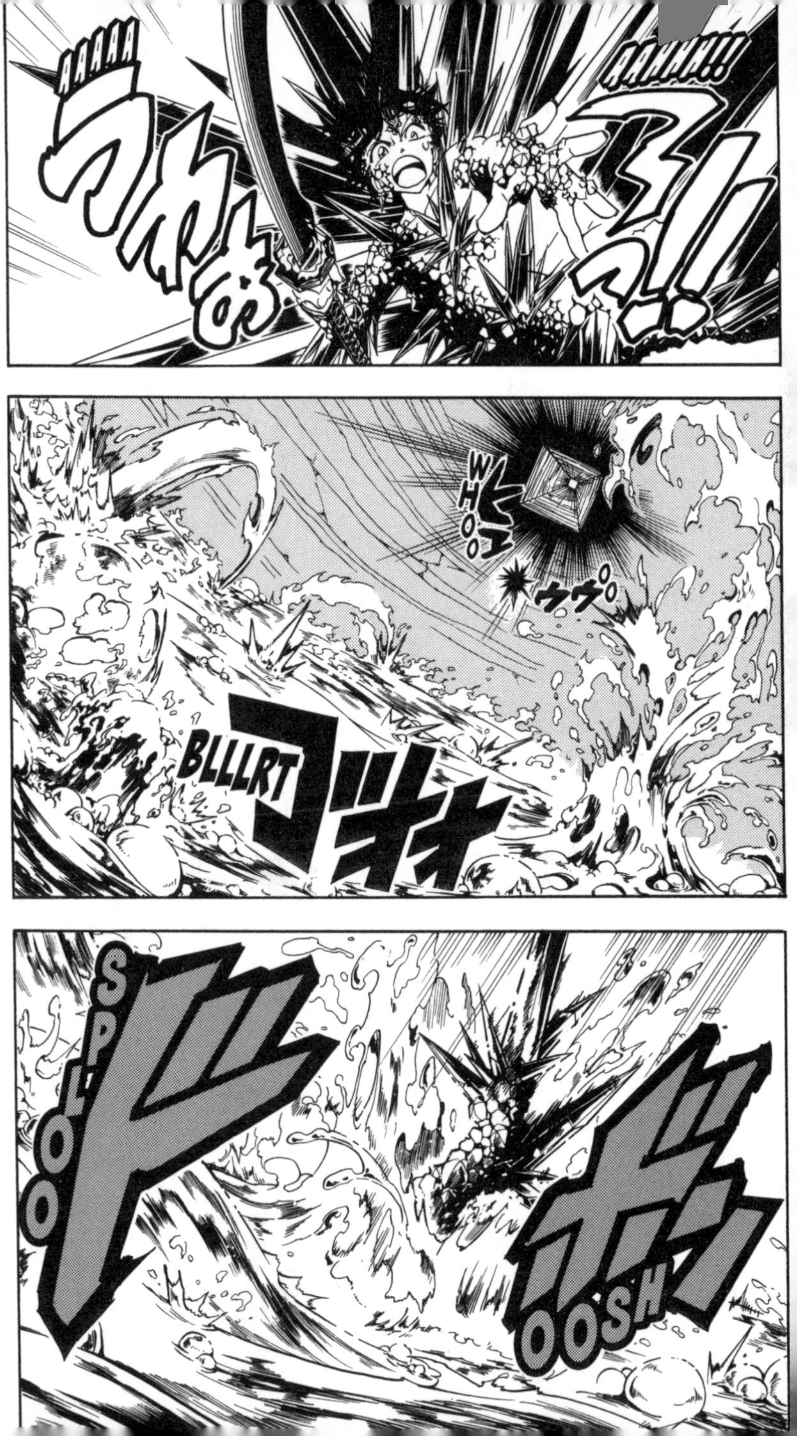

AAAAA
AAAAAA!!
WHOOM
BLLLRT
SPLOOO
OOSH

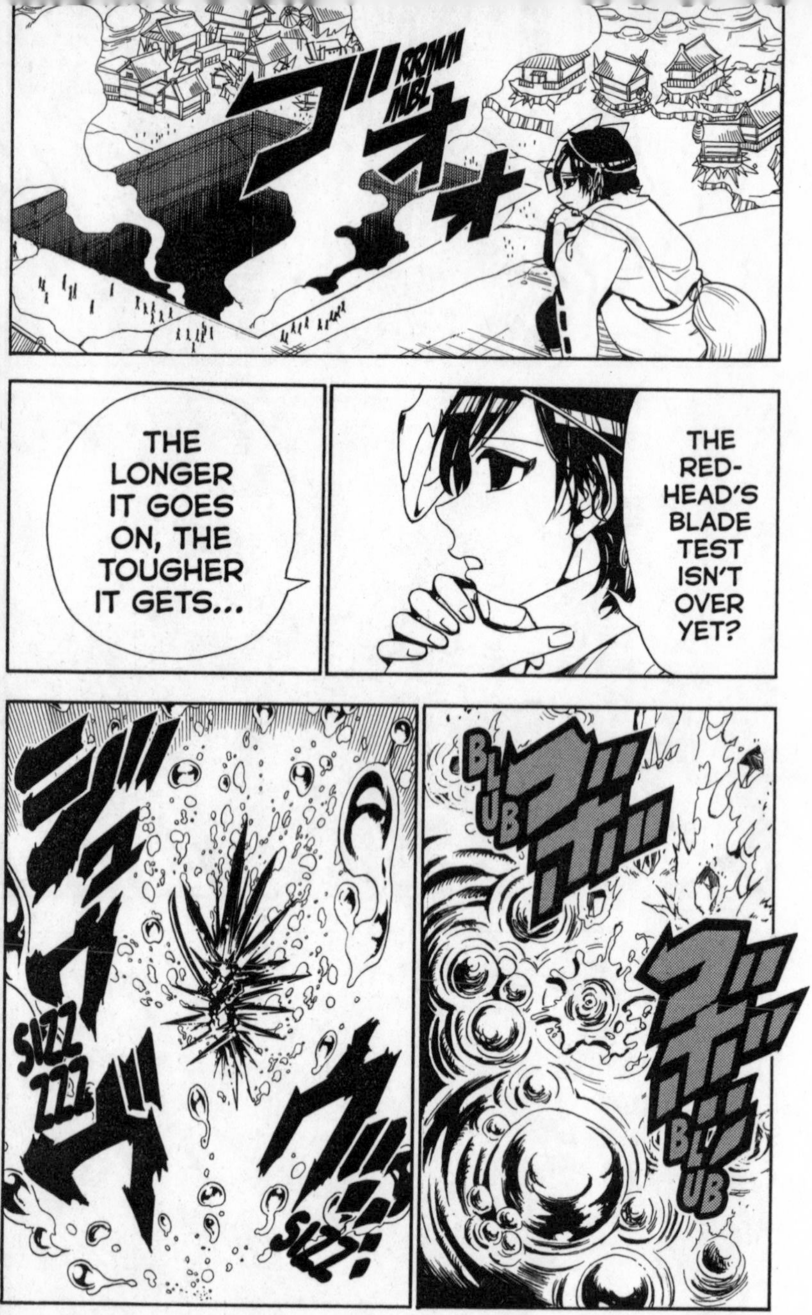
RRMMMBL
THE RED-HEAD'S BLADE TEST ISN'T OVER YET?
THE LONGER IT GOES ON, THE TOUGHER IT GETS...
BLUB
BLUB
SIZZZZZZ
SIZZ!

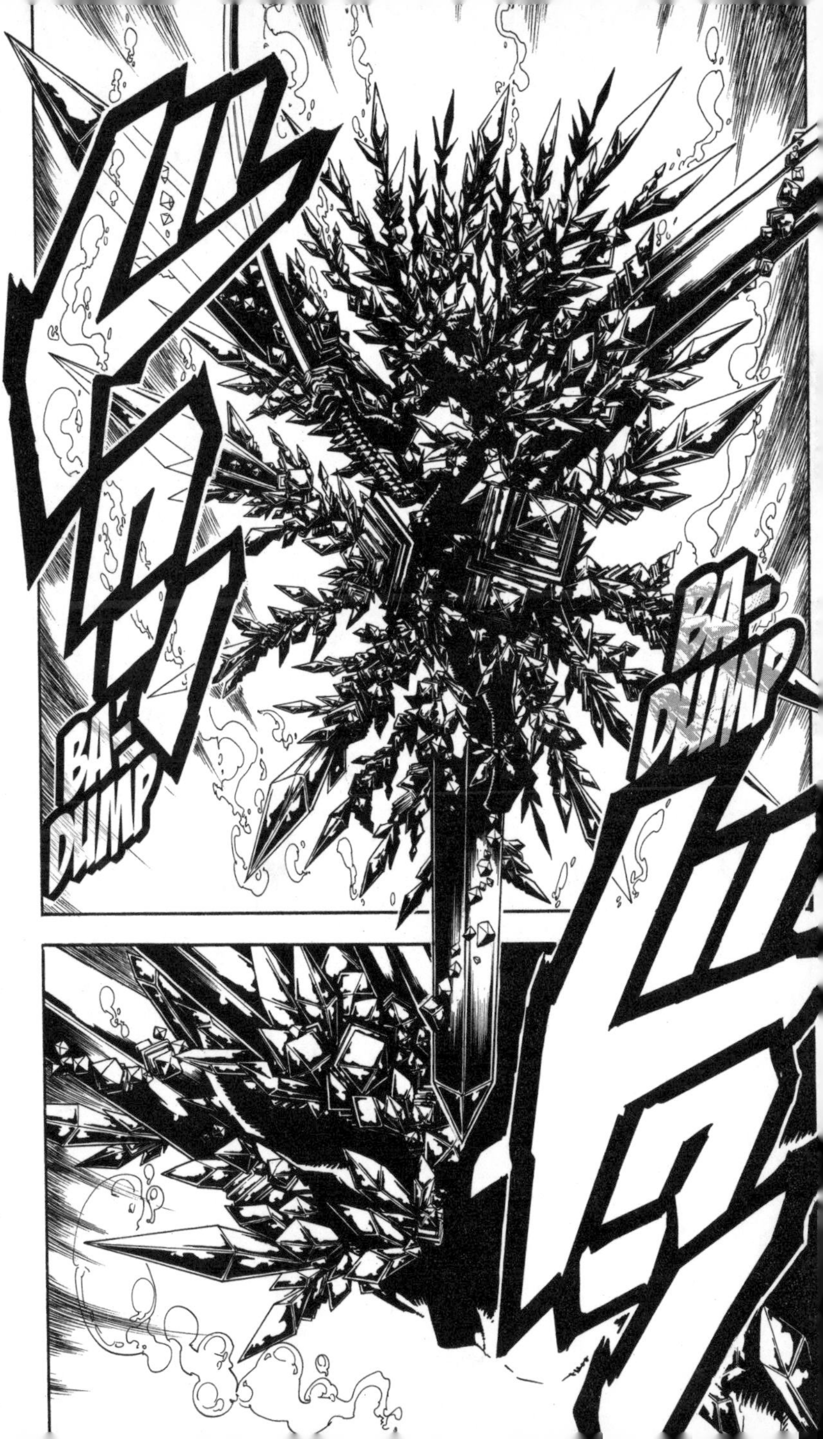
BA-DUMP
BA-DUMP

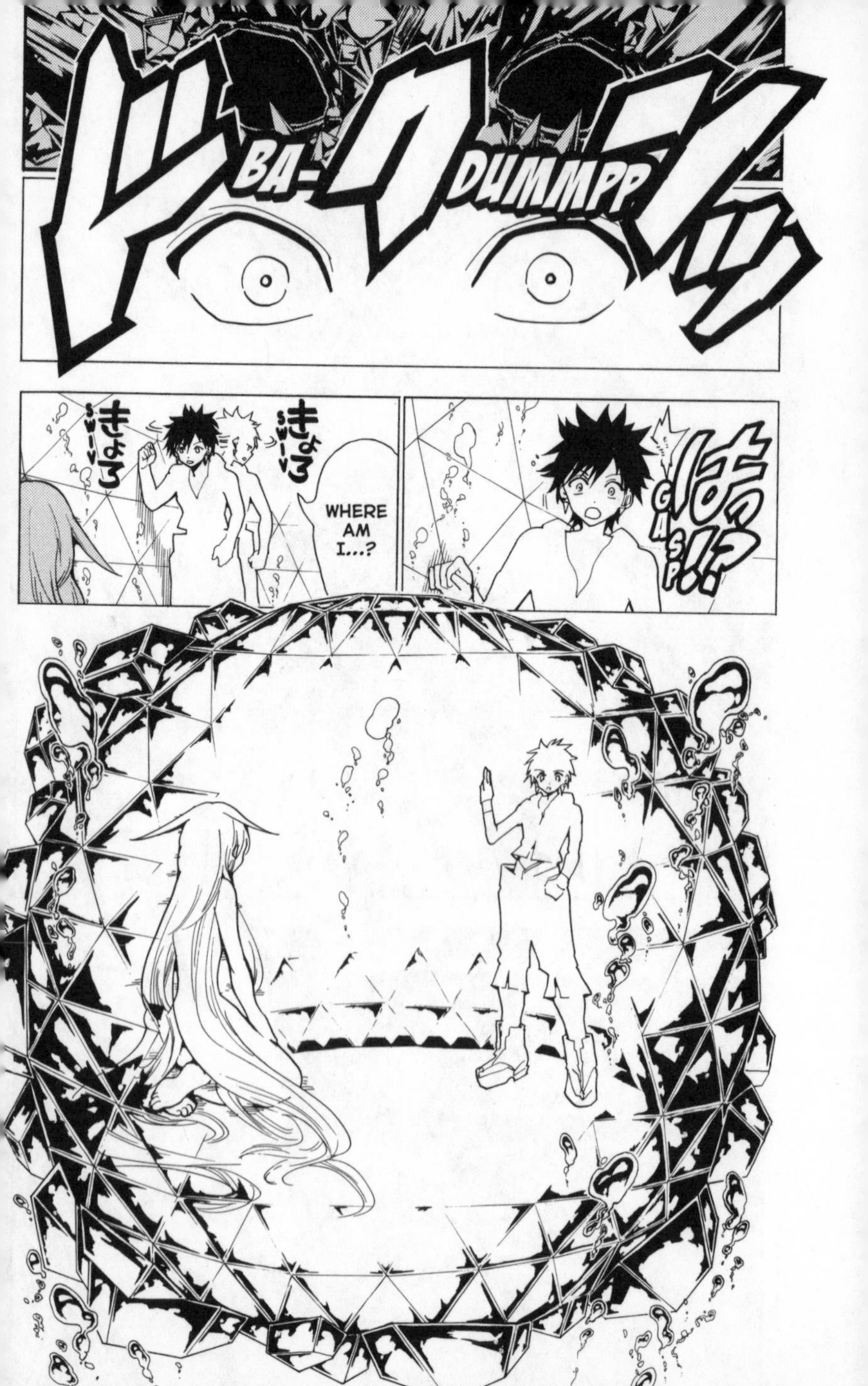
BA-DUMMPP
GASP!?
WHERE AM I...?
SWIV
SWIV

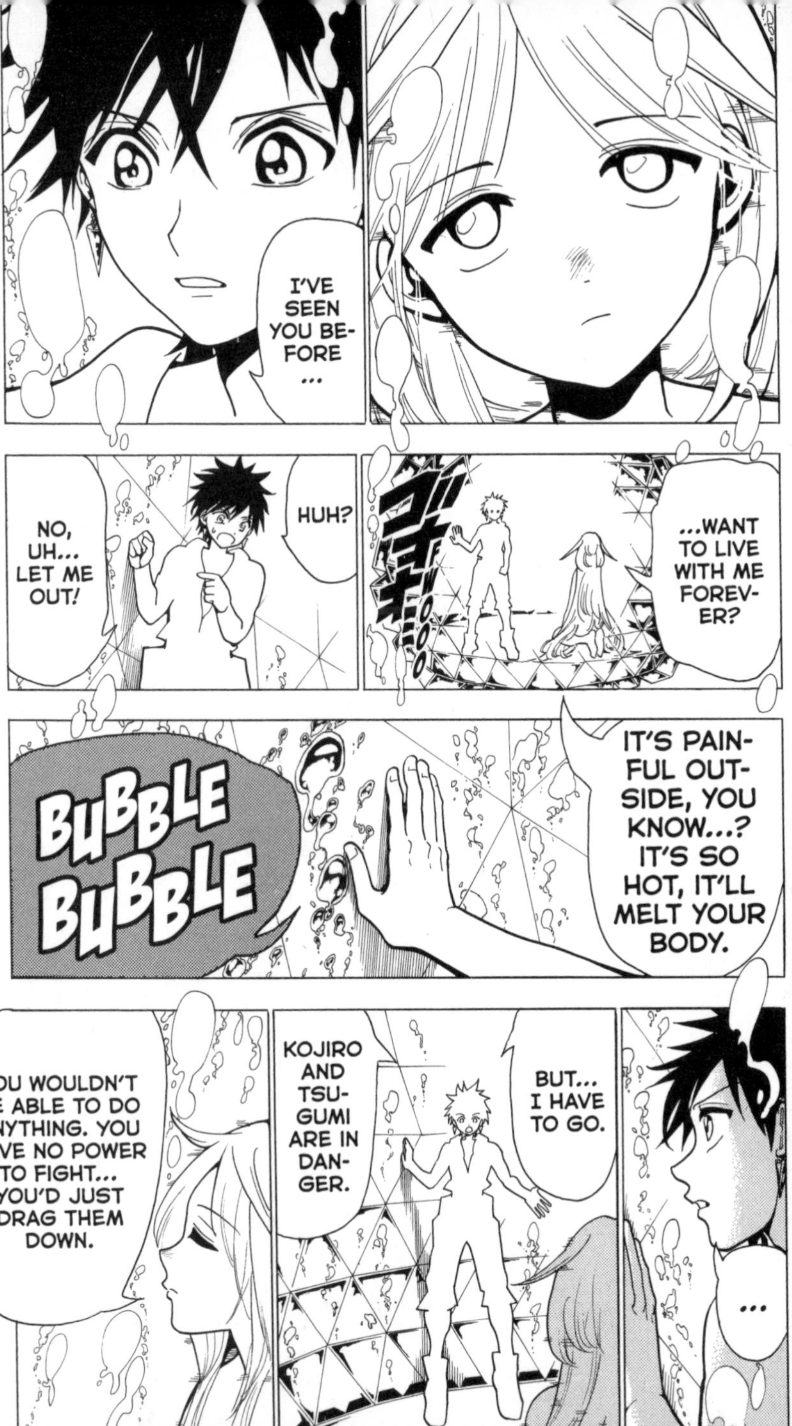
I'VE SEEN YOU BEFORE ...
...WANT TO LIVE WITH ME FOREVER?
FWOOO
HUH?
NO, UH... LET ME OUT!
IT'S PAINFUL OUTSIDE, YOU KNOW...? IT'S SO HOT, IT'LL MELT YOUR BODY.
BUBBLE BUBBLE
...
BUT... I HAVE TO GO.
KOJIRO AND TSUGUMI ARE IN DANGER.
YOU WOULDN'T BE ABLE TO DO ANYTHING. YOU HAVE NO POWER TO FIGHT... YOU'D JUST DRAG THEM DOWN.

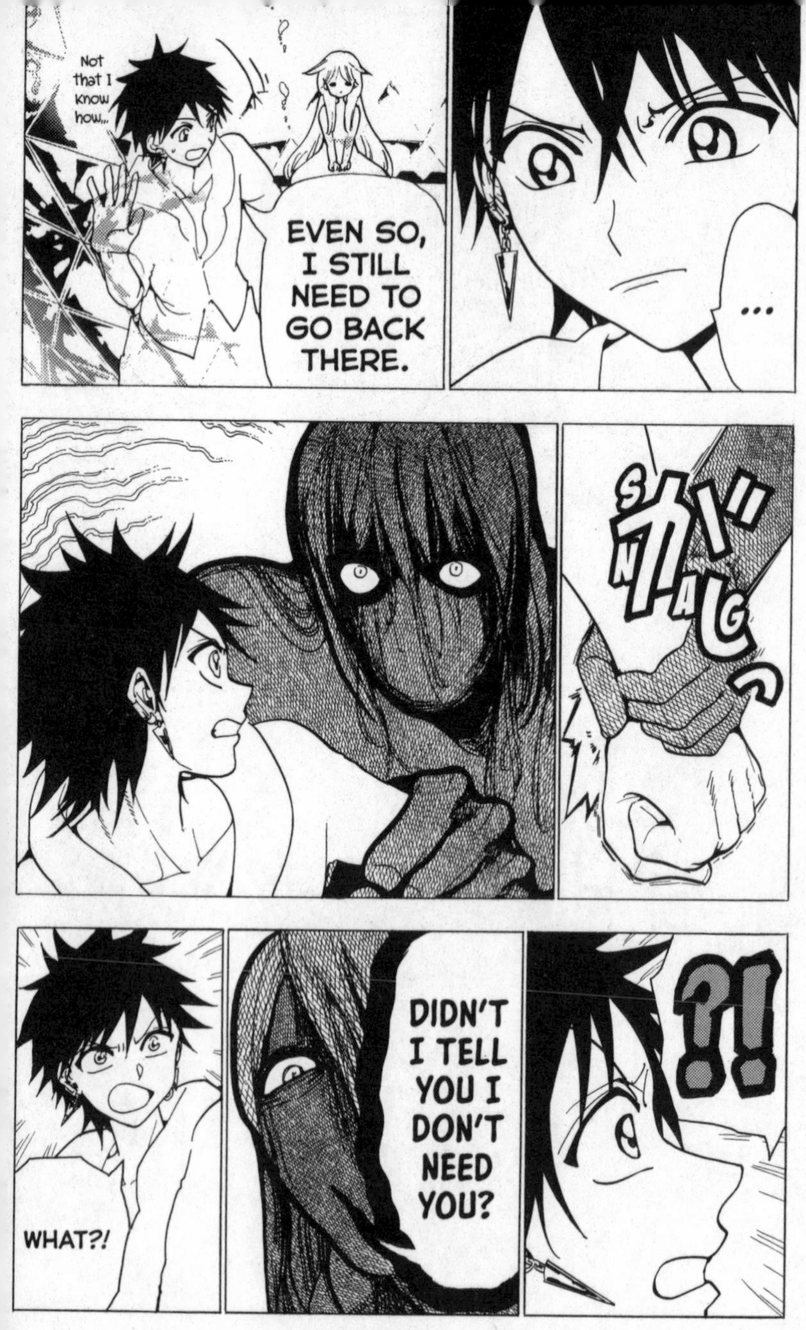
...
EVEN SO, I STILL NEED TO GO BACK THERE.
Not that I know how...
SNAG
?!
DIDN'T I TELL YOU I DON'T NEED YOU?
WHAT?!

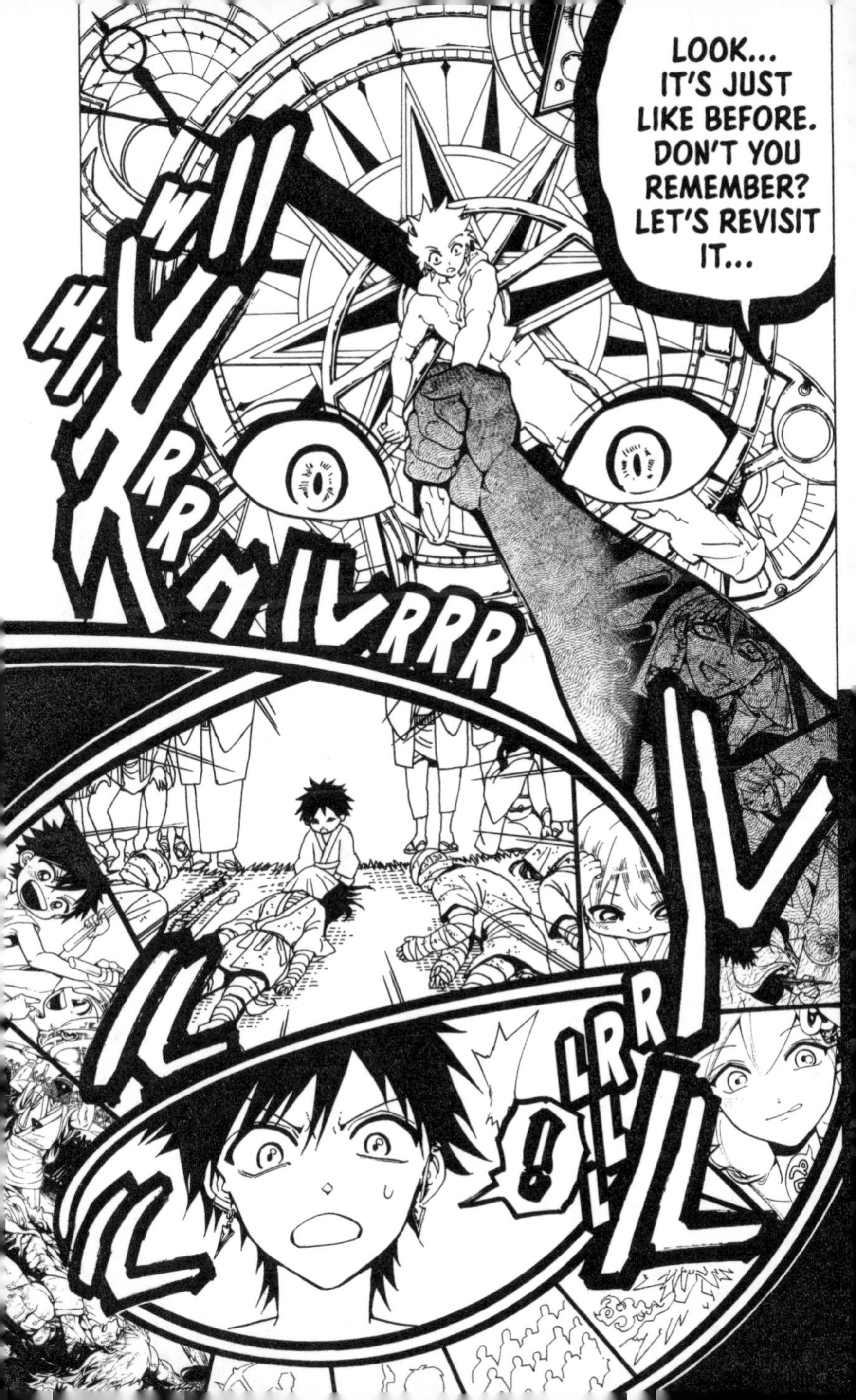
LOOK... IT'S JUST LIKE BEFORE. DON'T YOU REMEMBER? LET'S REVISIT IT...

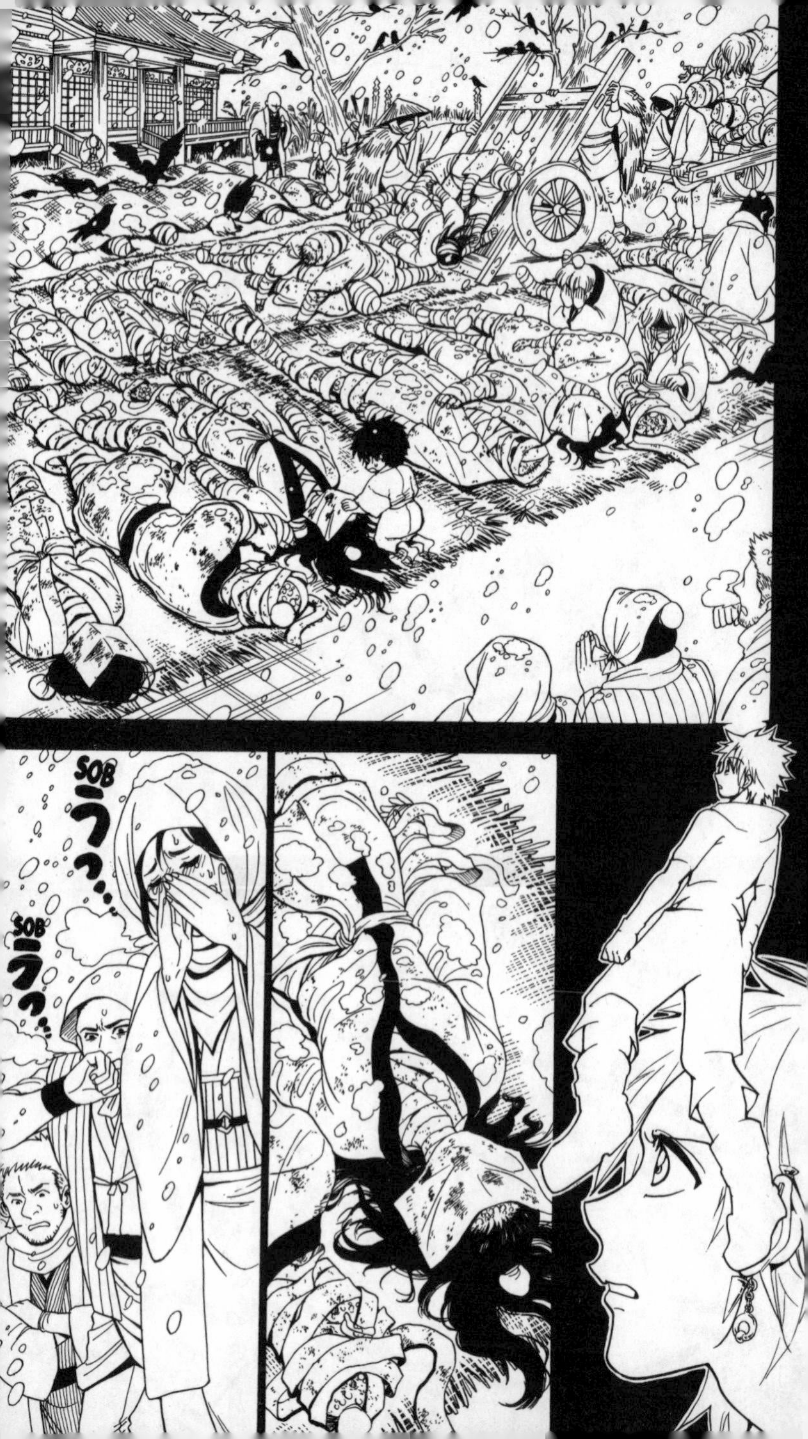
SOB
うっ…
SOB
うっ…

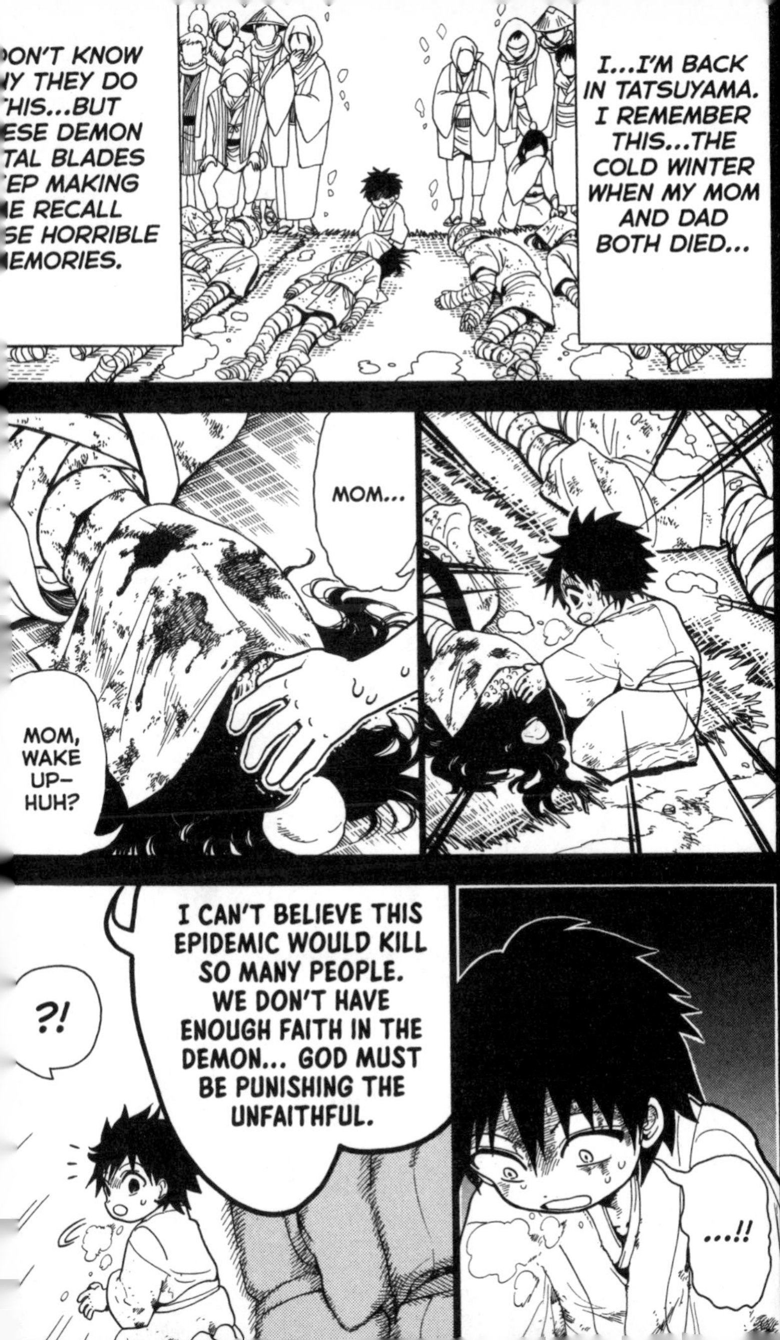
I...I'M BACK IN TATSUYAMA. I REMEMBER THIS...THE COLD WINTER WHEN MY MOM AND DAD BOTH DIED...
ON'T KNOW Y THEY DO THIS...BUT ESE DEMON TAL BLADES EP MAKING E RECALL SE HORRIBLE EMORIES.
MOM...
MOM, WAKE UP— HUH?
...!!
I CAN'T BELIEVE THIS EPIDEMIC WOULD KILL SO MANY PEOPLE. WE DON'T HAVE ENOUGH FAITH IN THE DEMON... GOD MUST BE PUNISHING THE UNFAITHFUL.
?!

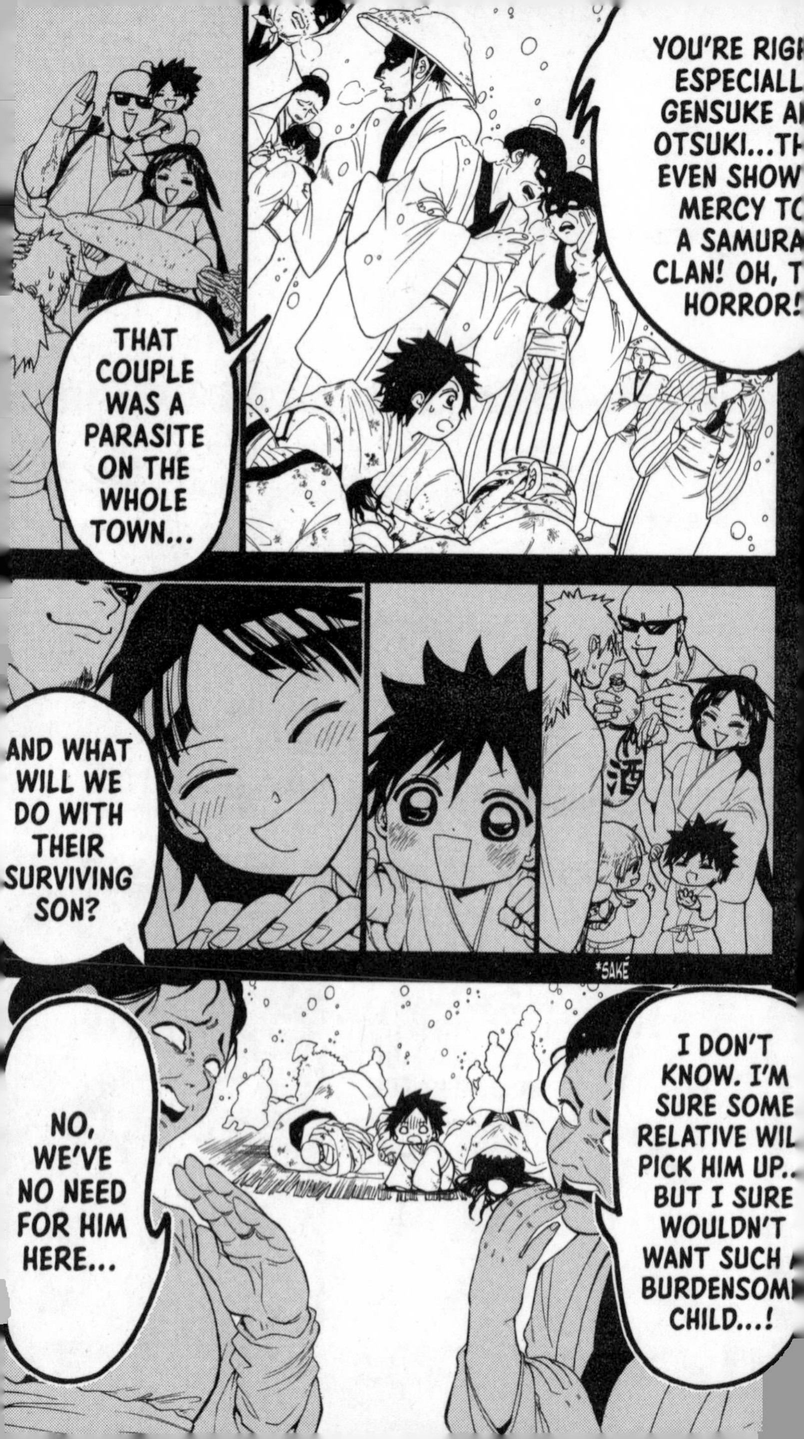
YOU'RE RIGI ESPECIALL GENSUKE A OTSUKI...TH EVEN SHOW MERCY TC A SAMURA CLAN! OH, T HORROR!
THAT COUPLE WAS A PARASITE ON THE WHOLE TOWN...
酒
*SAKÉ
AND WHAT WILL WE DO WITH THEIR SURVIVING SON?
I DON'T KNOW. I'M SURE SOME RELATIVE WIL PICK HIM UP... BUT I SURE WOULDN'T WANT SUCH BURDENSOM CHILD...!
NO, WE'VE NO NEED FOR HIM HERE...

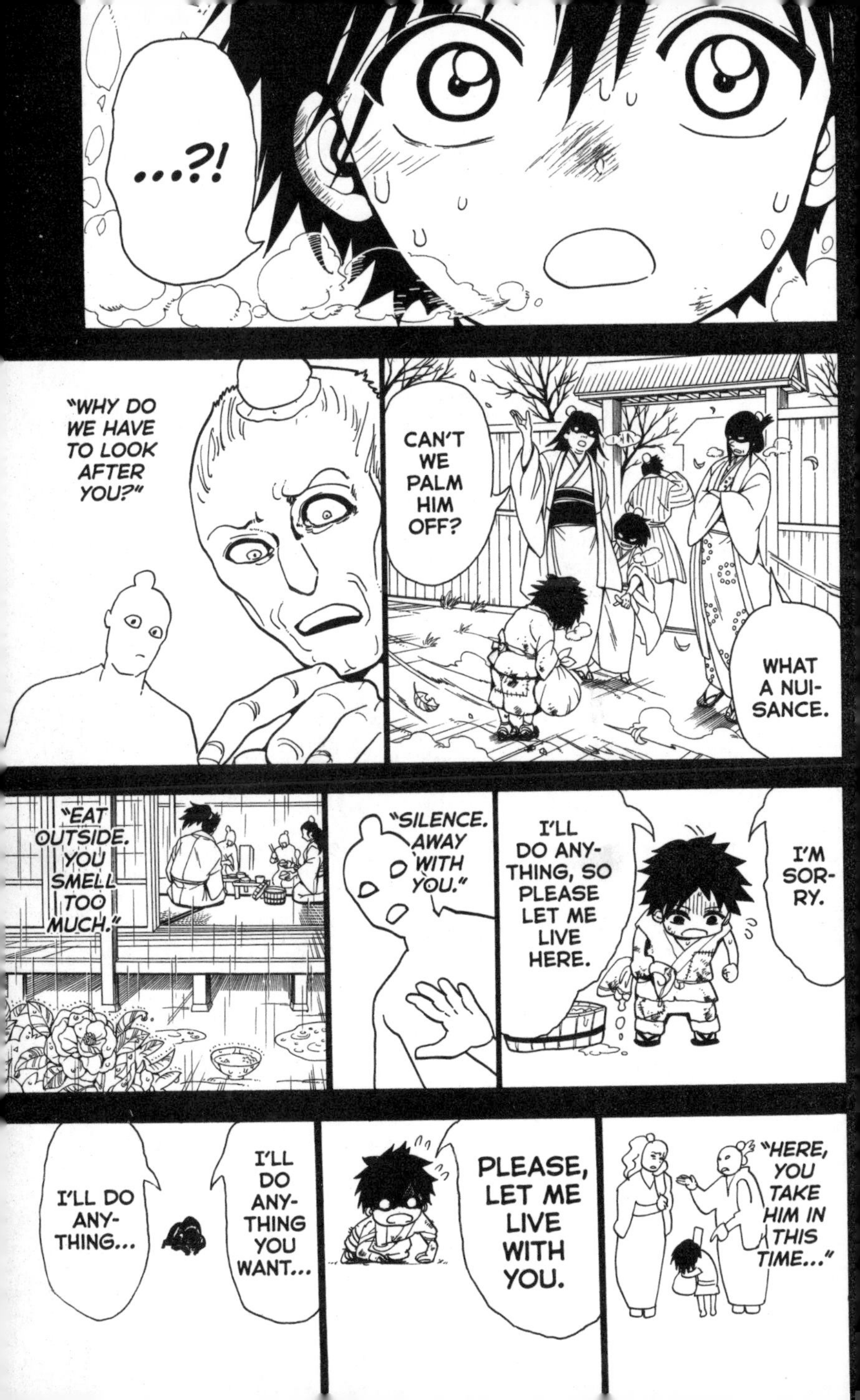
...?!
CAN'T WE PALM HIM OFF?
WHAT A NUI-SANCE.
"WHY DO WE HAVE TO LOOK AFTER YOU?"
I'M SOR-RY.
I'LL DO ANY-THING, SO PLEASE LET ME LIVE HERE.
"SILENCE. AWAY WITH YOU."
"EAT OUTSIDE. YOU SMELL TOO MUCH."
"HERE, YOU TAKE HIM IN THIS TIME..."
PLEASE, LET ME LIVE WITH YOU.
I'LL DO ANY-THING YOU WANT...
I'LL DO ANY-THING...

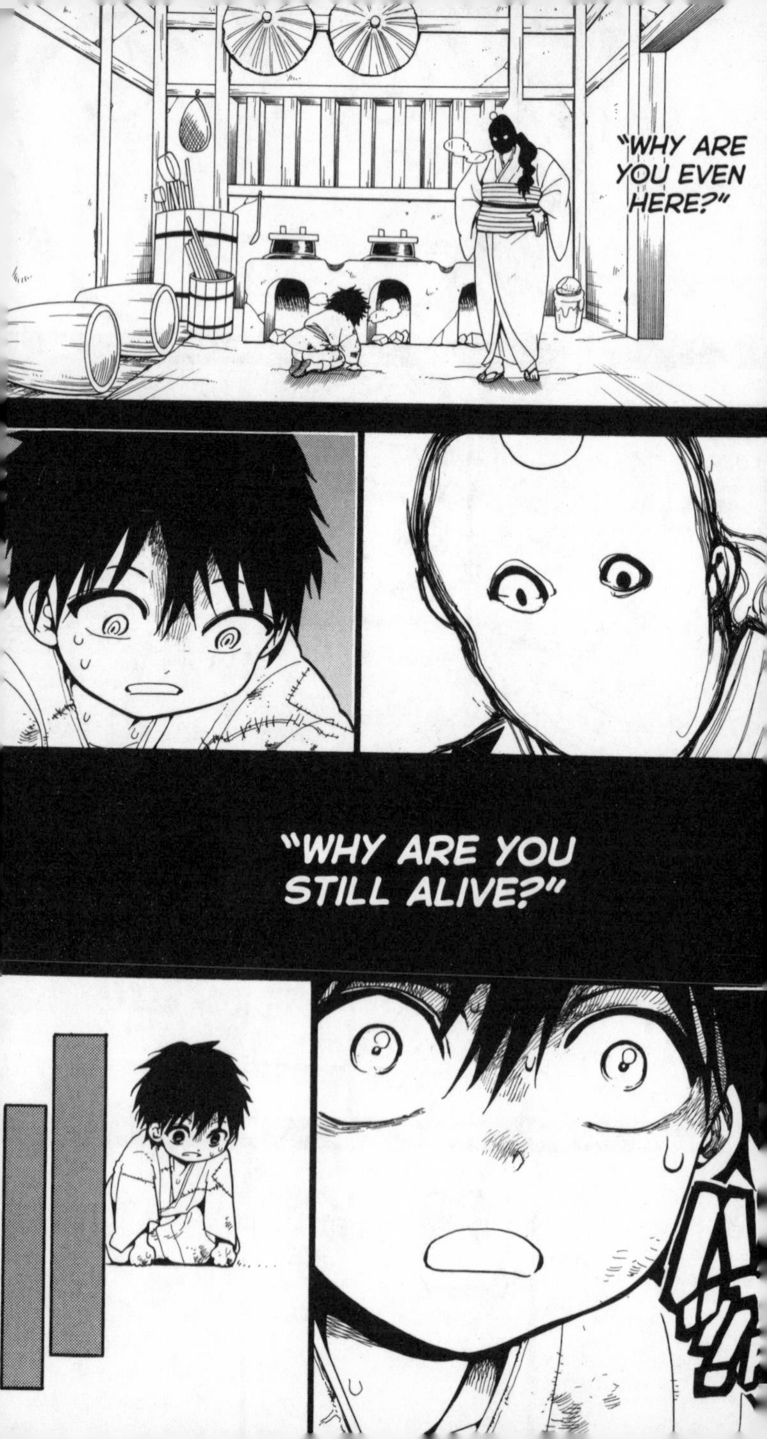
"WHY ARE YOU EVEN HERE?"
"WHY ARE YOU STILL ALIVE?"

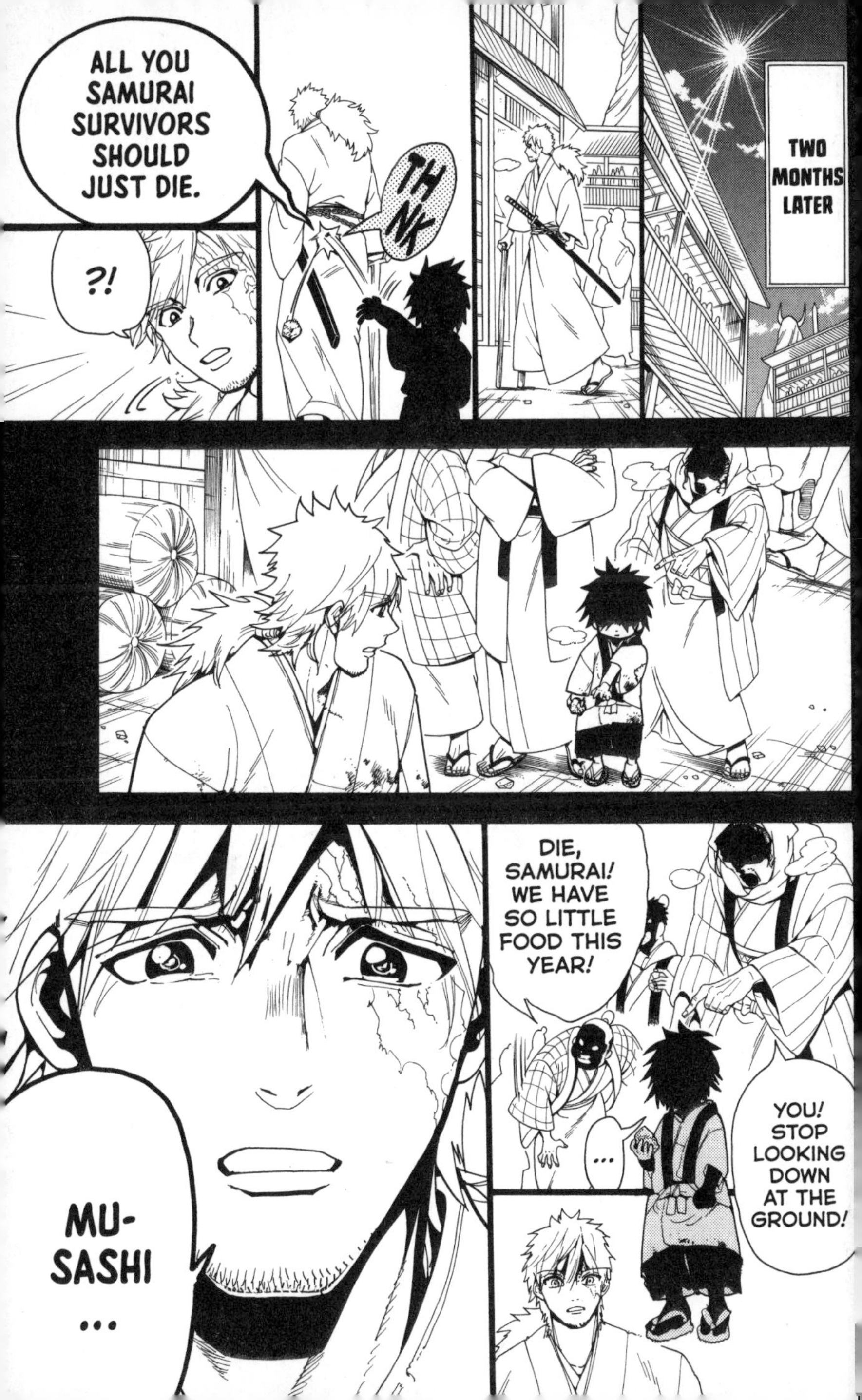
TWO MONTHS LATER
THNK
ALL YOU SAMURAI SURVIVORS SHOULD JUST DIE.
?!
DIE, SAMURAI! WE HAVE SO LITTLE FOOD THIS YEAR!
YOU! STOP LOOKING DOWN AT THE GROUND!
...
MU-SASHI ...

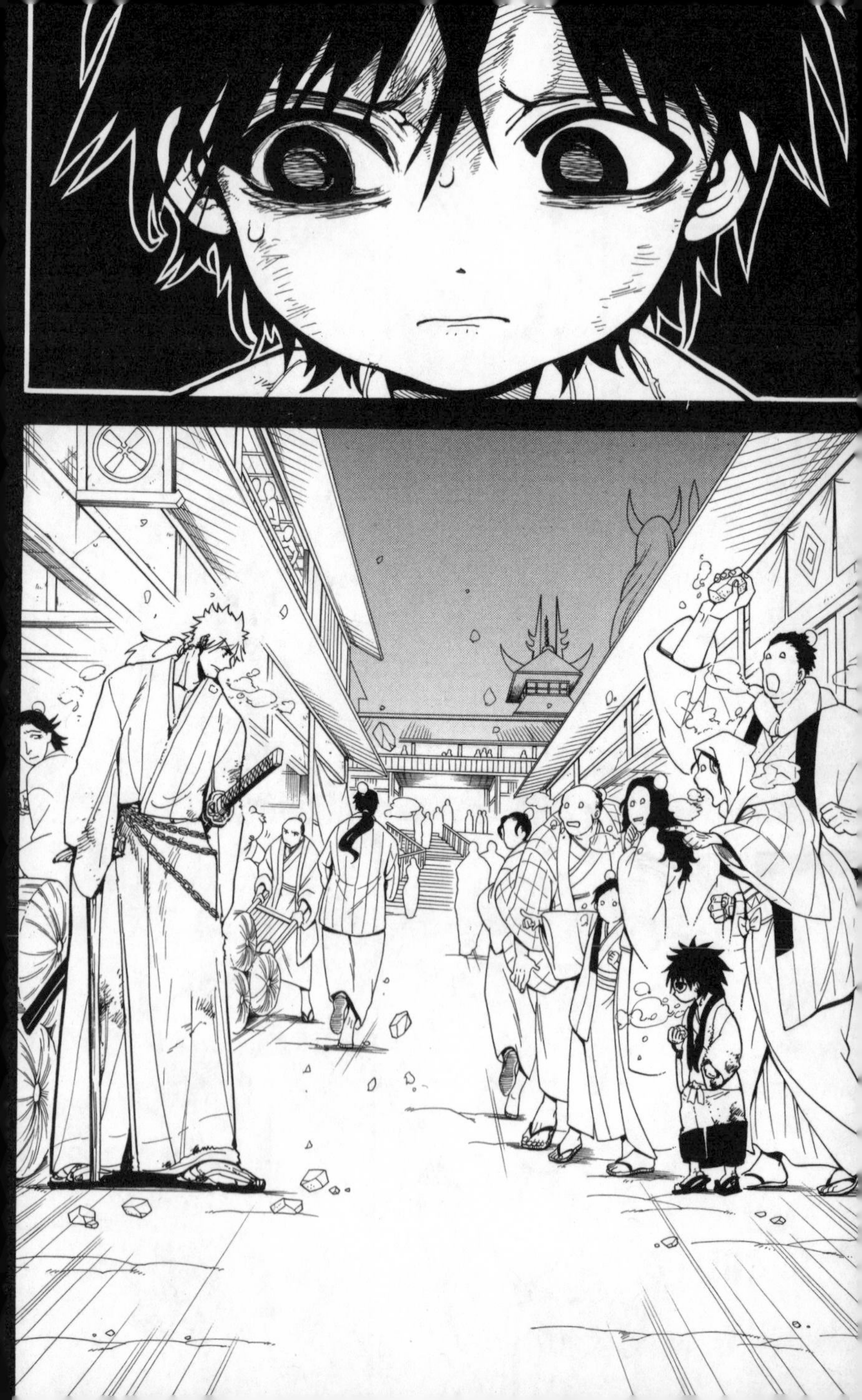

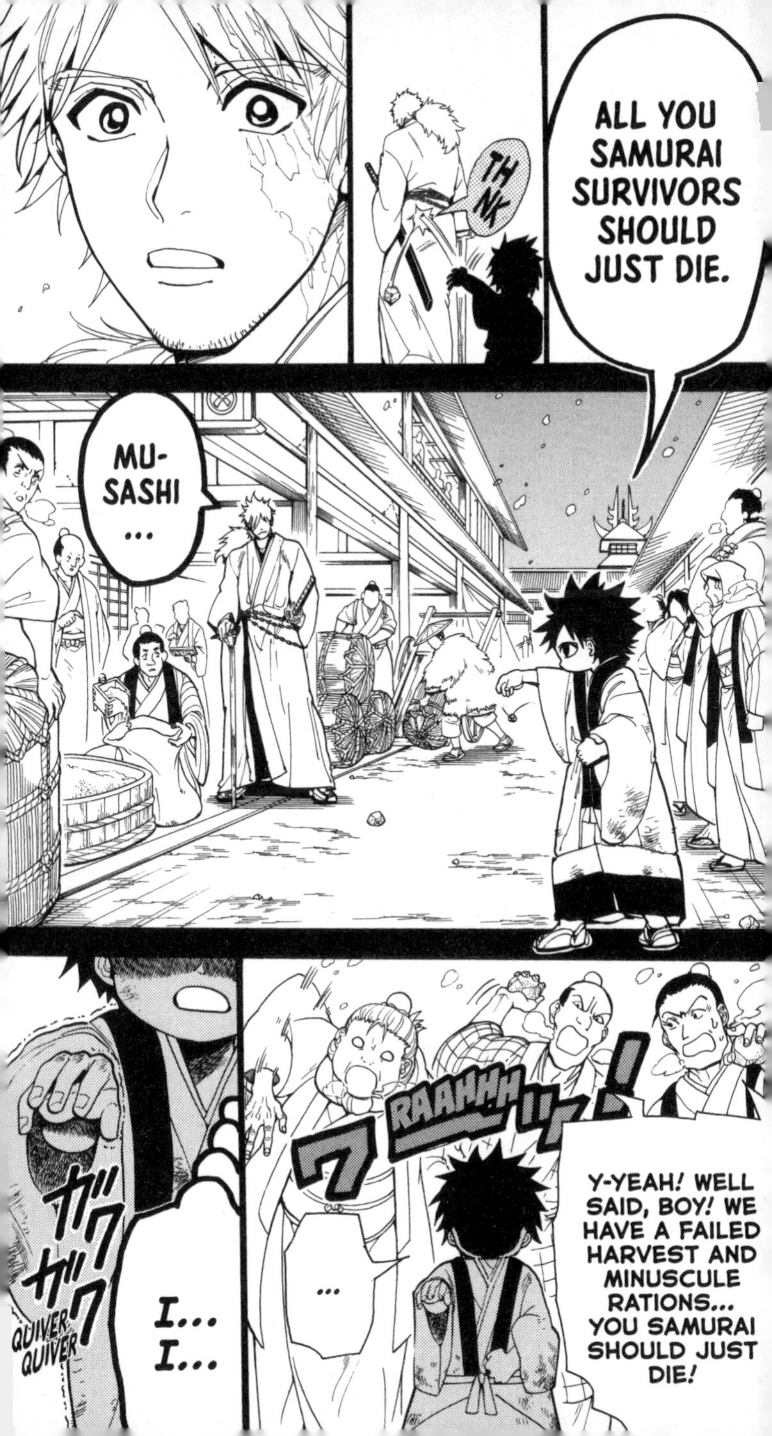
ALL YOU SAMURAI SURVIVORS SHOULD JUST DIE.
THNK
MU-SASHI ...
ワ
RAAHHH
Y-YEAH! WELL SAID, BOY! WE HAVE A FAILED HARVEST AND MINUSCULE RATIONS... YOU SAMURAI SHOULD JUST DIE!
...
I... I...
ガク ガク
QUIVER QUIVER

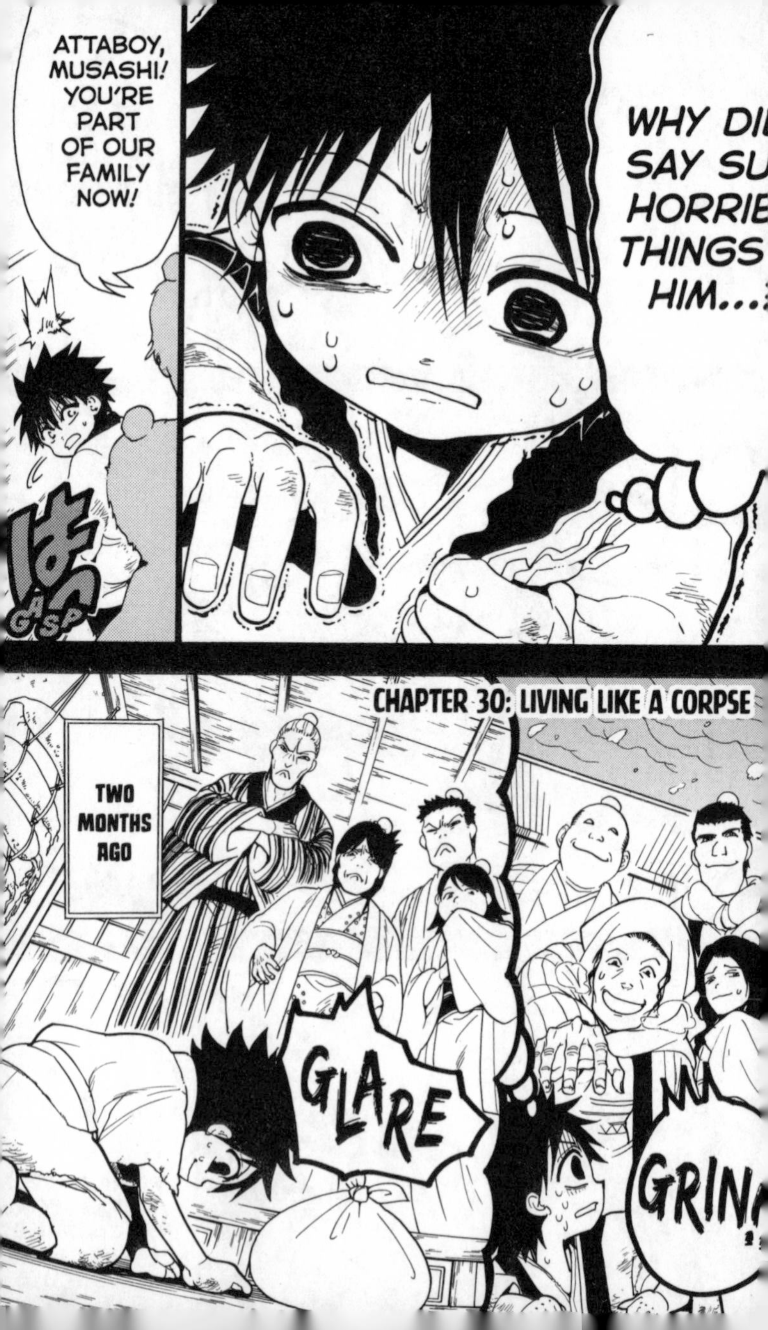
WHY DI SAY SU HORRIE THINGS HIM...
ATTABOY, MUSASHI! YOU'RE PART OF OUR FAMILY NOW!
はっ
GASP
CHAPTER 30: LIVING LIKE A CORPSE
TWO MONTHS AGO
GRIN
GLARE

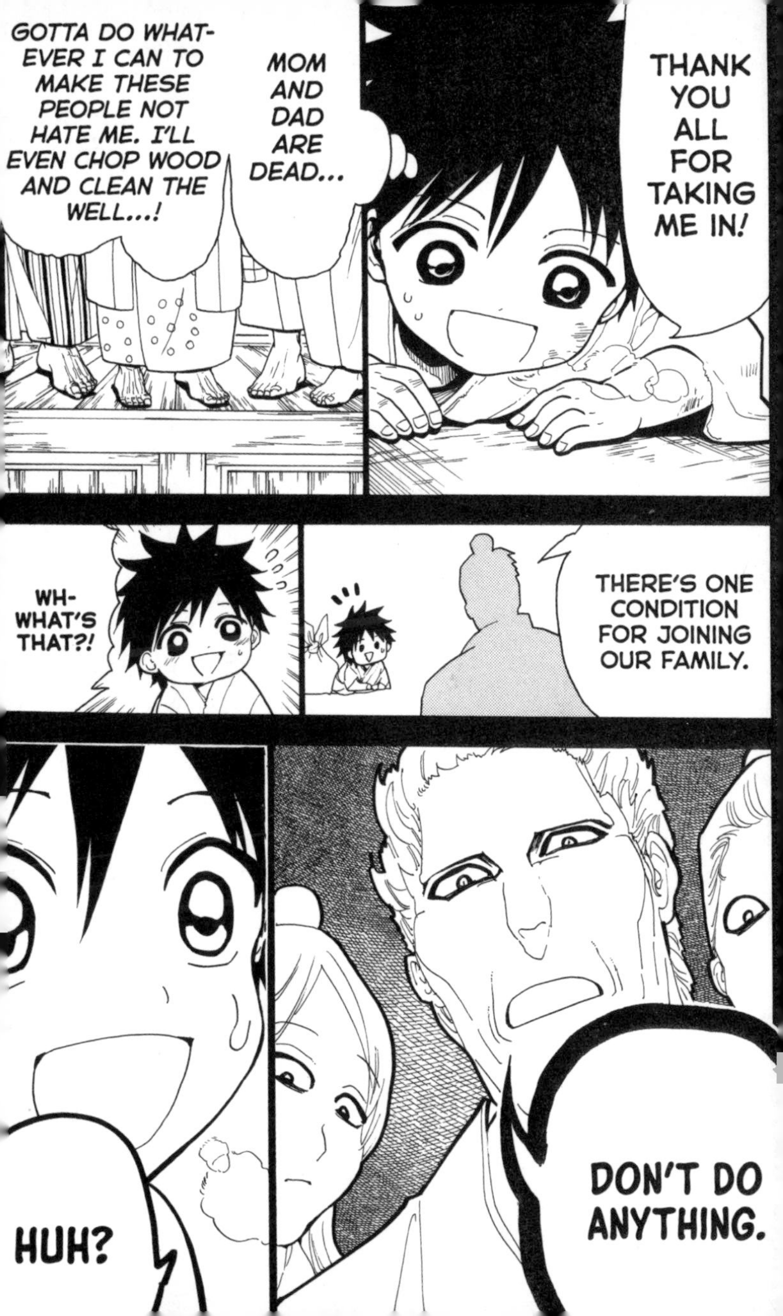
THANK YOU ALL FOR TAKING ME IN!
MOM AND DAD ARE DEAD...
GOTTA DO WHAT-EVER I CAN TO MAKE THESE PEOPLE NOT HATE ME. I'LL EVEN CHOP WOOD AND CLEAN THE WELL...!
THERE'S ONE CONDITION FOR JOINING OUR FAMILY.
WH- WHAT'S THAT?!
DON'T DO ANYTHING.
HUH?

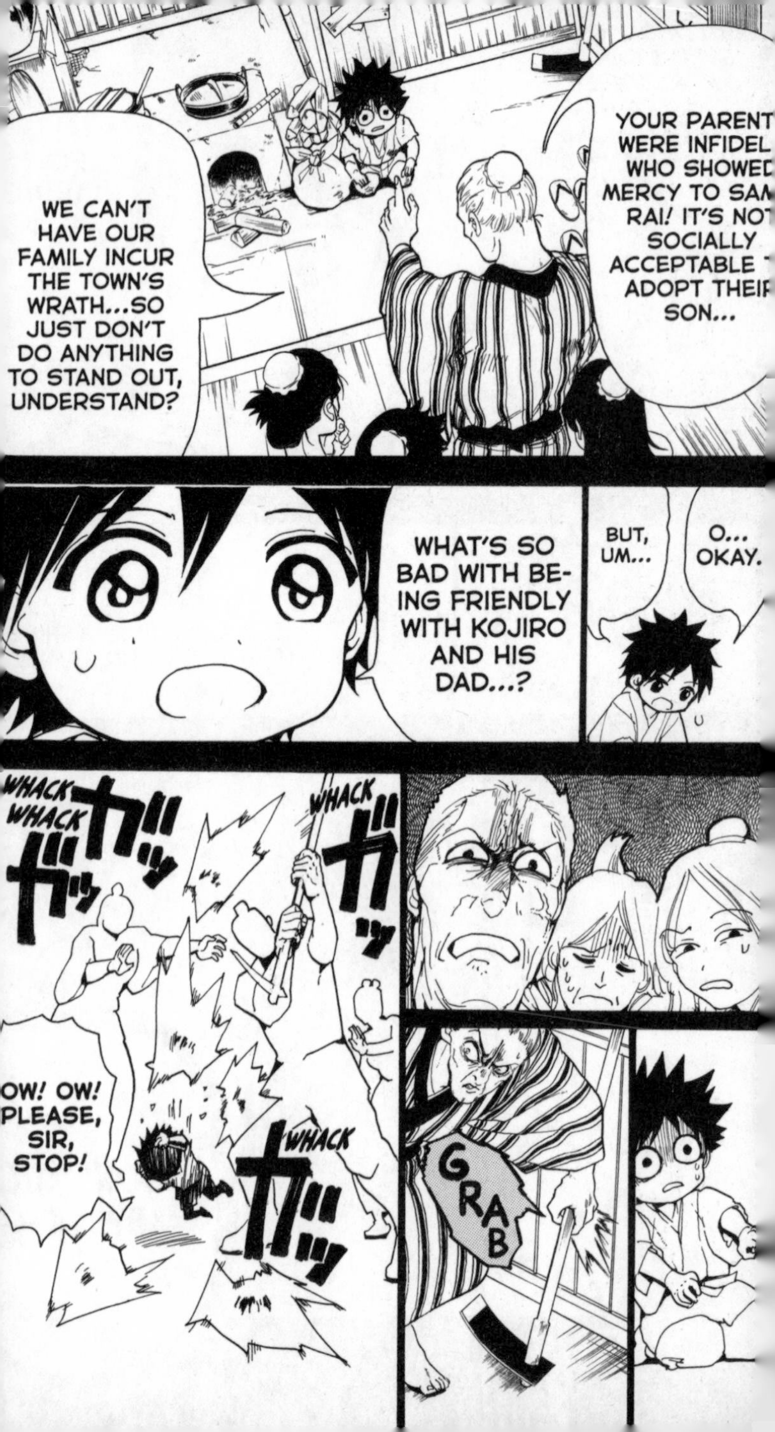
YOUR PARENT WERE INFIDEL WHO SHOWED MERCY TO SAM RAI! IT'S NOT SOCIALLY ACCEPTABLE T ADOPT THEIR SON...
WE CAN'T HAVE OUR FAMILY INCUR THE TOWN'S WRATH...SO JUST DON'T DO ANYTHING TO STAND OUT, UNDERSTAND?
O... OKAY.
BUT, UM...
WHAT'S SO BAD WITH BEING FRIENDLY WITH KOJIRO AND HIS DAD...?
GRAB
WHACK
ガッ
WHACK WHACK
ガッ
ガッ
OW! OW! PLEASE, SIR, STOP!
WHACK
ガッ

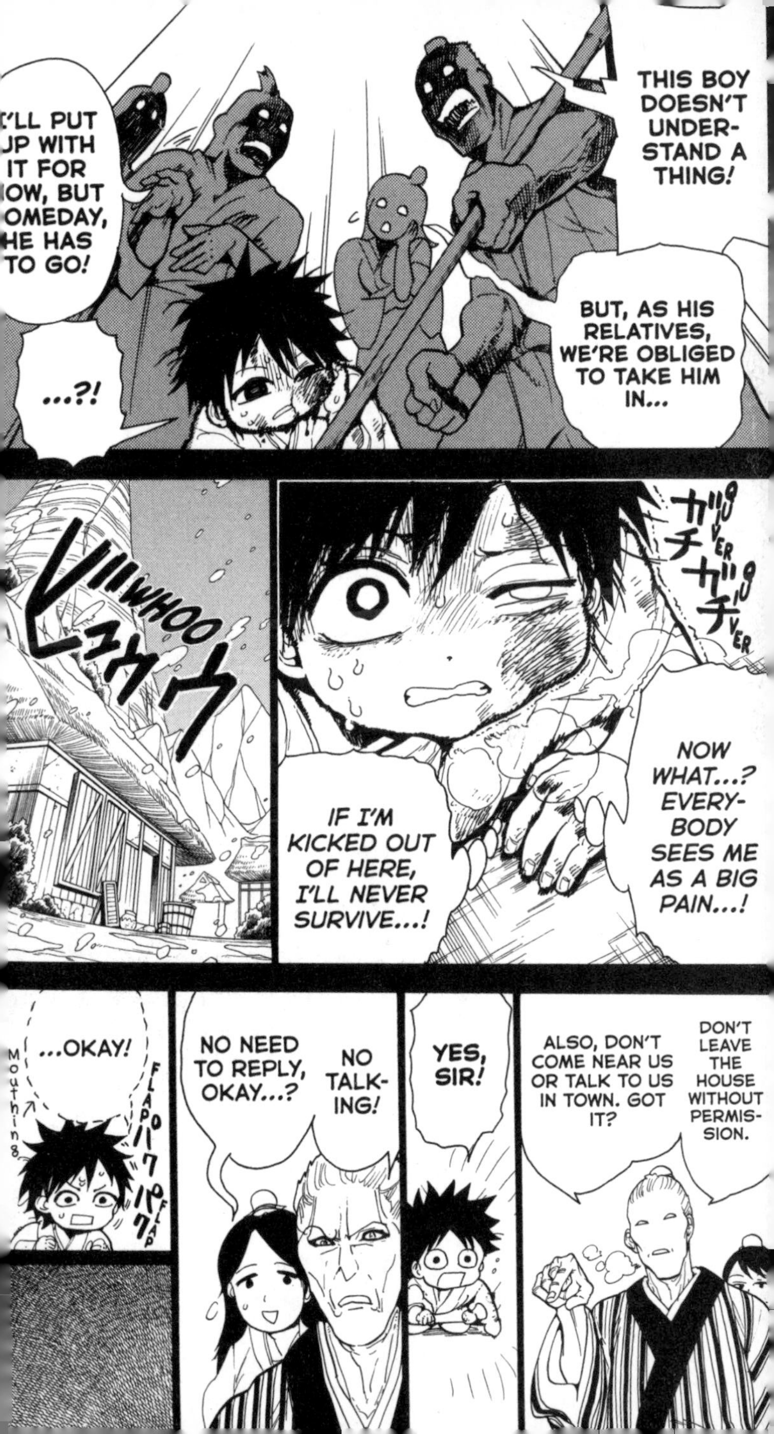
THIS BOY DOESN'T UNDER-STAND A THING!
BUT, AS HIS RELATIVES, WE'RE OBLIGED TO TAKE HIM IN...
'LL PUT JP WITH IT FOR OW, BUT OMEDAY, HE HAS TO GO!
...?!
ガチガチ JUVVER
NOW WHAT...? EVERY-BODY SEES ME AS A BIG PAIN...!
IF I'M KICKED OUT OF HERE, I'LL NEVER SURVIVE...!
VIIIWHOO
DON'T LEAVE THE HOUSE WITHOUT PERMIS-SION.
ALSO, DON'T COME NEAR US OR TALK TO US IN TOWN. GOT IT?
YES, SIR!
NO TALK-ING!
NO NEED TO REPLY, OKAY...?
...OKAY!
Mouthing
パクパク FLAP FLAP

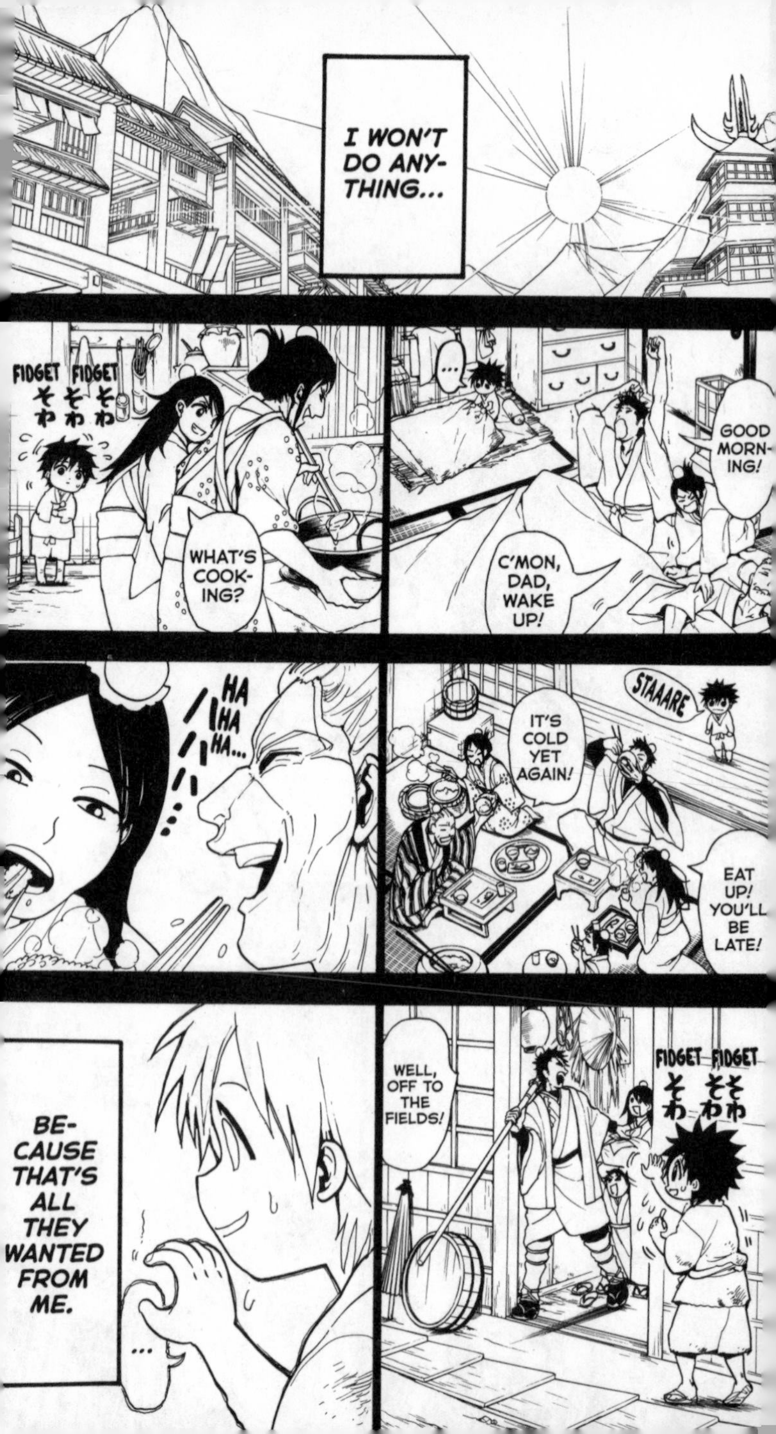
I WON'T DO ANY-THING...
GOOD MORN-ING!
...
C'MON, DAD, WAKE UP!
FIDGET FIDGET
そわそわ
WHAT'S COOK-ING?
STAAARE
IT'S COLD YET AGAIN!
EAT UP! YOU'LL BE LATE!
HA HA HA...
WELL, OFF TO THE FIELDS!
FIDGET FIDGET
そわそわ
BE-CAUSE THAT'S ALL THEY WANTED FROM ME.
...

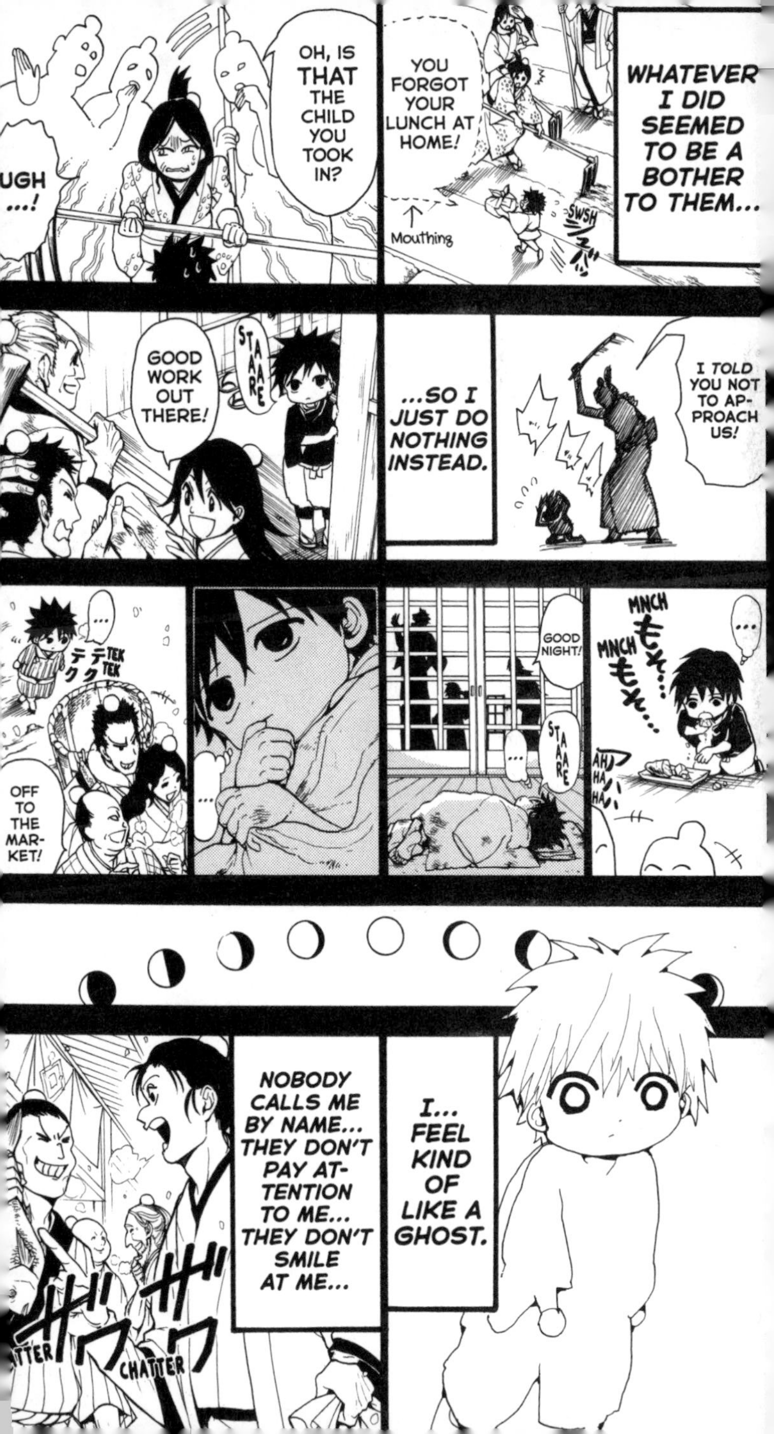
WHATEVER I DID SEEMED TO BE A BOTHER TO THEM...
YOU FORGOT YOUR LUNCH AT HOME!
Mouthing
SWSH
OH, IS THAT THE CHILD YOU TOOK IN?
UGH ...!
I TOLD YOU NOT TO AP-PROACH US!
...SO I JUST DO NOTHING INSTEAD.
STAAARE
GOOD WORK OUT THERE!
...
MNCH
MNCH
AHAHAHA
GOOD NIGHT!
STAAARE
...
...
...
TEK TEK
OFF TO THE MARKET!
I... FEEL KIND OF LIKE A GHOST.
NOBODY CALLS ME BY NAME... THEY DON'T PAY AT-TENTION TO ME... THEY DON'T SMILE AT ME...
CHATTER
CHATTER

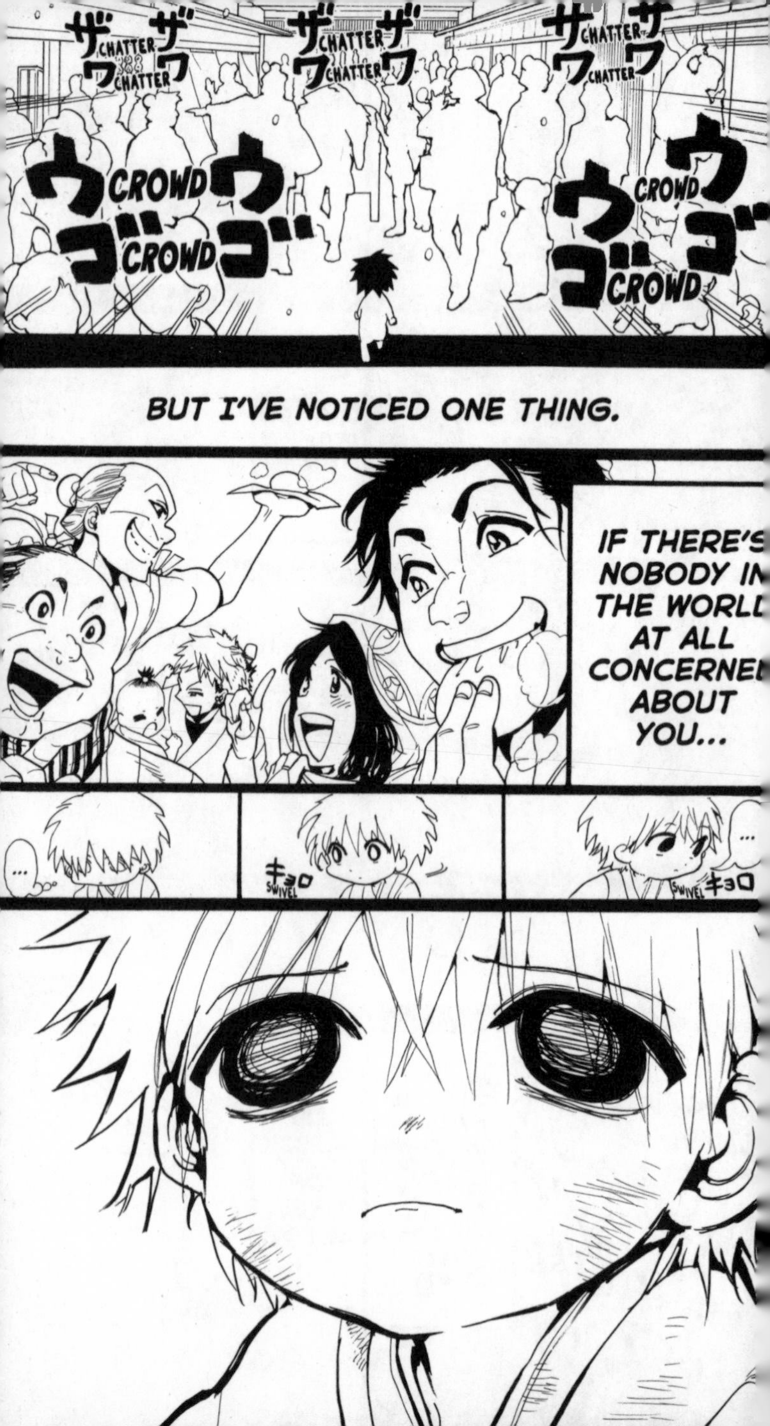
ザワ CHATTER ザワ CHATTER
ザワ CHATTER ザワ CHATTER
ザワ CHATTER ザワ CHATTER
ウゴ CROWD ウゴ CROWD
ウゴ CROWD ウゴ CROWD
BUT I'VE NOTICED ONE THING.
IF THERE'S NOBODY IN THE WORLD AT ALL CONCERNED ABOUT YOU...
...
キョロ SWIVEL
キョロ SWIVEL
...

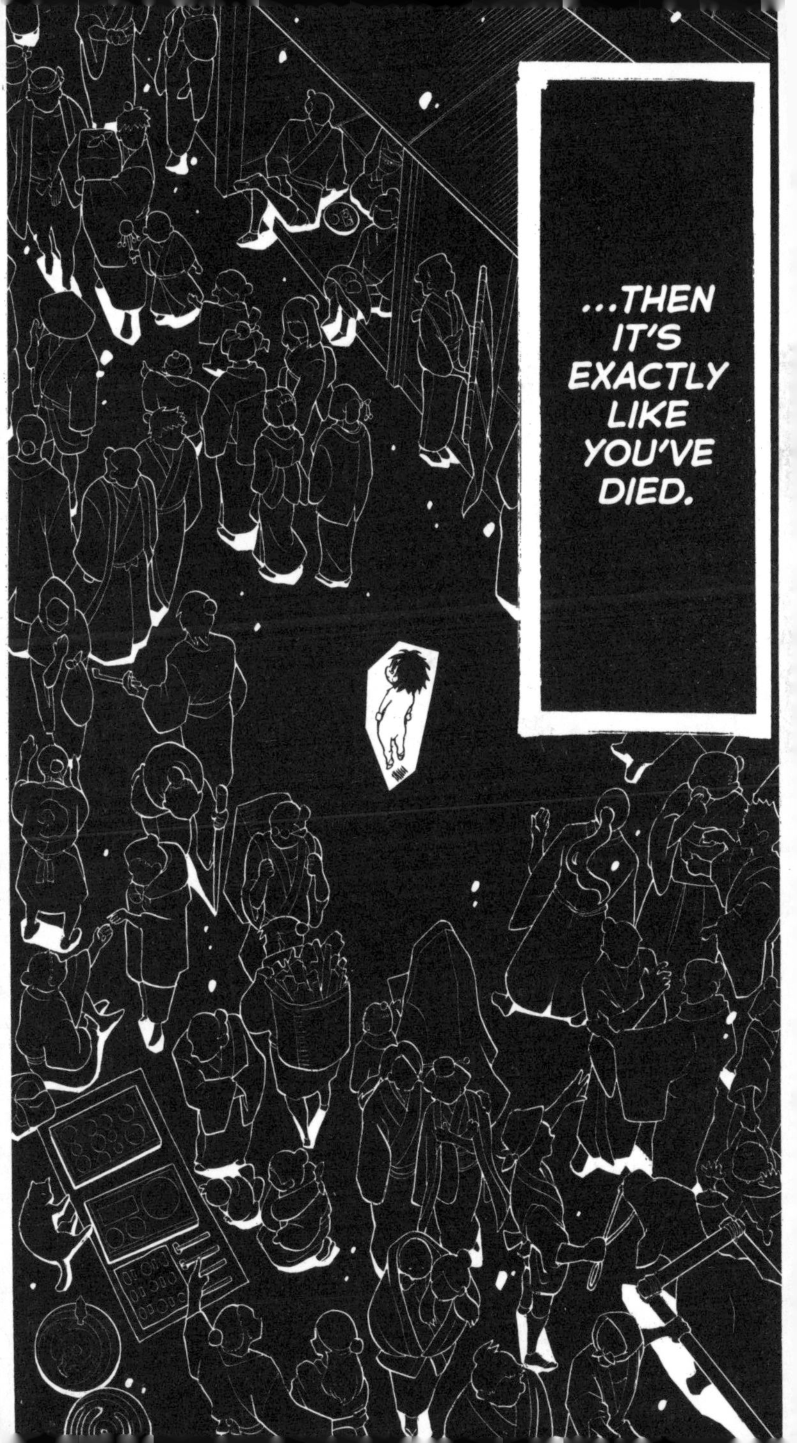
...THEN IT'S EXACTLY LIKE YOU'VE DIED.

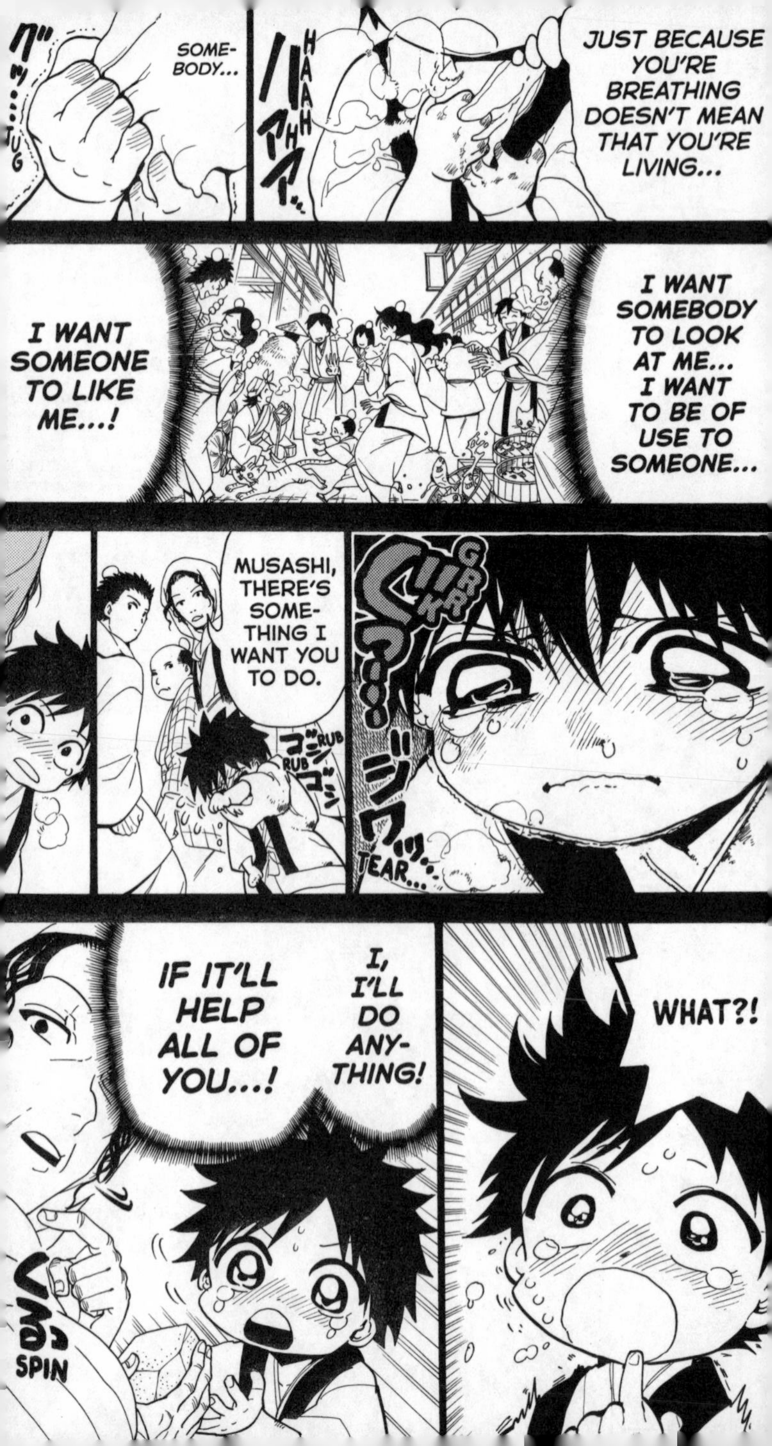
JUST BECAUSE YOU'RE BREATHING DOESN'T MEAN THAT YOU'RE LIVING...
HAAHH
SOME-BODY...
TUG
I WANT SOMEBODY TO LOOK AT ME... I WANT TO BE OF USE TO SOMEONE...
I WANT SOMEONE TO LIKE ME...!
TEAR...
MUSASHI, THERE'S SOME-THING I WANT YOU TO DO.
RUB
RUB
WHAT?!
I, I'LL DO ANY-THING!
IF IT'LL HELP ALL OF YOU...!
SPIN

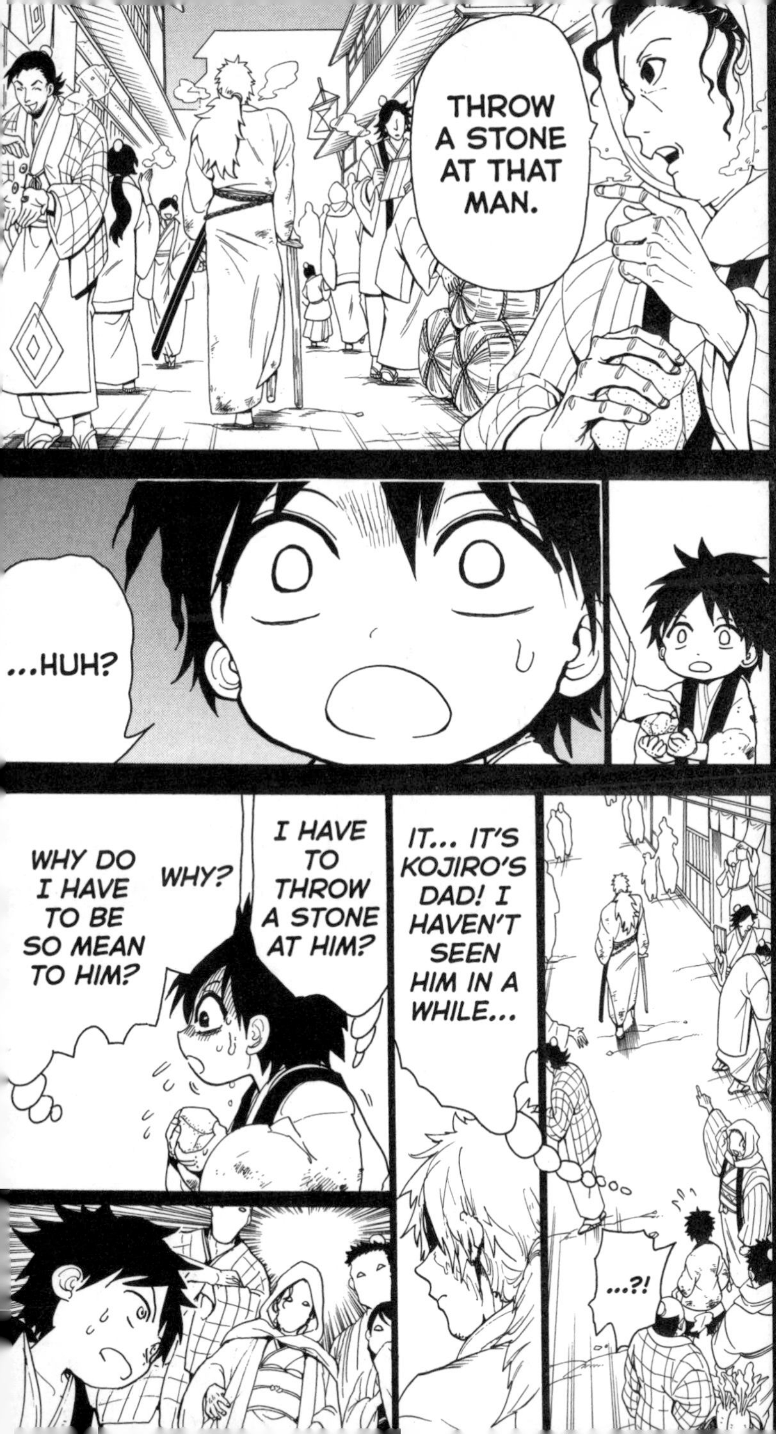
THROW A STONE AT THAT MAN.
...HUH?
...?!
IT... IT'S KOJIRO'S DAD! I HAVEN'T SEEN HIM IN A WHILE...
I HAVE TO THROW A STONE AT HIM?
WHY?
WHY DO I HAVE TO BE SO MEAN TO HIM?

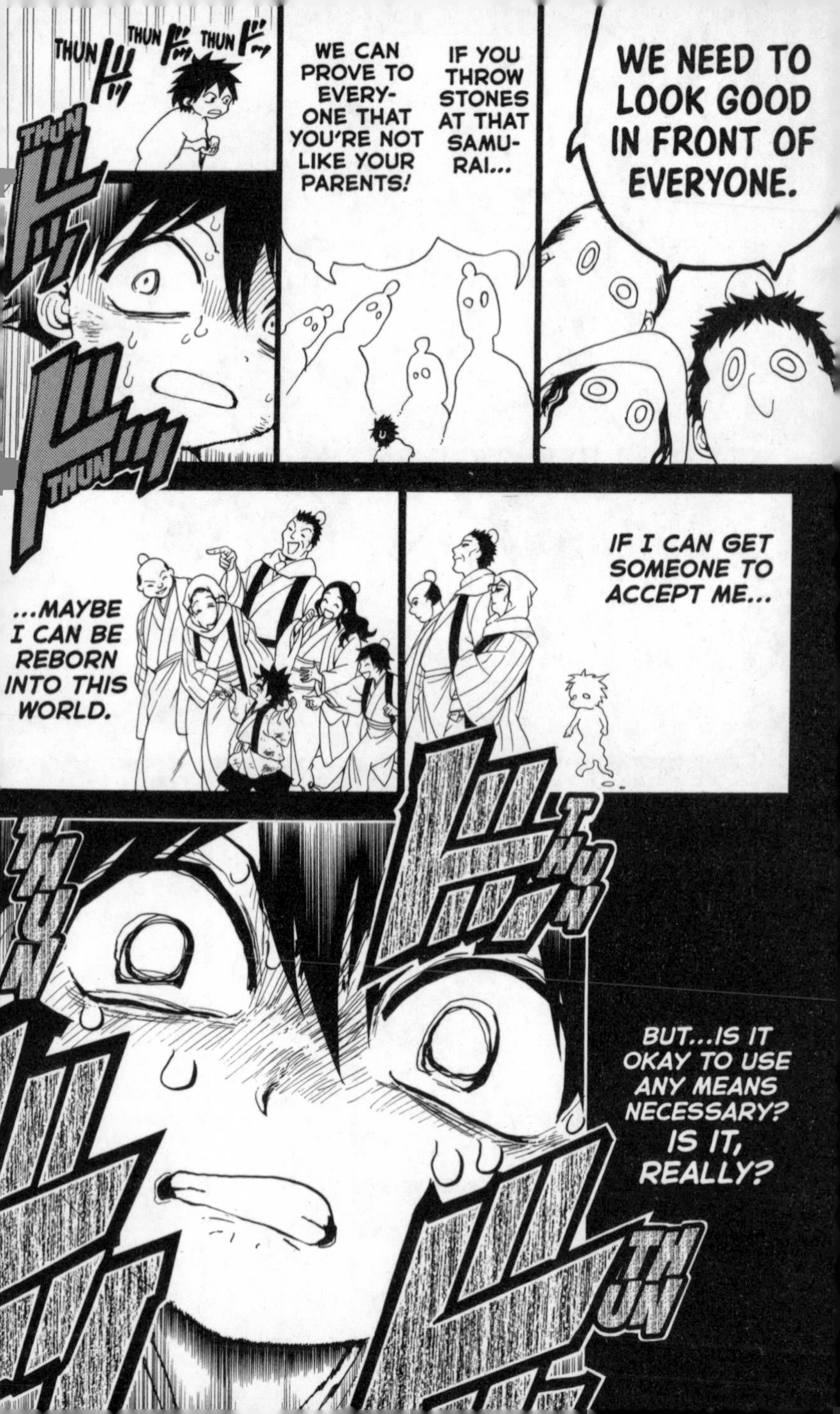
WE NEED TO LOOK GOOD IN FRONT OF EVERYONE.
IF YOU THROW STONES AT THAT SAMURAI...
WE CAN PROVE TO EVERYONE THAT YOU'RE NOT LIKE YOUR PARENTS!
THUN
THUN
THUN
THUN
THUN
IF I CAN GET SOMEONE TO ACCEPT ME...
...MAYBE I CAN BE REBORN INTO THIS WORLD.
THUN
THUN
BUT...IS IT OKAY TO USE ANY MEANS NECESSARY? IS IT, REALLY?
THUN

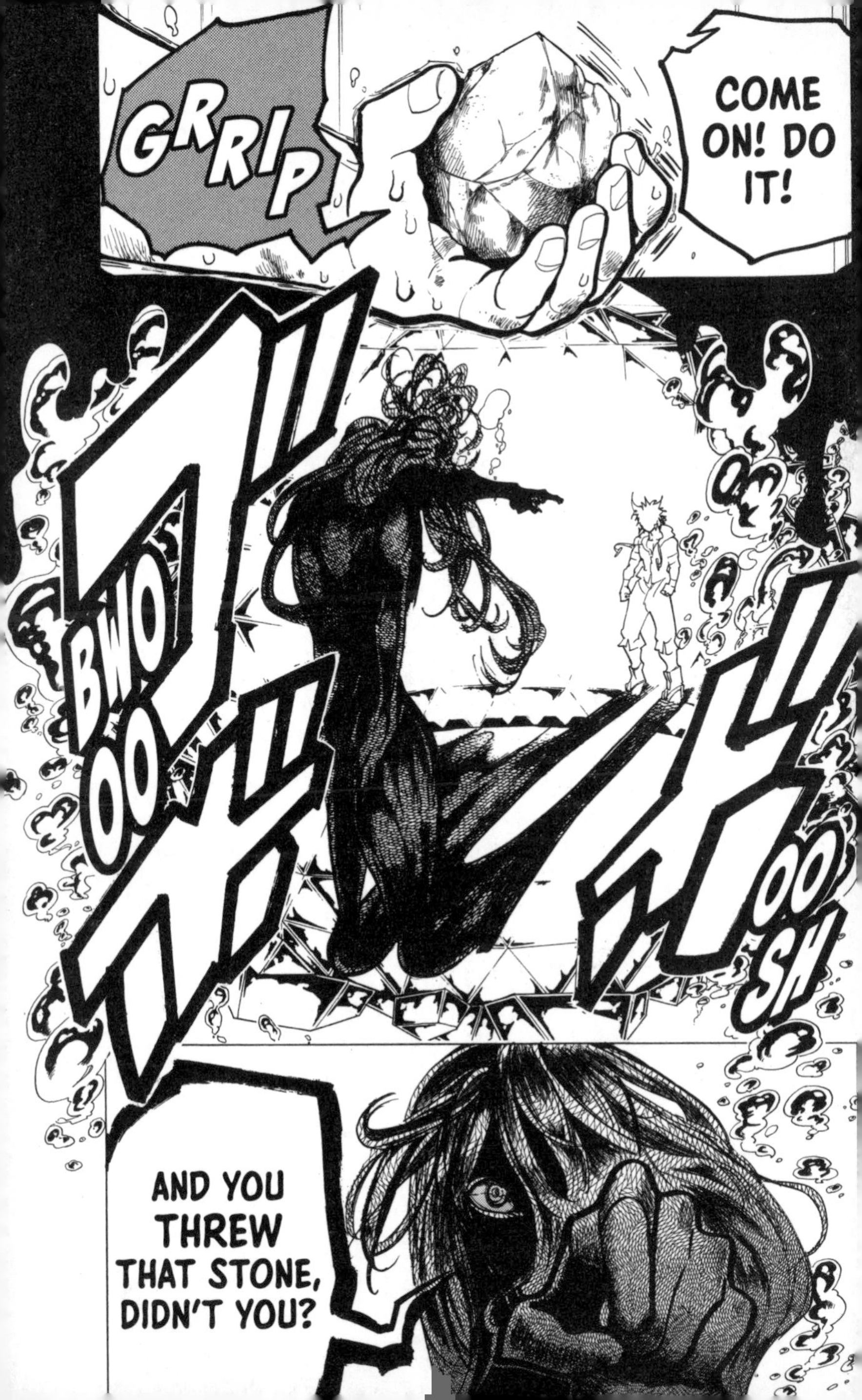
COME ON! DO IT!
GRRIP
BWOOO
OOSH
AND YOU THREW THAT STONE, DIDN'T YOU?

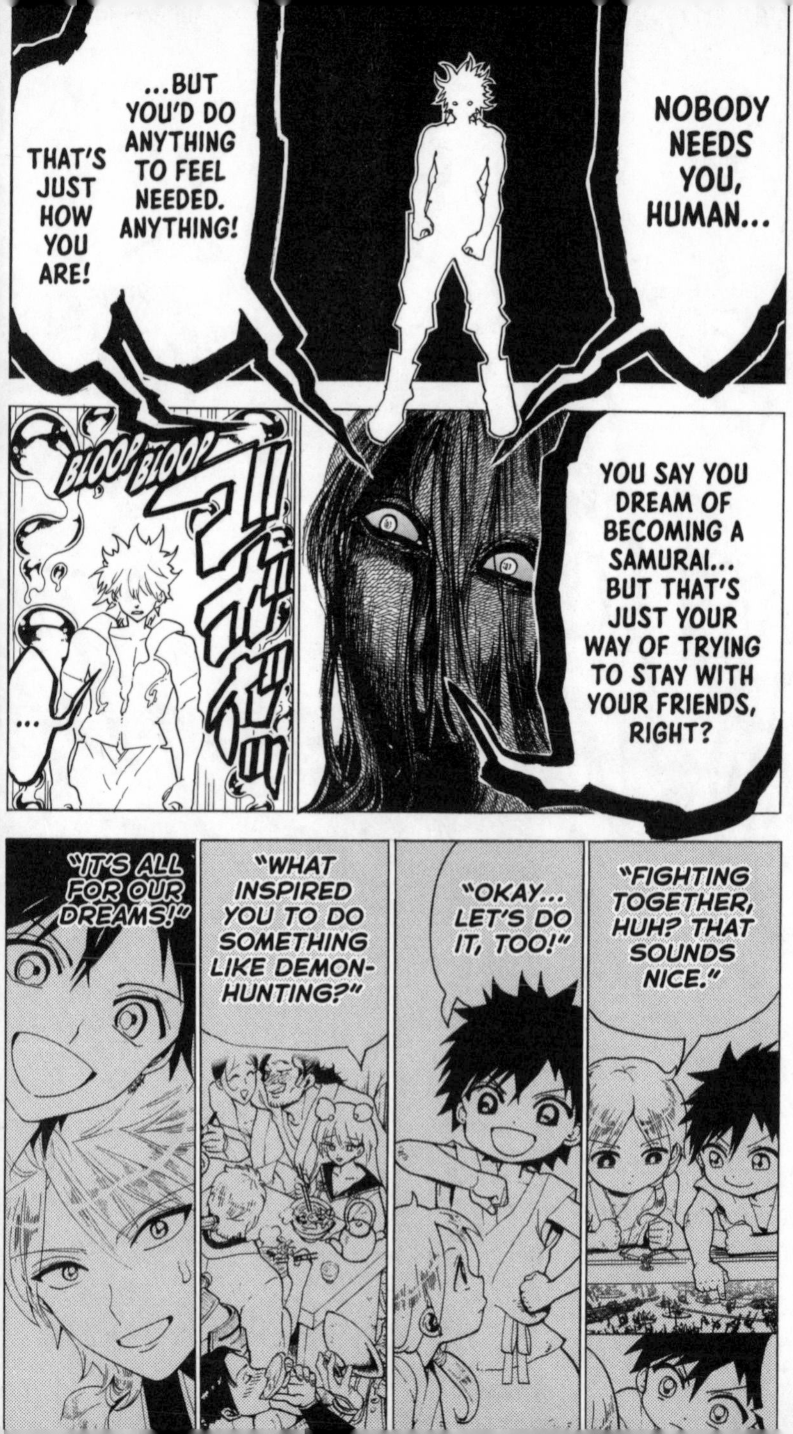
NOBODY NEEDS YOU, HUMAN...
...BUT YOU'D DO ANYTHING TO FEEL NEEDED. ANYTHING!
THAT'S JUST HOW YOU ARE!
YOU SAY YOU DREAM OF BECOMING A SAMURAI... BUT THAT'S JUST YOUR WAY OF TRYING TO STAY WITH YOUR FRIENDS, RIGHT?
BLOOP BLOOP
...
"FIGHTING TOGETHER, HUH? THAT SOUNDS NICE."
"OKAY... LET'S DO IT, TOO!"
"WHAT INSPIRED YOU TO DO SOMETHING LIKE DEMON-HUNTING?"
"IT'S ALL FOR OUR DREAMS!"

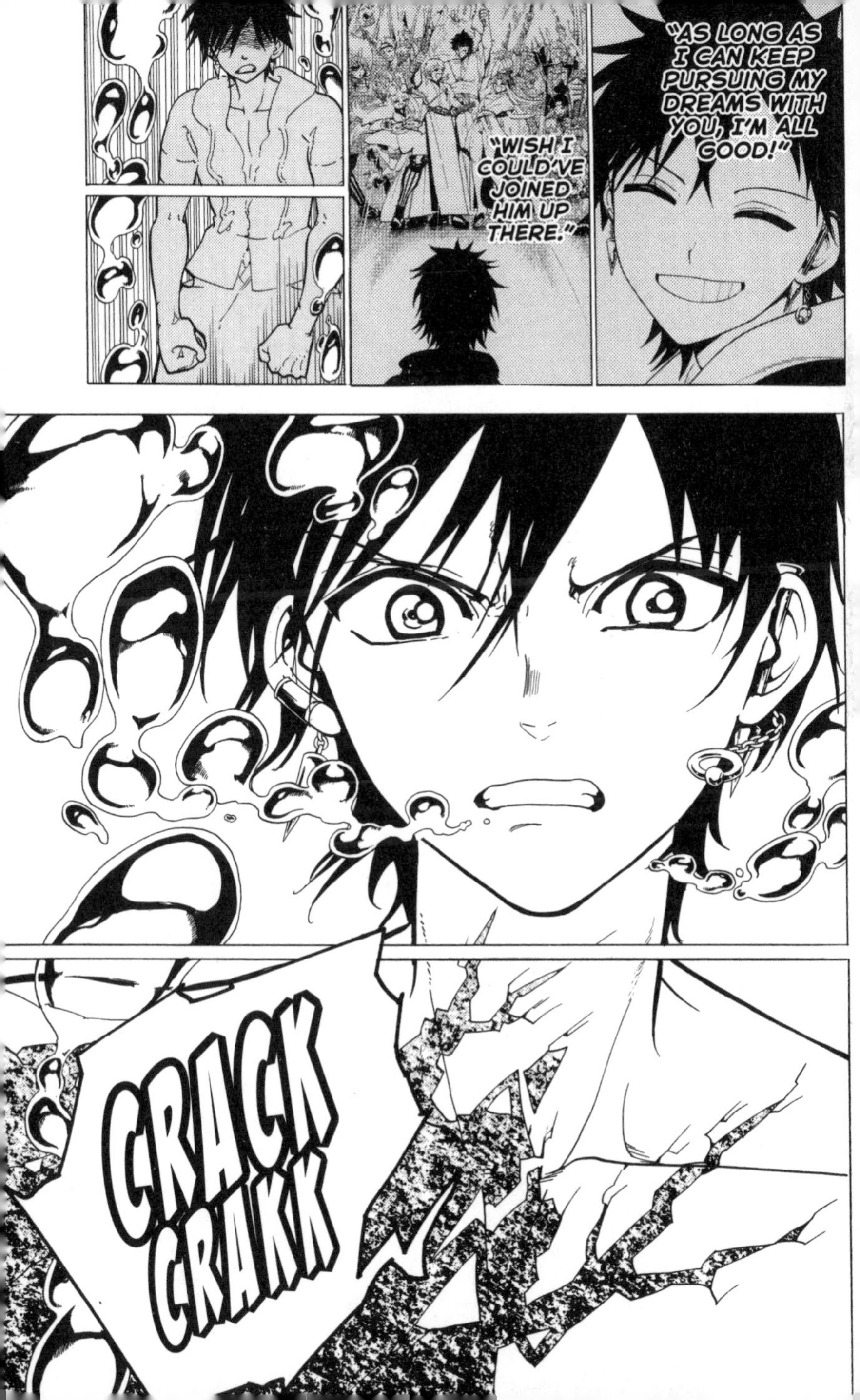
"AS LONG AS I CAN KEEP PURSUING MY DREAMS WITH YOU, I'M ALL GOOD!"
"WISH I COULD'VE JOINED HIM UP THERE."
CRACK CRAKK

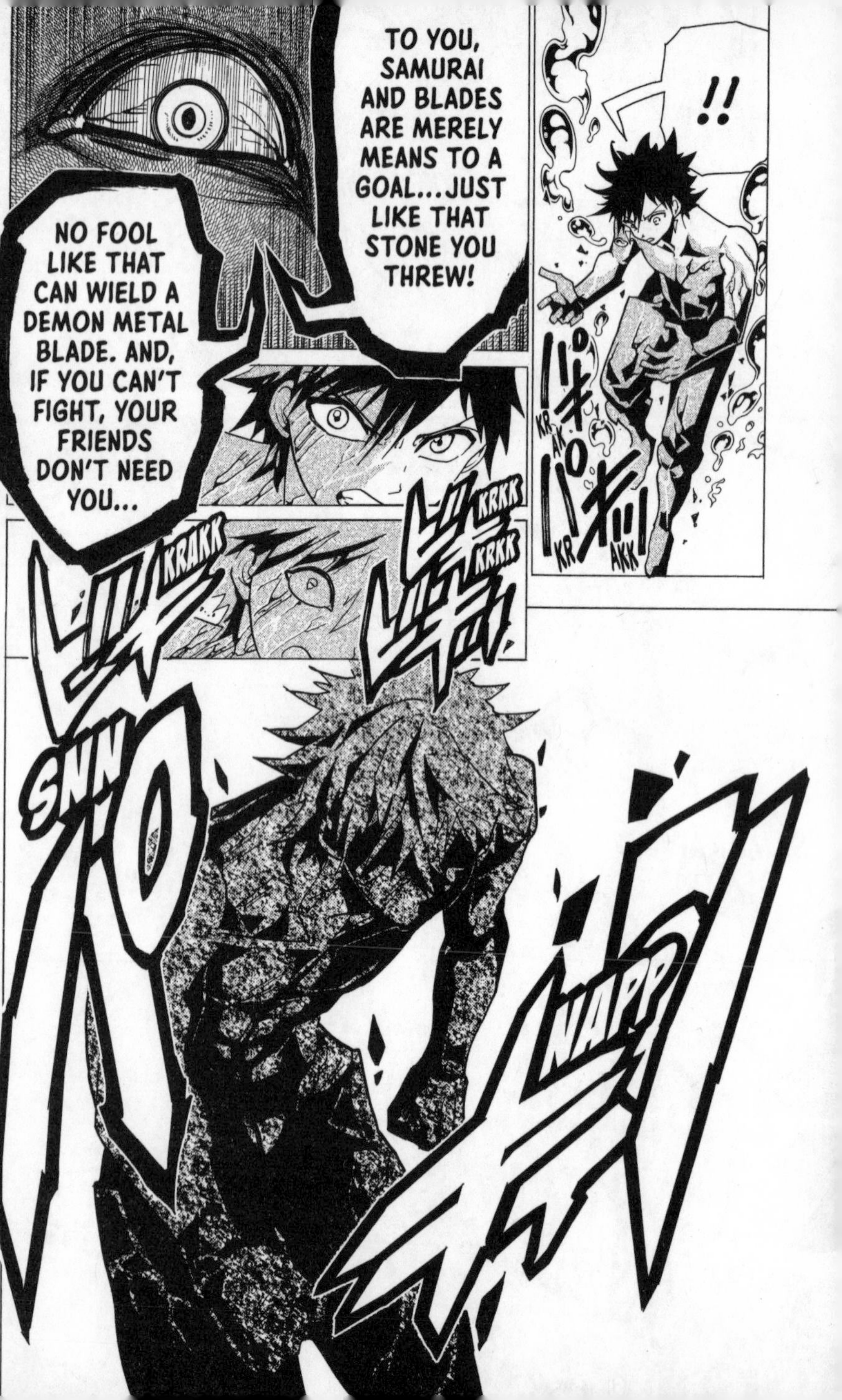
!!
KR AK
KR AKK
TO YOU, SAMURAI AND BLADES ARE MERELY MEANS TO A GOAL...JUST LIKE THAT STONE YOU THREW!
NO FOOL LIKE THAT CAN WIELD A DEMON METAL BLADE. AND, IF YOU CAN'T FIGHT, YOUR FRIENDS DON'T NEED YOU...
KRKK
KRKK
KRAKK
SNAPP
SNN

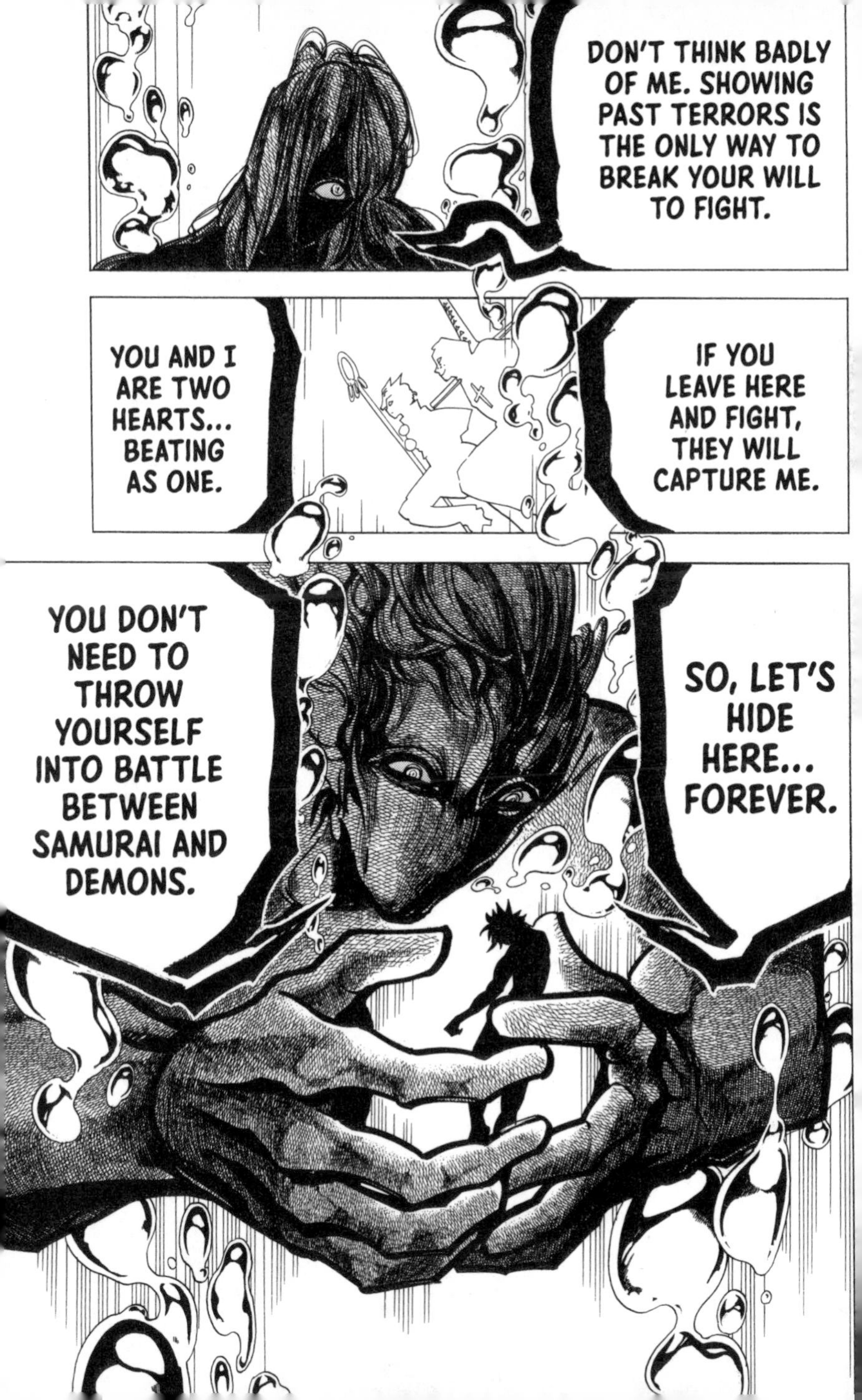
DON'T THINK BADLY OF ME. SHOWING PAST TERRORS IS THE ONLY WAY TO BREAK YOUR WILL TO FIGHT.
IF YOU LEAVE HERE AND FIGHT, THEY WILL CAPTURE ME.
YOU AND I ARE TWO HEARTS... BEATING AS ONE.
SO, LET'S HIDE HERE... FOREVER.
YOU DON'T NEED TO THROW YOURSELF INTO BATTLE BETWEEN SAMURAI AND DEMONS.

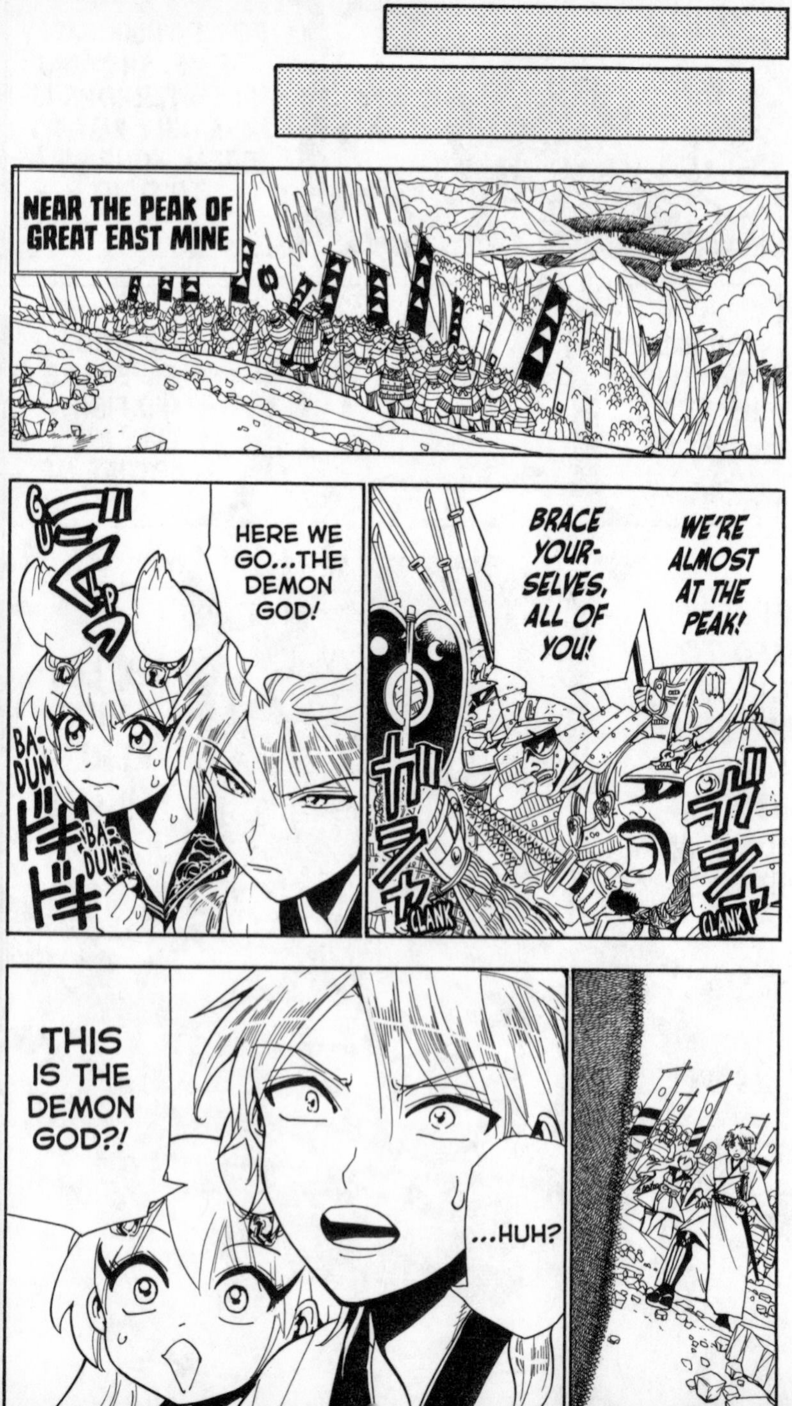
NEAR THE PEAK OF GREAT EAST MINE
WE'RE ALMOST AT THE PEAK!
BRACE YOURSELVES, ALL OF YOU!
CLANK
CLANK
HERE WE GO...THE DEMON GOD!
BA-DUM
BA-DUM
THIS IS THE DEMON GOD?!
...HUH?

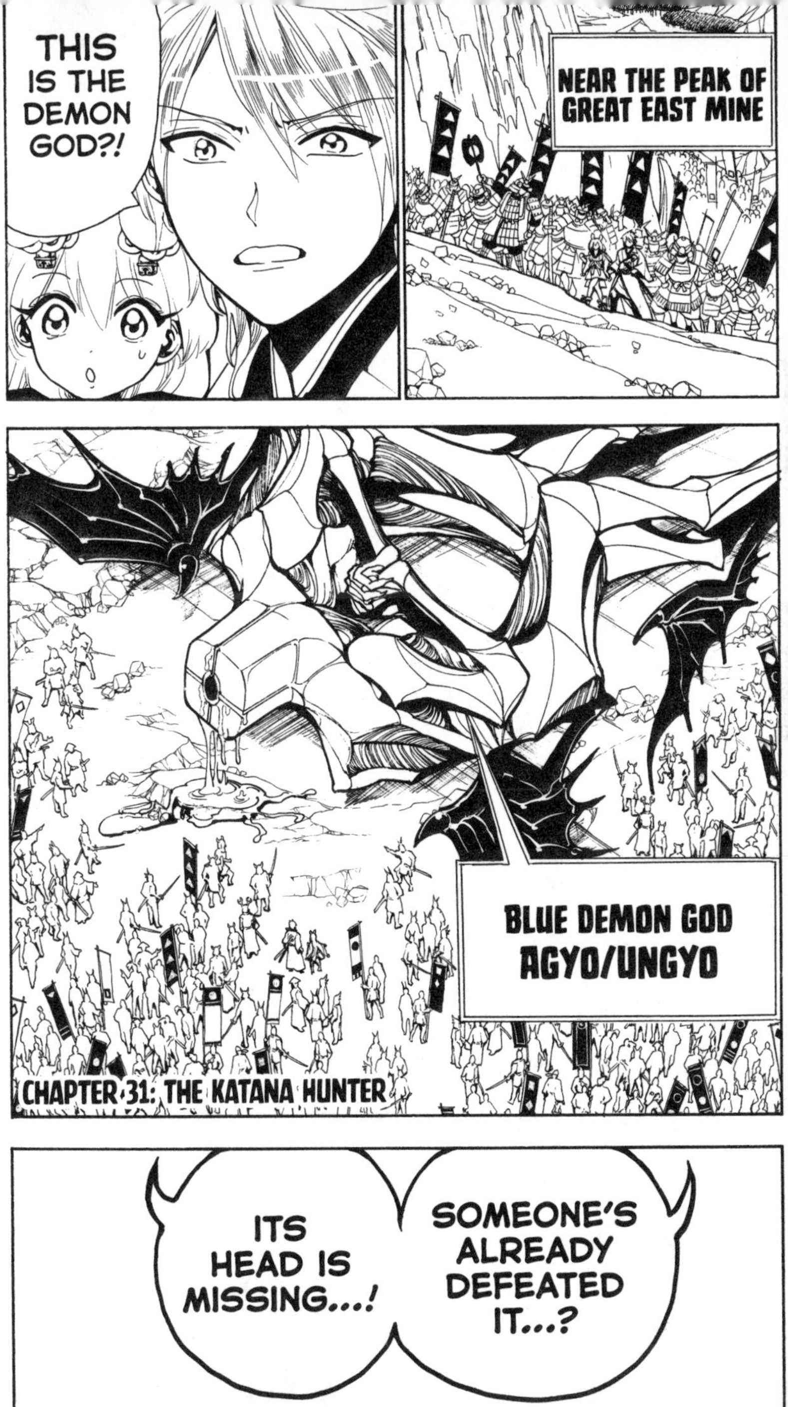
NEAR THE PEAK OF GREAT EAST MINE
THIS IS THE DEMON GOD?!
BLUE DEMON GOD AGYO/UNGYO
CHAPTER 31: THE KATANA HUNTER
SOMEONE'S ALREADY DEFEATED IT...?
ITS HEAD IS MISSING...!

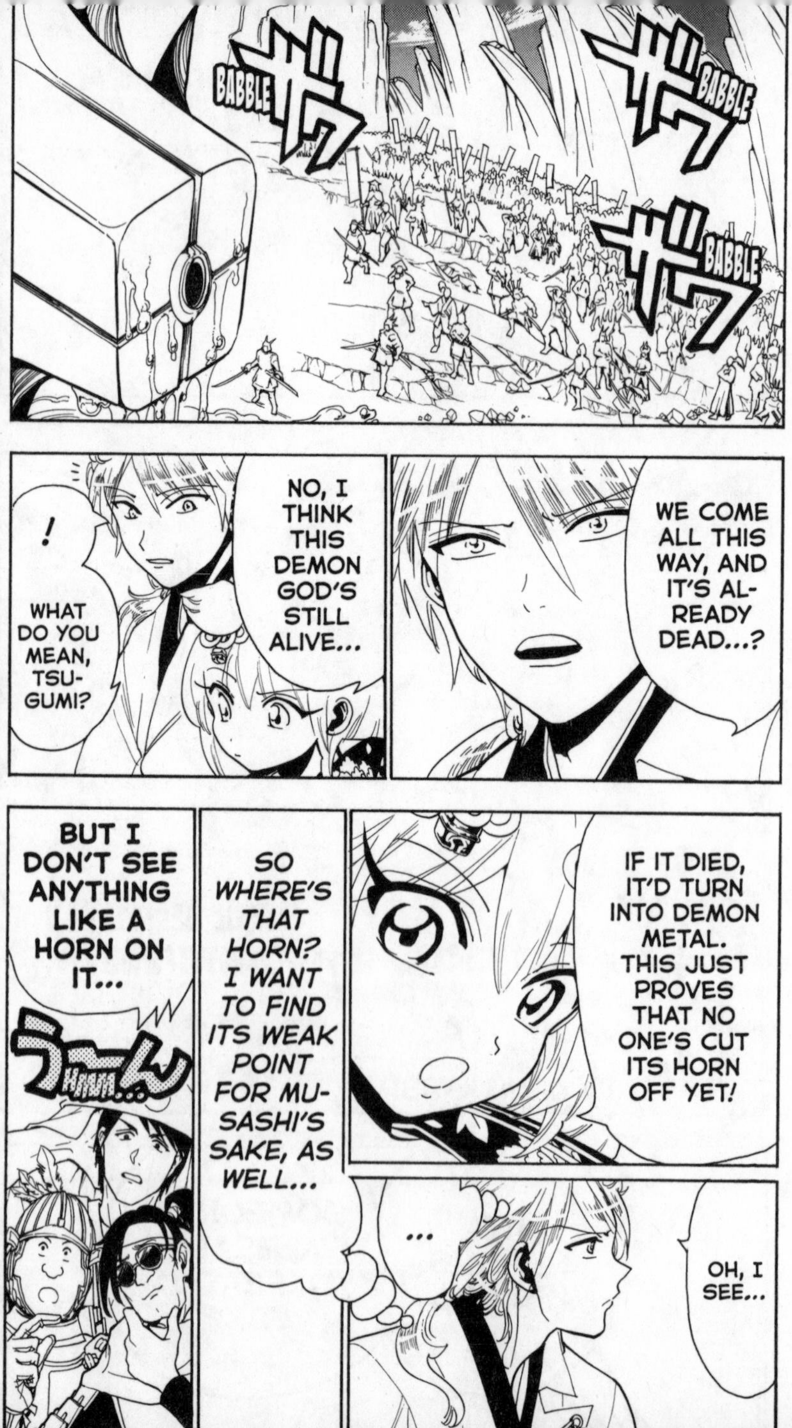
ザワ BABBLE
ザワ BABBLE
BABBLE ザワ
WE COME ALL THIS WAY, AND IT'S ALREADY DEAD...?
NO, I THINK THIS DEMON GOD'S STILL ALIVE...
!
WHAT DO YOU MEAN, TSUGUMI?
IF IT DIED, IT'D TURN INTO DEMON METAL. THIS JUST PROVES THAT NO ONE'S CUT ITS HORN OFF YET!
OH, I SEE...
...
SO *WHERE'S* THAT HORN? I WANT TO FIND ITS WEAK POINT FOR MUSASHI'S SAKE, AS WELL...
BUT I DON'T SEE ANYTHING LIKE A HORN ON IT...
うーん HMMM...

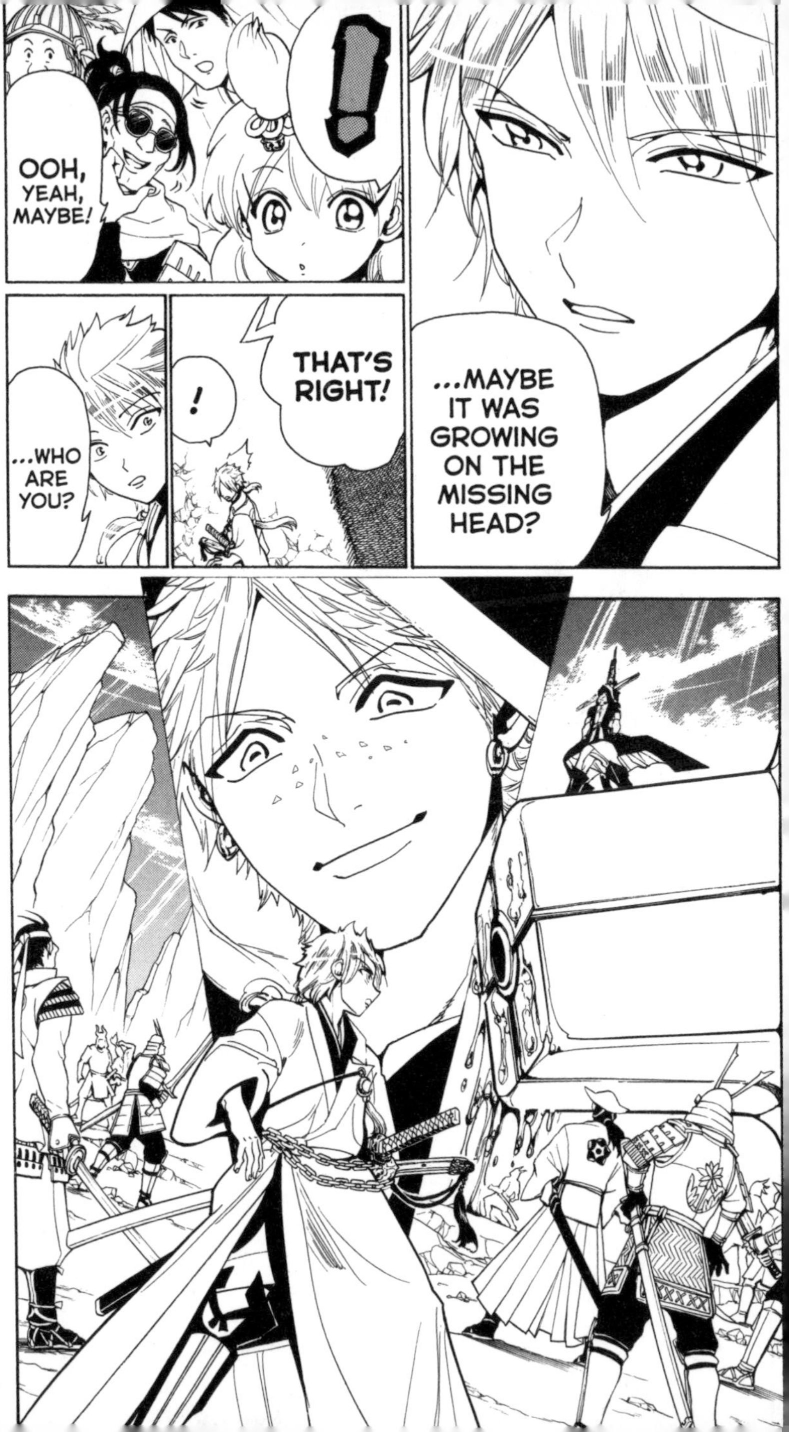
...MAYBE IT WAS GROWING ON THE MISSING HEAD?
!
OOH, YEAH, MAYBE!
THAT'S RIGHT!
!
...WHO ARE YOU?

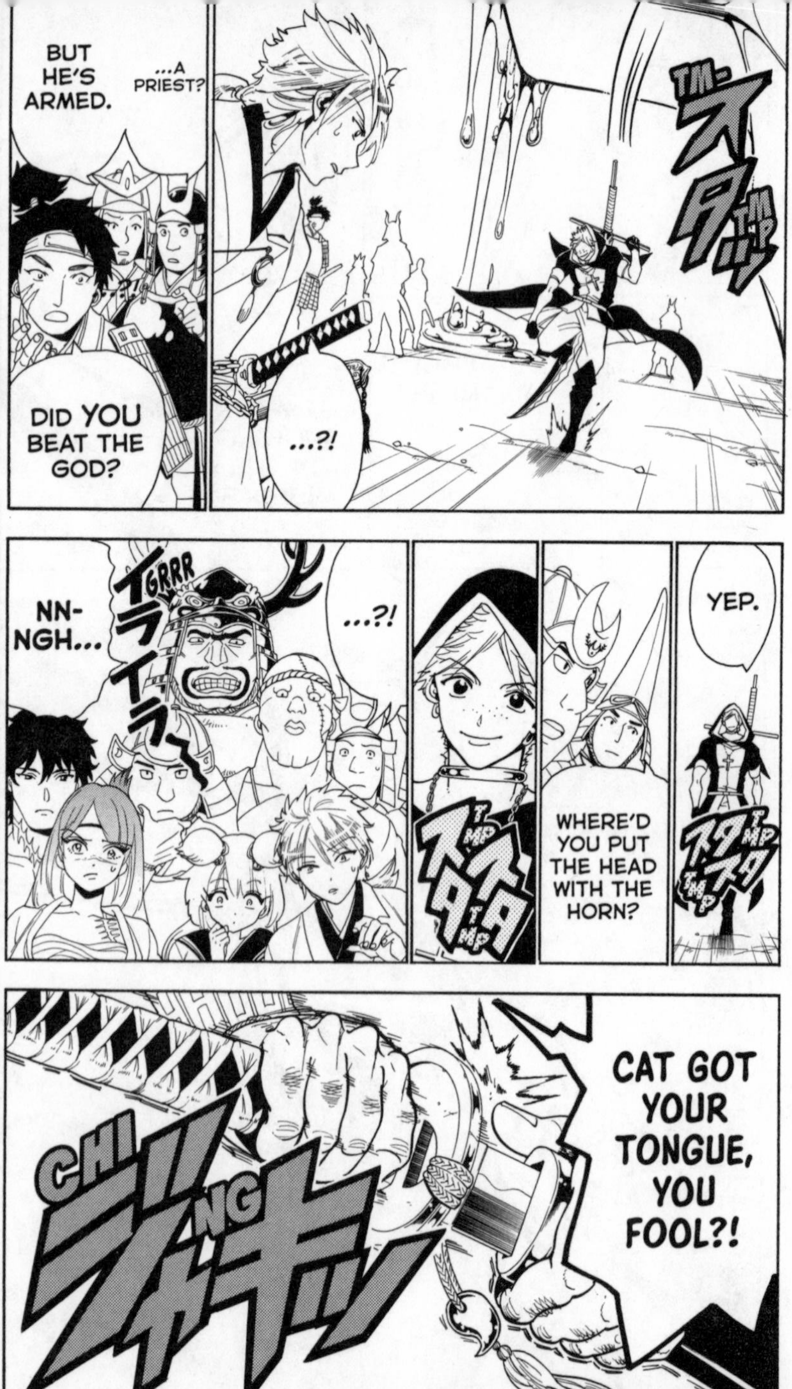
TM-
TMP
...?!
...A PRIEST?
BUT HE'S ARMED.
DID YOU BEAT THE GOD?
YEP.
TMP
WHERE'D YOU PUT THE HEAD WITH THE HORN?
TMP
...?!
GRRR
NN-NGH...
CAT GOT YOUR TONGUE, YOU FOOL?!
CHI
NG

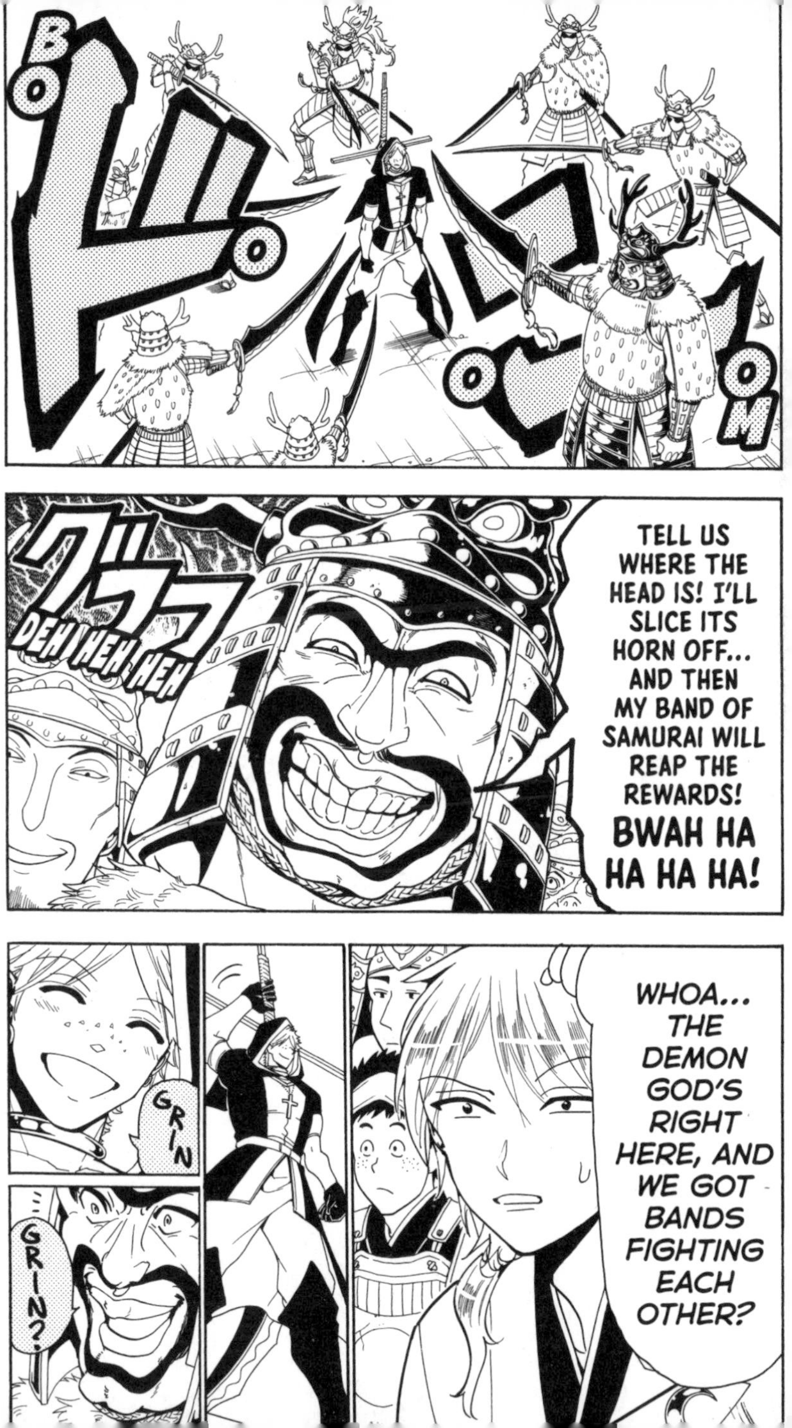
BOOOOM
DEH HEH HEH
TELL US WHERE THE HEAD IS! I'LL SLICE ITS HORN OFF... AND THEN MY BAND OF SAMURAI WILL REAP THE REWARDS! BWAH HA HA HA HA!
WHOA... THE DEMON GOD'S RIGHT HERE, AND WE GOT BANDS FIGHTING EACH OTHER?
GRIN
...GRIN?!

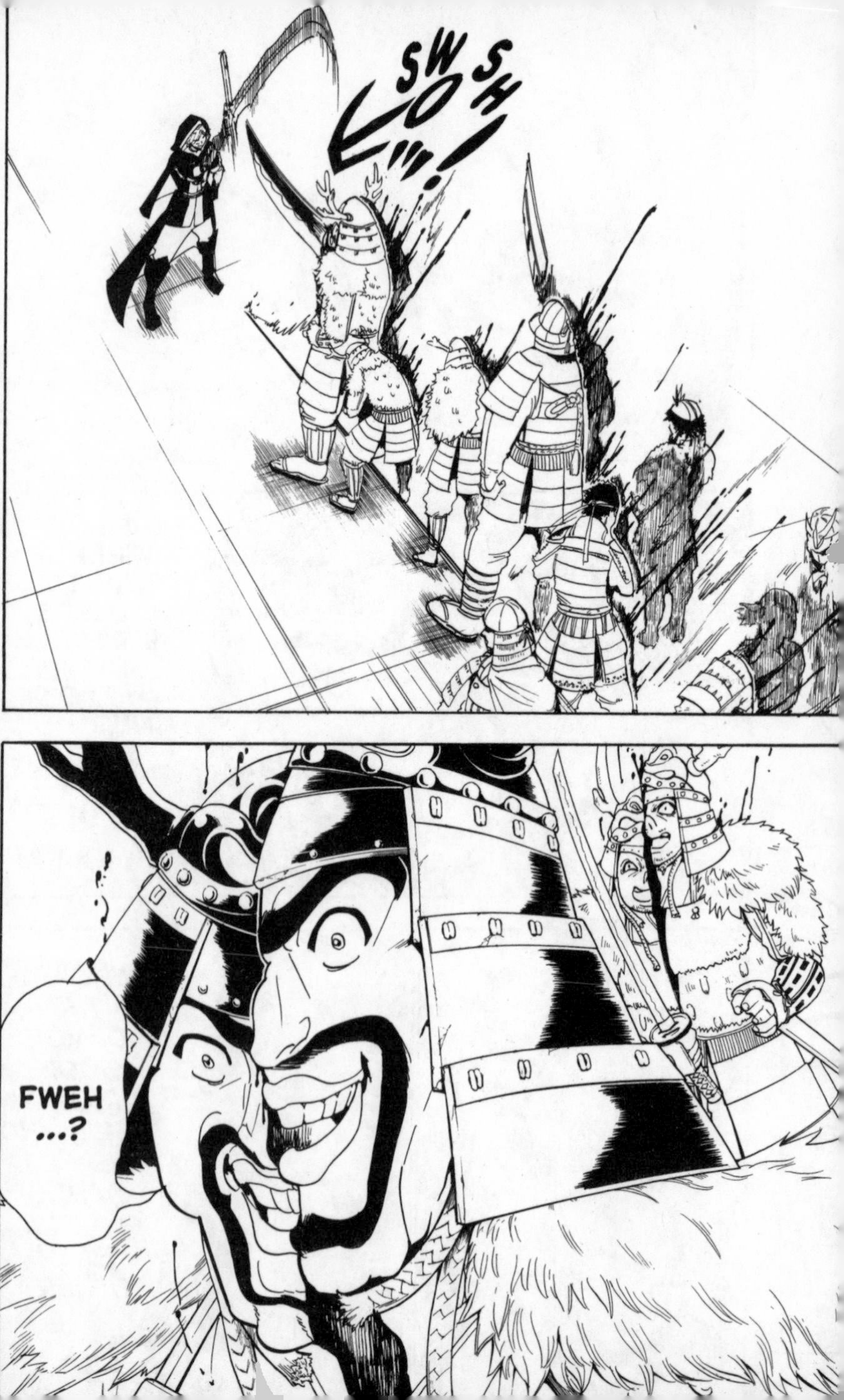
SWOSH!
FWEH ...?

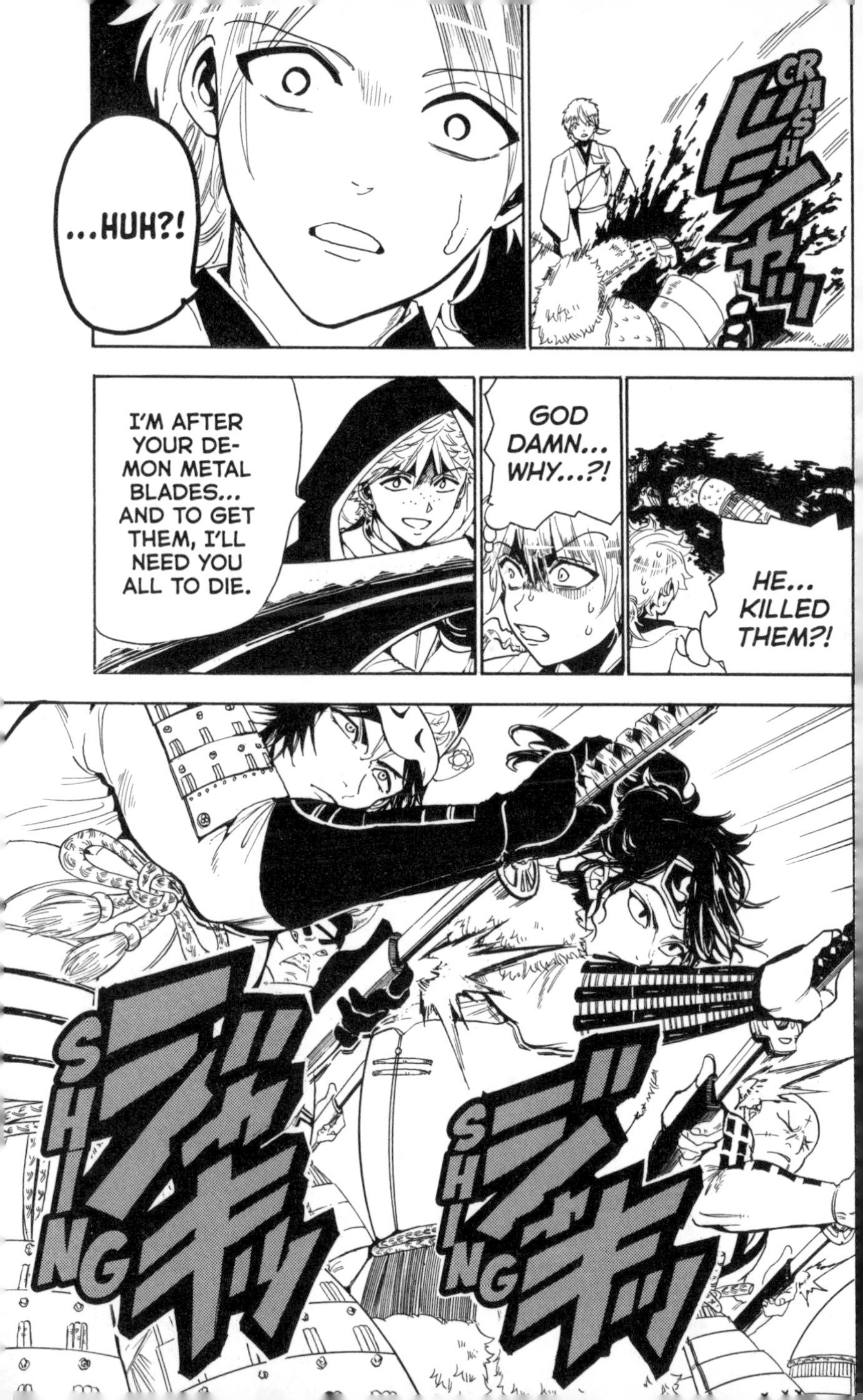
CRASH
...HUH?!
HE... KILLED THEM?!
GOD DAMN... WHY...?!
I'M AFTER YOUR DEMON METAL BLADES... AND TO GET THEM, I'LL NEED YOU ALL TO DIE.
SHING
SHING

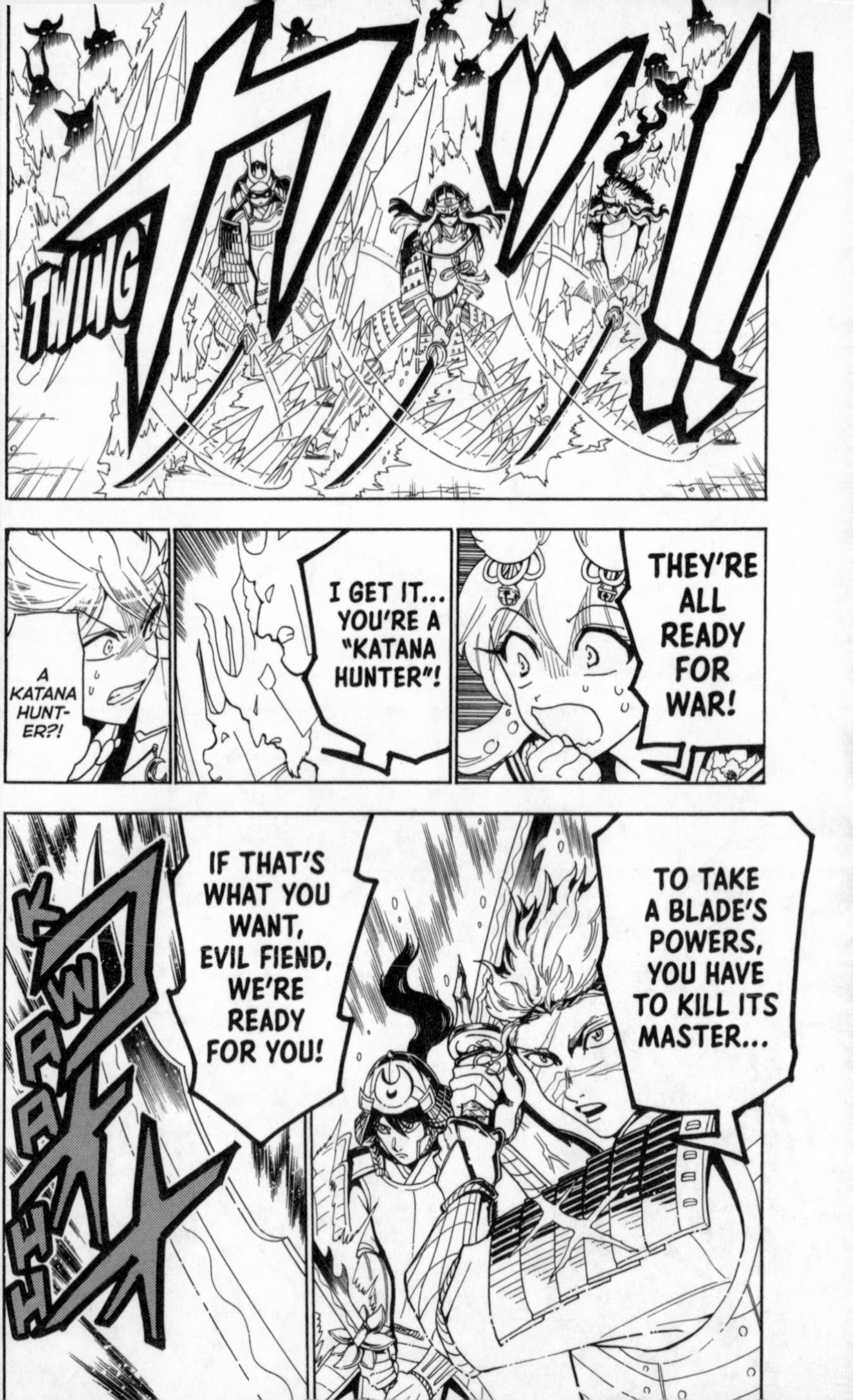

TWING
THEY'RE ALL READY FOR WAR!
I GET IT... YOU'RE A "KATANA HUNTER"!
A KATANA HUNT-ER?!
TO TAKE A BLADE'S POWERS, YOU HAVE TO KILL ITS MASTER...
IF THAT'S WHAT YOU WANT, EVIL FIEND, WE'RE READY FOR YOU!
KWAAHHH

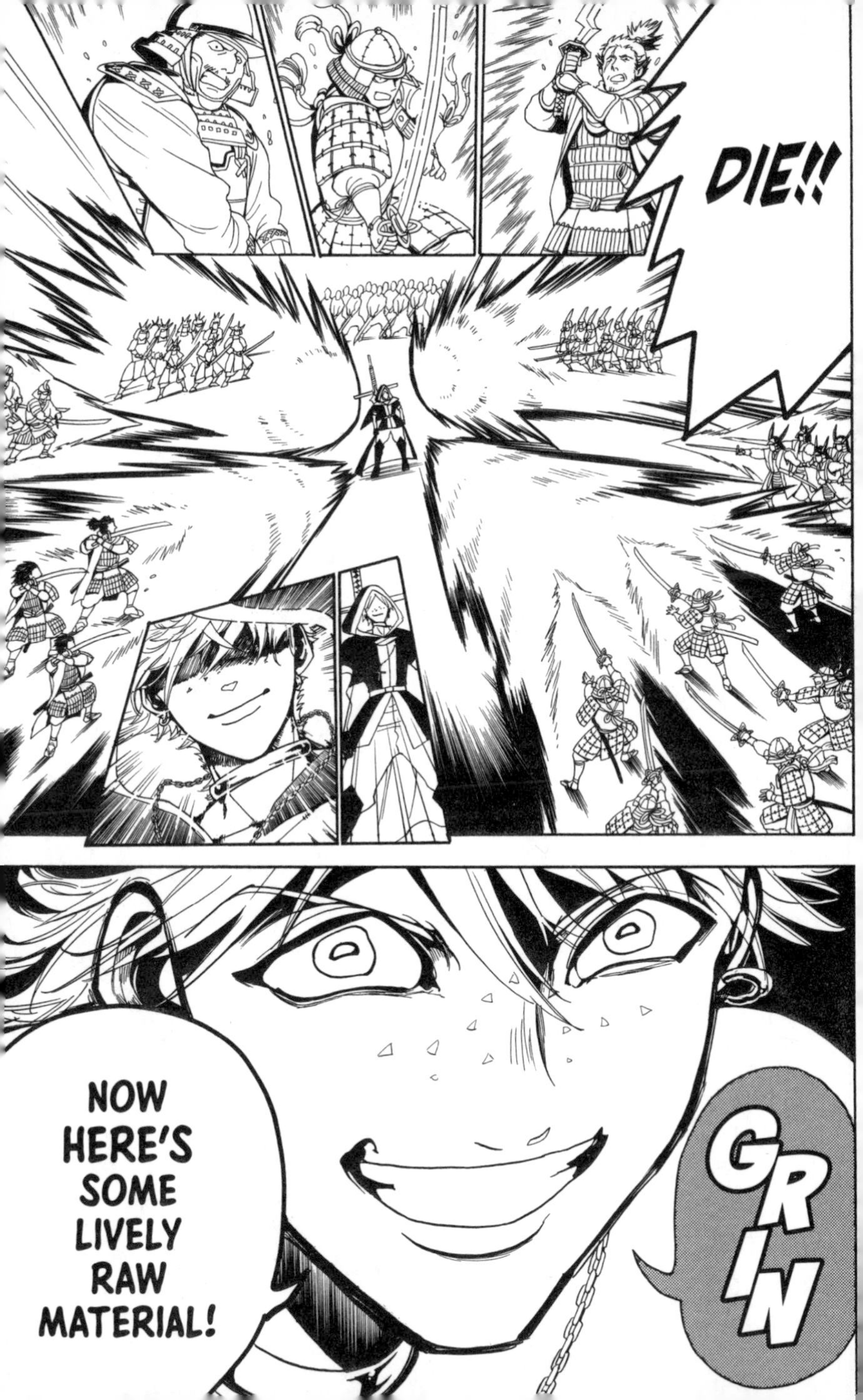
DIE!!
NOW HERE'S SOME LIVELY RAW MATERIAL!
GRIN

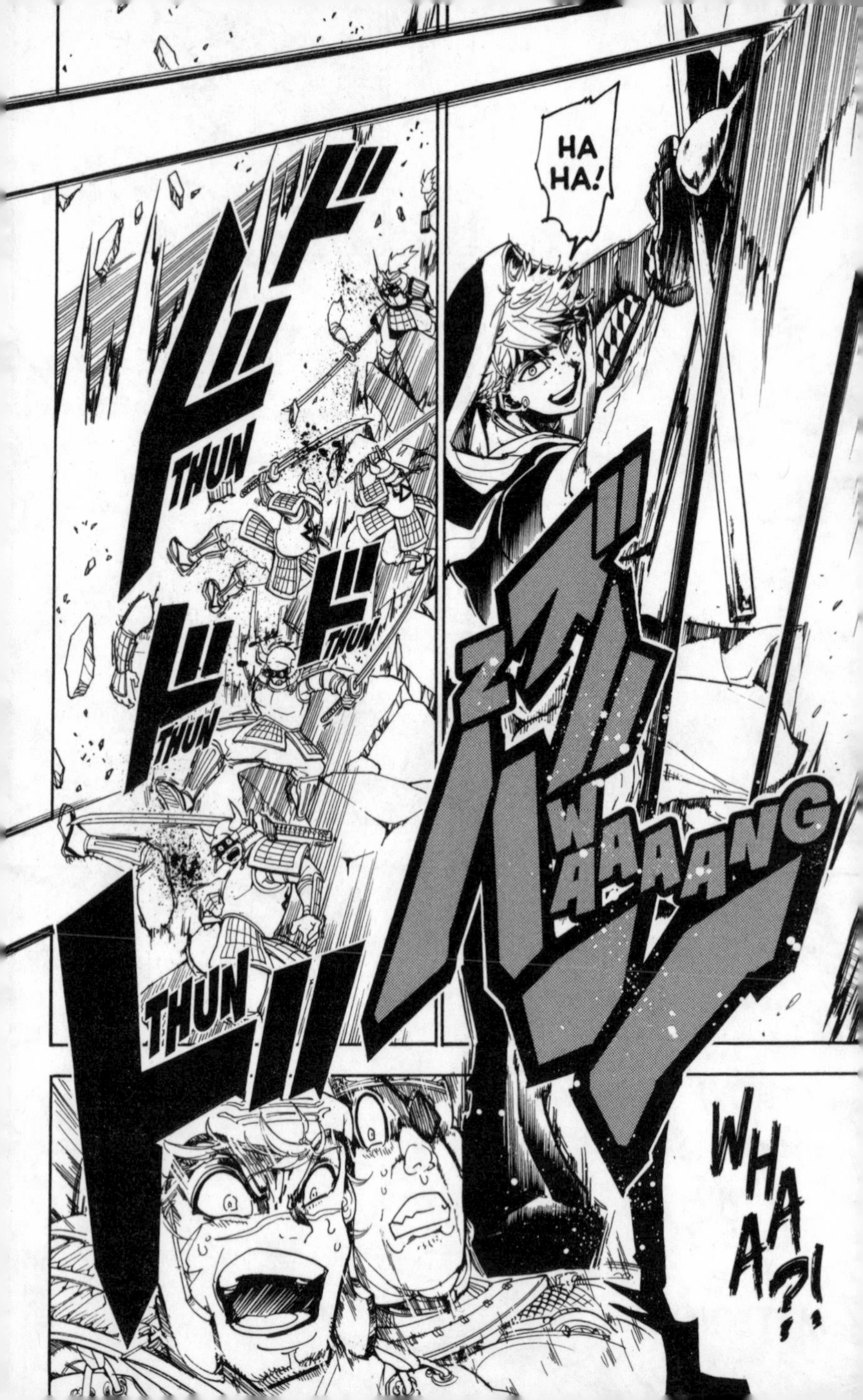
HA HA!
Z
WAAAANG
THUN
THUN
THUN
THUN
WHAAA?!

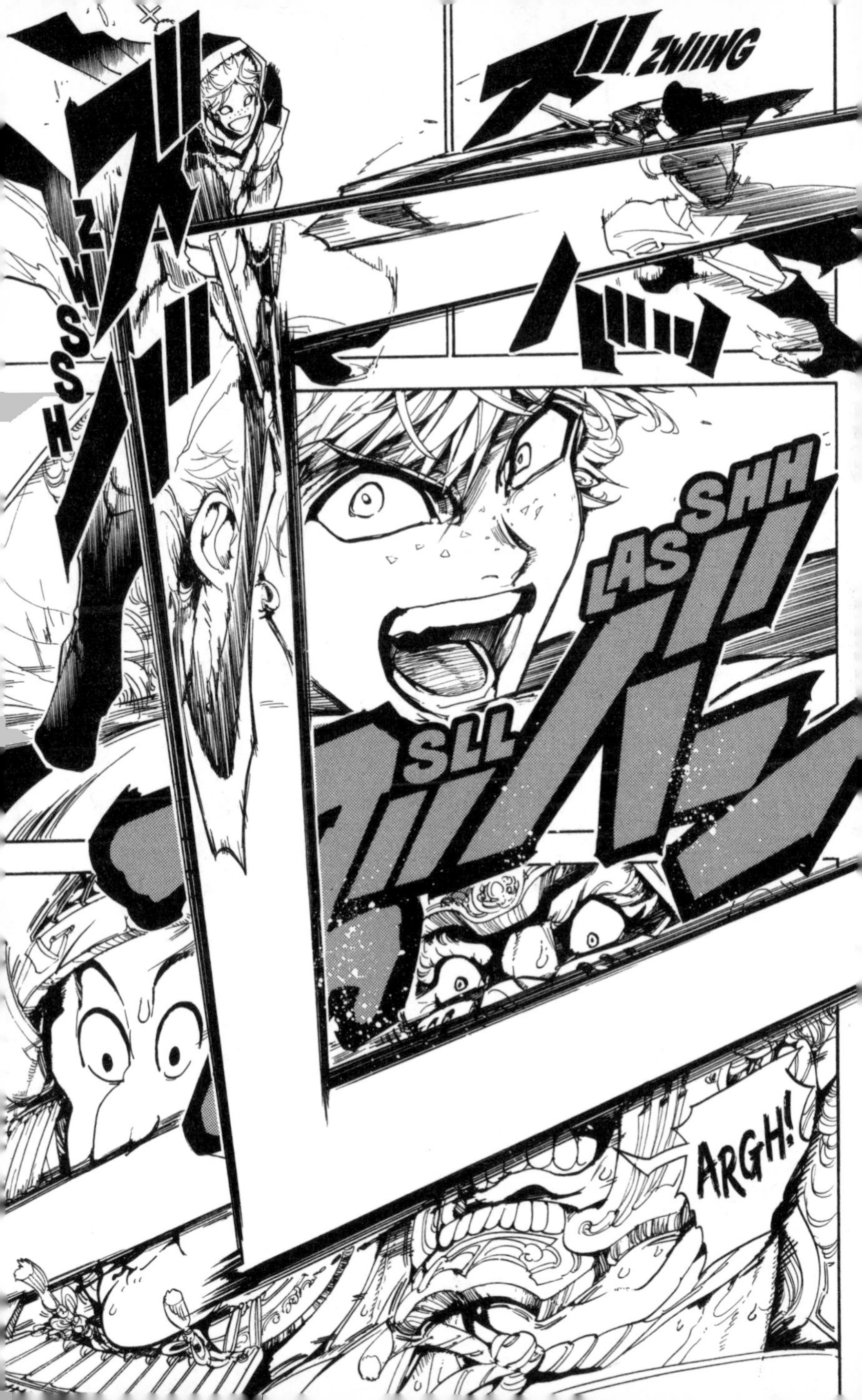
ZWIING
ZWSSH
SLLLASSHH
ARGH!

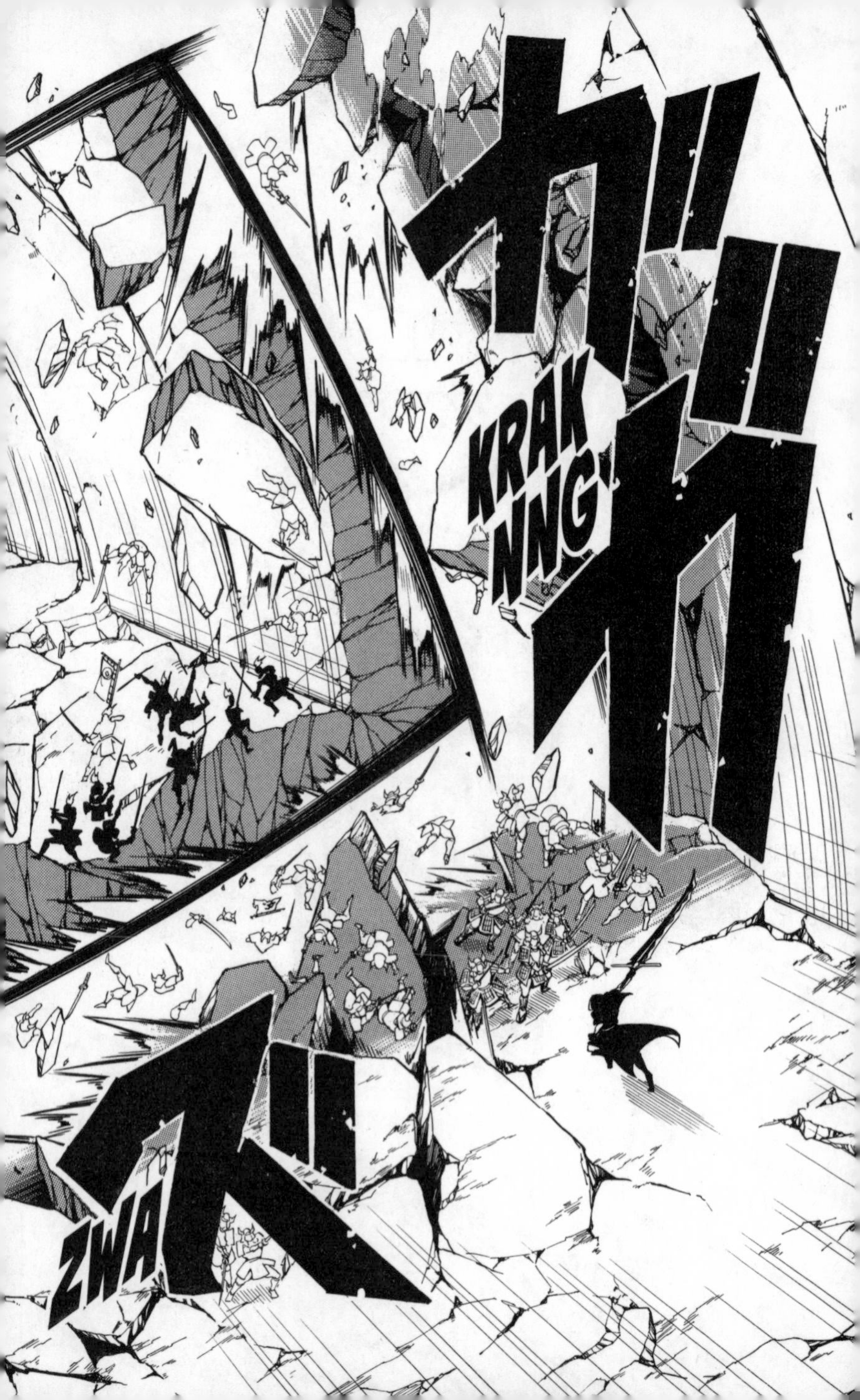
KRAK NNG!
ZWA

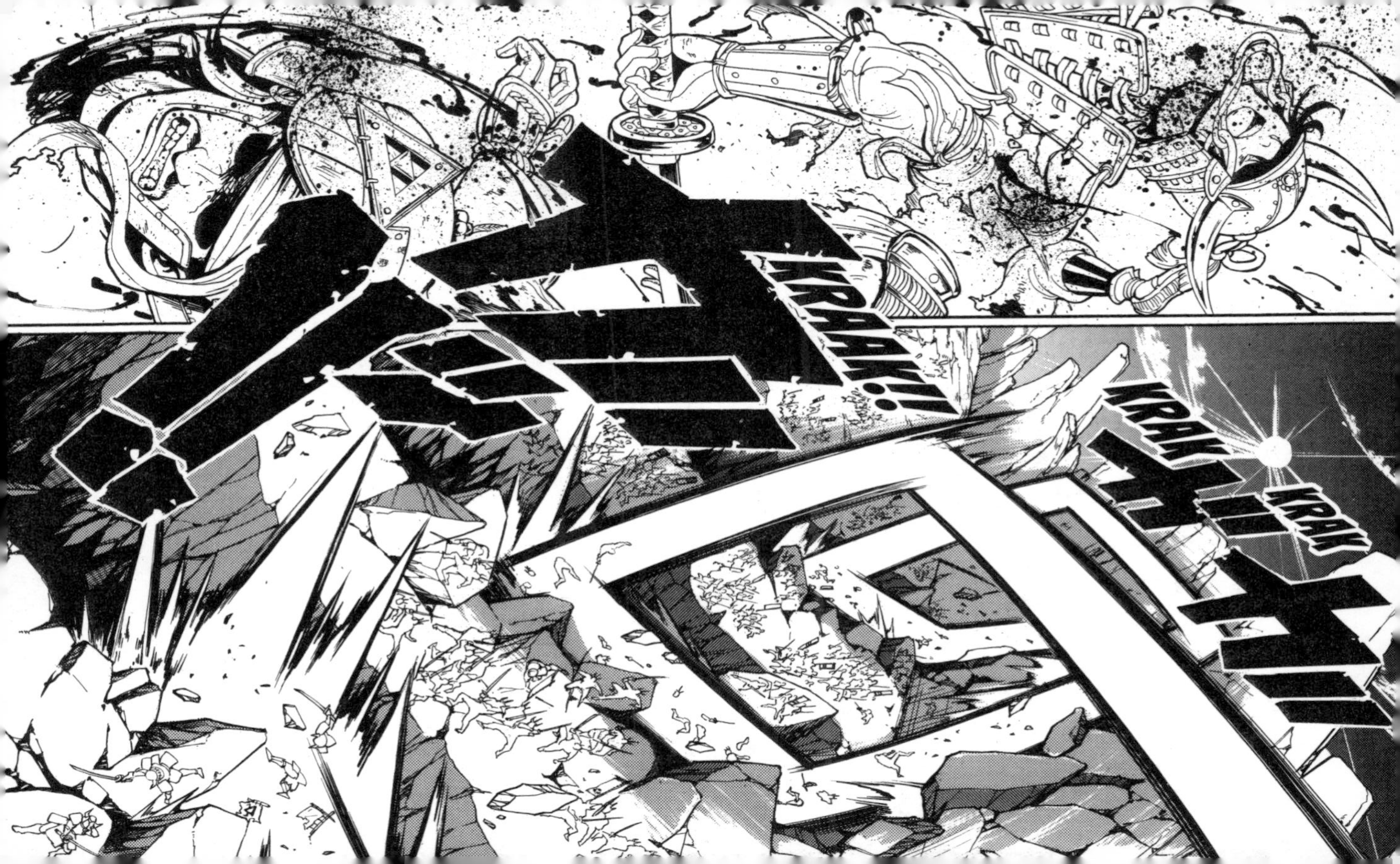
KRAAK!!
KRAK
KRAK

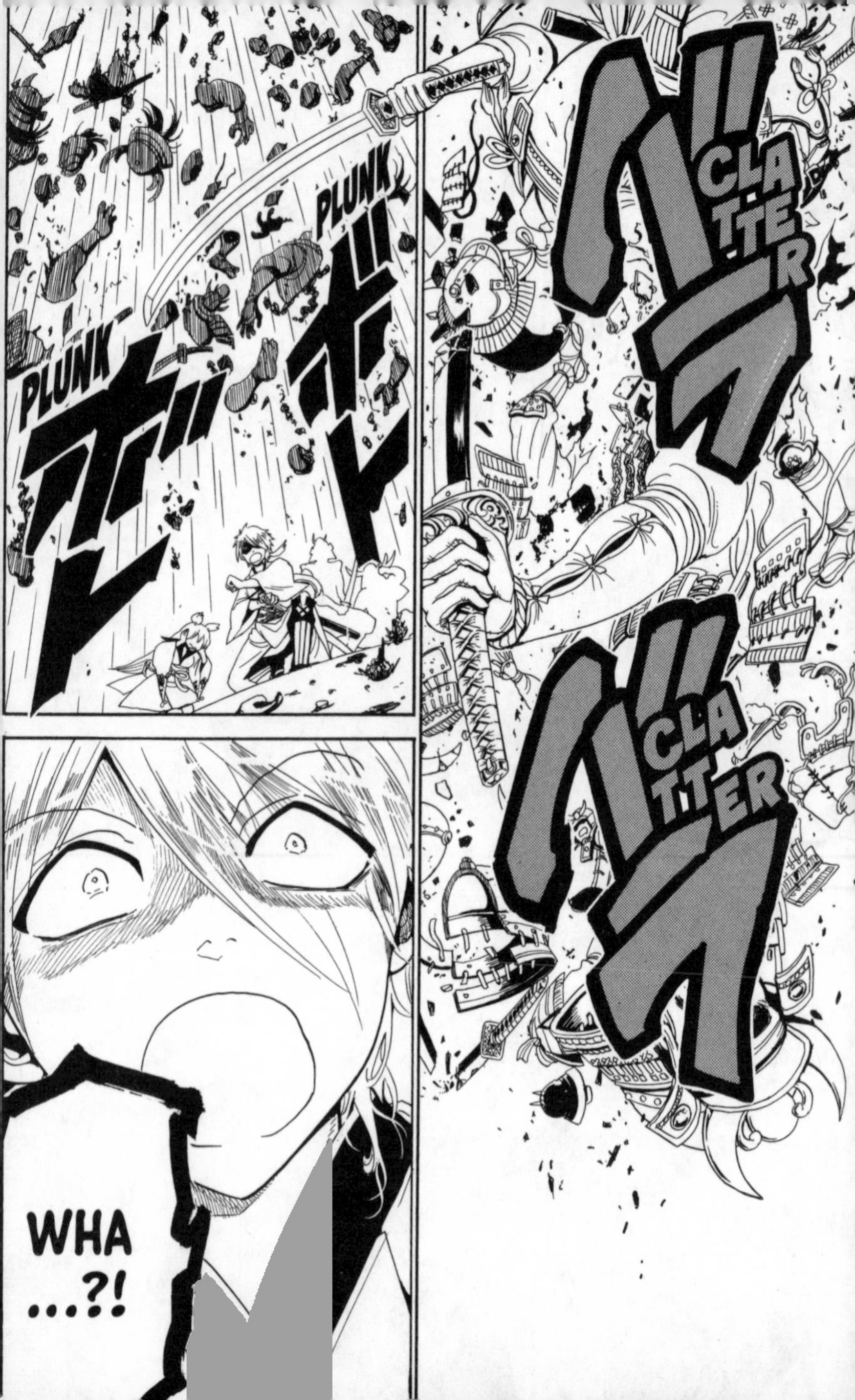
CLATTER
CLATTER
PLUNK
PLUNK
WHA ...?!

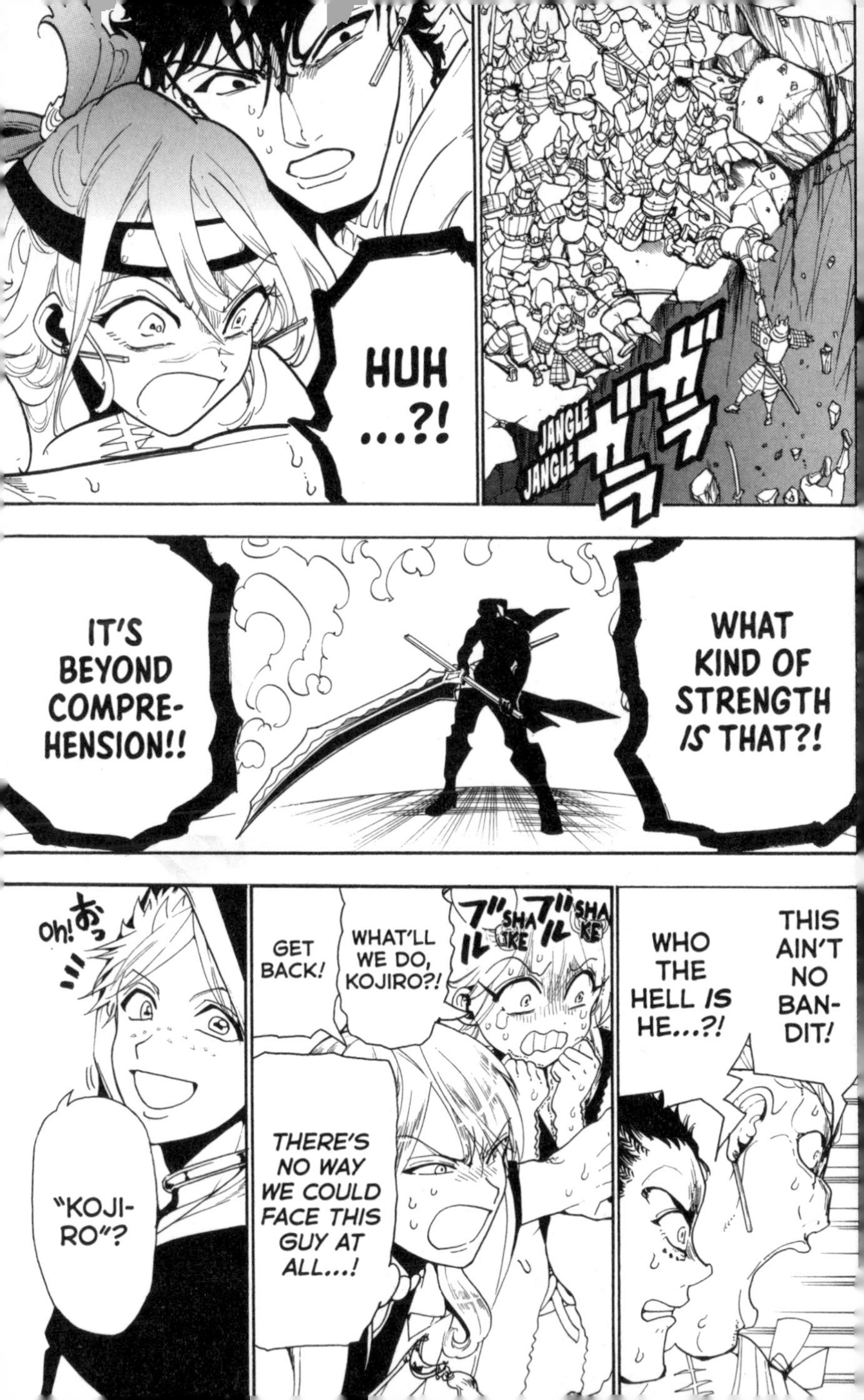
JANGLE JANGLE
ガラガラ
HUH ...?!
WHAT KIND OF STRENGTH IS THAT?!
IT'S BEYOND COMPRE-HENSION!!
THIS AIN'T NO BAN-DIT!
WHO THE HELL IS HE...?!
SHAKE SHAKE
ブルブル
WHAT'LL WE DO, KOJIRO?!
GET BACK!
THERE'S NO WAY WE COULD FACE THIS GUY AT ALL...!
Oh! おっ
"KOJI-RO"?

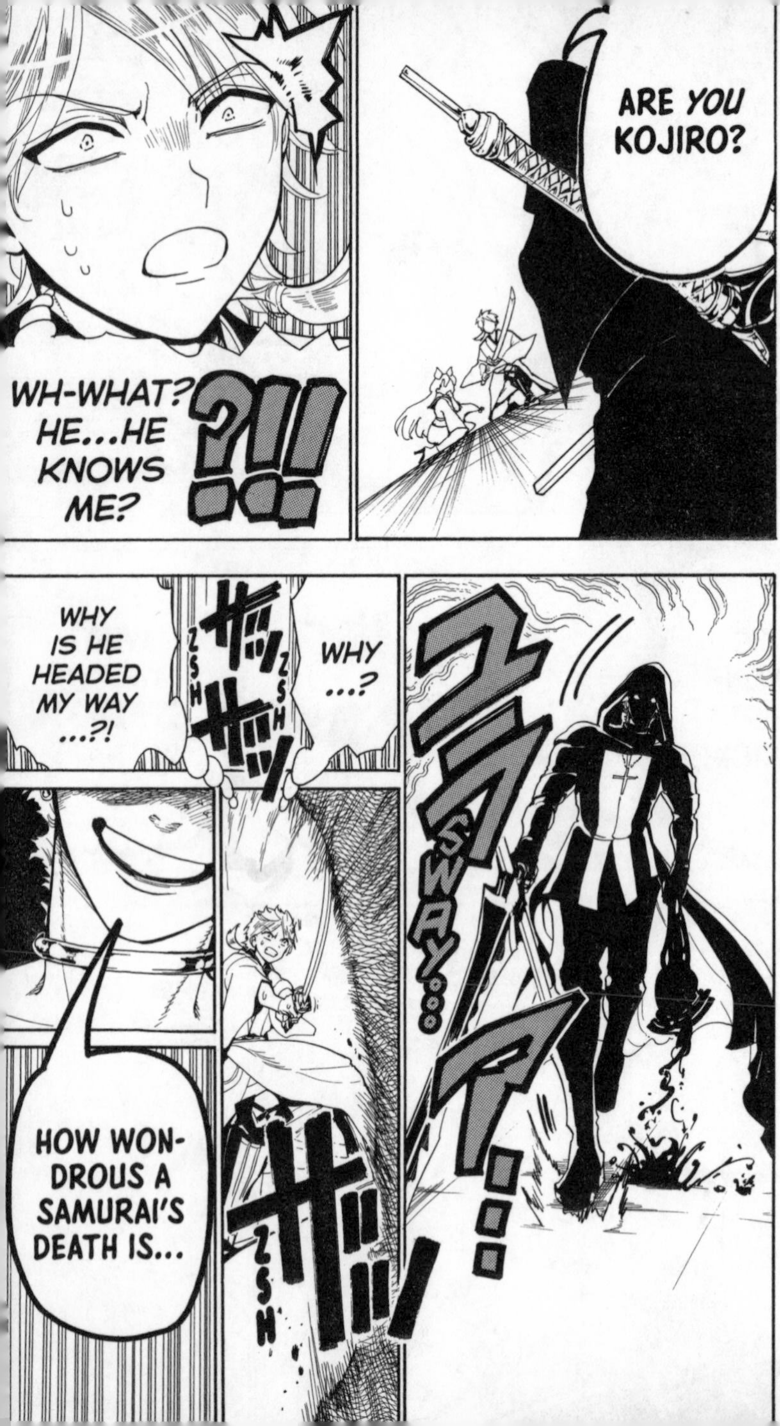
ARE YOU KOJIRO?
WH-WHAT? HE...HE KNOWS ME?
?!!
SWAY...
WHY...?
ZSH
ZSH
WHY IS HE HEADED MY WAY...?!
HOW WONDROUS A SAMURAI'S DEATH IS...
ZSH

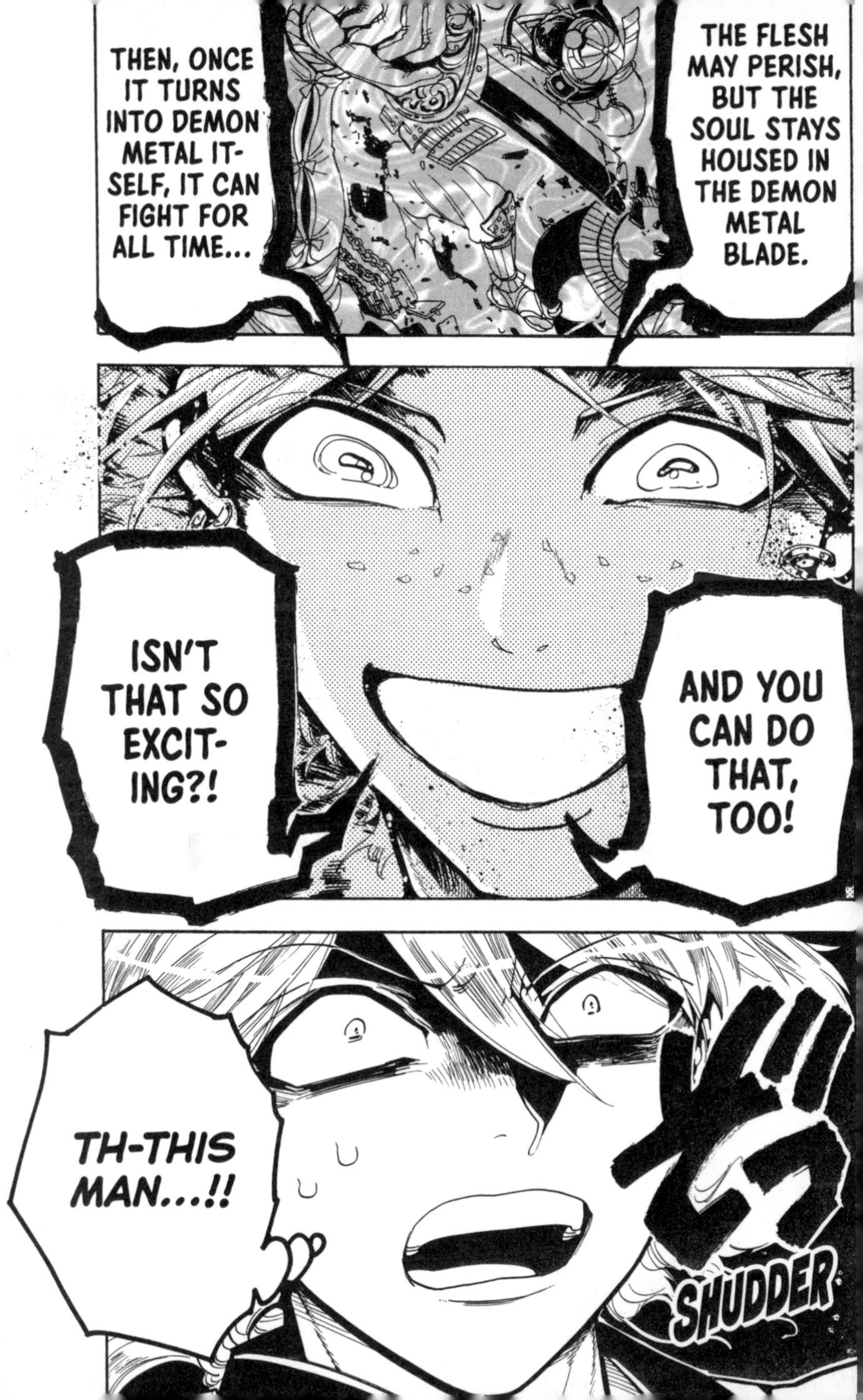
THE FLESH MAY PERISH, BUT THE SOUL STAYS HOUSED IN THE DEMON METAL BLADE.
THEN, ONCE IT TURNS INTO DEMON METAL IT-SELF, IT CAN FIGHT FOR ALL TIME...
AND YOU CAN DO THAT, TOO!
ISN'T THAT SO EXCIT-ING?!
SHUDDER
TH-THIS MAN...!!

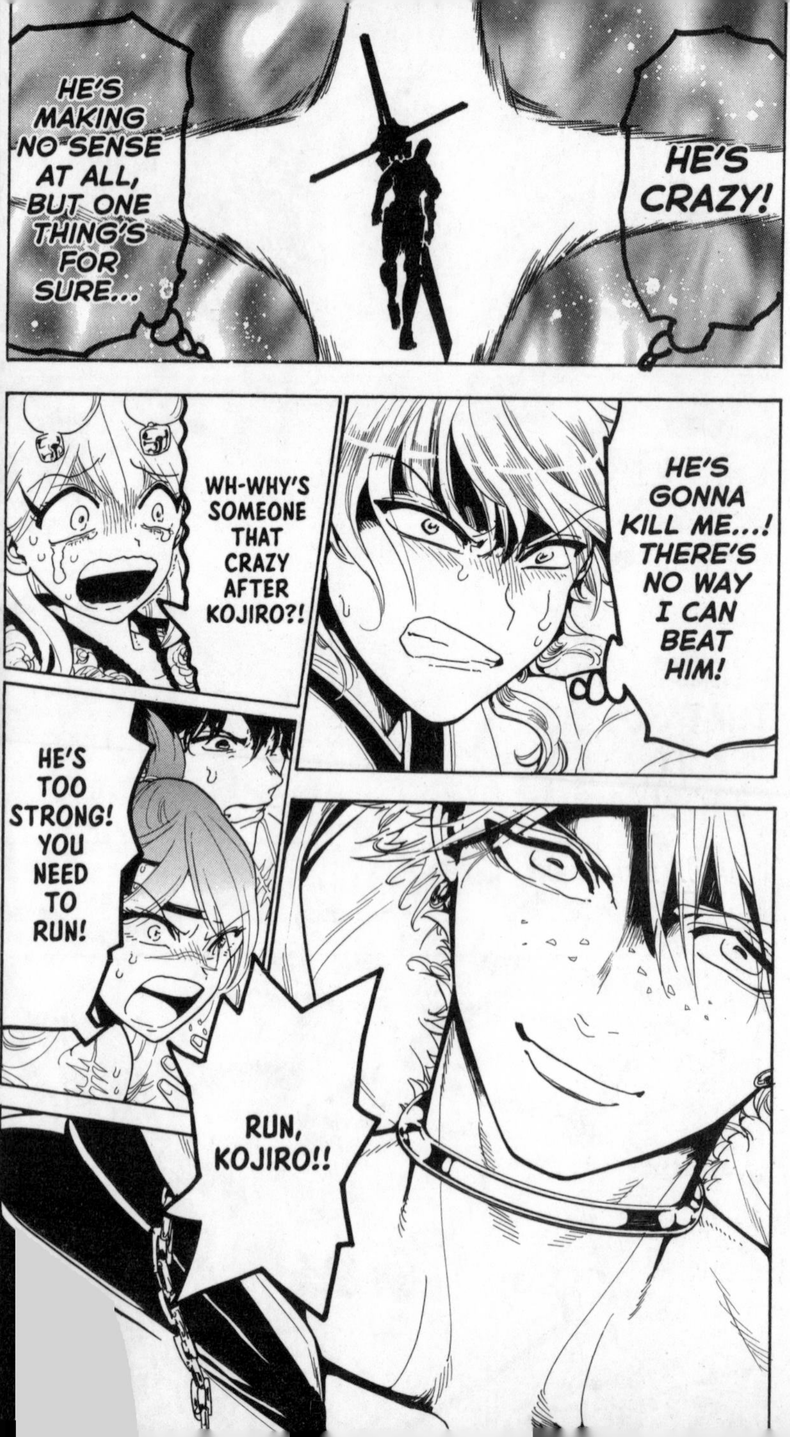
HE'S CRAZY!
HE'S MAKING NO SENSE AT ALL, BUT ONE THING'S FOR SURE...
HE'S GONNA KILL ME...! THERE'S NO WAY I CAN BEAT HIM!
WH-WHY'S SOMEONE THAT CRAZY AFTER KOJIRO?!
HE'S TOO STRONG! YOU NEED TO RUN!
RUN, KOJIRO!!

CHAPTER 32: THE WAY SAMURAI LIVE

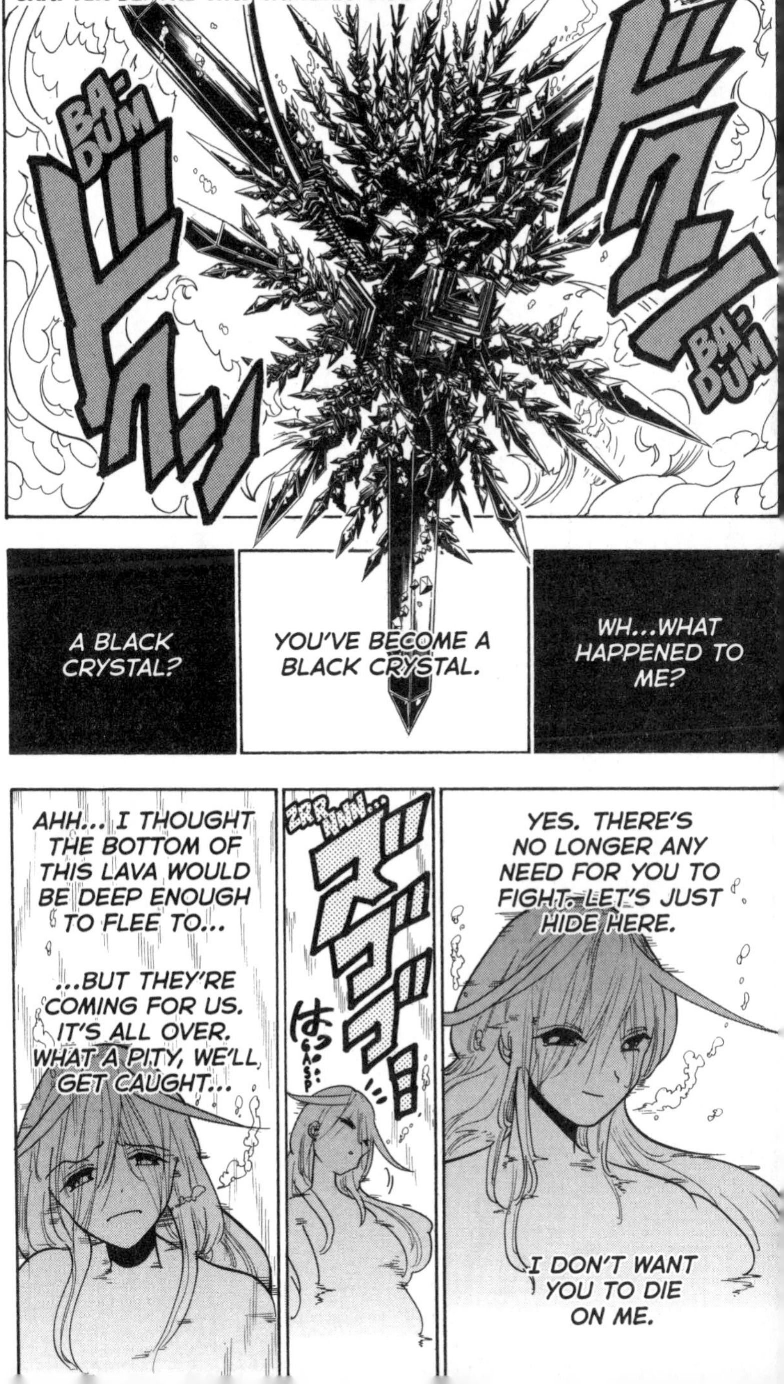
BA-DUM
BA-DUM
WH...WHAT HAPPENED TO ME?
YOU'VE BECOME A BLACK CRYSTAL.
A BLACK CRYSTAL?
YES. THERE'S NO LONGER ANY NEED FOR YOU TO FIGHT. LET'S JUST HIDE HERE.
I DON'T WANT YOU TO DIE ON ME.
ZRRVNN...
GASP
AHH... I THOUGHT THE BOTTOM OF THIS LAVA WOULD BE DEEP ENOUGH TO FLEE TO...
...BUT THEY'RE COMING FOR US. IT'S ALL OVER. WHAT A PITY, WE'LL GET CAUGHT...

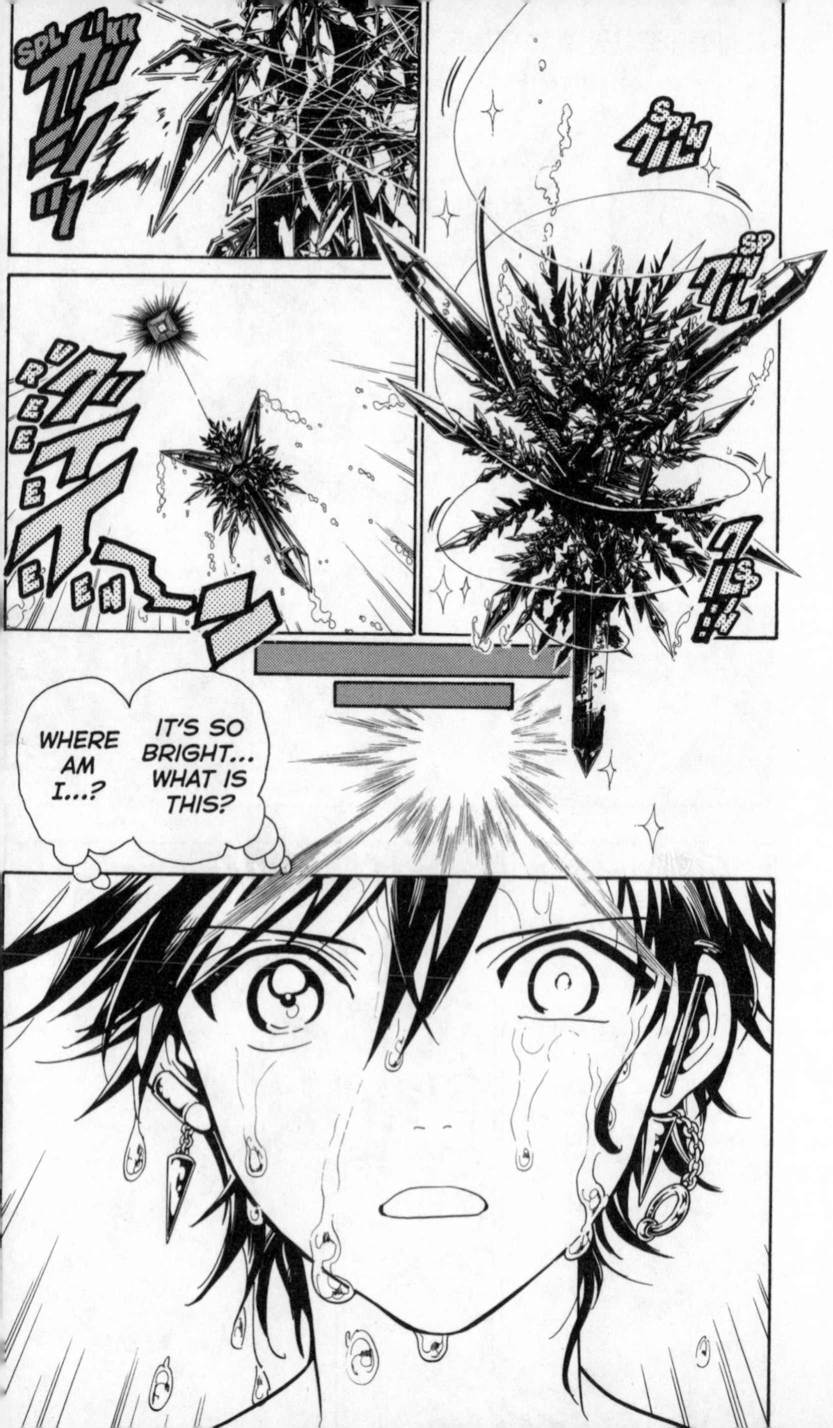
SPIN
SPIN
SPIN!!
SPLIKK
VREEEEEN
IT'S SO BRIGHT... WHAT IS THIS?
WHERE AM I...?

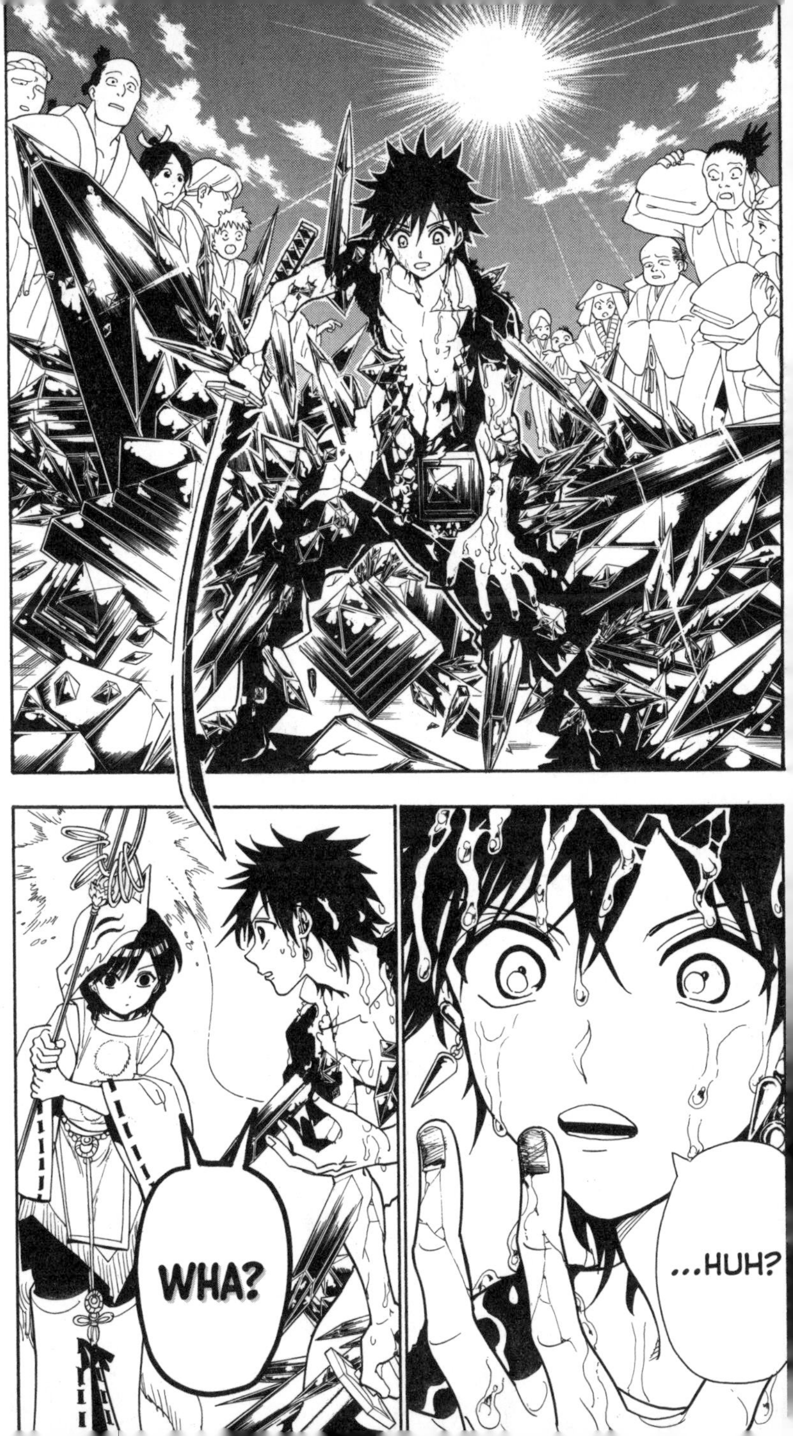
...HUH?
WHA?

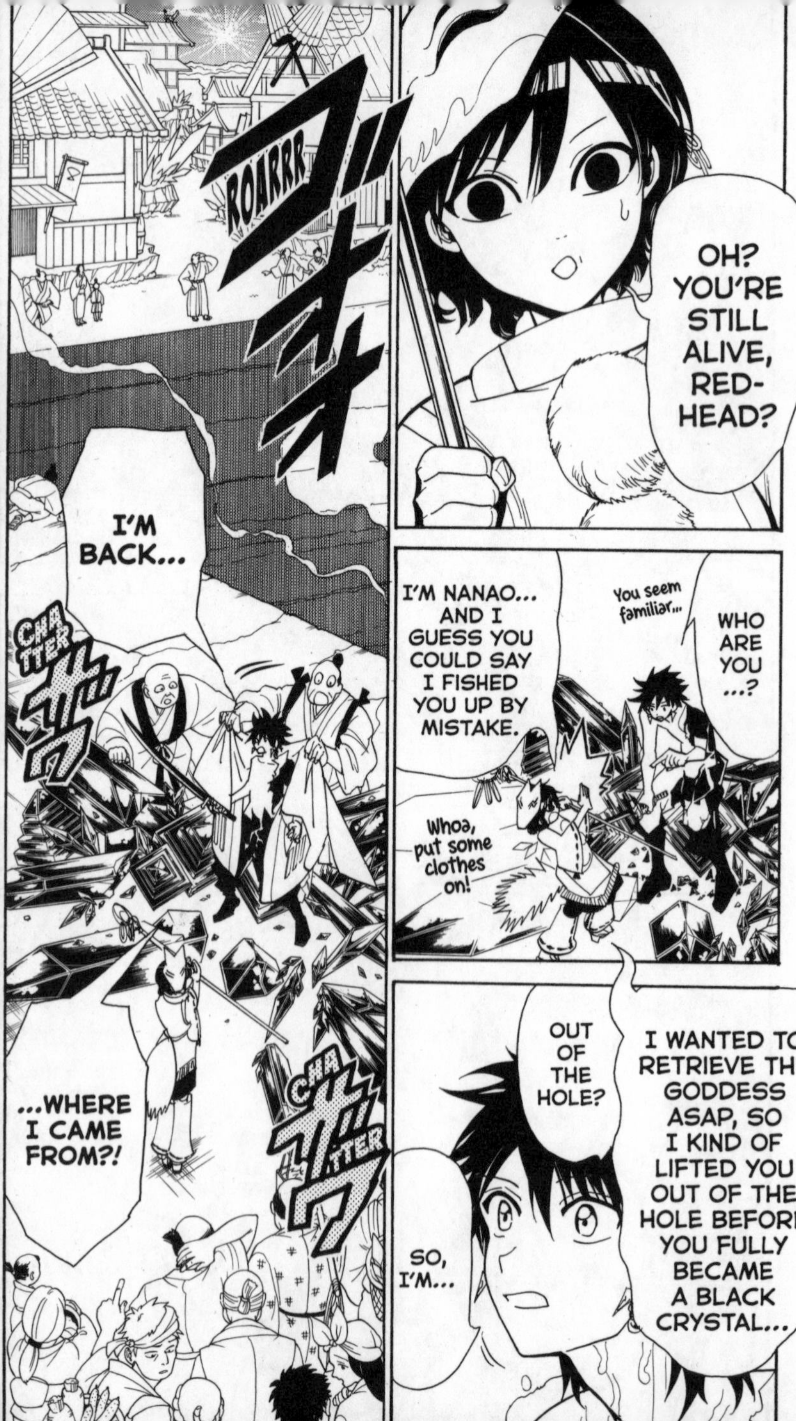
OH? YOU'RE STILL ALIVE, RED-HEAD?
WHO ARE YOU ...?
You seem familiar...
I'M NANAO... AND I GUESS YOU COULD SAY I FISHED YOU UP BY MISTAKE.
Whoa, put some clothes on!
I WANTED TO RETRIEVE THE GODDESS ASAP, SO I KIND OF LIFTED YOU OUT OF THE HOLE BEFORE YOU FULLY BECAME A BLACK CRYSTAL...
OUT OF THE HOLE?
SO, I'M...
ROARRR
I'M BACK...
CHATTER
...WHERE I CAME FROM?!
CHATTER

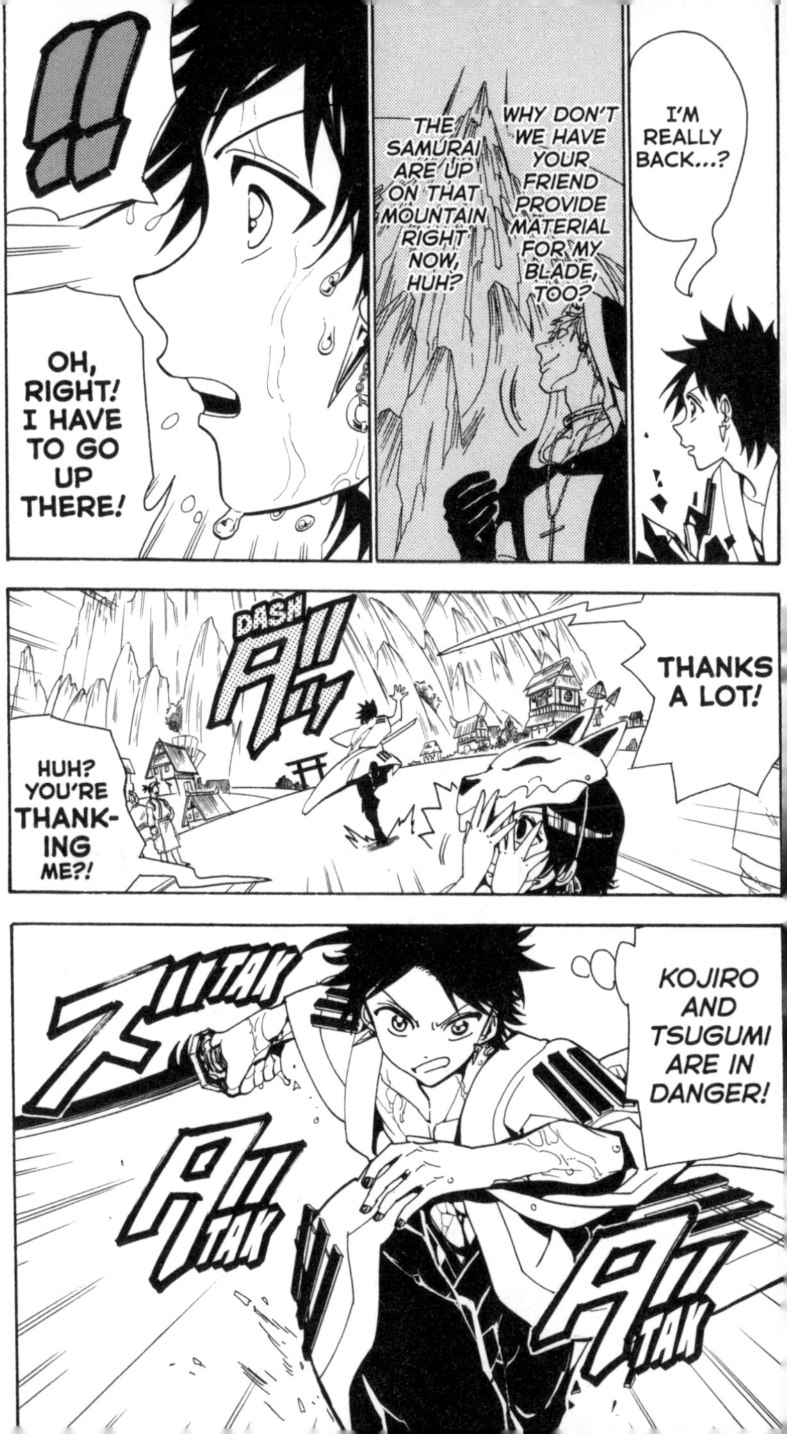
I'M REALLY BACK...?
WHY DON'T WE HAVE YOUR FRIEND PROVIDE MATERIAL FOR MY BLADE, TOO?
THE SAMURAI ARE UP ON THAT MOUNTAIN RIGHT NOW, HUH?
!!
OH, RIGHT! I HAVE TO GO UP THERE!
THANKS A LOT!
DASH
HUH? YOU'RE THANKING ME?!
KOJIRO AND TSUGUMI ARE IN DANGER!
TAK
TAK
TAK

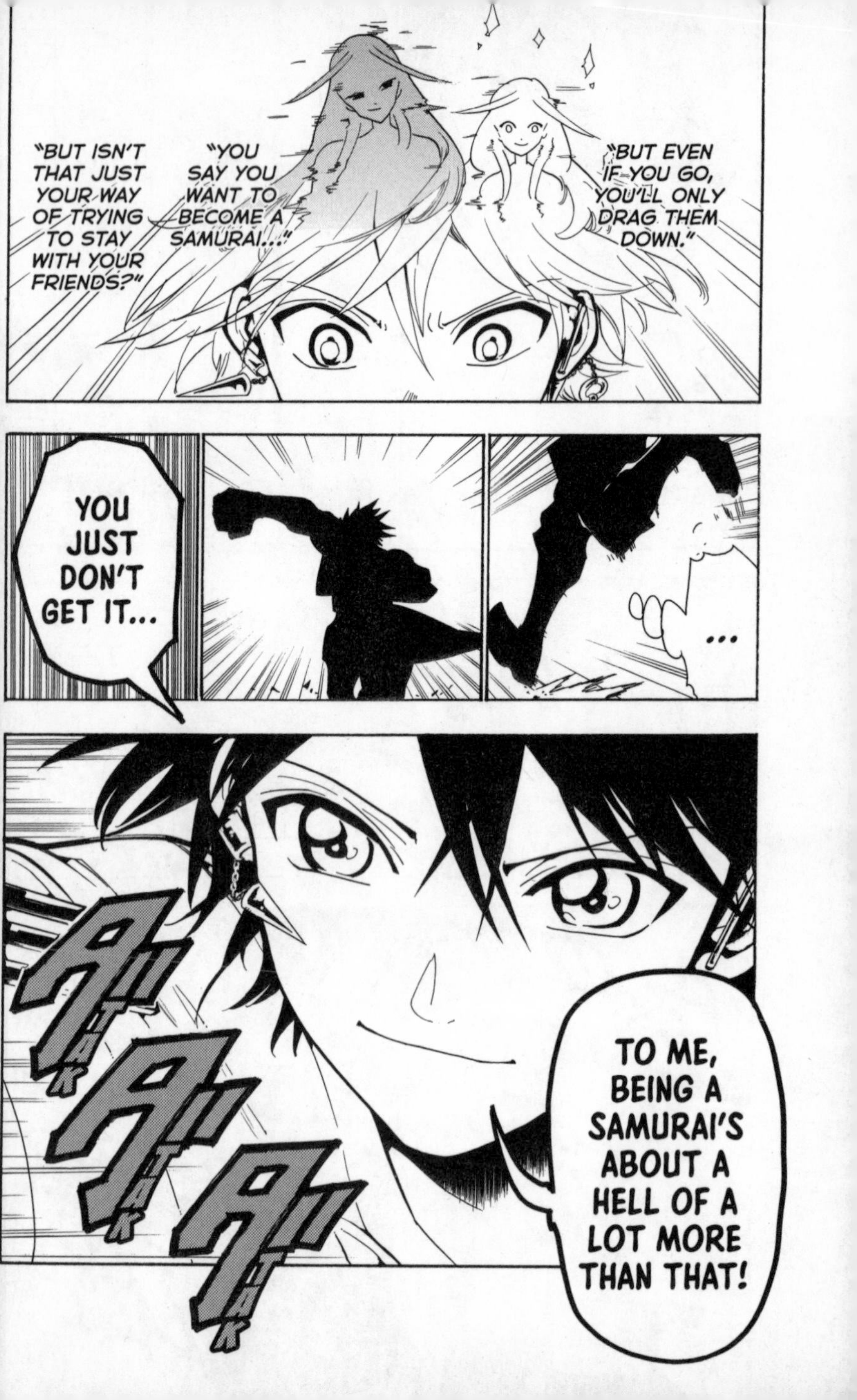
"BUT EVEN IF YOU GO, YOU'LL ONLY DRAG THEM DOWN."
"YOU SAY YOU WANT TO BECOME A SAMURAI..."
"BUT ISN'T THAT JUST YOUR WAY OF TRYING TO STAY WITH YOUR FRIENDS?"
...
YOU JUST DON'T GET IT...
TO ME, BEING A SAMURAI'S ABOUT A HELL OF A LOT MORE THAN THAT!

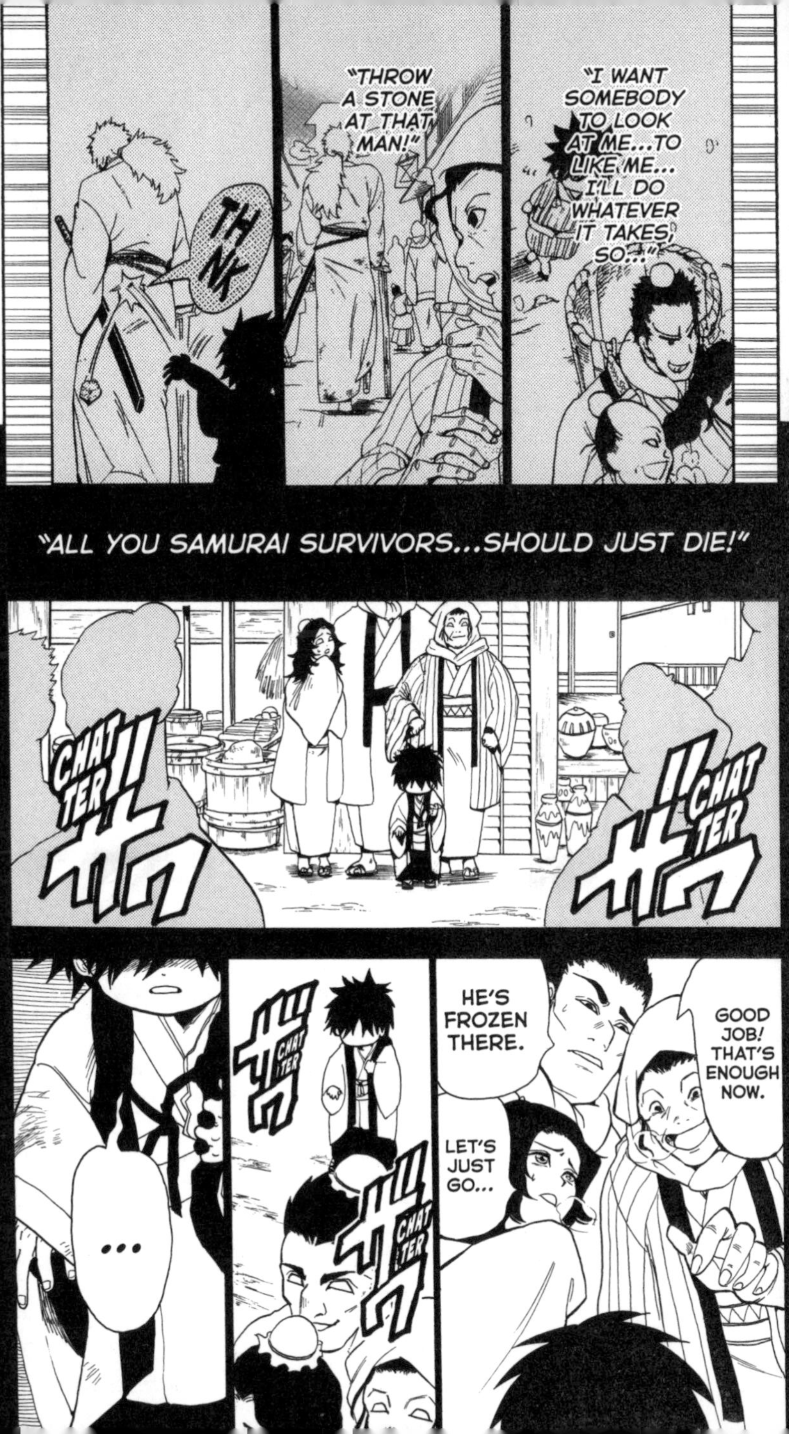
"I WANT SOMEBODY TO LOOK AT ME...TO LIKE ME... I'LL DO WHATEVER IT TAKES, SO..."
"THROW A STONE AT THAT MAN!"
THNK
"ALL YOU SAMURAI SURVIVORS...SHOULD JUST DIE!"
CHATTER
CHATTER
GOOD JOB! THAT'S ENOUGH NOW.
HE'S FROZEN THERE.
LET'S JUST GO...
CHATTER
CHATTER
...

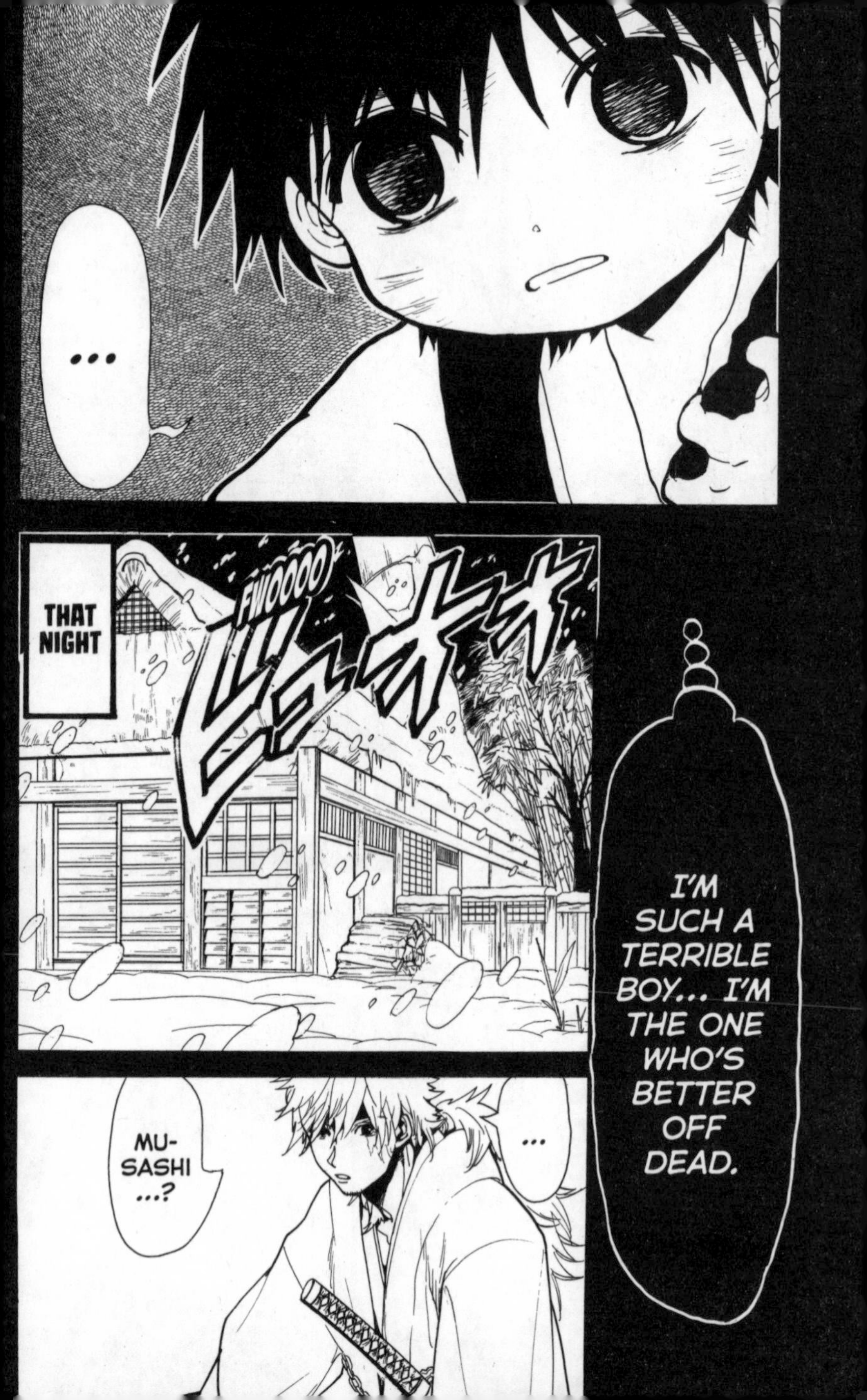
...
I'M SUCH A TERRIBLE BOY... I'M THE ONE WHO'S BETTER OFF DEAD.
THAT NIGHT
FWOOOO
...
MU-SASHI ...?

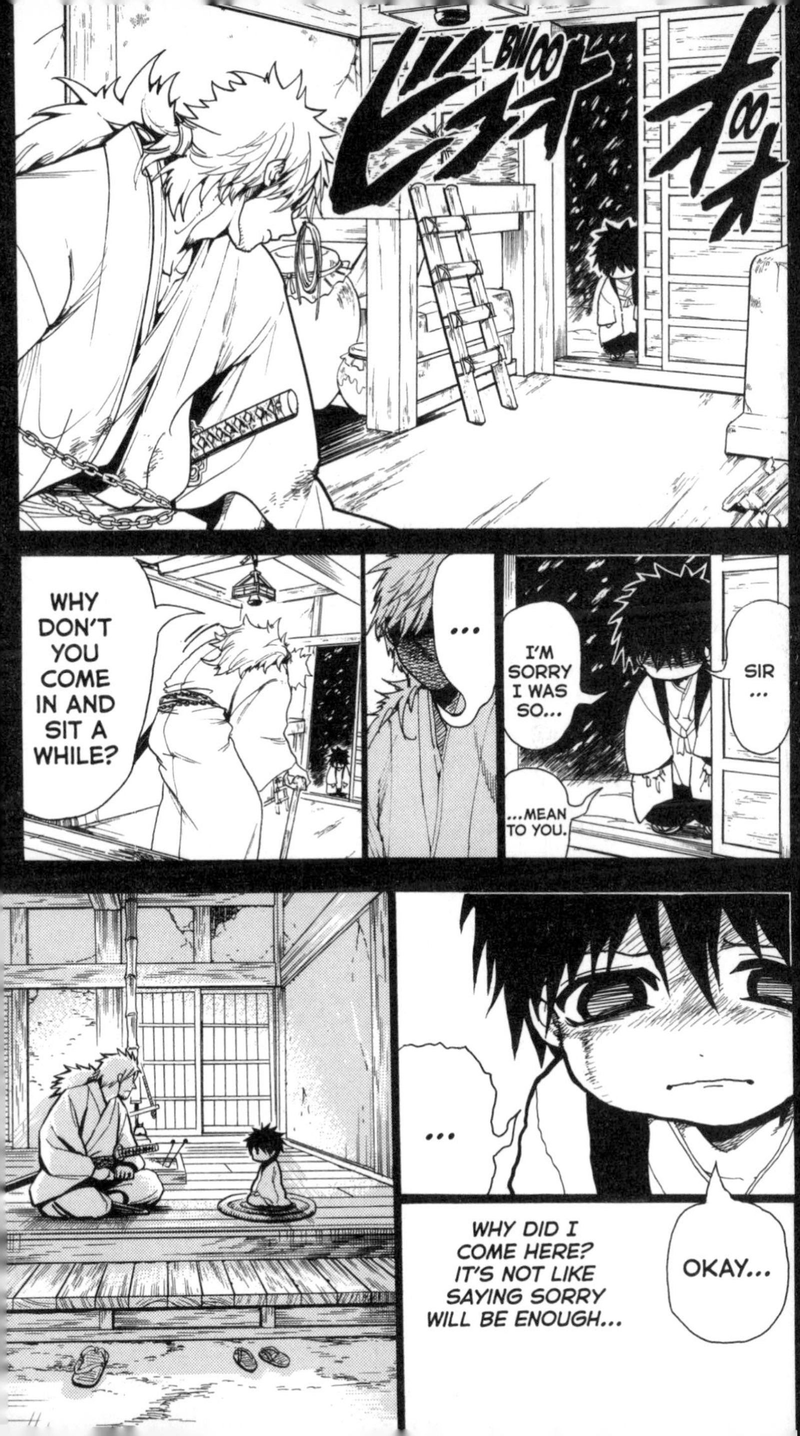
BWOO
SIR...
I'M SORRY I WAS SO...
...MEAN TO YOU.
...
WHY DON'T YOU COME IN AND SIT A WHILE?
...
OKAY...
WHY DID I COME HERE? IT'S NOT LIKE SAYING SORRY WILL BE ENOUGH...

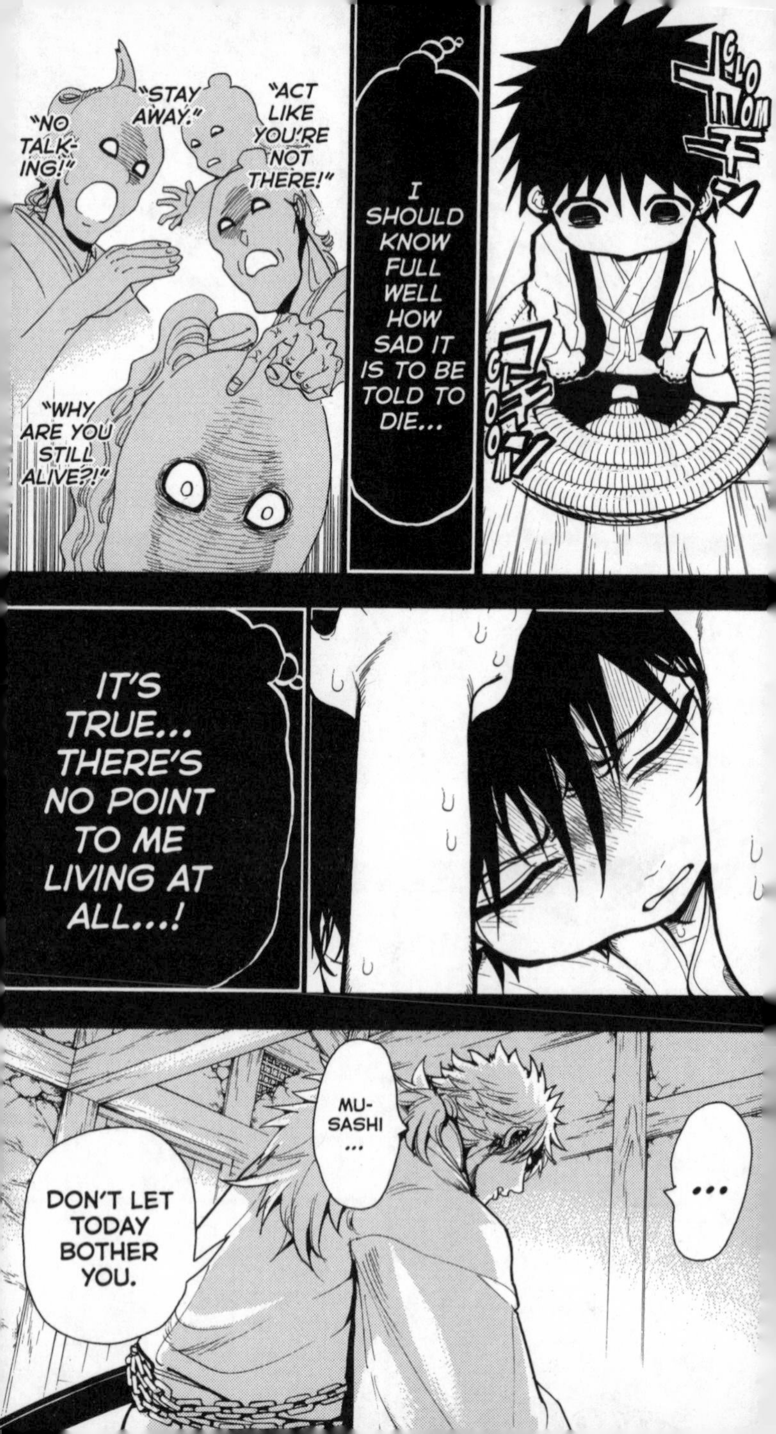
GLOOM
GLOOM
I SHOULD KNOW FULL WELL HOW SAD IT IS TO BE TOLD TO DIE...
"ACT LIKE YOU'RE NOT THERE!"
"STAY AWAY."
"NO TALKING!"
"WHY ARE YOU STILL ALIVE?!"
IT'S TRUE... THERE'S NO POINT TO ME LIVING AT ALL...!
...
MU-SASHI...
DON'T LET TODAY BOTHER YOU.

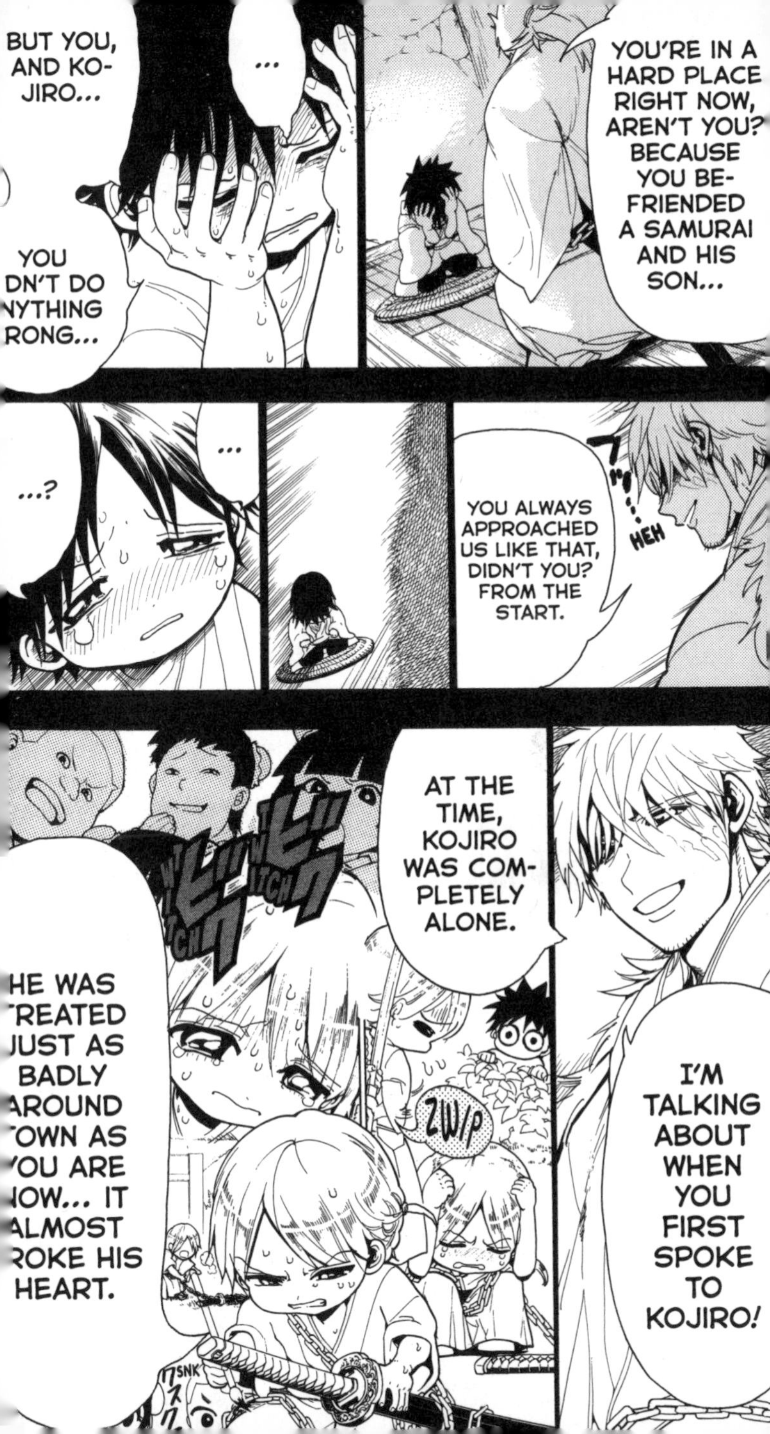
YOU'RE IN A HARD PLACE RIGHT NOW, AREN'T YOU? BECAUSE YOU BE-FRIENDED A SAMURAI AND HIS SON...
BUT YOU, AND KO-JIRO...
...
YOU DN'T DO NYTHING RONG...
HEH
YOU ALWAYS APPROACHED US LIKE THAT, DIDN'T YOU? FROM THE START.
...
...?
I'M TALKING ABOUT WHEN YOU FIRST SPOKE TO KOJIRO!
AT THE TIME, KOJIRO WAS COM-PLETELY ALONE.
TWITCH
TWITCH
HE WAS REATED JUST AS BADLY AROUND OWN AS OU ARE IOW... IT ALMOST ROKE HIS HEART.
ZWIP
SNK

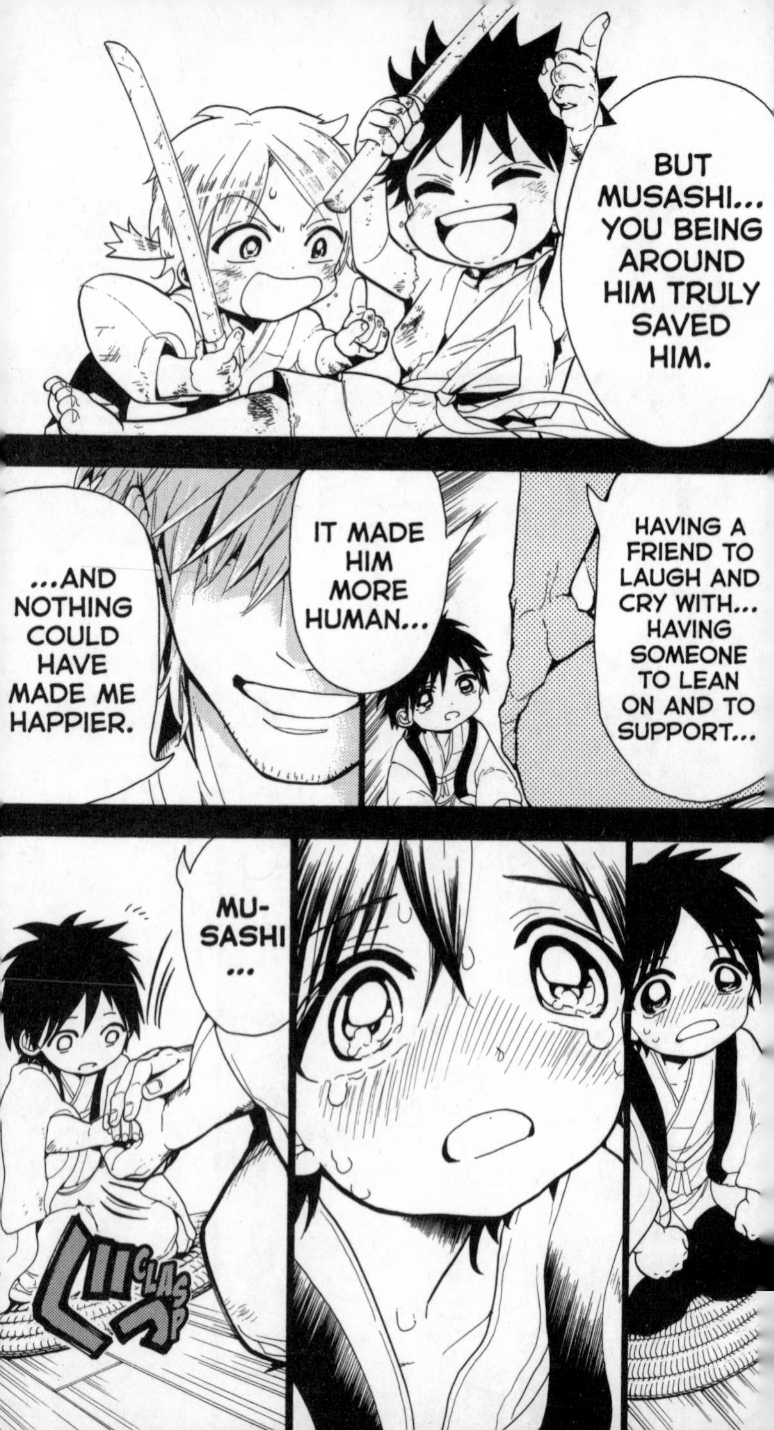
BUT MUSASHI... YOU BEING AROUND HIM TRULY SAVED HIM.
HAVING A FRIEND TO LAUGH AND CRY WITH... HAVING SOMEONE TO LEAN ON AND TO SUPPORT...
IT MADE HIM MORE HUMAN...
...AND NOTHING COULD HAVE MADE ME HAPPIER.
MU-SASHI...
CLASP

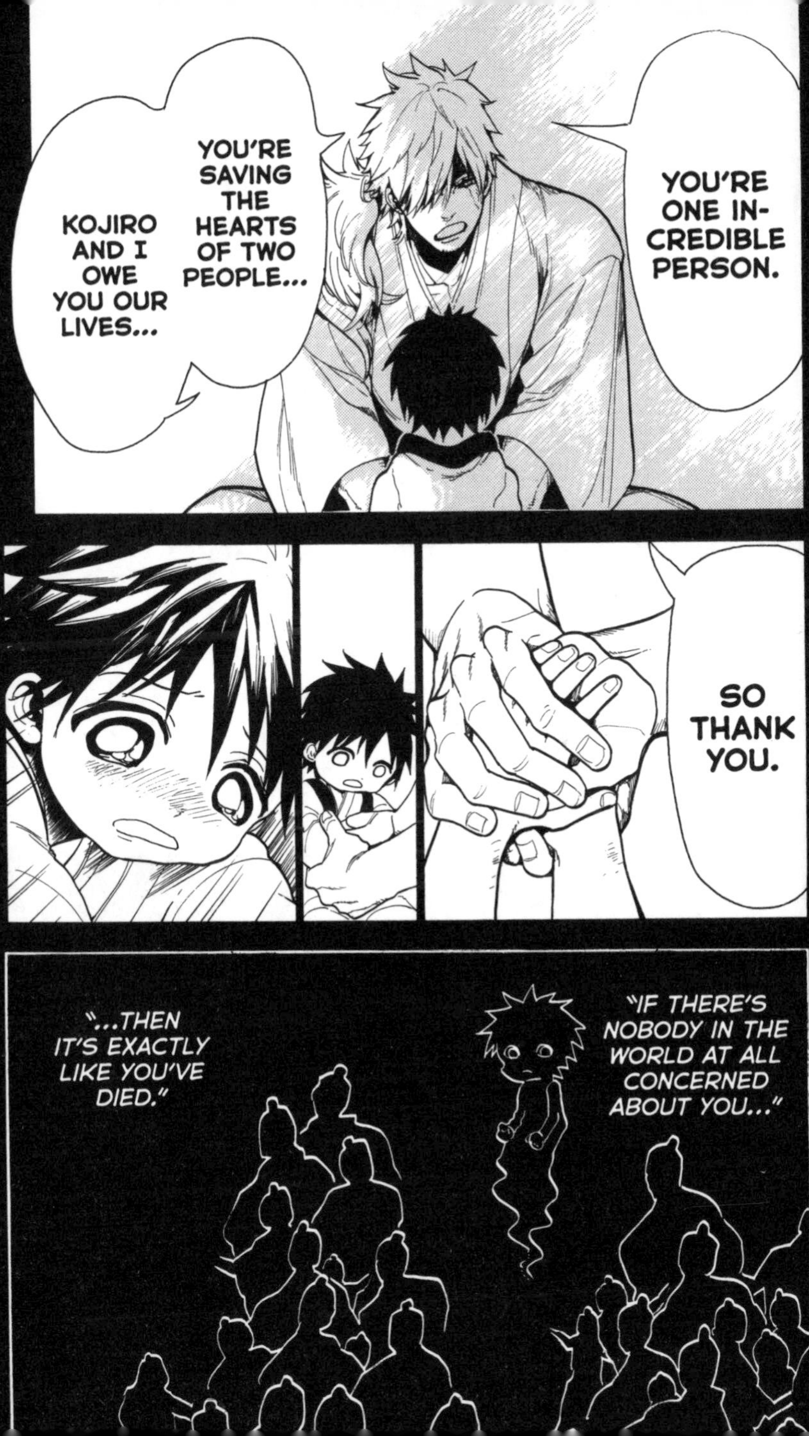
YOU'RE ONE IN-CREDIBLE PERSON.
YOU'RE SAVING THE HEARTS OF TWO PEOPLE...
KOJIRO AND I OWE YOU OUR LIVES...
SO THANK YOU.
"IF THERE'S NOBODY IN THE WORLD AT ALL CONCERNED ABOUT YOU..."
"...THEN IT'S EXACTLY LIKE YOU'VE DIED."

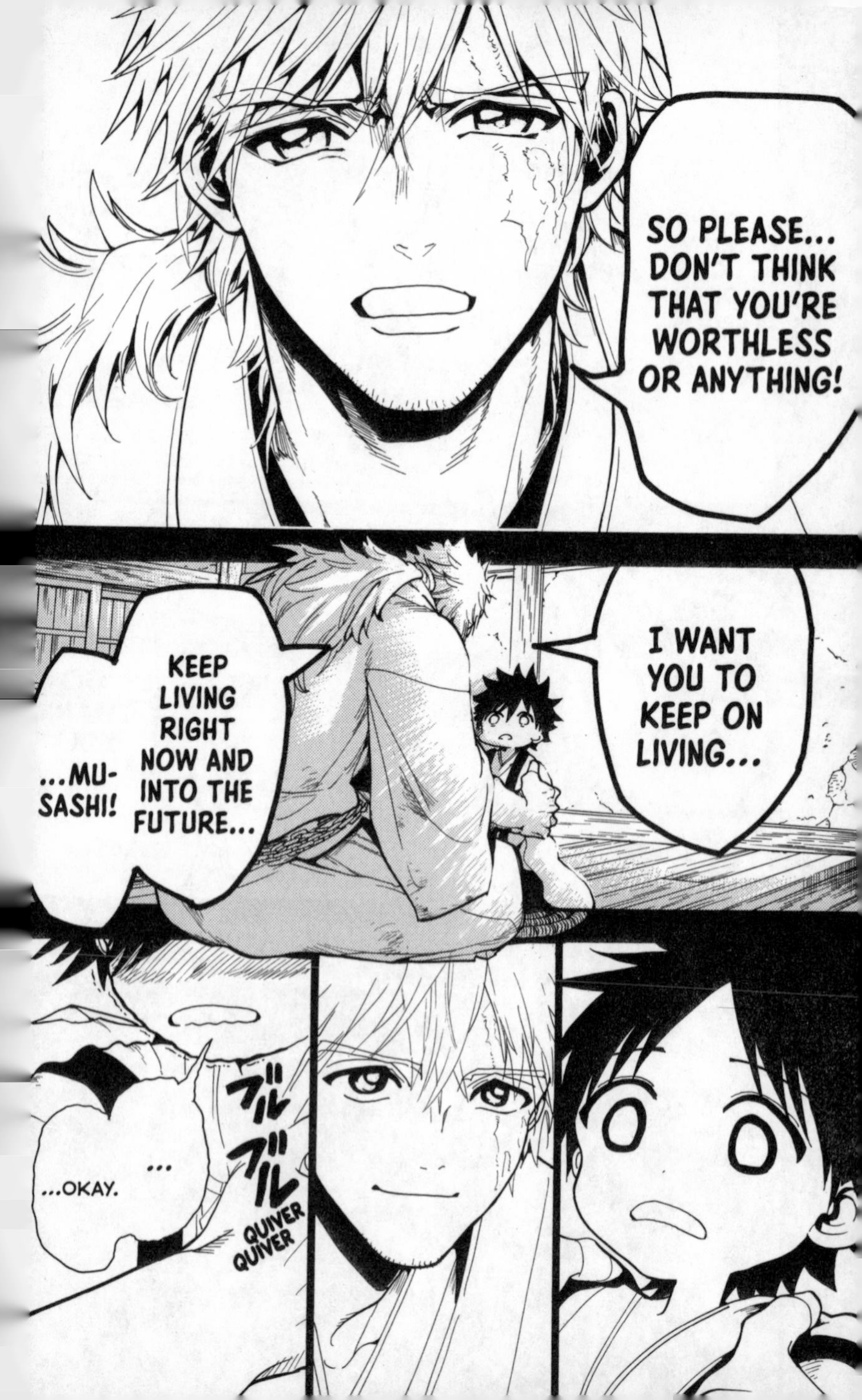
SO PLEASE... DON'T THINK THAT YOU'RE WORTHLESS OR ANYTHING!
I WANT YOU TO KEEP ON LIVING...
KEEP LIVING RIGHT NOW AND INTO THE FUTURE...
...MU-SASHI!
ブルブル
QUIVER QUIVER
...
...OKAY.

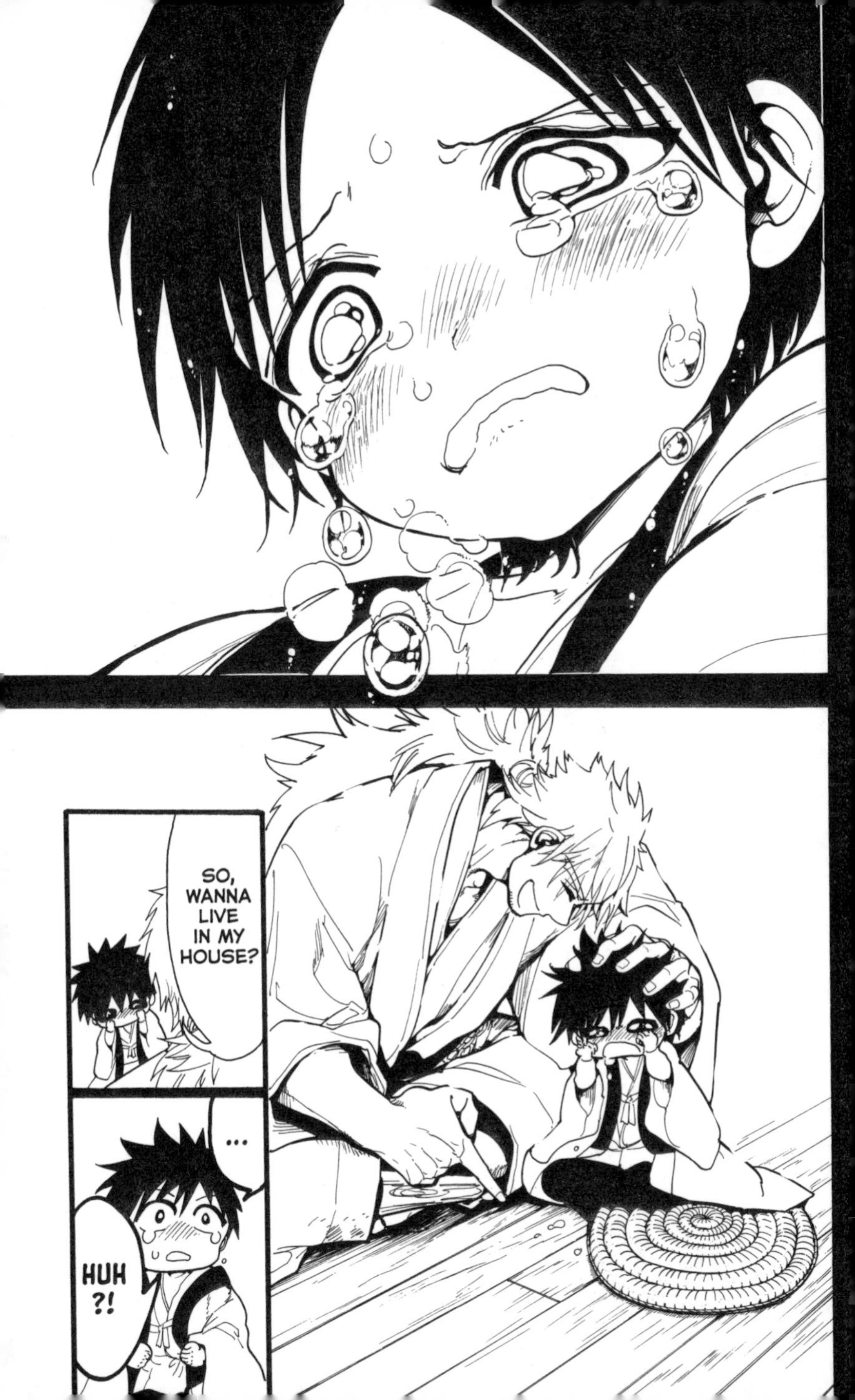
SO, WANNA LIVE IN MY HOUSE?
...
HUH ?!

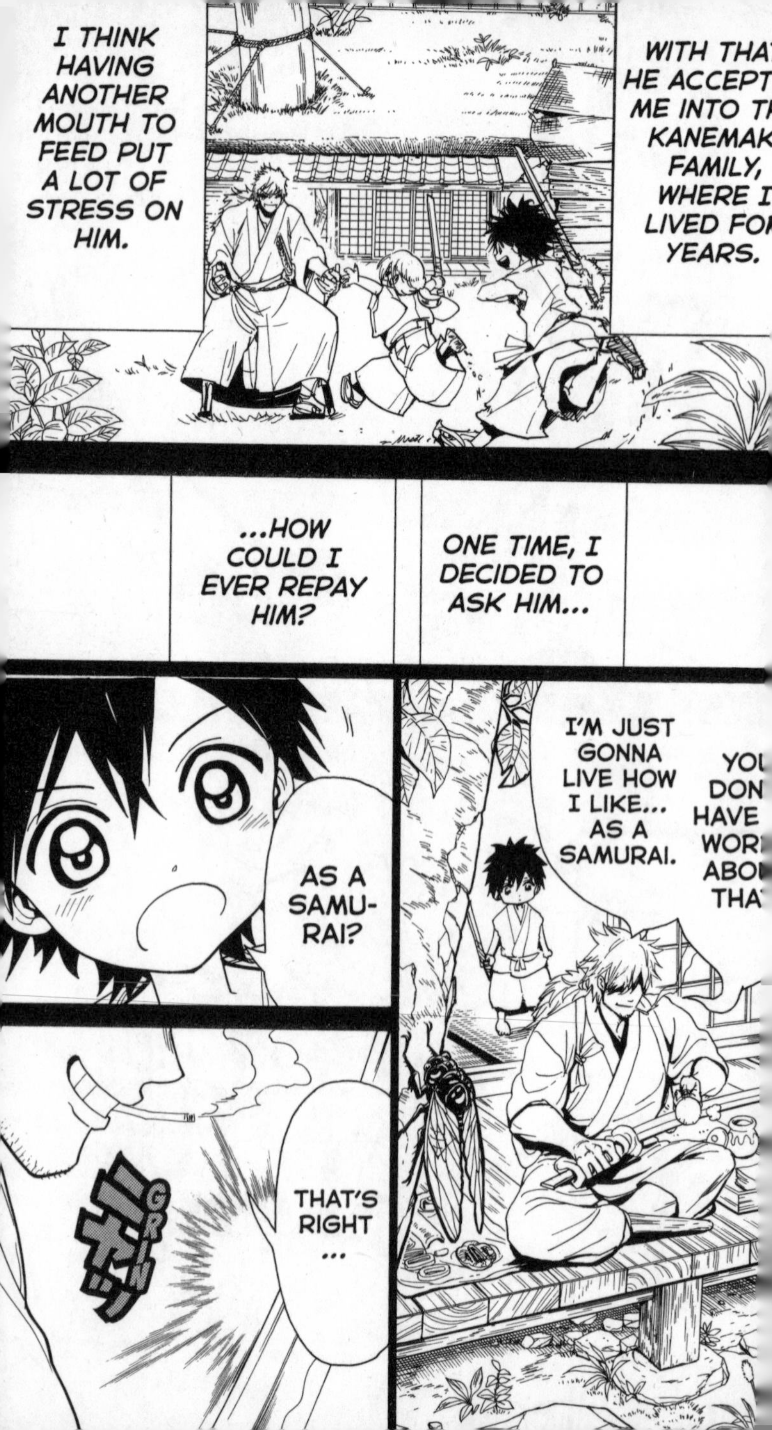

WITH THA HE ACCEPT ME INTO T KANEMAK FAMILY, WHERE I LIVED FO YEARS.
I THINK HAVING ANOTHER MOUTH TO FEED PUT A LOT OF STRESS ON HIM.
ONE TIME, I DECIDED TO ASK HIM...
...HOW COULD I EVER REPAY HIM?
YOU DON HAVE WOR ABO THA
I'M JUST GONNA LIVE HOW I LIKE... AS A SAMURAI.
AS A SAMU-RAI?
THAT'S RIGHT ...
GRIN

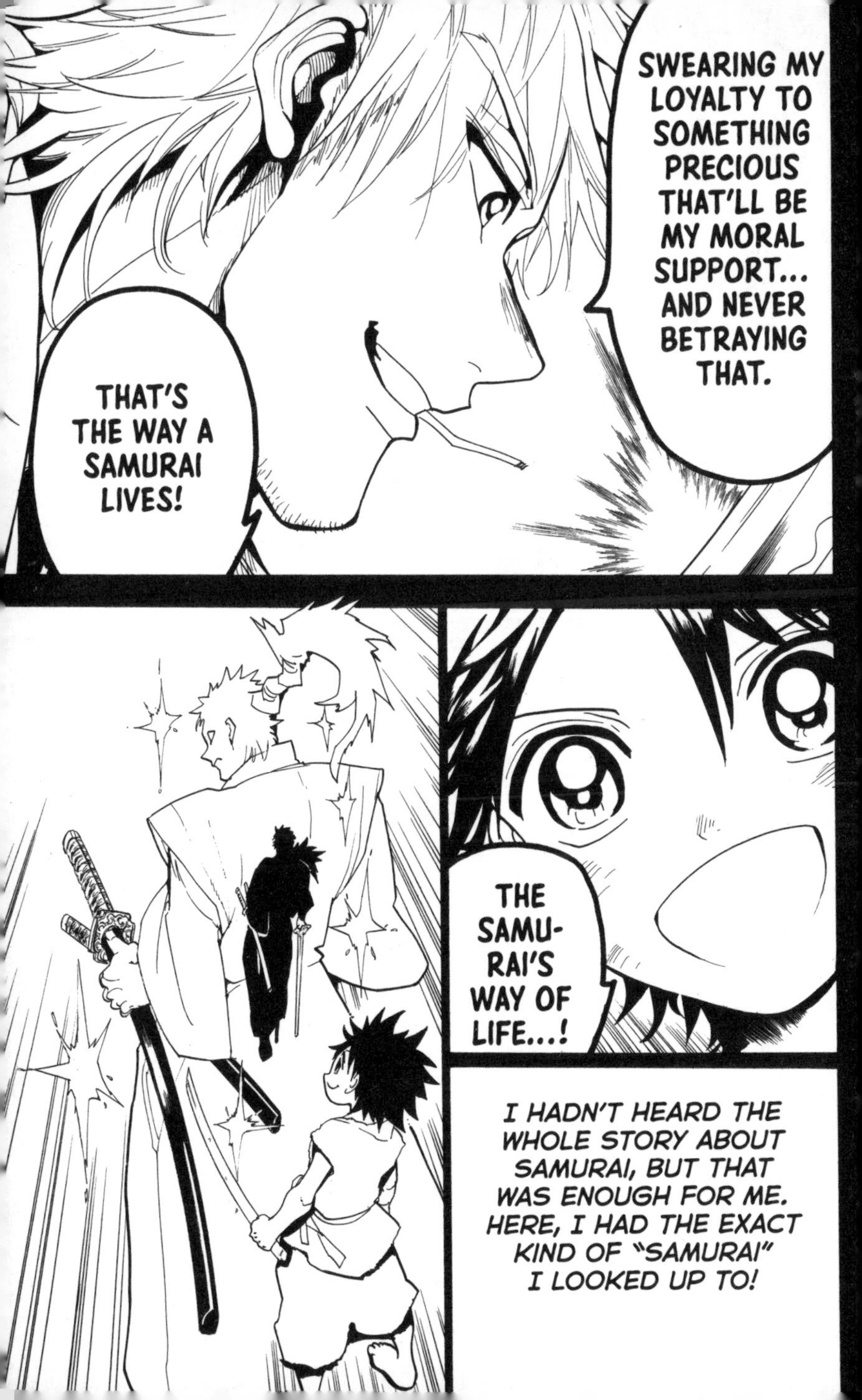
SWEARING MY LOYALTY TO SOMETHING PRECIOUS THAT'LL BE MY MORAL SUPPORT... AND NEVER BETRAYING THAT.
THAT'S THE WAY A SAMURAI LIVES!
THE SAMU-RAI'S WAY OF LIFE...!
I HADN'T HEARD THE WHOLE STORY ABOUT SAMURAI, BUT THAT WAS ENOUGH FOR ME. HERE, I HAD THE EXACT KIND OF "SAMURAI" I LOOKED UP TO!

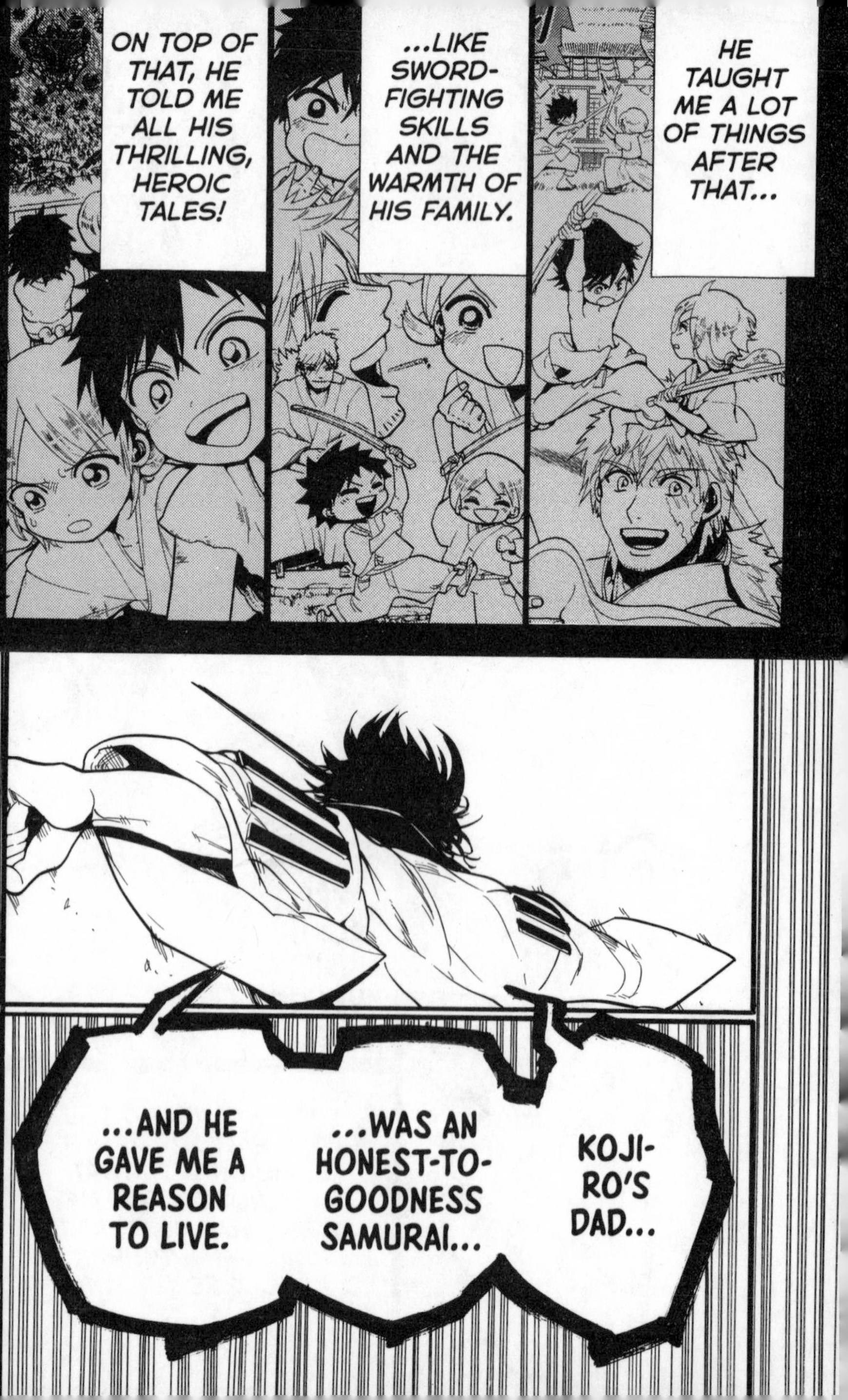
HE TAUGHT ME A LOT OF THINGS AFTER THAT...
...LIKE SWORD-FIGHTING SKILLS AND THE WARMTH OF HIS FAMILY.
ON TOP OF THAT, HE TOLD ME ALL HIS THRILLING, HEROIC TALES!
KOJI-RO'S DAD...
...WAS AN HONEST-TO-GOODNESS SAMURAI...
...AND HE GAVE ME A REASON TO LIVE.

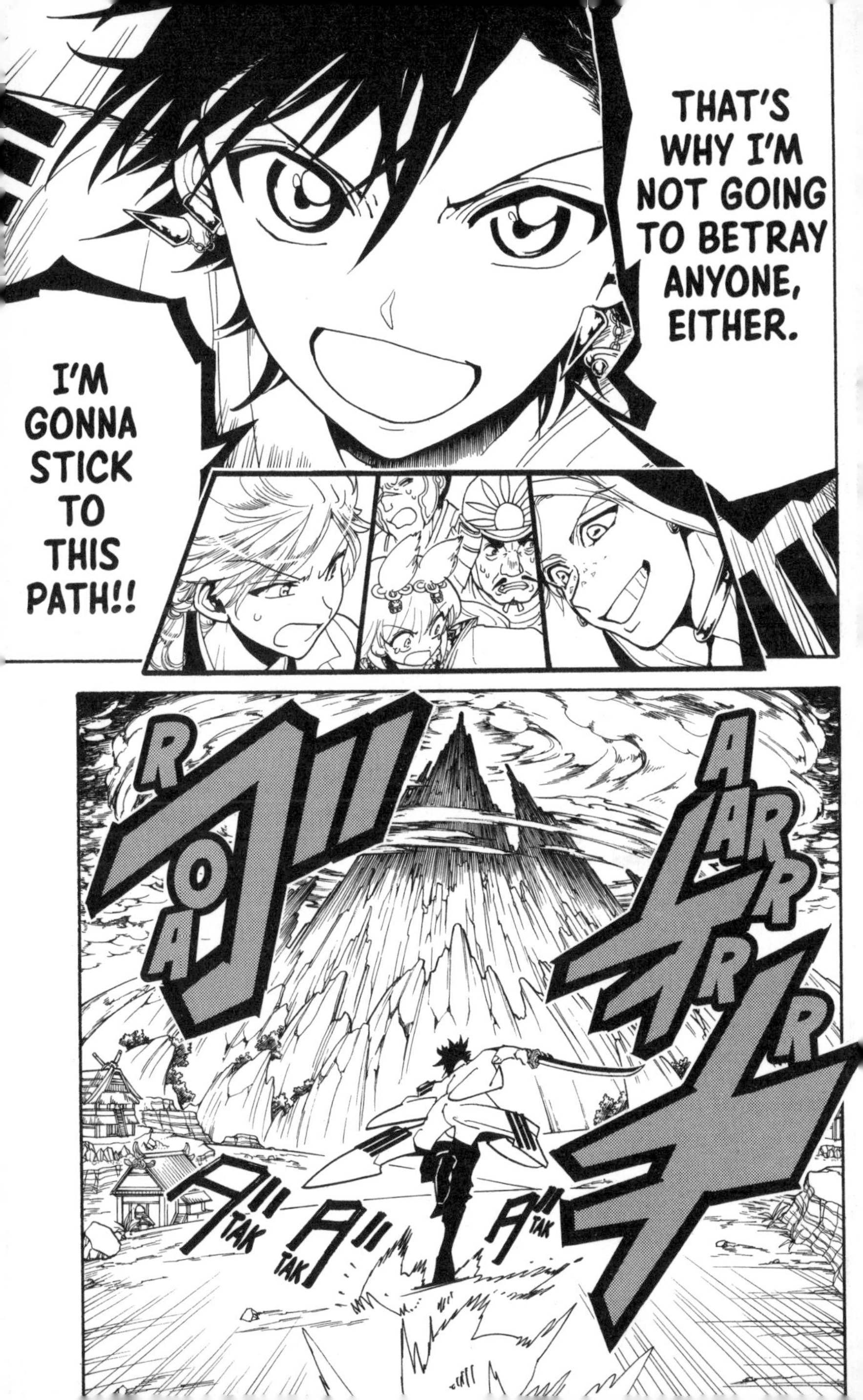
THAT'S WHY I'M NOT GOING TO BETRAY ANYONE, EITHER.
I'M GONNA STICK TO THIS PATH!!
ROA
AARRRR
TAK
TAK
TAK

ORIENT

STAFF

REGULAR ASSISTANTS

舞嶋 大
Hiro Maizima

秋山 有緒子
Yuiko Akiyama

メギ
Megi

吉田 真美
Mami Yoshida

石後 千鳥
Chidori Ishigo

中村 犬彦
Inuhiko Nakamura

EDITORIAL TEAM

詫摩 尚樹
Naoki Takuma

菊地 優斗
Yuto Kikuchi

長塚 雅彦
Masahiko Nagatsuka

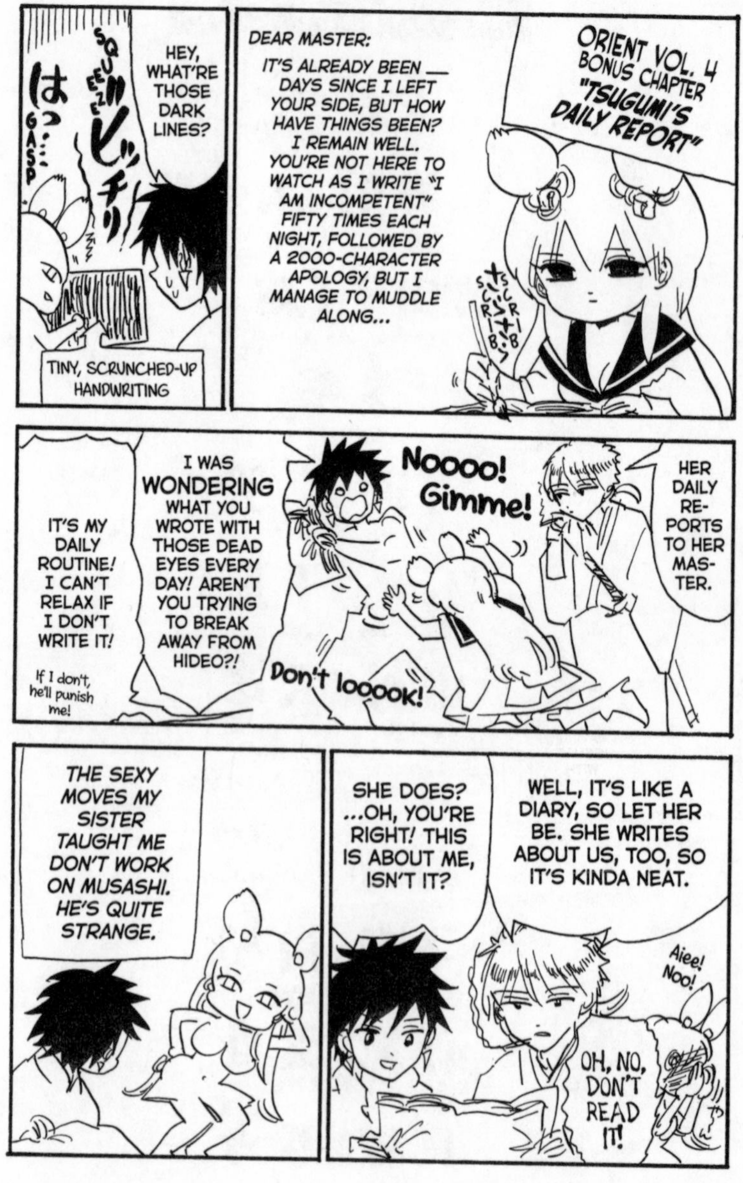
ORIENT VOL. 4 BONUS CHAPTER "TSUGUMI'S DAILY REPORT"
DEAR MASTER:
IT'S ALREADY BEEN __ DAYS SINCE I LEFT YOUR SIDE, BUT HOW HAVE THINGS BEEN? I REMAIN WELL. YOU'RE NOT HERE TO WATCH AS I WRITE "I AM INCOMPETENT" FIFTY TIMES EACH NIGHT, FOLLOWED BY A 2000-CHARACTER APOLOGY, BUT I MANAGE TO MUDDLE ALONG...
SCRIB SCRIB
HEY, WHAT'RE THOSE DARK LINES?
SQUEEZE
ビッチリ
はっ…
GASP
TINY, SCRUNCHED-UP HANDWRITING
HER DAILY REPORTS TO HER MASTER.
Noooo! Gimme!
I WAS WONDERING WHAT YOU WROTE WITH THOSE DEAD EYES EVERY DAY! AREN'T YOU TRYING TO BREAK AWAY FROM HIDEO?!
Don't looook!
IT'S MY DAILY ROUTINE! I CAN'T RELAX IF I DON'T WRITE IT!
If I don't, he'll punish me!
WELL, IT'S LIKE A DIARY, SO LET HER BE. SHE WRITES ABOUT US, TOO, SO IT'S KINDA NEAT.
SHE DOES? ...OH, YOU'RE RIGHT! THIS IS ABOUT ME, ISN'T IT?
Aiee! Noo!
OH, NO, DON'T READ IT!
THE SEXY MOVES MY SISTER TAUGHT ME DON'T WORK ON MUSASHI. HE'S QUITE STRANGE.

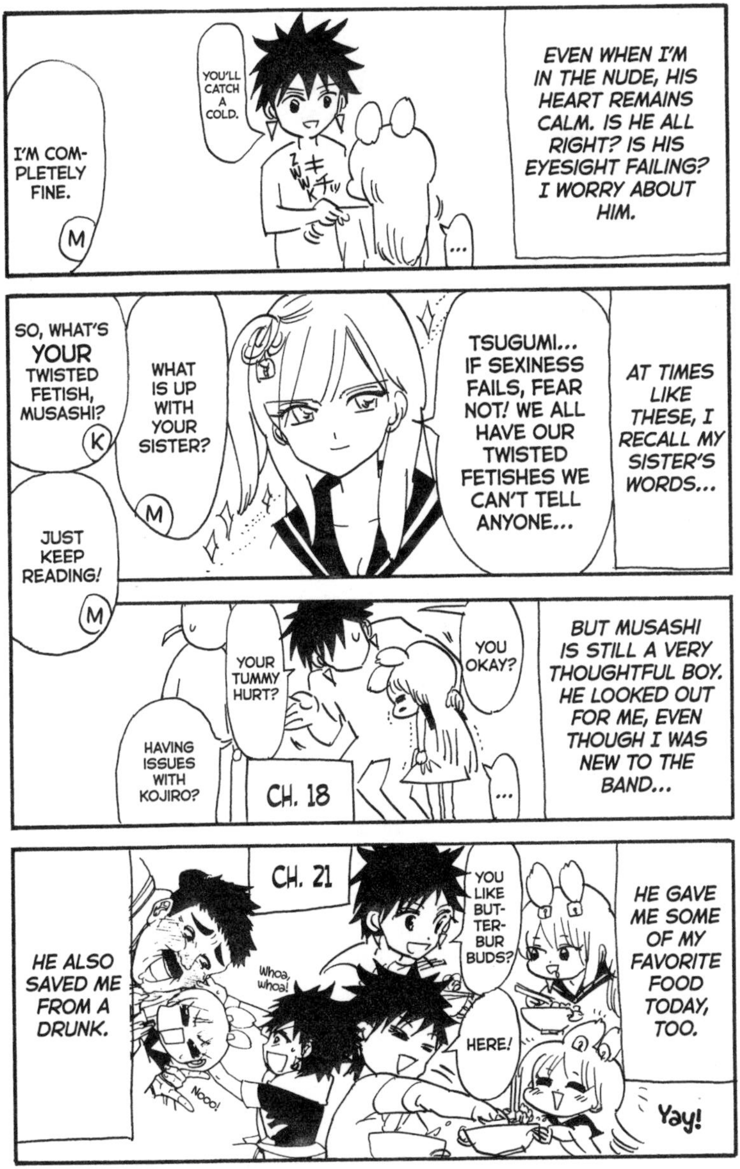
EVEN WHEN I'M IN THE NUDE, HIS HEART REMAINS CALM. IS HE ALL RIGHT? IS HIS EYESIGHT FAILING? I WORRY ABOUT HIM.
...
YOU'LL CATCH A COLD.
I'M COMPLETELY FINE. M
AT TIMES LIKE THESE, I RECALL MY SISTER'S WORDS...
TSUGUMI... IF SEXINESS FAILS, FEAR NOT! WE ALL HAVE OUR TWISTED FETISHES WE CAN'T TELL ANYONE...
WHAT IS UP WITH YOUR SISTER? M
SO, WHAT'S YOUR TWISTED FETISH, MUSASHI? K
JUST KEEP READING! M
BUT MUSASHI IS STILL A VERY THOUGHTFUL BOY. HE LOOKED OUT FOR ME, EVEN THOUGH I WAS NEW TO THE BAND...
YOU OKAY?
...
YOUR TUMMY HURT?
CH. 18
HAVING ISSUES WITH KOJIRO?
HE GAVE ME SOME OF MY FAVORITE FOOD TODAY, TOO.
Yay!
YOU LIKE BUTTERBUR BUDS?
HERE!
CH. 21
Whoa, whoa!
Nooo!
HE ALSO SAVED ME FROM A DRUNK.

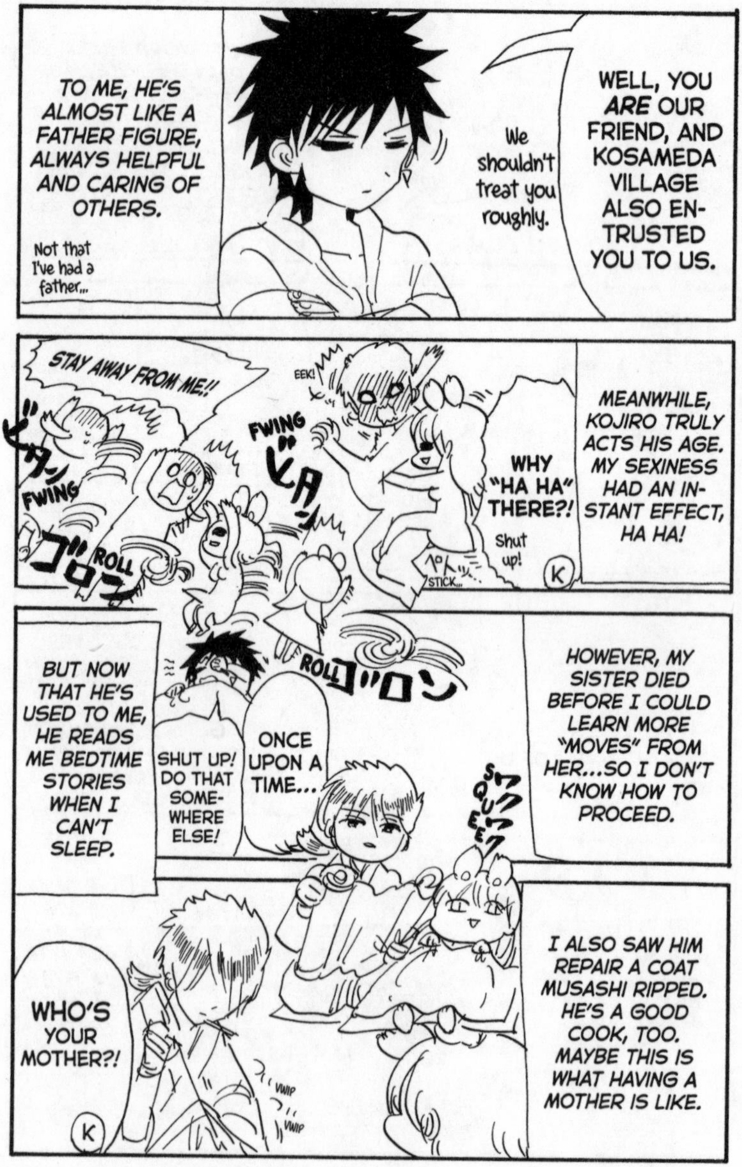
WELL, YOU ARE OUR FRIEND, AND KOSAMEDA VILLAGE ALSO EN-TRUSTED YOU TO US.
We shouldn't treat you roughly.
TO ME, HE'S ALMOST LIKE A FATHER FIGURE, ALWAYS HELPFUL AND CARING OF OTHERS.
Not that I've had a father...
MEANWHILE, KOJIRO TRULY ACTS HIS AGE. MY SEXINESS HAD AN IN-STANT EFFECT, HA HA!
WHY "HA HA" THERE?!
Shut up!
K
ペトッ
STICK...
EEK!
FWING
ビタン
STAY AWAY FROM ME!!
ビタン
FWING
ゴロン
ROLL
HOWEVER, MY SISTER DIED BEFORE I COULD LEARN MORE "MOVES" FROM HER...SO I DON'T KNOW HOW TO PROCEED.
SQUEEE
ROLL ゴロン
ONCE UPON A TIME...
SHUT UP! DO THAT SOME-WHERE ELSE!
BUT NOW THAT HE'S USED TO ME, HE READS ME BEDTIME STORIES WHEN I CAN'T SLEEP.
I ALSO SAW HIM REPAIR A COAT MUSASHI RIPPED. HE'S A GOOD COOK, TOO. MAYBE THIS IS WHAT HAVING A MOTHER IS LIKE.
VWIP
VWIP
WHO'S YOUR MOTHER?!
K

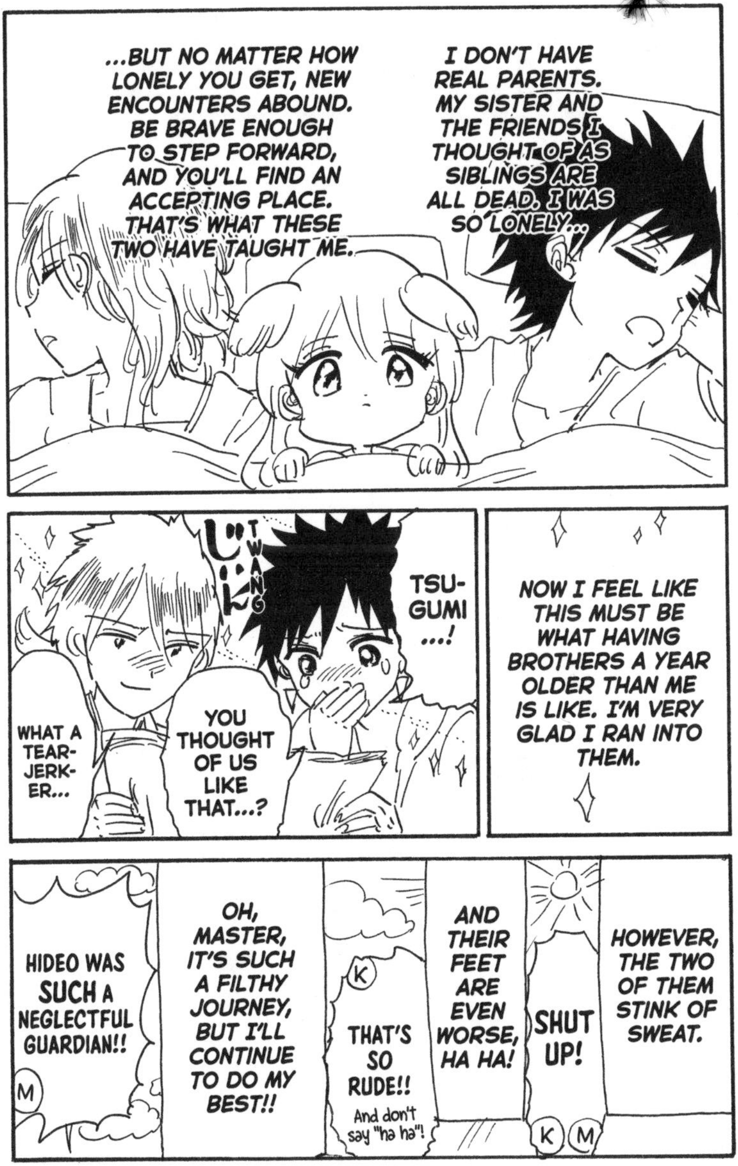
I DON'T HAVE REAL PARENTS. MY SISTER AND THE FRIENDS I THOUGHT OF AS SIBLINGS ARE ALL DEAD. I WAS SO LONELY...
...BUT NO MATTER HOW LONELY YOU GET, NEW ENCOUNTERS ABOUND. BE BRAVE ENOUGH TO STEP FORWARD, AND YOU'LL FIND AN ACCEPTING PLACE. THAT'S WHAT THESE TWO HAVE TAUGHT ME.
NOW I FEEL LIKE THIS MUST BE WHAT HAVING BROTHERS A YEAR OLDER THAN ME IS LIKE. I'M VERY GLAD I RAN INTO THEM.
TSU-GUMI...!
TWANG
YOU THOUGHT OF US LIKE THAT...?
WHAT A TEAR-JERK-ER...
HOWEVER, THE TWO OF THEM STINK OF SWEAT.
SHUT UP!
K M
AND THEIR FEET ARE EVEN WORSE, HA HA!
K
THAT'S SO RUDE!!
And don't say "ha ha"!
OH, MASTER, IT'S SUCH A FILTHY JOURNEY, BUT I'LL CONTINUE TO DO MY BEST!!
HIDEO WAS SUCH A NEGLECTFUL GUARDIAN!!
M

The End

A Kodansha Comics Trade Paperback Original
Orient 4 copyright © 2019 Shinobu Ohtaka
English translation copyright © 2021 Shinobu Ohtaka

Published in the United States by Kodansha Comics, an imprint of Kodansha USA Publishing, LLC, New York.

Publication rights for this English edition arranged through Kodansha Ltd., Tokyo.

First published in Japan in 2019 by Kodansha Ltd., Tokyo.

ISBN 978-1-64651-226-3

Printed in the United States of America.

www.kodansha.us

9 8 7 6 5 4 3 2 1
Translation: Nate Derr, Kevin Gifford
Lettering: Belynda Ungurath
Editing: Megan Ling
Kodansha Comics edition cover design by Phil Balsman
YKS Services LLC/SKY Japan, INC.

Publisher: Kiichiro Sugawara

Director of publishing services: Ben Applegate
Associate director of operations: Stephen Pakula
Publishing services managing editors: Madison Salters, Alanna Ruse
Production managers: Emi Lotto, Angela Zurlo
Logo and character art ©Kodansha USA Publishing, LLC